Exchange of Information in the EU

Exchange of Information in the EU

Taxpayers' Rights, Transparency and Effectiveness

Edited by

Marina Serrat Romaní

Beatriu de Pinós Research Fellow, Faculty of Law, University of Barcelona, Spain

Jasper Korving

Assistant Professor in Tax Law, Maastricht University and Senior Manager at the Netherlands Knowledge Management of Deloitte Belastingadviseurs BV, the Netherlands

Mariolina Eliantonio

Professor of European and Comparative Administrative Law and Procedure, Maastricht University, the Netherlands

EE Edward Elgar PUBLISHING

Cheltenham, UK • Northampton, MA, USA

Published by
Edward Elgar Publishing Limited
The Lypiatts
15 Lansdown Road
Cheltenham
Glos GL50 2JA
UK

Edward Elgar Publishing, Inc.
William Pratt House
9 Dewey Court
Northampton
Massachusetts 01060
USA

A catalogue record for this book
is available from the British Library

Library of Congress Control Number: 2024930468

This book is available electronically in the **Elgar**online
Law subject collection
http://dx.doi.org/10.4337/9781035314560

Printed on elemental chlorine free (ECF)
recycled paper containing 30% Post-Consumer Waste

ISBN 978 1 0353 1455 3 (cased)
ISBN 978 1 0353 1456 0 (eBook)

Printed and bound in the USA

Contents

Contributors

Aikaterini Antoniou DPhil student at Keble College, University of Oxford (United Kingdom)

Vasiliki Athanasaki Post-doc Researcher (Aristotle University of Thessaloniki, Greece), Collaborating Teaching Staff (Hellenic Open University)

Andrés Báez Moreno Associate Professor in Tax Law at Universidad Carlos III de Madrid (Spain)

Arthur Bianco PhD researcher at University of Luxembourg (Luxembourg)

Willem Boei Lecturer in Tax Law at Erasmus University Rotterdam (Netherlands) and Tax Advisor at Deloitte Belastingadviseurs BV (Netherlands)

Almut Breuer Assistant Professor in Tax Law at Maastricht University (Netherlands) and owner of Breuer Fiscale Advocatuur (Netherlands)

Alicja Brodzka Assistant Professor at Wrocław University of Economics and Business (Poland)

Chiara Cinotti PhD Candidate in Tax Law at "Sapienza" University of Rome (Italy), Teaching Assistant in Tax Law at University of Florence (Italy) and Lawyer at DS Tax & Legal (Italy)

Filip Debelva Professor in Tax Law at Catholic University of Leuven (Belgium) and attorney at Deloitte Legal – *Lawyers* (Belgium)

Stefano Dorigo Associate Professor in Tax Law at University of Florence (Italy) and Lawyer at DS Tax & Legal (Italy)

Sjoerd Douma Professor of International and European Procedural Tax Law at University of Amsterdam (Netherlands) and Partner at Lubbers, Boer & Douma (Netherlands)

Olivier Dubos Professor in Public Law at Bordeaux University (France)

Mariolina Eliantonio Professor in European Administrative Law and Procedure at Maastricht University (Netherlands)

Stefanie Geringer Postdoctoral Researcher in the Department of Tax Law at the University of Vienna (Austria) and Certified Tax Adviser and Manager at BDO Austria

Tatsiana Ivanchykava PhD Researcher at Bordeaux University (France) and at Maastricht University (Netherlands)

Tobias Koegl Research Assistant in International and Austrian Taxation at University of Liechtenstein in Vaduz (Liechtenstein)

Jasper Korving Assistant Professor in Tax Law at Maastricht University (Netherlands) and Senior Manager at the Netherlands Knowledge Management of Deloitte Belastingadviseurs BV (Netherlands)

Marianne Malmgrén Doctor of Laws, Docent in International Tax Law at the University of Eastern Finland (Finland) and founding-partner of Tax Services MSK Oy (Finland)

Saturnina Moreno González Professor in Tax Law at University of Castilla-La Mancha (Spain)

Katerina Pantazatou Associate Professor in Tax Law at University of Luxembourg (Luxembourg)

Luisa Scarcella Global Policy Lead in Taxation and Trade at International Chamber of Commerce (France)

Marina Serrat Romaní Beatriu de Pinós Research Fellow at University of Barcelona (Spain)

Alessia Tomo Postdoctoral Researcher at DigiTax – Centre of Excellence of University of Antwerp (Belgium)

Anne Van de Vijver Professor of Tax Law at University of Antwerp (Belgium) and of-counsel at Tiberghien Lawyers (Belgium)

Juan Manuel Vázquez PhD Researcher and Academic Coordinator of the CPT Project at University of Amsterdam (Netherlands) and Professional Support Lawyer at Loyens & Loeff (Netherlands)

Martin Wenz Professor for Business Taxation and the Laws of International and Liechtenstein Taxation at University of Liechtenstein in Vaduz (Liechtenstein)

Kasem Zotkaj PhD Candidate and Research Assistant in International Taxation at University of Liechtenstein in Vaduz (Liechtenstein)

Abbreviations

AEOI	Automatic Exchange of Information
AML	Anti-Money Laundering
AMLD	Anti-Money Laundering Directive
APA	Advance Pricing Agreements
ATR	Advance Tax Ruling
CbCR	Country-by-Country Reporting
CJEU	Court of Justice of the European Union
CRS	Common Reporting Standards
DAC	Consolidated version of Directive 2011/16 of 15 February 2011 on administrative cooperation in the field of taxation and repealing Directive 77/799/EEC
DAC1	Directive 2011/16 of 15 February 2011 on administrative cooperation in the field of taxation and repealing Directive 77/799/EEC
DAC2	Directive 2014/107/EU of 9 December 2014 amending Directive 2011/16/EU as regards mandatory automatic exchange of information in the field of taxation
DAC3	Directive (EU) 2015/2376 of 8 December 2015 amending Directive 2011/16/EU as regards mandatory automatic exchange of information in the field of taxation (cross-border rulings)
DAC4	Directive (EU) 2016/881 of 25 May 2016 amending Directive 2011/16/EU as regards mandatory automatic exchange of information in the field of taxation (CbCR)
DAC5	Directive (EU) 2016/2258 of 6 December 2016 amending Directive 2011/16/EU as regards access to anti-money-laundering information by tax authorities (AML information)

DAC6	Directive (EU) 2018/822 of 25 May 2018 amending Directive 2011/16/EU as regards mandatory automatic exchange of information in the field of taxation in relation to reportable cross-border arrangements
DAC7	Directive (EU) 2021/514 of 22 March 2021 amending Directive 2011/16/EU on administrative cooperation in the field of taxation (online platforms)
DAC8	Directive (EU) 2023/2226 of 17 October 2023 amending Directive 2011/16/EU on administrative cooperation in the field of taxation (crypto-assets and e-money)
EC	European Commission
EOI	Exchange of Information
EOIR	Exchange of Information upon Request
EU	European Union
OECD	Organisation for Economic Co-operation and Development
SEOI	Spontaneous Exchange of Information

Legislation

Directive 77/799/EEC of 19 December 1977 concerning mutual assistance by the competent authorities of the Member States in the field of direct taxation [1977] OJ L 336/15

Consolidated version of Directive 2011/16 of 15 February 2011 on administrative cooperation in the field of taxation and repealing Directive 77/799/EEC (DAC)

Directive 2011/16 of 15 February 2011 on administrative cooperation in the field of taxation and repealing Directive 77/799/EEC [2011] OJ L 64/1 (DAC1)

Directive 2014/107/EU of 9 December 2014 amending Directive 2011/16/EU as regards mandatory automatic exchange of information in the field of taxation [2014] OJ L 359/1 (DAC2)

Directive (EU) 2015/2376 of 8 December 2015 amending Directive 2011/16/EU as regards mandatory automatic exchange of information in the field of taxation (cross-border rulings) [2015] OJ L 332/1 (DAC3)

Directive (EU) 2016/881 of 25 May 2016 amending Directive 2011/16/EU as regards mandatory automatic exchange of information in the field of taxation (CbCR) [2016] OJ L 146/8 (DAC4)

Directive (EU) 2016/2258 of 6 December 2016 amending Directive 2011/16/EU as regards access to anti-money-laundering information by tax authorities (AML information) [2016] OJ L 342/1 (DAC5)

Directive (EU) 2018/822 of 25 May 2018 amending Directive 2011/16/EU as regards mandatory automatic exchange of information in the field of taxation in relation to reportable cross-border arrangements [2018] OJ L 139/1 (DAC6)

Directive (EU) 2021/514 of 22 March 2021 amending Directive 2011/16/EU on administrative cooperation in the field of taxation (online platforms) [2021] OJ L 107/1 (DAC7)

Directive (EU) 2023/2226 of 17 October 2023 amending Directive 2011/16/EU on administrative cooperation in the field of taxation (crypto-assets and e-money) [2023] OJ L 2023/2226 (DAC8)

Proposal for a Council Directive laying down rules to prevent the misuse of shell entities for tax purposes and amending Directive 2011/16/EU [2021] COM(2021) 565 final (Unshell Directive)

Introduction: *exchange of information in the EU – taxpayers' rights, transparency and effectiveness*

Marina Serrat Romaní, Jasper Korving and Mariolina Eliantonio

EXCHANGE OF INFORMATION: AN ESSENTIAL TOOL IN THE HANDS OF THE TAX AUTHORITIES

The exchange of information is a tool that public administrations have long been using as an administrative cooperation mechanism to execute their mandates and accomplish their public policies. The exchange of information for tax purposes between tax administrations has been present in bilateral treaties for decades. Nevertheless, it has become increasingly relevant in the last decade as a tool to improve the ability of tax authorities to deter, detect and disrupt tax evasion and avoidance.

The collapse of the economic bubble in 2008 left public treasuries in a fragile state, exacerbated by the discovery of dramatic tax evasion cases. Many of these cases were related to financial entities located in what were considered tax havens or countries with a significantly enhanced tax secrecy, and to the reticence of countries to adapt their domestic legislation to cooperate in the taxation field. This made it clear that the (then) current norms concerning tax cooperation among countries were outdated for the current social and economic reality. After the G20's 2009 London meeting, the different G20 authorities pushed for the implementation of an adequate standard of exchange of information for tax purposes. Shortly after that proposal, during the 2012 meeting in Los Cabos, the G20 and all the representatives of the OECD countries agreed to improve transparency standards and the exchange of information methods as the best way to solve both the problem of the public treasuries and tax avoidance and evasion.[1]

[1] G20 Los Cabos Summit, G20 Leaders Declaration (18–19 June 2012) 48, <https://www.oecd.org/g20/summits/los-cabos/2012-0619-loscabos.pdf> accessed 5 December 2023.

The OECD and the EU initially regulated the exchange of information rules via a system of exchange upon request, but the number of situations where information needed to be exchanged automatically has exploded over the last few years. At first, the increased call for transparency related in particular to financial information aiming to end bank secrecy. However, in the meantime, EU tax policy expanded the situations in which the automatic exchange of information is required. Gradually, the information to be exchanged automatically shifted from a limited number of items of income to be included in tax assessments, to information before a tax assessment had even been issued, such as tax rulings concluded with tax authorities (DAC3) and information on tax advice relating to potentially aggressive tax arrangements (DAC6). This policy of expansion has not ended here, since certain sectors of collaborative platforms (DAC7) and crypto-actives (DAC8) will soon extend the amount of information that can be exchanged.

The triangle formed by fiscal transparency, mutual assistance and the exchange of information has been part of the European dynamic for decades. Nevertheless, due to the growing importance of international operations, the previous regulations had too many legal loopholes to face present-day challenges and the context of globalisation. In recent years, the debate regarding the exchange of information and transparency has become a matter of interest not only for the EU and its Member States, but also for international organisations, such as the OECD and the UN, as well as other interested countries. This evolution and continuous expansion of the exchange of information, especially within the EU, as well as the lack of comprehensive research in this area prompted the establishment of this research project, which aims to cover the historical development of the exchange of information, its application and limits (if any), its relation to taxpayers' rights and the necessity and effectiveness of continuously extending the exchange of information requirements, from the perspectives of both tax and administrative law.

THE OBJECTIVES OF THIS BOOK

The aim of this book is twofold. First, to examine the concepts and general issues that contributed to shaping the current state of the EU exchange of information system, such as transparency, digitalisation, taxpayers' rights and the effectiveness of the current legal framework to comply with the purposes of exchange of information and administrative cooperation from the perspective of both tax and administrative law. Both fields of law have an overlapping interest in the topic, as it materially concerns information that is necessary for taxation purposes and connects to the relationship between, on the one hand, a government and, on the other, individual and corporate taxpayers. Legal aspects in relation to the exchange of information have thus far been limited to each respective field of law, even though rules on transparency are just as relevant to tax law as well.[2] This book hopes to close that gap.

The second aim is to shed light on all the amendments that the EU Council Directive on Administrative Cooperation has undergone (and is still undergoing) by analysing the main characteristics of each of its modifications, their strong and weak points, as well as their potential for improvement, effectiveness with respect to their objectives and their impact on taxpayers' rights.

As a whole, the aim of this book is to develop a comprehensive analysis of the exchange of information process for tax purposes within the EU from both a philosophical and theoretical perspective and a practical perspective (i.e., considering the EU legislation regulating the matter). In order to achieve these objectives, the book will cover the historical development of the exchange of information, its application, limits (if any), effects on taxpayers' rights and the necessity and effectiveness of continuously extending the exchange of information requirements, from both a tax and an administrative law perspective.

Part I of the book will elucidate the main concepts and legal effects of the exchange of information procedures for transparency purposes. Some authors will approach the regulatory framework from a tax law perspective, while others will tackle it from the perspective of administrative law. Part II provides an analysis of each EU legislative instrument that regulates the procedures

---

[2] See, for instance, Viktoria Wöhrer, *Data Protection and Taxpayers' Rights: Challenges created by Automatic Exchange of Information* (IBFD 2018); Xavier Oberson, *International Exchange of Information in Tax Matters. Towards Global Transparency* (Elgar Tax Law and Practice 2023); Giuseppe Marino (ed), *New Exchange of Information versus Tax Solutions of Equivalent Effect* (EATLP International Tax Series, IBFD 2016); Oliver-Christoph Günther and Nicole Tüchler, 'Exchange of Information for Tax Purposes' in Michael Lang (ed), *Series on International Tax Law* (Volume 80, Vienna, Linde Verlag 2013); Marcel GH Schaper, 'Data protection rights and tax information exchange in the European Union: an uneasy combination' (2016) 23 Maastricht Journal of European and Comparative Law 514; Saturnina Moreno González, 'The automatic exchange of tax information and the protection of personal data in the European Union: reflections on the latest jurisprudential and normative advances' (2016) 25 EC Tax Review 146; Maryte Somare and Veronika Wöhrer, 'Automatic exchange of financial information under the Directive on administrative cooperation in the light of the global movement towards transparency' (2015) 43 Intertax 804; Aleksandar Josimovski, 'Tax cooperation among member states of European Union and Directive on administrative cooperation in the field of taxation' (2013) 47 Zbornik Radova: Pravni Fakultet U Novom Sadu 537; Roman Seer, 'Recent development in exchange of information within the EU for tax matters' (2013) 22 EC Tax Review 66; Marius Vascega and Servaas Van Thiel, 'Assessment of taxes in cross-border situations: the new EU directive on administrative cooperation in the field of taxation' (2011) 20 EC Tax Review 148; Dennis Weber, 'Proposal for a council directive on administrative cooperation in the field of taxation: bank secrecy' (2009) 2(4) Highlights & Insights on European Taxation 29.

for exchanging information for tax purposes. This part aims to illustrate the general considerations made in Part I.

The scope of this volume necessarily comes with some limitations. First, even though the book will focus in Part I on the development of conceptual and theoretical lenses to analyse the features and effects of the standards of tax transparency within the exchange of information procedures, such analysis does not seek to offer a comprehensive analysis of the EU legislation. That will take place in Part II. Second, the book's conceptual analysis on the effects of the standards of transparency on taxpayers' rights will not include a study of all the taxpayers' rights that might possibly be affected during an exchange of information procedure. Instead, we have selected the most relevant and common rights currently present in court cases or being addressed in academic literature.

STRUCTURE OF THE VOLUME

In light of the abovementioned aims, the volume is organised in two parts.

Part I includes chapters that relate to general principles and concepts that impact the exchange of information in the field of taxation. The chapters in this part will discuss, among other things, the notions of 'tax transparency' and 'foreseeable relevance'. The chapters show how these general concepts have progressively evolved and what their impact is on taxpayers' rights in the field of exchange of information. As increased transparency can limit taxpayers' rights, it might be necessary to set boundaries for the exchange of information. The concept of 'foreseeable relevance' should be viewed from that perspective, as, broadly speaking, it requires tax authorities to determine the extent to which the requested information is actually necessary for determining a taxpayer's tax base, avoiding so-called 'fishing expeditions'. To that end, research is conducted as to whether it is possible to move towards an internationally agreed standard of 'foreseeable relevance' in which there is a reasonable balance between the need to guarantee effective administrative cooperation and to respect taxpayers' fundamental rights.

In this first part, the shaping of the administrative cooperation procedures for tax purposes in the EU will be discussed as well. First, the research addresses the consequences of the mechanisms of exchange of information as a form of transnational administrative law. When, for instance, a request for information is made by one state, that decision as well as the information shared have legal effects in another state. This transnationality of administrative decisions may jeopardise taxpayers' rights to effective judicial protection.

Second, in a more globalised and digitalised world, taxpayers' rights should be protected against governments' use of digital infrastructure. The exponentially fast development of communications technology combined with the progressive digitalisation of all fields of society have been decisive factors for tax administrations to implement those exchange of information methods that allow massive transfers of data. The combination of the simplicity of collecting and exchanging information through the internet together with the enormous amounts of data that can be processed gives rise to the question of whether the rights, guarantees and obligations surrounding the procedures of exchange of information that were appropriate a few decades ago are still suitable in the current context.

Furthermore, the relationship between transparency and exchange of information policies and several taxpayers' rights will be addressed. This analysis will focus on the EU perspective, especially considering the position of the Court of Justice of the European Union and the European Court of Human Rights, including their different interpretation and application of the relevant fundamental rights. The analysis will focus on the right to privacy and the treatment of data by the tax administrations during the procedure; the right of the taxpayer and other involved parties to be heard and the right to judicial protection within an exchange of information procedure.

Besides the legal aspects in relation to the increased exchange of information, this part will also analyse the effectiveness of the exchange of information legislation and procedures within the EU. Although the European Commission has provided a transparent legislative framework, some forms of income may still escape taxation. And, even if all information is actually exchanged, it can be questioned whether all information is actually used by the tax authorities. Therefore, the question of whether the current exchange of information practice achieves its full potential of the system will be investigated.

Finally, in this part the relationship between the exchange of information and certain non-EU Member States is explored. The existence of sufficient exchange of information processes in certain non-EU jurisdictions is relevant for the determination of whether that jurisdiction should be considered a Non-Cooperative Jurisdiction. Such a qualification has consequences across the EU, as the individual Member States are supposed to take defensive measures against the use of entities in the list of Non-Cooperative Jurisdictions. In Part I, the relevance of using exchange of information as a listing criterion is looked at. Besides that, the existence of legally guaranteed possibilities to exchange information, e.g. by means of bilateral treaties including provisions on the exchange of information, can be relevant in cases where domestic law provisions potentially infringe EU law. An established infringement can, after all, be justified due to a lack of effective fiscal supervision, which in turn would often not occur when a treaty foreseeing an exchange of information is in force.

Part II of the book will consist of chapters that address the evolution of the exchange of information within the EU. As the exchange of information was first addressed by the OECD in its Model Tax Convention, and the concepts used in this convention formed the inspiration for EU legislation in the field of exchange of information, this part will start by analysing the influence of the OECD and its guidelines on the European legislation. The evolution at OECD and, to some extent, EU level is also contextualised with their political, societal, economic and legal environment to explain the status quo and illustrates the implications and significance for the exchange of tax information within the EU territory.

Subsequently, the EU initiatives on the (increasing) exchange of information will be examined, starting with a focus on the early stages of legislation. Part II, Chapter 11 will start with an analysis of the old 1977 Directive on Administrative Cooperation and its 2011 replacement. In this chapter, the concepts and particularities governing this Directive will be critically examined, in a contextual framework. In this respect, the way in which certain concepts in the Directives were developed will be analysed, alongside how they are interpreted and what influenced the final legislative text, taking into account developments at an international level, especially in the US.

Subsequent chapters will focus on the almost yearly amendments to the Directive to widen the standard of transparency and the number of situations where information is automatically exchanged: tax rulings (DAC3), country-by-country reporting (DAC4), anti-money laundering (DAC5), potentially aggressive tax arrangements (DAC6) and online platforms (DAC7). The individual chapters dealing with these amendments to the original Directive on Administrative Cooperation all analyse the material scope of the amendment and its necessity, the interpretational circumstances and difficulties of the rules in the respective Directives, and the effectiveness of the exchange of information on the selected topic. Furthermore, the relationship between the amendments and taxpayers' fundamental rights, as elaborated on in Part I, will be addressed critically.

Further expansion of the Directive is already in progress. The upcoming amendments, which entail extending the fields in which automatic exchange of information is required, will cover the data on cryptocurrencies and other digital assets (DAC8) and minimum substance requirements for entities (Unshell). This book will also dedicate a separate chapter to DAC8. As there is still a great lack of clarity on the wording of the Unshell Directive, this proposal will not be discussed in this book.

PART I

General principles and concepts impacting the exchange of information

1. Transparency and foreseeable relevance in exchange of information procedures

Saturnina Moreno González

1.1 INTRODUCTION

In the context of international exchange of information upon request (EoIR), 'foreseeable relevance' is a condition for the obligation of the requested state to provide information to the requesting state. However, 'foreseeable relevance' is a vague concept, which, traditionally, has not been explicitly defined in either international conventions or in European legislation, which has resulted in the emergence of discrepancies between the requesting and requested authorities, hindering the effectiveness of international administrative cooperation. In the global trend towards intensifying the fight against tax evasion and avoidance, the search for greater transparency has led to a broad interpretation of the 'foreseeable relevance' requirement so as not to frustrate the effectiveness of administrative cooperation.

One of the original objectives of Directive 2011/16/EU on administrative cooperation in the field of taxation (DAC1) was to align European legislation with the international standard of transparency in the exchange of information on request. The Directive itself advocates a flexible interpretation of this requirement to enhance the effectiveness of cross-border information exchange. However, the Directive, and thus the requirement of foreseeable relevance contained therein, must be interpreted in the light of primary EU law.

The recent case law of the Court of Justice of the European Union (CJEU) has contributed to clarifying and delimiting the concept of 'foreseeable relevance' as a requirement for tax information requests. In the same vein, Directive (EU) 2021/514 of 22 March amending Directive 2011/16/EU on administrative cooperation in the field of taxation has codified the concept of 'foreseeable relevance' and clarified its meaning in cases of group requests. Moreover, the effective control of this requirement connects directly to several fundamental rights, such as the right to privacy (Article 7 of the Charter of

Fundamental Rights of the EU – the 'Charter'), the protection of personal data (Article 8 of the Charter) and the right to effective judicial protection (Article 47 of the Charter).

The purpose of this chapter is to analyse the evolution of the 'foreseeable relevance' requirement in EU law and the tension between this requirement and the search for greater transparency and efficiency of exchanges. This will allow us to identify certain developments related to the guarantees to be granted to subjects concerned by EoIR procedures. It will also allow us to reflect on the need to find a reasonable balance, as necessary as it is complex, between the effectiveness of administrative cooperation and mutual assistance between Member States and the protection of the taxpayers' fundamental rights, especially in the context of EU law, presided over by the Charter of Fundamental Rights.[1]

1.2 TRANSPARENCY IN CROSS-BORDER EXCHANGE OF TAX INFORMATION

In the literal sense, the term 'transparency' refers to a quality of objects that allows them to be easily seen through. It is also related to clarity, in the sense of being evident, that something can be understood without doubt or ambiguity. From a legal perspective, transparency is a diffuse and multifaceted concept, with various aspects or manifestations.[2] As an example, the notion of 'tax transparency' is used in some tax systems as a metaphorical reference to denote a certain special corporate taxation regime.[3]

Going beyond this, in terms of drafting legal rules (including tax rules), transparency is one of the principles of good regulation that should govern how they are set out, advocating 'better regulation', not only from an economic perspective, but also from that of a more transparent form of making law that is open to citizen participation.[4] Transparency is also related to the requirements

---

[1] This work has been carried out within the framework of the research Project: Ministerio de Ciencia, Innovación y Universidades de España, 'El cumplimiento cooperativo de las obligaciones tributarias en la era post-BEPS: nuevos retos' (2019-2022) PGC2018-097713-B-100 State Program for the Generation of Knowledge and Scientific and Technological Strengthening of the R+D+i System.

[2] See Johanna Hey, 'The Notion and Concept of Tax Transparency' in Funda Başaran Yavaşlar and Johanna Hey, *Tax Transparency* (IBFD - EATLP International Tax Series, vol. 17, IBFD 2019) 3–4.

[3] For instance, in Spain, the Corporate Income Tax Act (Law 27/2014 of 27 November), Chapter X, art 100 contains the controlled foreign companies (CFC) regime (*transparencia fiscal internacional*).

[4] See Communication From The Commission To The European Parliament, The Council, The European Economic And Social Committee And The Committee Of The

of clarity and precision of rules and is often invoked in the debate on improving the quality and simplification of tax legislation and procedures.[5]

In the relations between the tax administration and taxpayers, transparency is two-way in nature, although there are greater demands for transparency on the taxpayer than on the administration.[6]

The transparency of taxpayers (and of other third parties) is tied to obligations of collaboration and, in particular, to their obligation to provide the tax administration with different kinds of tax-relevant data that may be useful for the application of taxes. Therefore, it 'can be named as a *sine qua non* condition for an effective tax procedure system based on the fundamental principles of legality and equality'.[7] Additionally, transparency is one of the guiding principles of the cooperative relationship and seeks to encourage and facilitate taxpayers' voluntary compliance with their obligations, in exchange for greater legal certainty.

The transparency of the tax administration involves the responsibility to inform and assist taxpayers in complying with their tax obligations, by means of different tools, data and information that safeguard predictability in the application of taxes and facilitate voluntary compliance with tax obligations. Furthermore, the specific legislation on transparency in place in different countries obliges public bodies and administrations to actively make public and guarantee citizens' access to public information, files, and registers, with certain constraints based on reasons of public interest or the protection of personal data. Similarly, in European and national legislation on the protection of personal data, transparency is enshrined as one of the principles of the processing of such information, the most significant manifestation of which is the duty to inform the data subject about the processing of their personal data, a right that may also be subject to necessary and proportionate limitations, to protect objectives of public interest.

Without prejudice to these (and other) legal dimensions of transparency in the design and application of tax systems,[8] the term 'tax transparency' is closely related to administrative cooperation and international mutual assis-

---

Regions: Better regulation for better results – An EU agenda [2015] COM(2015) 215 Final, 4–6.

[5] See Recommendation to Improve the Situation of Taxpayers in the Single Market [2020] (Roadmap-Ares (2020) 6140272, European Commission 2020).

[6] Roman Seer, 'Purpose and Problems of Tax Transparency: The Legal Perspective' in Funda Başaran Yavaşlar and Johanna Hey (eds), *Tax Transparency* (IBFD - EATLP International Tax Series, vol. 17, IBFD 2019) 20–21.

[7] See ibid 19.

[8] Another dimension of transparency is the protection of democracy and the public through a naming-and-shaming approach. On this new dimension of tax transparency and the risks it entails, see Seer (n 6) 24.

tance.[9] Indeed, one of the most significant trends in the international tax framework in recent years is the escalation of administrative cooperation through: (i) the strengthening of minimum standards of transparency to improve the effectiveness of the regulatory instruments that enable tax-relevant data and information to be obtained upon request;[10] and (ii) the progressive implementation, thanks to advances in technology, of a new model of administrative cooperation based on the generalisation of the automatic exchange of tax-relevant information.[11] This dual strategy is logical, given the complementarity of the two forms of information exchange.

This trend responds to the logic that only through greater transparency and more intense and efficacious administrative cooperation can proper compliance with tax obligations be ensured, in order to more effectively combat phenomena such as aggressive tax planning, tax avoidance, tax evasion and harmful tax competition in a context of a globalised and digitalised economy.

---

[9] Hey (n 2) 3.

[10] Between 2009 and 2010, the OECD's Global Forum on Transparency and Exchange of Information worked to ensure the effective and rapid implementation of the minimum transparency standards for the exchange of information upon request, i.e., the minimum conditions of transparency that the different states were obliged to meet in order to achieve a level playing field in questions of taxation. This minimum standard entailed compliance with the following requirements: the generalised provision of tax information upon request by any state, without the possibility of invoking bank secrecy or the requested state's absence of interest in providing it; the exchange of all information foreseeably relevant to the proper application of the tax system of the requesting state; and the confidentiality of the information provided, with the aim of protecting the rights and interests of the taxpayers concerned. In March 2010, the Global Forum initiated a peer review process to verify the effective implementation of this minimum standard in the different countries. Effective exchange of tax information revolves around three essential elements: the availability of adequate, accurate and up-to-date information; adequate access to information; and the existence of information exchange mechanisms. The standard was revised in 2016, to adapt it to the 2012 update of Article 26 of the OECD MC. See OECD, *Exchange of Information on Request: Handbook for Peer Reviews 2016–2020* (Global Forum on Transparency and Exchange of Information for Tax Purposes, 3rd edn, OECD 2017) 16–26.

[11] A decisive step towards establishing the standard for transparency in AEoI was the approval in July 2014 by the OECD Council of the new international standard for the automatic exchange of financial account information (Common Reporting Standard). To ensure effective implementation of the AEoI Standard, the Global Forum works on three fronts: calling for commitments to implement the AEoI Standard and monitoring compliance in real time; reviewing the implementation of the AEoI Standard, including its effectiveness in practice; and assisting in the implementation of the AEoI Standard. See OECD, *Peer Review of the Automatic Exchange of Financial Account Information 2021* (Global Forum on Transparency and Exchange of Information for Tax Purposes, OECD 2021).

The above ideas are confirmed if we analyse the OECD/G20 BEPS Project, where transparency, one of the pillars on which the project is based, is given concrete expression in a series of actions (5, 12 and 13) in which administrative cooperation, through the (mainly automatic) exchange of information plays a decisive role.[12] The European Union is a leader in the global race towards greater transparency and administrative cooperation, although its objectives go beyond those described above, aiming also to promote fairer taxation and safeguard the proper functioning of the internal market. Among its aims, DAC1 sought to align European legislation on administrative cooperation with the international context of strengthening and improving the minimum standard of transparency and the exchange of information on request.[13]

Furthermore, since the Communication of 6 December 2012 on an action plan to strengthen the fight against tax fraud and tax evasion, the Commission has emphasised the need to forcefully promote automatic exchange of information (AEoI) as a European and international standard for transparency and administrative cooperation in the tax field.[14] Accordingly, since its adoption, DAC1 has undergone seven amendments, which have essentially introduced new reporting obligations on taxpayers, third parties (financial institutions, tax intermediaries, digital platform operators, crypto-asset service providers) and tax administrations. The data and information reported under these new obligations are subject to automatic exchange of information between Member States. These data and information refer to certain financial accounts,[15] advance cross-border tax rulings and advance pricing arrangements (DAC3), country-by-country reports filed by certain multinational groups (DAC4), potentially aggressive cross-border tax planning arrangements, certain data available to digital platform operators (DAC6) and transactions with crypto-assets, e-money and central bank digital currencies (DAC 8).

---

[12] OECD, 'BEPS Actions' (BEPS: Inclusive Framework on Base Erosion and Profit Shifting, 2023), <https://www.oecd.org/tax/beps/beps-actions/> accessed 5 December 2023.

[13] DAC1, recitals 4 and 5.

[14] Communication from The Commission to The European Parliament and The Council 'An Action Plan to Strengthen the Fight against Tax Fraud and Tax Evasion' [2012] COM(2012) 722 final, 4.

[15] See DAC2. Furthermore, DAC5 amended DAC1 to permit access to anti-money-laundering information by tax authorities. DAC5 does not extend the scope of the AEoI but guarantees the access of tax authorities to information on beneficial ownership in accordance with anti-money-laundering legislation which is essential to ensure the effectiveness of automatic exchange of financial account information in tax matters.

It is worth underlining the effects of strengthening tax transparency through international administrative cooperation:

1. The tax administrations of cooperating States can more efficiently prevent and control proper compliance of taxpayers' tax obligations in a cross-border scenario. As a result, their tax powers are reinforced.[16]
2. The new requirements for communication of data with 'tax relevance' and the automatic exchange of such information have brought about a change in the dynamics of the relationship between the administration and taxpayers. Thanks to the analysis of data collected through big data and artificial intelligence technologies, it is possible to develop preventive tools that increase taxpayers' voluntary compliance with tax obligations, as well as to detect potential non-compliance in a way that was, until recently, not thought to be possible.
3. From a tax policy viewpoint, the rapid advances made in recent years in tax transparency and administrative cooperation can be explained, at least partly, by the lower costs that such measures involve for countries, while allowing them to continue to develop an economic and fiscal policy intended to attract investment and economic activity to their territory. Meanwhile, measures to genuinely reform the rules on which the international and European corporate tax framework is built are more complex to implement, given that they involve higher costs for some countries to the benefit of others and further ceding of fiscal sovereignty.[17] These reflections make even greater sense after taking note of the difficulties in: (i) reaching consensus on the solution to the tax challenges arising from the digitalisation of the economy proposed by the OECD/G20 Inclusive Framework and established under so-called Pillars One and Two, and (ii) achieving its adoption in EU law.[18]

---

[16] José Manuel Calderón Carrero, 'Intercambio de información y asistencia mutua' in Nestor Carmona Fernández and José Manuel Calderón Carerro (coords), *Convenios Fiscales Internacionales y Fiscalidad de la Unión Europea* (CISS-Wolters Kluwer 2017) 829; Francisco Alfredo Garcia Prats, 'La política de la Unión Europea en materia de lucha contra la planificación fiscal agresiva ¿propuesta necesaria y adecuada)' in Francisco Alfredo Garcia Prats (ed), *Gobernanza económica e integración fiscal en la Unión Europea* (Tirant lo Blanch 2016) 15.

[17] Michael Devereux, *Tax transparency and tax co-ordination: a new era for tax reforms in a globalised world* (Policy Paper Series, Oxford University Centre for Business Taxation 2016) 5.

[18] The European Union has supported the OECD/G20 Inclusive Framework on BEPS and is committed to a swift implementation of the Pillars One and Two by means of Union Law. In that context, it has adopted the Council Directive 2022/2523 of 14 December 2022 on ensuring a global minimum level of taxation for multinational enterprise groups and large-scale domestic groups in the Union.

However, as discussed in tax literature for several years, this model of stronger tax transparency and administrative cooperation has largely been built with the rights of those affected by it being somewhat neglected. In other words, it has failed to take into account the need to reconcile the public interest with adequate protection of the rights of taxpayers and third persons affected by the actions and procedures involved in cross-border exchange of information.[19]

In the European arena, the Directive on Administrative Cooperation is addressed to the Member States and does not assign specific rights to taxpayers.[20] Under the principle of procedural autonomy, it is the Member States that are responsible for taking action to safeguard the appropriate application of the mechanisms for cross-border exchange of tax information provided for in the Directive and to reconcile them with the protection of the rights of persons affected by such actions or procedures. Consequently, the form and degree of protection of those rights may vary across States. However, the provisions of the Charter of Fundamental Rights are applicable to the Member States when they implement Union law (Article 51(1) of the Charter), such that the principle of procedural autonomy must not jeopardise the effectiveness of EU law itself, nor affect the essential content of the rights and principles set out in the Charter.

It is thus straightforward to understand the importance of the role to be played by the CJEU in the current state of development of EU law (without prejudice to the work of the European Court of Human Rights and national courts) both in the progressive integration of national tax actions and procedures that govern exchange of information, and in the definition of the outlines of the legal position of taxpayers and third persons affected by such procedures. An example of this is the recent case law of the Court of Justice on the nature, conditions of compliance and administrative and judicial enforcement of the 'foreseeable relevance' requirement.

---

[19] The specialised literature on this question is quite extensive. It can be consulted in Saturnina Moreno Gonzaléz, *The Council Directive 2011/16/EU in the Global context of Tax Transparency and Automatic Exchange of Information* (1st edn, Francis Lefebvre 2018).

[20] Case C-276/12 *Jiří Sabou v Finanční ředitelství pro hlavní město Prahu* [2013] ECLI:EU:C:2013:678, para 36.

1.3 DEFINITION OF THE CONCEPT OF 'FORESEEABLE RELEVANCE' IN THE CASE LAW OF THE COURT OF JUSTICE OF THE EU AND DIRECTIVE 2011/16/EU

1.3.1 A Preliminary Question: The Impact of the Commentary on Article 26(1) of the OECD Model Convention on the Interpretation of the Directive

No explicit definition of the concept of 'foreseeable relevance' was included in Directive 2011/16/EU on administrative cooperation in the field of taxation,[21] nor in Article 26 of the OECD Model Tax Convention on Income and on Capital (OECD MC).[22] The Directive, in Article 1(1), states that its purpose is to lay down the 'the rules and procedures under which Member States shall cooperate with each other with a view to exchanging information that is *fore-seeably* relevant to the administration and enforcement of the domestic laws of the Member States' concerning the taxes included within its scope.[23]

---

[21] The situation has changed following the adoption of DAC7.

[22] Similarly, Article 4(1) (general provision on exchange of information) of the OECD Multilateral Convention on Mutual Assistance in Tax Matters refers generically to this requirement, without defining it. The OECD Model Agreement on Exchange of Information in Tax Matters mentions the 'foreseeable interest' of the information in Articles 1 (purpose and scope of the Agreement) and 5(5) (exchange of information upon request).

[23] Article 1(1) of the Directive raises the question of whether the requirement of 'foreseeable relevance' applies to all forms of cross-border exchange of information, including automatic exchange. The literal interpretation and systematic placement of Article 1(1) (located in Chapter I of the Directive, which deals with 'general provisions') suggests the answer is positive. However, the different role played by the automatic exchange of information must be considered. This modality is intended to provide tax administrations with more extensive and commonly used information. Thus, the necessity and relevance of the data gathered and automatically transferred for the tax purposes pursued must be demonstrated *ex ante*, i.e., at the time of drafting the content and scope of the legal rules facilitating automatic exchange of information. This will allow data subjects to have certainty and predictability as regards the type of data collected and transmitted, who is responsible for their processing and the purposes for which the transmitted data will be used. The principle of proportionality is of absolute importance in this form of information exchange. See F. Alfredo García Prats, 'The Legitimacy of AEOI and Measures other than AEOI' in Giuseppe Marino (ed), *New Exchange of Information versus Tax Solutions of Equivalent Effect* (EATLP International Tax Series, volume 13, IBFD 2015) 143; Pasquale Pistone 'Foreseeable relevance and the impact of taxpayers' rights in the EU' (*Review of European Administrative Law Blog*, 18 March 2022), <https://realaw.blog/?p=1124> accessed 5 December 2023.

Furthermore, when regulating the procedure for the exchange of information on request, provided for in Section I of Chapter II of the Directive, Article 5 expressly sets out the obligation for the requested authority to communicate 'to the requesting authority any information referred to in Article 1(1) that it has in its possession or that it obtains as a result of administrative enquiries'. Recital 9 of Directive 2011/16/EU clarifies that the requirement of foreseeable relevance pursues two objectives: 'to provide for exchange of information in tax matters to the widest possible extent and, at the same time, to clarify that Member States are not at liberty to engage in "fishing expeditions" or to request information that is unlikely to be relevant to the tax affairs of a given taxpayer.'

Although the 'foreseeable relevance' requirement should be interpreted in such a way as not to hinder the effectiveness of the exchange of information, it is necessary to insist on the need for there to be, in any event, an open investigation or examination procedure in the framework of which the request for information is made. In the absence of a link between the information requested and specific control operations in respect of one or more taxpayers being carried out in the requesting State, the requirement of foreseeable relevance would not be met.[24]

Additionally, the Directive establishes certain limits on the exchange of information on request, requiring the requesting authority to have exhausted its usual sources of information before making the request and to have been unable to obtain such information (in line with the principle of subsidiarity) and that the provision of the requested information must not lead to the disclosure of a commercial, industrial or professional secret or of a commercial process, or of information whose disclosure would be contrary to the public interest.[25]

Furthermore, Article 20 of the Directive regulates the standard forms on which requests for information (and administrative enquiries) are to be sent and the computerised formats to be used for the exchange of information between Member States. Paragraph 2 of this Article, as originally worded, established that the standard form for requests for information should include at least the following information: (a) the identity of the person under examination or investigation; and (b) the tax purpose for which the information is sought. If both requirements, are not met, this would prevent the requirement of foreseeable relevance of the requested information from being considered as met. The requesting authority may also provide, to the extent known and in line with

---

[24] Esther Machanoses Garcia, *El intercambio de información entre Administraciones en materia tributaria* (Instituto de Estudios Fiscales 2018) 228.

[25] DAC art 17.

the international situation, the name and address of any person believed to be in possession of the requested information, as well as any element that might facilitate the gathering of information by the requested authority.

Beyond the aforementioned aspects, Directive 2011/16/EU failed to address fundamental questions for the interpretation of the criterion of foreseeable relevance – for example, how the term 'identity of the person under examination or investigation' should be interpreted and, in particular, whether this requires providing the name and/or address of the person under investigation. A further question would be whether requests for information on a specific taxpayer subject to an examination could include a request for unspecified or general information relating to that taxpayer, or whether, in light of recital 9 (referring to a 'given taxpayer') and Article 20(2)(a) of the Directive (which requires the 'identity' of the person under investigation to be provided), a request for information on a group of unidentified taxpayers would satisfy the requirement of foreseeable relevance. Moreover, questions also arise as to whether requests for information (and information orders) can be disputed, by means of what type of appeal, and by whom (the third party holding the information, the taxpayer under investigation or third parties concerned). These are, broadly speaking, the questions underlying the preliminary rulings that gave rise to several judgments, namely the *Berlioz*,[26] *Grand Duchy of Luxembourg v B and F.C.*,[27] and *Grand Duchy of Luxembourg v L*[28] rulings.

Nonetheless, these rulings also raise the no less important question of the impact of the OECD MC and its Commentary on the interpretation of the Directive. In particular, the question is raised as to whether the interpretation of the 'foreseeable relevance' requirement in Directive 2011/16/EU should be interpreted considering the modifications in Article 26(1) of the OECD MC and its Commentary in 2012, subsequent to the publication of the Directive.

Although the 1963 OECD MC already included a clause on exchange of information, the wording of Article 26 has been amended several times over the years, reflecting the OECD's wish to render the exchange of information between tax administrations as more operational. Regarding the changes affecting the 'foreseeable relevance' requirement, the 2005 revision amended the first paragraph of Article 26 of the OECD MC, replacing the term 'necessary information' with 'foreseeably relevant information', in order to align the terminology used in this Article with the 2002 OECD Model Agreement on

---

[26] Case C-682/15 *Berlioz Investment Fund SA v Directeur de l'administration des contributions directes* [2017] ECLI:EU:C:2017:373.

[27] Joined Cases C-245/19 and C-246/19 *État luxembourgeois v B and Others* [2020] ECLI:EU:C:2020:795.

[28] Case C-437/19 *État du Grand-duché de Luxembourg v L* [2021] ECLI:EU:C:2021:953.

exchange of information in tax matters. However, this did not alter the material scope of the provision. The aim of the reform was to clarify that the standard of exchange of information should be as broad as possible, but without it covering so-called 'fishing expeditions' or requests for information irrelevant to examining the tax situation of a given taxpayer. Subsequently, in 2012, both Article 26 and its Commentaries were newly amended. On this occasion, the Commentary on Article 26(1) of the OECD MC underwent significant changes (in paragraphs 5, 5(1), 5(2) and 8), amongst which it is worth noting the easing of the 'foreseeable relevance' threshold for the purposes of the information request, the specific treatment of requests for information in relation to a group of taxpayers not individually identified and the recommendation of time limits for the provision of information, among other aspects.

In the *Berlioz* judgment, the Court of Justice recognised that the concept of 'foreseeable relevance' used in Articles 1(1) and 5 of Directive 2011/16/EU reflects that used in Article 26 of the OECD MC.[29] Furthermore, the explanatory memorandum of the proposal leading to the adoption of Directive 2011/16/EU refers several times to the OECD MC.[30] However, the latter was drawn up between 2009 and 2011, a period in which the OECD recommendations on interpreting the criterion of 'foreseeable relevance' criterion were those included in the 2005 version of the Model Convention, a circumstance which raised concerns about a possible automatic application of the subsequent amendments to Article 26 and its Commentary for purposes of interpreting Directive 2011/16/EU.

In contrast to this supposed automatic interpretation, it is worth noting that, as pointed out by the Advocate General Kokott, the OECD MC and its Commentaries are not legally binding international conventions but are the unilateral acts of an international organisation in the form of recommendations to its member countries. Thus, although the terms used in the OECD MC and the Directive are identical, the former simply reflects the opinion of experts representing the governments of the OECD member countries, and not that of the legislature of the Union or its Member States.[31] The Court of Justice has stated on various occasions that a clause in a double taxation agreement (DTA), interpreted in the light of the commentaries on the OECD MC, cannot

---

[29] Case C-682/15 (n 27) para 67.

[30] Proposal for a Council Directive on administrative cooperation in the field of taxation [2009] COM (2009) 29 final, Explanatory Memorandum, para 8.

[31] Case C–245/19 *Berlioz Investment Fund SA v Directeur de l'administration des contributions directes*, Opinion of Advocate General Kokott [2017] ECLI:EU:C:2017:2, paras 118 and 119.

restrict EU law.[32] In addition, simply adopting the interpretation set out by the Commentaries on Article 26 of the OECD MC following the adoption of the Directive would result in OECD member countries, which are not necessarily Member States of the European Union, being able to decide on the interpretation of an EU Directive, modifying the obligations of the Member States established in the Council, even though Article 20(2) of the Directive remains unalterable.[33]

Furthermore, an unconsidered extension of the OECD's proposed and maintained approach to Directive 2011/16/EU ignores the fact that, despite the Directive on Administrative Cooperation being addressed to the Member States and not assigning specific rights to taxpayers,[34] the provisions of the Charter are applicable both to the EU legislature and to the Member States when they implement EU law. Thus, interferences with the fundamental rights of Union citizens in the context of cross-border exchange of tax information activities carried out under the Directive must comply with Article 52(1) of the Charter, which requires such limitations be provided for by law, the essential content of those rights and freedoms be respected and such limitations be proportional and necessary.[35] Such requirements would not be met by the OECD MC and its Commentaries as they are not based on a decision made by the national or EU legislature.[36] This does not prevent, as will be seen, the interpretation of Articles 1(1), 5 and 20(2) of the Directive made by the CJEU

---

32 C-265/04 *Margaretha Bouanich v Skatteverktet* [2006] ECLI:EU:C:2006:51, paras 50 and 56.

33 Opinion of Advocate General Kokott (n 32) para 120.

34 C-276/12 (n 21) para 36.

35 The CJEU judgment in Case C-694/20 *Orde van Vlaamse Balies and Others v Vlaamse Regering* [2022] ECLI:EU:C:2022:963, is proof of this. It ruled that Article 8ab(5) of DAC1 (introduced by DAC6) violates Article 7 of the Charter that protects the confidentiality of all correspondence between individuals, and in particular with the lawyers. The reporting obligations of the Directive provides for a dispensation to intermediaries that are subject to legal professional privilege in their home state such that they are not required to report relevant arrangements to the tax authority. However, according to Article 8ab(5), such intermediaries are required to notify other intermediaries (or, in their absence, the taxpayer) of their reporting obligations. The CJEU considered that, although the Directive's objective is to prevent aggressive tax planning and is therefore in the general interest, Article 8ab(5) contains an unnecessary limitation of Article 7 of the Charter. For a more detailed analysis of this judgment, see Part II, Chapter 15 in this book.

36 Opinion of Advocate General Kokott (n 32) para 124. In a similar vein, see: Enrique Sánchez De Castro Martín-Luengo, 'Intercambio de información previa solicitud bajo la Directiva 2011/16/UE y protección de datos: Alguna casuística sobre la identidad de la persona bajo investigación e información con pertinencia previsible' in Isaac Merino Jara (ed), *Derechos fundamentales y tributación: Monográfico Nueva Fiscalidad* (Dykinson 2020) 280.

in the cases of *Grand Duchy of Luxembourg v B and F.C.* and *Grand Duchy of Luxembourg v L* from being aligned with the most recent international standards on the criterion of foreseeable relevance.

1.3.2 'Foreseeable Relevance' in the Case Law of the CJEU

The three judgments all answer questions referred for a preliminary ruling by the Luxembourg Supreme Administrative Court under the Law of 25 November 2014 on the procedure applicable to the exchange of information on request in the field of taxation. Reading these three judgments reveals the progress that each one represents compared with the previous one as regards defining the contours of the concept of foreseeable relevance.

In the *Berlioz* case, the CJEU observed that it is apparent from the wording of Articles 1(1) and 5 of Directive 2011/16/EU that the term 'foreseeable relevance' describes the *characteristic* that the requested information must possess, such that the obligation imposed on the requested authority to cooperate with the requesting authority does not extend to the provision of information that does not have that characteristic. In other words, the requirement of 'foreseeable relevance' of the requested information is a condition of the legality of the request for information for the requested Member State to be obliged to process it and, at the same time, of the information order derived from that request.

The CJEU also addressed the question of who is responsible for assessing whether this condition is met. In principle, it is for the requesting authority, which is in charge of the investigation giving rise to the request for information, to assess, according to the circumstances of the case, the foreseeable relevance of the information requested for that investigation based on the progress made in the proceedings and after having exhausted the usual sources of information which it has been able to use. In so doing, the requesting authority has a certain margin of discretion, which does not, nonetheless, authorise it to request information without relevance to the investigation. However, the requested authority must verify that such information is not devoid of any foreseeable relevance to the investigation undertaken by the requesting authority. In order for the requested authority to be able to carry out such verification, the requesting authority must provide adequate reasons explaining the purpose of the information sought in the tax procedure in respect of the taxpayer identified in the request for information. In addition, where necessary, the requested authority may, for the purpose of this verification, ask the requesting authority for additional information required to rule out the manifest lack of foreseeable relevance of the information requested. Hence, 'the review to be carried out by the requested authority is not limited to a brief and formal verification of the regularity of the request for information' in the light of these questions, but must also 'enable that authority to satisfy itself that the information sought is not devoid of any foreseeable relevance having regard to the identity of the taxpayer concerned and that of any third party asked to provide the information, and to the requirements of the tax investigation concerned.'[37]

In this way, in the *Berlioz* case, the Court of Justice makes a first approximation to the legal nature and scope of this concept, as well as to the scope of the control that the tax (and judicial) authorities of the requested state must exercise over it, but gives no indications as to the degree of reasoning and detail of the requests for information for these (and the requests issued by the authorities of the requested state) to be considered foreseeably relevant.[38] These questions are dealt with in the following two judgments.

The *Grand Duchy of Luxembourg v B and F.C.* examines whether, under Articles 1(1) and 5 of the Directive, the requirement of foreseeable relevance is met by requests for information (and the subsequent decisions requesting information) concerning multiple data on unspecified contracts, invoices and payments, delimited by criteria based on the identity of the taxpayer concerned, the period to which the investigation in the requesting State relates and the identity of the person in possession of the information involved.

In light of the evidence set out in the *Berlioz* case, the Court had no doubt that the decision requesting information at issue in the main proceedings, together with the request for exchange of information on which it is based, was not manifestly devoid of any foreseeable relevance, as it states the identity of the taxpayer concerned by the investigation giving rise to the request, the period covered by that investigation and the identity of the third person holding the information relating to contracts, invoices and payments concluded or carried out during that period and connected to the taxpayer concerned.

The fact that the information order refers to contracts, invoices and payments that are imprecisely identified does not make it a random request, because, in the information order, the contracts, invoices and payments are delimited by criteria based on: (i) the fact that they were concluded or carried out with the person holding the information; (ii) the fact that they were concluded or carried out during the period covered by the investigation; and (iii) their relationship with the taxpayer under investigation. Moreover, both the request

---

37 Case C-682/15 (n 27) para 82.

38 Marina Serrat Romaní, 'La relevancia de la pertinencia previsible: Comentario crítico a la Sentencia del Tribunal de Justicia de la Unión Europea de 6 de octubre de 2020, asuntos acumulados C-245/19 y C-246/19' (*CJEU Leading Cases*, 1 May 2021), <https://ecjleadingcases.wordpress.com/2021/05/01/marina-serrat-romani-la-relevancia-de-la-pertinencia-previsible-comentario-critico-a-la-sentencia-del-tribunal-de-justicia-de-la-union-europea-de-6-de-octubre-de-2020-asuntos-acumulados-c%e2%80%912/> accessed 5 December 2023.

for information and the decision requiring the requested information during the preliminary stage of the investigation, the purpose of which is to gather information of which the requesting authority, by definition, does not have full and precise knowledge. It is thus foreseeable that some of the information relating to the decision ordering the provision of the information (together with the request for information) will ultimately prove to be irrelevant in light of the results of the investigation conducted by the requesting authority, without this circumstance indicating that the information in question can be regarded as manifestly devoid of any foreseeable relevance.[39]

The last of the rulings, thus far, is *Grand Duchy of Luxembourg v L*. This was a long-awaited judgment because, in contrast to the previous cases, the CJEU was called upon to decide whether (and how) requests for information about a group of identifiable, but neither named nor individually distinguished, taxpayers meet the requirement of foreseeable relevance. Specifically, in the first two questions referred for a preliminary ruling, the national court asks, in essence, whether, in accordance with Articles 1(1), 5 and 20(2)(a) of Directive 2011/16/EU, it is possible to conclude that a request for information is manifestly not devoid of any foreseeable relevance when the persons under examination or investigation are not identified by name and individually by that request, but the requesting authority substantiates, by means of a clear and sufficient explanation, that it is conducting out a targeted investigation into a limited group of persons, justified by reasonable suspicions of non-compliance with a specific legal obligation.

One of the main contributions of this judgment is that it clarifies the interpretation of the term 'identity' contained in Article 20(2)(a) of the Directive. Furthermore, drawing on a systematic interpretation of this provision, together with Articles 1(1) and 5 of Directive 2011/16/EU, the Court concludes that the 'identity of the taxpayer under examination or investigation' is an element that the statement of reasons for the request for information must necessarily contain in order to enable the requested authority to establish that the information requested is not devoid of any foreseeable relevance and to require that authority to comply with the request.

Article 20(2)(a) of the Directive makes no reference to domestic law as regards the meaning of the term. It is therefore an autonomous concept of EU law that must be interpreted uniformly based on its literal, contextual, and teleological interpretation. The term 'identity' denotes, in its typically accepted or common meaning, 'the data that allow a person to be recognised as a person, and which are not limited to identifying them by their name.'[40]

---

39 Joined Cases C-245/19 and C-246/19 (n 28) paras 117–23.

40 Case C-437/19 (n 29) para 51.

Regarding the context of this concept, it is worth noting, on the one hand, that the term 'person', as defined in Article 3(11) of the Directive also includes an association of legal persons whose identity cannot be established on the basis of personal data such as those relating to the civil status of a natural person, with it being necessary that those persons can be identified by a set of distinctive factual and legal characteristics; on the other hand, since the 'foreseeable relevance' rule is intended to facilitate, as much as possible, the exchange of information in tax matters, the procedural rules laid down in Article 20 of the Directive 'need to be interpreted liberally in order not to frustrate the effective exchange of information.' Accordingly, the requirement imposed by Article 20(2)(a) of the Directive to provide in the request for information elements of reasoning relating to the identity of the persons under examination or investigation 'needs to be interpreted flexibly, in the sense that it does not necessarily require identifying those persons individually and by name.'[41]

Finally, under a teleological interpretation of the Directive, 'an interpretation of the concept of "identity of the person under examination or investigation" amounting to a prohibition of any request for information in which the requesting authority does not refer to persons individually and by name would risk depriving the instrument of cooperation that is the request for information of its practical effect and would thus run counter to the objective of combating international tax fraud and tax evasion that that instrument is pursuing.'[42] Hence, the concept of 'identity of the person' in Article 20(2)(a) of the Directive refers not only to the name and other personal data, but also the distinctive qualities or characteristics that make it possible to identify the person or persons subject to an examination or investigation based on a common set of distinguishing qualities or characteristics. However, when the request for information made by the requesting authority concerns a group of taxpayers not identified by name and individually, there is a substantial risk of opening a random investigation that manifestly exceeds the framework of the tax investigation carried out, imposing an excessive burden on the requested authority. The Court is therefore particularly careful with the requirements for the requesting authority to state reasons for its request for information, going

---

41 ibid paras 52 and 55.

42 ibid para 58. Although the Court of Justice uses the terms 'tax fraud and tax evasion', this terminology in fact refers to tax avoidance and evasion. For more about the meaning of tax avoidance (and aggressive tax planning) in European Tax Law see Pasquale Pistone, 'The Meaning of Tax Avoidance and Aggressive Tax Planning in European Union Tax Law: Some Thoughts in Connection with the Reaction to Such Practices by the European Union' in Ana Paula Dourado (ed), *Tax Avoidance Revisited in the EU BEPS Context* (IBFD 2017) 78.

a step further than in the case of the *Grand Duchy of Luxembourg v B and F.C.* ruling.

Indeed, in *Grand Duchy of Luxembourg v B and F.C.*, the Court of Justice underscored the importance of the statement of reasons for the request for information made by the requesting authority being sufficient for: (i) the identity of the taxpayer concerned by the investigation giving rise to that request, (ii) the requirements of such an investigation, and (iii) where it is necessary to obtain the information in question from a person holding that information, the identity of that person. This requirement for the statement of reasons is critical for the requested authority to be able, first, to verify that the request for information is not manifestly devoid of any foreseeable relevance and to accept the request and, if the decision to issue the request is disputed, for the court to determine that the reasons for that decision and for the request on which it is based are sufficient to conclude that they are not manifestly devoid of any foreseeable relevance.[43] Moreover, in Case C-437/19, the Court insists on greater depth in the statement of reasons for requests for information when they concern data and information on a group of unidentified persons, so as to rule out the risk that such requests are made for the purpose of 'fishing expeditions'. Thus, it requires the requesting authority to provide, first, a description 'as detailed and complete as possible of the group of taxpayers under examination or investigation, specifying the common set of qualities or distinguishing characteristics of the persons comprising that group', such that the requested authority is able to identify them; second, to explain 'the specific tax obligations to which those persons are subject'; and finally, to set out 'the reasons for which those persons are suspected of having committed the omissions or infringements under examination or investigation.'[44]

In summary, the judgments of *Grand Duchy of Luxembourg v B and F.C.* and *Grand Duchy of Luxembourg v L* have the virtue of underlining, first, the importance of the requesting state's request for information always being sufficiently reasoned, and, second, in the case of requests for information on unidentified but identifiable persons, their requiring a more complete or more detailed statement of reasons from the requesting state, such that the requirement of foreseeable relevance can be considered to be met. Thus, the aspect of the reasoning of the request must be based on the circumstances of each case and cannot be fulfilled by simply individualising the request. In short, the requirement of a statement of reasons is the *counterpoint* to the flexibility of the concept of 'foreseeable relevance' and is embodied in the material content

---

[43] Joined Cases C-245/19 and C-246/19 (n 28) paras 115 and 116.

[44] Case C-437/19 (n 29) para 67.

of requests for information, which must be adapted, as regards degree of reasoning, to the circumstances of each case.[45]

1.3.3 Codification of the Concept of 'Foreseeable Relevance' in DAC7

Prior to the publication of the case of the *Grand Duchy of Luxembourg v L*, the EU Council adopted DAC7 which, among other amendments to Directive 2011/16/EU,[46] codified, for the first time, the indeterminate legal concept of 'foreseeable relevance' in the cross-border exchange of information between tax administrations. The 'declaratory value' of its inclusion in the Directive[47] should not detract from this improvement, given that its intention is to provide a clear legal framework to safeguard the effectiveness of exchanges of information (avoiding the refusal of requests) and to provide legal certainty for both tax administrations and taxpayers.[48] To this end, DAC7 introduces a new Article 5a into Directive 2011/16/EU and amends Article 20(2).[49]

The new Article 5a, in its first paragraph, defines the requirement of foreseeable relevance as follows: 'For the purposes of a request referred to in Article 5, the requested information is foreseeably relevant where, at the time the request is made, the requesting authority considers that, in accordance with its national law, there is a reasonable possibility that the requested information will be relevant to the tax affairs of one or several taxpayers, whether identified by name or otherwise, and be justified for the purposes of the investigation.'

To demonstrate the foreseeable relevance of the requested information, paragraph 2 of Article 5a obliges the requested authority to provide its requesting counterpart with at least the following information: 'a) the tax purpose for which the information is sought, and b) specification of the information required for the administration or enforcement of its national law.' Nevertheless, where the request refers to a group of taxpayers who cannot

---

45 María Esther Sanchez Lopez, 'Las garantías del contribuyente en el intercambio de información entre estados. Examen de la STJUE de 25 de noviembre de 2021, asunto *État luxemburgeois*' (2022) 10 Quincena Fiscal.

46 In particular, DAC7 introduces two fundamental innovations. On the one hand, it establishes a 'standardized reporting requirement' for digital platform operators to enhance tax compliance in relation to their sellers. On the other hand, it clarifies the framework and principles applied in cases of joint audits between tax administrations of different Member States. For an in-depth analysis of the DAC7 rules for reporting by online platform operators in terms of proportionality and legal certainty see Part II, Chapter 16 in this book.

47 See Opinion of Advocate General Kokott (n 32) para 72.

48 DAC7, recital 4.

49 Member States generally have until 31 December 2022 to transpose the Directive.

be individually identified, paragraph 3 of Article 5a states that the requesting State shall provide at least the following information: (a) a detailed description of the group; (b) an explanation of the applicable law and of the facts based on which there is reason to believe that the taxpayers in the group have not complied with the applicable law; (c) an explanation how the requested information would assist in determining compliance by the taxpayers in the group; and (d) where relevant, facts and circumstances related to the involvement of a third party that actively contributed to the potential non-compliance of the taxpayers in the group with the applicable law. This provision is aligned with the case law of the CJEU and the Commentaries on Article 26, paragraph 1 of the 2012 OECD MC.[50]

Under the new wording of Article 20(2), the information on the standard form used in the information request shall include at least: (a) the identity of the person under examination or investigation and, in the case of group requests, a detailed description of the group; and (b) the tax purpose for which the information is sought. Consequently, following the amendments made to Directive 2011/16/EU by DAC7, the doubts regarding the interpretation on the scope of the concept of foreseeable relevance are allayed in favour of a broad interpretation that includes cases of requests for information on several taxpayers that cannot be identified individually. It is worth noting that one of the objectives of Directive 2011/16/EU is to ensure the maximum effectiveness of all forms of cross-border exchange of information and, from this viewpoint, a broad concept of foreseeable relevance is consistent with the aim of enhancing the exchange of information on request between tax administrations.

However, as an important counterpoint, Article 5a of the Directive bolsters the assessment of foreseeable relevance by enhancing the requirement to state reasons in two ways: first, by obliging the requesting authority to justify that, under its national law, it is reasonably possible that the information requested will be relevant to the tax affairs of one or several taxpayers and will be justified for the purpose of the investigation; and second, by increasing the information that the requesting authority must provide in order to demonstrate this requirement is met, especially in cases of requests for information concerning a group of taxpayers.

At this point, it should be emphasised that the statement of reasons is important not only to enable the requested authority to verify the foreseeable relevance of the information requested, but also to ensure that actions aimed at processing information involving personal data of natural person respect

[50] See OECD, Commentaries on the Articles of the Model Tax Convention (OECD 2010), commentary on Article 26(1), para 5.2.

the principles of purpose limitation and data minimisation.[51] It should be recalled, in this regard, that Article 25(1) of Directive 2011/16/EU, as drafted by DAC7, states that 'all exchanges of information pursuant to this Directive shall be subject to Regulation (EU) 2016/679 of the European Parliament and of the Council'. By virtue of the principle of proactive responsibility set out in Articles 5(2) and 24 of the General Data Protection Regulation (GDPR), data controllers must be able to demonstrate that they have taken appropriate measures to ensure compliance with the principles relating to the processing of personal data. Moreover, the CJEU has recently held that in a case where the communication of the personal data with tax relevance is not based directly on a legal provision that constitutes its basis, but results from a request from the competent public authority, it is necessary for that request to specify the specific purposes of the collection of the data in the light of the task carried out in the public interest or the exercise of public powers, in order to enable the addressee of that request to ensure that 'the transmission of the personal data in question is lawful and the national courts concerned to exercise a review of the lawfulness of the processing operations in question'.[52]

In this sense, it is important to highlight an amendment made to Article 6(2) of Directive 2011/16/EU under DAC7. This provision, in its wording prior to the amendment, stated that the requesting authority 'may' include 'a reasoned request for a specific administrative enquiry' to be undertaken by the requested authority. DAC7 omits the adjective 'specific' from this provision, an omission that gives the requested authority greater room for manoeuvre to carry

---

[51] According to Article 5 of the General Data Protection Regulation (GDPR) (Regulation (EU) 2016/679 of the European Parliament and of the Council of 27 April 2016 on the protection of natural persons with regard to the processing of personal data and on the free movement of such data, and repealing Directive 95/46/EC (General Data Protection Regulation) [2016] OJ L 119/1), personal data shall be: (b) 'collected for specified, explicit and legitimate purposes and not further processed in a manner that is incompatible with those purposes'; and (c) 'adequate, relevant and limited to what is necessary in relation to the purposes for which they are processed'. According to Article 4(9) of the GDPR, Public authorities to which personal data are disclosed in accordance with a legal obligation for the exercise of their official mission, such as tax and customs authorities, should not be regarded as recipients if they receive personal data which are necessary to carry out a particular inquiry in the general interest, in accordance with Union or member state law. However, recital 31 of the GDPR states that in these cases, the 'requests for disclosure sent by the public authorities should always be in writing, *reasoned* and occasional, and should not concern the entirety of a filing system or lead to the interconnection of filing systems'.

[52] Case C-175/20 *SIA 'SS' v Valsts ieņēmumu dienests* [2022] ECLI:EU:C:2022:124, para 71.

out the enquiry or enquiries it deems appropriate.[53] However, the most striking aspect of the amendment of Article 6(2) of the Directive is that opportunity has been lost to establish the obligation (not the mere possibility) for all requests for information (not only for those involving the need for the requested State to carry out a certain administrative activity) to include a *sufficient statement of reasons* on the foreseeable relevance of the information requested for the tax purposes sought, with the material content provided for in Article 5a.[54]

Finally, DAC7 reduces the time limit from six to three months for the requested authority to send the requested information, where, at the time of the request it does not have such information in its possession, or to inform of the reasons for its delay and the date by which it will be able to provide it. This amendment has the effect of aligning the Directive, in matters of time limits, with other international and European rules on mutual assistance and administrative cooperation, but beyond that, its practical consequences remain limited.[55]

1.4 'FORESEEABLE RELEVANCE' AND FUNDAMENTAL RIGHTS

As noted in Part I, Chapters 5 and 6 in this book, one of the most complex and sensitive questions related to the cross-border exchange of tax information on request is finding an appropriate balance between the public interest (ensuring tax compliance, preventing tax avoidance and evasion) and the so-called taxpayer's participatory rights (the right to be informed, the right to be heard and the right to appeal). Despite the significance of these rights,[56] the international instruments designed to enable the exchange of information leave it to the

---

[53] Mercedes Fuster Gómez, 'Avances en la interpretación de la "pertinencia previsible" en el intercambio de información tras los pronunciamientos del TJUE y la DAC7' (2021) 3 Nueva Fiscalidad 147, 151.

[54] See Sánchez López (n 46); Bernardo D. Olivares Olivares, *Protección de datos, administración tributaria y tratamientos de alto riesgo en la Unión Europea* (Thomson Reuters-Aranzadi 2018) 152.

[55] As regards the effects of non-compliance with the three-month time limit referred to in Article 10 of Council Regulation (EU) 904/2010 of 7 October 2010 on administrative cooperation and combating fraud in the field of value added tax (recast) [2020] OJ L 268/1, see the judgment of CJEU of 30 September 2021, Case C-186/20 *HYDINA SK s.r.o. v Finančné riaditeľstvo Slovenskej republiky* [2021] ECLI:EU:C:2021:786, para 37.

[56] OECD *Committee of Fiscal Affairs Working Party No. 8, Taxpayers' rights and obligations – A survey of the legal situation in OECD countries* (volume 19, OECD 1990); OECD, *Tax Information Exchange between OECD Countries (a survey of current practices)* (OECD Publishing 1994), para 65; OECD, *Taxpayer Rights and Obligations* (OECD Publishing 2003); OECD, *Report on Tax Administrations in*

domestic laws of the co-operating states to actually apply them. Comparative law studies show that the recognition and scope of these rights vary significantly between countries,[57] and coincide in underlining that, as a result of the global trend towards greater effectiveness in cross-border exchange of information through the removal of obstacles to its fulfilment, some countries tend to limit or even remove participatory rights previously recognised in their legal systems where the outcome of the exchange of tax information may be compromised.[58]

The CJEU has stated on several occasions that the rules governing the exchange of tax information are addressed only to tax administrations – not to individuals – and only on the former do they confer rights and obligations.[59] This explains 'the traditional shortcoming of these rules as regards regulating the rights and guarantees of individuals affected by the exchange of information'.[60]

However, from the perspective of EU law, the existence of general principles of EU law that can be applied to the exchange of tax information, together with the possibility that such actions may affect certain fundamental rights recognised in the EU Charter of Fundamental Rights, make it possible to affirm the existence of 'legal framework of reference for individuals affected by the exchange of information that may offer protection different from that offered by the States themselves and even from that provided by international legal systems'.[61]

In the context of the EU, the right to an effective remedy is enshrined in both Article 6(1) of the Convention for the Protection of Human Rights and Fundamental Freedoms (ECHR) and in Article 47 of the Charter. The latter states in its first paragraph that 'Everyone whose rights and freedoms guaran-

---

OECD Countries and other Advanced and Emerging Economies (OECD Publishing 2015).

[57] Philip Baker and Pasquale Pistone, 'General Report' in Werner Haslehner, *The Practical Protection of Taxpayers' Rights* (Cahier de Droit Fiscal International, Volume 100B, SDU 2015); Giuseppe Marino, *New Exchange of Information versus Tax Solutions of Equivalent Effect* (EATLP International Tax Series, Volume 13, IBFD 2015) 39–46. See also the national and regional reports published annually by the IBFD's *Observatory on the Protection of Taxpayers' Rights*, <https://www.ibfd.org/ibfd-academic/publications/observatory-protection-taxpayers-rights-optr> accessed 5 December 2023.

[58] Menita Giusy de Flora, 'Protection of the Taxpayer in the Information Exchange Procedure' (2017) 45(6–7) Intertax 449.

[59] Case C-276/12 (n 21) para 36; Case C-682/15 (n 27) para 45.

[60] Fernando Fernández Marín, 'El Derecho de defensa y el intercambio de información tributaria en el Derecho de la UE' (2018) 8 Studi Tributari Europei 59, 60.

[61] ibid.

teed by the law of the Union are violated has the right to an effective remedy before a tribunal in compliance with the conditions laid down in this Article'. The second paragraph of said Article recognises the right of all individuals to 'a fair and public hearing within a reasonable time by an independent and impartial tribunal previously established by law'. In EU law, this right must be safeguarded not only in court proceedings, but also in administrative procedures undertaken by EU institutions and organisations, and in those conducted by Member States in the application of EU law, to allow individuals to exercise their rights before the administration.[62]

The judgments analysed in the previous section address the right to effective remedy in the exchange of tax information as regards the right to submit cases to jurisdiction, to access Justice. This right corresponds to the obligation that the second paragraph of Article 19(1) of the TFEU imposes on the Member States to 'provide the necessary means of redress to ensure an effective remedy in the areas covered by Union law'.

Let us recall that those judgments respond to various questions referred for a preliminary ruling by the Luxembourg Supreme Administrative Court under the Law of 25 November 2014 on the procedure applicable to the exchange of information on request in the field of taxation. This law, in the wording applicable to the facts of the main proceedings, prevented those named in the information order from lodging a direct appeal against it. The order could only be disputed indirectly in the context of an administrative appeal against the penalty imposed for failing to comply with the reporting obligation.[63]

In this context, the aforementioned judgments mark an important step forward in clarifying the scope of the right to effective remedy in cross-border exchange of information procedures, specifically in relation to the contestability of information orders.[64] This progress is twofold. On the one hand, it ensures that the addressee of the information order has a direct and effective appeal, not only incidental, against this decision, prior to the cross-border transfer of information, which allows them to respond to arbitrary or disproportionate administrative actions. On the other, the addressee of the order shall have access to the information referred to in Article 20(2) of the Directive in the context of any judicial proceedings in which the legality of the order deci-

---

62 ibid 62.

63 Article 6 of that Law provided that 'no appeal may be lodged against the request for exchange of information or against the decision of requirement referred to in Article 3(1) and (3)'. The Law of 1 March 2019 redrafted this provision to allow for a direct appeal against the decision.

64 See Aurora Ribes Ribes, 'Comentario a la Sentencia del TJUE (Gran Sala) de 6 de octubre de 2020: Joined Cases C-245/19 and C-246-19' (2021) 1(132) Revista Técnica Tributaria 213, 219.

sion is discussed, such that their case can be given a fair hearing as regards the requirement of foreseeable relevance.

However, the judgments in the cases of *Berlioz* and *Grand Duchy of Luxembourg v L* are inconclusive as to whether the addressee of the information order should have access to the minimum content of the request for information submitted by the requesting authority together with the order decision itself. The *Berlioz* judgment recognised that, in the context of court proceedings, the defendant should have access to the information in Article 20(2) of the Directive for his case to be heard fairly in relation to the requirement of foreseeable relevance, although the right of access to the entire request for information was denied on the grounds of the secrecy of the information (Article 16 of Directive 2011/16/EU). However, in the words of Advocate General Kokott, if, in accordance with the case law of the CJEU, the addressee of the information order must have access to that information in the judicial proceedings, there is no reason why that information should not be communicated to them in the information order itself, so that they can defend their rights effectively and decide whether or not to dispute that decision.[65] This is corroborated by the fact that, according to the Court, the same criteria apply to the review to be carried out by the requested authority and the Court hearing the case as regards the examination of foreseeable relevance. Additionally, the addressee's access to that minimum information, together with the decision to issue the order, is supported by the principle of judicial economy, as it would avoid the filing of unnecessary appeals, the only reason for which is to access that information to see whether the information order is challengeable.[66] Moreover, the Court of Justice finds that the right to effective remedy does not require Member States to provide the taxpayer who is the subject of an investigation (or third parties affected by the information order) with a direct appeal against the decision to issue an order to the holder of the information, since the taxpayer is not the addressee of such an order and is not bound by it, with the possibility of challenging the subsequent tax assessment being a sufficient guarantee.

In our view, the Court's reasoning on this point is not satisfactory, as, despite recognising the complementary nature of the fundamental rights to privacy (Article 7 Charter) and the protection of personal data (Article 8 Charter) and the right to effective remedy in the framework of a request for information in accordance with Directive 2011/16/EU, it does not address the fact that an indirect appeal against the tax assessment is not capable of preventing interference with the personal data of the taxpayer, a physical person,

---

65 Opinion of Advocate General Kokott (n 32) para 137.

66 Opinion of Advocate General Kokott (n 32) para 91.

which occurs when the data is collected. A subsequent possible use of the data only perpetuates this interference, meaning that a legal remedy against the use of the data in the course of the tax proceedings, even if it prohibited such use, it would prevent the perpetuation of the interference, but not the interference itself.[67] This is, to a certain extent, in line with the judgment in the *Sabou* case, the first in which the Court ruled on the taxpayer's right to be informed of a request for information in a procedure of exchange of information on request. The judgment stated that, given the silence of the Directive, the right to an effective remedy does not oblige the requested state to inform the taxpayer of the request for information nor to take part in the request, nor does it require that the taxpayer should be heard at the point when inquiries, which may include the examination of witnesses, are carried out, or before that State sends the information to the requesting state.

The Court based its judgment on an argument subsequently reiterated in those analysed in this work. It distinguishes, in the context of tax inspection procedures, between 'the investigation stage, during which information is collected and which includes the request for information by one tax authority to another' and 'the contentious stage, between the tax authorities and the taxpayer, which begins when the taxpayer is sent the proposed adjustment.'[68] In short, the Court refers the protection of the taxpayer to the domestic rules of each Member State at the stage following the gathering of information, although it notes that 'there is nothing to prevent a Member State from extending the right to be heard to other parts of the investigation stage, by involving the taxpayer in various stages of the gathering of information, in particular the examination of witnesses.'[69]

In sum, EU law, as interpreted by the CJEU, does not recognise the right of the taxpayer under investigation to take part in the cross-border exchange of tax information, on the understanding that these are part of a preliminary phase or a stage prior to the inspection procedure, it is then in the subsequent contentious phase that the taxpayer under investigation may have access to all relevant documentation and exercise their right of defence. This conclusion is, however, unsatisfactory, as it ignores the complementary nature of the right to an effective remedy and the rights to privacy and the protection of personal data in the exchange of tax information. It may thus lead to situations in which the taxpayer's legitimate rights and interests are seriously affected, without their being able to defend them effectively.[70]

---

[67] Opinion of Advocate General Kokott (n 32) para 74.

[68] C-276/12 (n 21) para 40.

[69] ibid para 45.

[70] This opinion is also defended, among others, by José Manuel Calderón Carrero and Alberto Quintas Seara, 'The Taxpayer's Right of Defense in Cross-Border

In the current state of development of EU law, the central role of the CJEU in defining the contours of the legal position of taxpayers (and third parties) affected by such proceedings is undeniable. However, the CJEU necessarily adopts a case-by-case approach which does not inevitably lead to the establishment of a general and consistent minimum standard of protection for persons affected by such proceedings.[71] As will be pointed out in Part I, Chapter 6 later in this book, 'the existing regime, in particular the concept of *ex post facto* judicial protection, and the ensuing reviewability of foreign decisions, fails to guarantee adequate protection to taxpayers and to affected third parties'.[72]

1.5 CONCLUDING REFLECTIONS

It is undoubtedly no simple task to strike the right balance between respect for taxpayers' fundamental rights and the need for tax authorities to have tools at their disposal to effectively control compliance with tax obligations and to combat tax avoidance and evasion. Nonetheless, however complex and sensitive it may be, it appears necessary to set out a common regulatory framework for the participatory rights of taxpayers in cross-border exchanges of information, as individuals with rights that need protection, such that they can effectively exercise their substantive or material rights, without prejudice to the possibility of some of these rights being limited where there are objective reasons to justify it and such limitations are interpreted in light of Article 52(1) of the Charter. This common treatment would also help make the principle of procedural autonomy more flexible, which, despite being complemented by the principles of equivalence and effectiveness, does not safeguard a similar level of protection of the fundamental rights of persons affected by these

---

Exchange of Information Procedures' (2014) 68(9) Bulletin for International Taxation, 506; Niels Diepvens and Filip Debelva, 'The Evolution of the Exchange of Information in Direct Tax Matters: The Taxpayer's Rights Under Pressure' (2015) 24(4) EC Tax Review 210, 218; G Melis, 'AEOI and Protection of Taxpayers' Procedural Rights' in Giuseppe Marino, *New Exchange of Information versus Tax Solutions of Equivalent Effect* (EATLP International Tax Series, Volume 13, IBFD 2015) 179; Xavier Oberson, *International Exchange of Information in Tax Matters: Towards Global Transparency* (Elgar Tax Law and Practice Series, 3rd edn, Edward Elgar 2023) 240; Philip Baker and Pasquale Pistone, 'Action 16: The Taxpayers' Right to an Effective Legal Remedy Under European Law in Cross-Border Situations' (2016) 25(5) EC Tax Review 335, 344; Luis Alfonso Martinez Giner, 'El intercambio automático de información en materia tributaria: retos e incertidumbres jurídicas' (2017) 173 Revista Española de Derecho Financiero 97, 163.

[71] Filip Debelva and Irma Johanna Mosquera Valderrama, 'Privacy and Confidentiality in Exchange of Information Procedures: Some Uncertainties, Many Issues, but Few Solutions' (2017) 45(5) Intertax 362, 374.

[72] See Part I, Chapter 6 in this book.

actions across the EU. It would also help make the exchange of information more effective, given that a higher level of protection of taxpayers' rights and guarantees might have a positive impact on the level of cooperation between taxpayers and tax administrations, enhancing the relationship between them.[73]

In this sense, the adoption of the GDPR is a most positive step in ensuring a more consistent and coherent protection of the rights and freedoms of European citizens regarding the processing of their personal data. The aims of this regulation include achieving 'a consistent and high level of protection for natural persons'.[74] This equivalent level of protection with regard to personal data represents an improvement in the recognition of taxpayers as data subjects,[75] since the controller, according to Article 5 of the GDPR, is responsible for the fair, lawful and transparent processing of personal data. However, a pending and relevant issue – into which the CJEU has not delved so far – is the connection between 'foreseeable relevance' and the principles related to the quality of the processing of personal data in the EoIR, with the purpose of bridging the principle of data minimisation with the content of the request of information (and the subsequent request decision).

The European Commission's project to enhance taxpayers' rights in the internal market is intended to improve the coordination of national legislation on taxpayers' rights at a European level and to identify and promote best administrative practices in this area.[76] This initiative is a step in the right direction and can perhaps be complemented with specific and minor changes in secondary EU law, which should be formulated and interpreted in accordance with the case law of the CJEU and taking into account the principles of effectiveness and equivalence between cross-border and domestic situations.[77]

Indeed, Article 25 of Directive 2011/16/EU has undergone successive amendments, leading to significant progress as regards respect for the fundamental right to the protection of personal data in the automatic exchange of information, including the recognition of the right of the data subject to be

---

[73] Luis Alfonso Martinez Giner, *La protección jurídica del contribuyente en el intercambio de información entre Estados* (Iustel 2009) 22 and 25.

[74] GDPR (n 52) recital 10.

[75] Marina Serrat Romani, *Los derechos y garantías de los contribuyentes en la era digital. Transparencia e intercambio de información tributaria* (Thomson Reuters-Aranzadi 2018) 356. In any case, it is a limited improvement, since legal persons are generally excluded from the scope of this fundamental right.

[76] This Project is part of the Communication for fair and simple taxation supporting the recovery strategy Tax Action Plan [2020] COM(2020) 312 Final. The Project consists of the presentation of a Communication and a Recommendation (n 5). The Commission's submission of both documents was initially scheduled for the third quarter of 2021.

[77] Baker and Pistone (n 71) 335.

informed *ex ante*, in certain cases, of the processing and transmission of their personal data, such that they can immediately and effectively control them.[78]

This would help provide taxpayers and national authorities with certainty regarding the contours and limits of the rights of participation in the exchange of tax information in EU law. Additionally, it would provide an equivalent minimum level of protection of taxpayers' rights, regardless of the Member State in which they are resident or in which they exercise their fundamental freedoms.[79] Moreover, given the certainty it would afford, it could contribute to developing a closer relationship between taxpayers and tax administrations, which, in turn, would help improve tax compliance.[80]

---

[78] Following the amendment of Article 25 of Directive 2011/16/EU by Directive 2023/2226/EU, the obligation to inform data subjects *ex ante* about the processing and transmission of personal data extends not only to financial institutions, with respect to financial account information, but also to intermediaries obliged to communicate potentially aggressive tax planning arrangements, reporting platform operators and crypto-asset service providers.

[79] Observatory on The Protection of Taxpayers' Rights, *Report on the Taxpayers' Rights in the EU*, 27.11.2020, p. 13; European Commission 'EU Taxpayers' Rights in the Single Market (Communication)' (Law, 2021), <https://ec.europa.eu/info/law/better-regulation/have-your-say/initiatives/12626-EU-taxpayers-rights-in-the-single-market-Communication-> accessed 5 December 2023.

[80] Maria Teresa Soler, 'Tax Administration versus Taxpayer – A New Deal?' (2012) 4(3) World Tax Journal 282.

2. Exchange of information procedures between composite administration and transnational administrative acts

Olivier Dubos, Mariolina Eliantonio and Tatsiana Ivanchykava

2.1 INTRODUCTION

The Directive on Administrative Cooperation provides for the exchange of tax information in three forms: spontaneous, automatic and on request. All three types of decision-making proceedings can be qualified as 'composite procedures' and generate a number of situations of so-called 'transnationality', in which the acts adopted, or the actions performed by the administrative authorities of the Member States concerned, are based on or have effects outside the territory of the legal systems in which the authorities themselves are located. These procedures, and the transnational administrative acts they generate, are not peculiar to the tax cooperation field, but are particularly prevalent in the area due to the intertwined nature of the administrative decision-making proceedings set out by EU secondary law. Because of the weight attached to situations of composite procedures and transnationality in the field of tax cooperation and the lack of research in this area, this chapter aims to consider the steps of the various mechanisms of exchange of information in tax matters and conceptualise them as acts of transnational imputation and transnational effects, and, subsequently, as a form of horizontal composite procedure. Thereafter, some thoughts will be offered on the implications of these conceptualisations for the question of access to justice and judicial control of exchange of information procedures, before a conclusion presents the main findings.

2.2 THE VARIEGATED UNIVERSE OF TRANSNATIONAL ADMINISTRATIVE ACTS: FUNCTIONS AND TYPES OF TRANSNATIONALITY IN THE EU AND ITS RELATIONSHIP TO COMPOSITE PROCEDURES

2.2.1 The Notion of Transnational Administrative Acts and their Functions in the EU

At the outset of this investigation, it ought to be noted that, despite its existence since the process of European integration, the notion of a 'transnational administrative act' has been neglected by legal scholarship and currently lacks full systematisation and conceptualisation.[1] Despite this neglect, transnational administrative acts have seen an immense proliferation in virtually all policy fields of the EU, including competition law, the environment, asylum and marketing authorisations (for example medicines). In fact, it would not be an overstatement to say that the very foundations of the EU internal market are grounded on the notion of transnationality.

Drawing from the definition of extraterritoriality by Brigitte Stern, we consider transnational administrative acts to be acts whose decision-making process or application takes place (at least in part) outside the territory of the State that issued it.[2] Borrowing from Prosper Weil's distinction of two dimen-

---

[1] See however Estelle Chambas, 'L'acte administratif unilatéral transnational' (DPhil Thesis, Université Paris II Panthéon-Assas 2022); Damien Elkind, 'L'efficacité des décisions administratives étrangères dans l'Union européenne. Étude de droit administratif transnational' (DPhil Thesis, University of Bordeaux 2018); Marie Gautier, 'Acte administratif transnational et droit de l'Union européenne' in Jean-Bernard Auby and Jacqueline Dutheil de la Rochère (eds), *Traité de droit administratif Européen* (Bruylant 2007) 1303; Clara I Velasco Rico, 'L'acte administratif national dans le contexte du droit de l'Union européenne' in Jean-Bernard Auby and Jacqueline Dutheil de la Rochère (eds), *Traité de droit administratif Européen* (3rd edn, Bruylant 2022) 915; Angelos S. Gerontas, 'Deterritorialization in Administrative Law: Exploring Transnational Administrative Decisions' (2013) 19(3) Columbia Journal of European Law 1; Matthias Ruffert, 'European Composite Administration: The transnational administrative act' in Oswald Jansen and Bettina Schöndorf-Haubold (eds), *The European Composite Administration* (Intersentia 2011) 277; Emilie Chevalier and Oliver Dubos, 'The Notion of "Transnationality" in Administrative Law: Taxonomy and Judicial Review' (2021) 22(3) German Law Journal 325; Luca De Lucia, 'From Mutual Recognition to EU Authorization: A Decline of Transnational Administrative Acts?' (2016) 8(1) Italian Journal of Public Law 90, 95–96.

[2] Brigette Stern, 'Une tentative d'élucidation du concept d'application extraterritoriale' (1986) 3 Revue Québécoise de Droit International 49, 51: 'There is extraterri-

sions of extraterritoriality, we furthermore identify transnational administrative acts which are (or are not) the product of a recognition process.[3]

In the context of the EU (but not solely), transnational administrative acts are used as a regulatory instrument by the legislator for a variety of different reasons, ranging from the need to facilitate the free movement of persons, the need to build the internal market of goods, or to protect the environment and personal data.

For example, in the context of visas and migration, the abolition of border controls between the Member States has necessitated legislation creating systems of information exchange, not dissimilar from those which are being explored in the field of tax cooperation.[4] Similarly, EU law provides a system for coordinating social security schemes and mutual administrative assistance between the various bodies of the Member States.[5] To ensure the free movement of persons, EU law establishes a mechanism for the mutual recognition of driver's licences[6] as well as of professional qualifications.[7] As will be explained below, mutual recognition is a typical regulatory scheme generating transnational administrative acts. It is also important to note in the context of

---

toriality in the application of a norm, if all or part of the application process takes place outside the territory of the State that issued it'.

3 Prosper Weil, 'International Law Limitation on State Jurisdiction' in Cecil J. Olmstead (ed), *Extraterritorial Application of Laws and Responses Thereto* (Oxford University Press 1984) 34.

4 See further on those mechanisms Niovi Vavoula, 'Information Sharing in the Dublin System: Remedies for Asylum Seekers In-Between Gaps in Judicial Protection and Interstate Trust' (2021) 22(3) German Law Journal 391.

5 Council Regulation (EC) No 883/2004 of the European Parliament and of the Council of 29 April 2004 on the coordination of social security systems [2004] OJ L 166/1. See further Henrik Wenander, 'Sincere Cooperation, Mutual Trust, and Mutual Recognition in Social Security Coordination' (2020) 13(3) Review of European Administrative Law 89.

6 Directive 2006/126/EC of the European Parliament and of the Council of 20 December 2006 on driving licences [2006] OJ L 403/18. See further for the evolution of the legislation and case law Meinhard Schröder, 'Mutual Recognition of Driving Licences in the EU – Current State of Integration and Perspectives' (2020) 3(1) Review of European Administrative Law 37.

7 Directive 2005/36/EC of the European Parliament and of the Council of 7 September 2005 on the recognition of professional qualifications [2005] OJ L 255/22. There is also sectoral legislation, such as Directive 98/5/EC of the European Parliament and of the Council of 16 February 1998 to facilitate practice of the profession of lawyer on a permanent basis in a Member State other than that in which the qualification was obtained, Directive 98/5/EC of the European Parliament and of the Council of 16 February 1998 to facilitate practice of the profession of lawyer on a permanent basis in a Member State other than that in which the qualification was obtained [1998] OJ L 77/36.

the free movement of goods that EU law and the CJEU's case law may provide for mutual recognition schemes, both through the *Cassis de Dijon* mechanism of negative integration,[8] and through the harmonisation of certain authorisation schemes, such as in field of medicine.[9]

2.2.2 The Types of Transnational Administrative Acts: Between Imputation and Effects

Departing from the earlier definition of transnational administrative acts as acts whose decision-making process or application takes place (at least in part) outside the territory of the State that issued it, one can distinguish between acts of transnational imputation and acts with transnational effects. In the first case, the transnational aspect is to be found in the decision-making process for the adoption of the act, while, in the second case, transnationality emerges in the application of the act.

In turn, acts of transnational imputation can find their 'transnational elements' in different places. There can be, first of all, acts that are of transnational imputation because they are (partly) based on a foreign factual ground. For example, the decision of a national competition authority concerning an undertaking whose conduct has an effect on the market of another EU Member State, or an environmental permit issued or refused in view of its impact on the territory of another Member State, would fall into this category of acts of transnational imputation.[10]

Second, the transnational imputation of an act can be shown in the legal grounds of an act, which can be (partly) foreign. For example, within the framework of the Schengen Information System, if the administration of a Member State has communicated that a foreigner has been the subject of a deportation order, the administration of another Member State may rely on

---

[8] Case 120/78 *Rewe-Zentral AG v. Bundesmonopolverwaltung für Branntwein* [1979] ECLI:EU:C:1979:42.

[9] Directive 2001/83/EC of the European Parliament and of the Council of 6 November 2001 on the Community code relating to medicinal products for human use [2001] OJ L 311/67. See further Sabrina Röttger-Wirtz, 'Mutual Recognition and the Ever-incomplete Internal Market for Pharmaceuticals' (2020) 13(3) Review of European Administrative Law 61.

[10] This flows indirectly from Council Regulation (EC) No 1/2003 of 16 December 2002 on the implementation of the rules on competition laid down in Articles 81 and 82 of the Treaty, [2003] OJ L 1/1, art 22 and Directive 2011/92/EU of the European Parliament and of the Council of 13 December 2011 on the assessment of the effects of certain public and private projects on the environment [2011] OJ L 26/1, art 7.

this information resulting from a foreign act to refuse a visa.[11] This act refusing a visa is an act of transnational imputation because (at least some of) its legal ground(s) are based on a foreign act.

Third, acts of transnational imputation can be acts of recognition. An act of recognition is, in general, an act through which an administrative body gives effects in its legal order to an act which has no such effects *de plano*. Such acts are adopted in the framework of the mutual recognition schemes mentioned above.[12]

Fourth, acts of transnational imputation can give execution to foreign acts. For example, in the field of taxation, Article 10(1) of Council Directive 2010/24/EU provides that '[A]t the request of the applicant authority, the requested authority shall recover claims which are the subject of an instrument permitting enforcement in the applicant Member State'.[13] The acts through which the requested authority will recover foreign tax claims may therefore be defined as an act of execution of transnational imputation, as it is taken on the basis of the request of a foreign authority to execute a foreign claim.

Moving from the decision-making process to the application of an administrative act, we can identify three categories of acts with transnational effects, according to the nature of these effects, namely: (i) acts with transnational factual effects, (ii) acts constituting the legal basis of a foreign act, and (iii) acts with transnational legal effects.

Some administrative acts, without affecting legal situations located in a foreign legal order, produce a *de facto* effect on the territory of a foreign State. For example, an authorisation for an installation is likely, at least potentially, to have environmental consequences on the territory of a bordering State. Precisely because of this potential factual effect, EU law foresees transnational public inquiries and transnational impact assessment procedures.[14]

Second, administrative acts can have transnational effects because they are the legal basis of acts adopted by a foreign authority. Taking again an example introduced above, a deportation order which constitutes the ground for the

---

[11] Convention implementing the Schengen Agreement of 14 June 1985 between the Governments of the States of the Benelux Economic Union, the Federal Republic of Germany and the French Republic on the gradual abolition of checks at their common borders [1985] OJ L 239/19, art 5(1)(d).

[12] See further on this concept Luis Arroyo Jiménez, 'Effective Judicial Protection and Mutual Recognition in the European Administrative Space' (2021) 22(3) German Law Journal 344.

[13] Council Directive 2010/24/EU of 16 March 2010 on mutual assistance for the recovery of claims relating to taxes, duties and other measures [2010] OJ L 84/1.

[14] Directive 2011/92/EU of the European Parliament and of the Council of 13 December 2011 on the assessment of the effects of certain public and private projects on the environment (codification) [2012] OJ L 26/1, art 7.

refusal of a visa by the administration of another Member State is an act with such transnational effects.

Third, administrative acts can produce transnational legal effects. This is the case when this act is potentially or actually capable of determining the legal situation of those to whom it applies. This is the case, for example, in mutual recognition schemes discussed above. An act which, subject to the recognition of another Member State, is capable of producing legal effects in the territory of the recognising Member State is an example of this type of administrative acts with transnational effects. There are also examples of acts having automatic transnational effects, which do not need recognition from a foreign authority to produce effects on the latter's territory. For example, EU legislation determines that a licence for the export of a cultural good obtained in one Member State is valid (and hence produces effects) through the entire territory of the EU.[15]

Finally, administrative acts can have legal effects outside their territory because EU legislation may allow an administrative authority to carry out acts of enforcement on foreign territory. For example, Article 35(9) of Directive 2014/65/EU provides that '[E]ach Member State shall provide that, where an investment firm authorised in another Member State has established a branch within its territory, the competent authority of the home Member State of the investment firm, in the exercise of its responsibilities and after informing the competent authority of the host Member State, may carry out on-site inspections in that branch'.[16]

2.2.3 Composite Procedures in the EU

Unlike the phenomenon of transnational administrative acts, the notion of 'composite procedures' has been widely discussed in literature, although the attention on this phenomenon is rather recent.[17] This term refers to administra-

[15] Council Regulation No 116/2009 of 18 December 2008 on the export of cultural goods [2009] OJ L 39/1, art 2(3).

[16] Directive 2014/65/EU of the European Parliament and of the Council of 15 May 2014 on markets in financial instruments and amending Directive 2002/92/EC and Directive 2011/61/EU [2014] OJ L 173/349.

[17] See *ex multis* Herwig C.H. Hofmann and Alexander H. Türk (eds), *Legal Challenges in EU Administrative Law – Towards an Integrated Administration* (Edward Elgar 2009); Sergio Alonso de León, 'Composite Administrative Procedures in the European Union' (DPhil Thesis, University Carlos III Madrid 2016), <https://e-archivo.uc3m.es/bitstream/handle/10016/23445/Tesis_Sergio_Alonso_de_Leon_2016.pdf> accessed 5 December 2023; Filipe Brito Bastos, 'Derivative Illegality in the European Composite Administrative Procedures' (2018) 55(1) Common Market Law Review 101; Mariolina Eliantonio, 'Review in an Integrated Administration: The

tive decision-making procedures which foresee the involvement of administrative authorities belonging to more than one legal system at various stages of the procedures and with different intensities.[18]

Importantly, for the purposes of this contribution, it should be highlighted that a basic sub-division of composite procedures is the division between 'horizontal' and 'vertical' composite procedures, on the basis of the involvement (or lack thereof) of the EU administrative authorities. Examples of vertical composite procedures, entailing cooperation between national and EU authorities, exist in several policy fields, such as marketing authorisations for genetically modified organisms (GMOs),[19] or the management of EU funds.[20] In these procedures, national authorities cooperate in various ways with the EU Commission or the EU agencies, in decision-making processes which are concluded through either a national administrative decision or a European measure.

Horizontal procedures, meanwhile, do not foresee the involvement of EU administrative authorities. These procedures exist in various policy fields and may take various shapes.

In terms of functions, horizontal composite procedures may have, first of all, a decision-making purpose. For example, a transboundary consultation in the framework of the environmental impact assessment of a project entails the creation of a horizontal composite procedure concluded with an authorisation (or a denial thereof) for a project.[21] These procedures can also have an enforcement purpose, as in the case of cooperation in inspection activities. For example, in the case of the implementation of EU fisheries policy, the legislative framework foresees the creation of joint inspection teams with inspectors of at least

---

Case of "Composite Procedures"' (2014) 7(2) Review of European Administrative Law 65.

[18] The term was famously coined by H. Hofmann. See Herwig C.H. Hofmann, 'Composite decision-making procedures in EU administrative law' in Hofmann and Türk (n 17) 136.

[19] Directive 2001/18/EC of the European Parliament and of the Council of 12 March 2001 on the deliberate release into the environment of genetically modified organisms and repealing Council Directive 90/220/EEC [2001] OJ L 106/1.

[20] Regulation (EU) 2021/1057 of the European Parliament and of the Council of 24 June 2021 establishing the European Social Fund Plus (ESF+) and repealing Regulation (EU) 1296/2013 [2021] OJ L 231/21.

[21] Directive 2011/92/EU of the European Parliament and of the Council of 13 December 2011 on the assessment of the effects of certain public and private projects on the environment (codification) [2012] OJ L 26/1, art 7.

two Member States carrying out an inspection in a specific area (under the operational coordination of the European Fisheries Control Agency).[22]

Finally, it should be mentioned that horizontal composite procedures can take more or less formalised shapes. In some cases, the cooperation entails the raising of a formal objection: according to the applicable EU legislation, a Member State may require the authorities of other Member States to state whether they have grounds for objecting to the issuing of a visa.[23] In other cases, the cooperation can be much more fluid and intangible: for example, the Water Framework Directive requires the creation of 'river basins' as basic operational entities of water management, independent of administrative and political borders. A river basin extending over the territory of more than one Member State should be integrated into an international river basin district, involving the constant cooperation of administrative authorities of several Members States.[24] As is the case with the procedures discussed below, horizontal composite procedures can also materialise in the exchange of information.

Having introduced the functions and types of transnational administrative acts, as well as the notion of horizontal composite procedure, the next section will conceptualise the procedures of exchange of information foreseen in the Directive on Administrative Cooperation and the acts generated therefrom as composite procedures and transnational administrative acts, before offering some reflections on the implications of this categorisation specifically for judicial protection.

2.3 EXCHANGE OF INFORMATION AS A PLAYGROUND FOR COMPOSITE PROCEDURES AND TRANSNATIONAL ADMINISTRATIVE ACTS

The Directive on Administrative Cooperation contains the legal regime for administrative cooperation between Member States in the tax field. According to its Article 1, the Directive 'lays down the rules and procedures under which the Member States shall cooperate with each other with a view to exchanging

---

22 Regulation (EU) 2019/473 of the European Parliament and of the Council of 19 March 2019 on the European Fisheries Control Agency (codification) [2019] OJ L 83/18, arts 5 and 7(d).

23 Regulation (EC) 810/2009 of the European Parliament and of the Council of 13 July 2009 establishing a Community Code on Visas (Visa Code) [2009] OJ L 243/1, art 22.

24 Directive 2000/60/EC of the European Parliament and of the Council of 23 October 2000 establishing a framework for Community action in the field of water policy [2000] OJ L 327/1.

information that is foreseeably relevant to the administration and enforcement of the domestic laws of the Member States concerning the taxes'. As such, the Directive foresees several types of cooperation between the national administrations of the Member States. For example, it provides for the mechanism of exchange of information,[25] the presence and participation of the officials of the requesting authority in administrative enquiries carried out by the requested authority,[26] simultaneous controls,[27] and administrative notifications.[28] In all of these cases, various national authorities cooperate for the implementation of EU law. Hence, these procedures clearly qualify as horizontal composite procedures and may generate transnational administrative acts.

In line with the focus of this collection, this chapter will further only consider the transnational administrative acts generated by exchange of information procedures. Zooming in on these mechanisms, a distinction should be made between the spontaneous or automatic exchange of information (i.e., without prior request) and that upon request. These will be examined in turn.

2.3.1 Exchange of Information Upon Request

Under the Directive on Administrative Cooperation, the competent authority of one Member State may request the competent authority of another Member State to provide information that is foreseeably relevant to the administration of the requesting Member State. This mechanism of exchange of information may lead to the adoption of transnational administrative acts by both the requested authority and the requesting authority.

The request of the requesting Member State aims to produce an effect outside its territory, in particular on the competent authority of another Member State. From this position, the request can be considered as an administrative act with transnational effects in the requested Member State.

From the perspective of the requested authority, once it has received the information request from a competent authority of another Member State, it has to communicate the requested information to the requesting authority.[29] In this context, two scenarios can be distinguished. If the requested authority is already in possession of the requested information, it must transmit it to the requesting authority. This act would qualify, from the perspective of the requested State, as an act of transnational imputation, because it is adopted on the basis of the request for information received from a foreign authority.

---

25 DAC1, arts 5, 8 and 9.

26 ibid art 11.

27 ibid art 12.

28 ibid art 13.

29 ibid art 5.

From the perspective of the requesting State, it is instead an act with potential transnational effects, because it may (but does not have to, as will be explained below) lead to the further adoption of acts in the requesting State.

It may also happen that the requested authority does not have this information in its possession, so, in order to fulfil its obligation of cooperation, it must carry out an administrative enquiry to collect requested information and then transmit it to the requesting authority.[30] In this case, the acts adopted by the requested authority in order to collect the requested information are based on the request coming from a foreign authority. On this basis, they should be considered as acts of transnational imputation. The act through which the information collected is subsequently shared with the requesting State qualifies, in turn – as in the case above –as an act of transnational imputation for the requested State and one with potential transnational effects for the requesting State.

The exchange of information upon request may also lead to the adoption of transnational administrative acts by the requesting authority. Indeed, after having sent a request for certain information foreseeably relevant for particular tax purposes, the requesting authority will receive the sought-after information from the requested authority (unless the requested authority is unable or unwilling to provide it).[31] Once the requesting authority receives the requested information, it may use the information as a basis for an administrative decision. It should be underlined that EU law does not specify any obligation on the requesting authority to follow up on the information received from the requested authority. The mechanism of exchange of information upon request focuses rather on the obligation of transmission of information by the requested authority, and does not impose any obligation on the follow-up on the part of the requesting competent authority. However, the Directive does state that the requesting authority may use the information received for the administration and enforcement of domestic tax law,[32] as well as for evidence on the same basis as similar information provided by one of its own authorities.[33] The requesting authority can even use the information for purposes other than those covered by the Directive with the permission of the competent authority of the Member State that communicated it.[34]

---

[30] ibid art 6. It should be noted that the Directive specifies that the requested authority must procure the information, 'even though that Member State may not need such information for its own tax purposes' (art 18(1)) and it is allowed to refuse to transmit the information or carry out the necessary enquiries only in certain situations listed in art 17.

[31] Further on the notion of foreseeable relevance see Part I, Chapter 1 in this book.

[32] DAC1 (n 25) art 16(1).

[33] ibid art 16(5).

[34] ibid art 16(2).

Thus, administrative acts adopted by the requesting authority that take information provided by the competent authority of another EU Member State into account will contain foreign elements and can, therefore, be considered as acts of transnational imputation.

2.3.2 Exchange of Information Without Prior Request

The Directive also foresees situations in which an information exchange takes place without a prior request from the competent authority. This means that each competent authority may, or must, transmit certain information which it possesses to the competent authority of any other Member State, either spontaneously or automatically. As pointed out in literature, the crucial difference between the mechanisms of information exchange without prior request and those upon request is that the information transmitted without prior request was originally collected by the transmitting authority for its own purposes and not in the interest of the competent authority of another Member State.[35] From this perspective, unlike in the case of the exchange of information upon request, there is no foreign element in the acts carried out when the information is collected, hence there is no transnational administrative act. In turn, the exchange of information without prior request may be automatic, compulsory or may be spontaneous. Each of these methods may lead to the adoption of transnational administrative acts by both the authority sending the information and the authority receiving the information.

Article 8 of the Directive provides for a mechanism of mandatory automatic exchange of information: it establishes that the competent authority of each Member State shall automatically communicate to the competent authority of any other Member State, information regarding taxable periods that is available concerning residents in that other Member State.[36] In such cases, and unlike the situation of an exchange of information upon request, the act through which the information is shared can be qualified, from the perspective of the receiving State, as an act with potential transnational effects. However, it will not be an act of transnational imputation for the State of the sending authority, as the sharing does not happen on the basis of a foreign element, but only on the basis of the applicable legislation.

As with respect to information exchanged upon request, while the competent authority of a Member State has an obligation to transmit the information under the Directive, the competent authority of another Member State that

---

[35] Jens-Peter Schneider, 'Basic Structures of Information Management in the European Administrative Union' (2014) 20(1) European Public Law 101.

[36] DAC1 (n 25) art 8.

receives the automatically transmitted information has no obligation to use it. However, in the case that the receiving competent authority adopts an administrative act on the basis of the information received from the authority of another Member State, the act adopted on its grounds should be considered as an act of transnational imputation, because it is (at least partly) based on the information originating from a different legal order.

Finally, the Directive foresees cases of spontaneous exchange of information. This mechanism is triggered in particular circumstances, such as a risk for the tax policy of a Member State.[37] In general, the competent authority of a Member State may transmit to the competent authorities of the other Member States any information at its disposal which may be useful to the competent authorities of the other Member States.[38] Thus it can be considered as the 'manifestation of shared administrative responsibilities'[39] between EU Member States. The Directive also provides that the sending authority may ask the receiving authority to give feedback on the transmitted information and to specify the follow-up given to it.[40]

As in the case of the mandatory automatic exchange of information, the act of sharing information spontaneously will not be qualified as an act of transnational imputation (because it is not based on an objective foreign element), but it does have the features of an act with potential transnational effects. In turn, the competent authority that receives the information spontaneously shared from the competent authority of another Member State, may (but is not obliged to) adopt an administrative act on the basis of received information. This act must be considered of transnational imputation.

2.4 THE IMPLICATIONS OF COMPOSITE PROCEDURES AND TRANSNATIONAL ADMINISTRATIVE ACTS IN THE EU MULTI-LEVEL SYSTEM OF JUDICIAL PROTECTION

Having conceptualised the mechanisms of exchange of information as a form of horizontal composite procedure, and as generating a number of transnational administrative acts, this section aims at providing some reflections on the possible gaps in judicial control within the framework of these procedures. While the reader should be referred to Part I, Chapter 6 of this book for the

37 ibid art 9(1).
38 ibid art 9(2).
39 Schneider (n 35).
40 DAC1 (n 25) art 14.

details on the system of judicial protection, and the case law of the CJEU on the exchange of information procedures, we aim here to present the *problématique* in the context of the general European administrative law framework.

The starting point of our reflection is that horizontal composite procedures and the ensuing transnational administrative acts challenge the traditional approach to judicial review of administrative action, which is based on the principle of territoriality. On this basis, the jurisdiction of the courts is limited to the review of the administrative action stemming from authorities belonging to its domestic legal system.[41] Furthermore, judicial control of foreign acts would entail a practical difficulty: the judge in one State would not be best placed to scrutinise a foreign act because of language barriers, different legal cultures, and legal technicalities. In addition, transnational judicial review of a foreign preparatory administrative act is also regarded as entailing an intrusion on State's sovereignty and democratic processes.[42] Along the same lines, an administrative act must be seen as the execution by a State, under its own political responsibility *vis-à-vis* its citizens, of the law adopted by the legislature of its own polity, in whose name its judiciary would be exercising the judicial function. Another State judiciary would, from that perspective, have little say in a legal and political process aiming at serving the needs of a different political community.[43] In the EU context, finally, the principle of mutual trust, famously enunciated by the CJEU in Opinion 1/13, would seem to speak against the possibility of national courts reviewing decisions stemming from other legal systems.[44]

The procedural integration at the level of decision-making (of which tax cooperation is a prime example), however, sits uncomfortably with this strict separation of judicial control of administrative action and may create difficulties in access to justice. These are likely to arise because the preliminary steps leading to a final decision within a composite procedure (i.e., acts of

---

41 Arroyo Jiménez (n 12) 355–56.

42 Angelos S. Gerontas (n 1).

43 See further on this point Paolo Mazzotti and Mariolina Eliantonio, 'Transnational Judicial Review in Horizontal Composite Procedures: Berlioz, Donnellan, and the Constitutional Law of the Union' (2020) 5(1) European Papers 41; Filipe Brito Bastos, 'Berlioz, B AND L: Some doubts on how to balance effective judicial protection and territoriality' (*Review of European Administrative Law Blog*, 1 April 2019), <https://realaw.blog/2022/04/01/berlioz-b-and-l-some-doubts-on-how-to-balance-effective-judicial-protection-and-territoriality-by-filipe-brito-bastos/> accessed 5 December 2023.

44 According to the CJEU, this principle 'requires [...] each of those States, save in exceptional circumstances, to consider all the other Member States to be complying with EU law and particularly with the fundamental rights recognised by EU law.' Opinion 2/13 of 18 December 2014 [2014] ECLI:EU:C:2014:2454, para 191.

transnational imputation in our categorisation above) might not constitute a reviewable act in the legal system to which an act or action belongs (in light of their preparatory nature), and, at the same time, might not be subject to judicial control in the court of the legal system adopting the final decision because of the limitations generated by the principle of territoriality.

This approach, however, might be in violation of the right to an effective remedy under Article 47 of the EU Charter on Fundamental Rights ('the Charter'). Furthermore, since horizontal cooperation takes place in the implementation of EU law obligations (i.e., a legal order common to all judiciaries), the difficulties traditionally affecting transnational judicial review, and those referred to above, do not arise, at least in as far as review against EU law standards is concerned. The argument based on the sovereignty of Member States is also not a hurdle for the judicial review of foreign acts: EU law forms part and parcel of the law which national judges are called upon to apply, and, to the extent that a national authority is acting within the scope of EU law, it does not act as fully sovereign administration, but rather as the executive of the European polity as a whole.[45]

As detailed in Part I, Chapter 6 of this title, the *Berlioz* line of case law has tackled the dilemma of transnational judicial review in exchange of information procedures, and concluded that national courts should be able, in application of Article 47 of the Charter, to review foreign preparatory measures against the relevant EU law standards.[46] While this case law seems to open the door to transnational judicial review of foreign preparatory acts in the context of exchange of information procedures, it leaves a number of questions (and possible gaps in judicial review) unanswered.

First of all, it seems that transnational judicial review is limited in scope to EU law-related errors in the actions of the foreign authority. While this solution seems the only feasible one to preserve the sovereignty of the national legal orders, and the only practicable one in view of the impossibility of a national court to engage with the minutiae of the national law of all other Member States, it does beg the question: *quid iuris* if the foreign preparatory measure has been adopted in violation of provisions of national law, such as fundamental procedural principles of the domestic legal system in which it was adopted? Should judicial protection be sought then in the domestic courts? Would time limits (likely expired once the individual becomes aware of the

---

[45] This aspect is nicely captured by the Italian administrative law scholarship through the notion of *amministrazione nazionale in funzione comunitaria* (national administration exercising EU functions), on which see, comprehensively, Lorenzo Saltari, *Amministrazioni nazionali in funzione comunitaria* (Giuffré Editore 2007).

[46] Case C-682/95 *Berlioz Investment Fund SA v. Directeur de l'administration des contributions directes* [2017] ECLI:EU:C:2017:373.

possible invalidity of the national preparatory measure) need to be by-passed by the court seized of this dispute?

Furthermore, *Berlioz* does not address the question of the 'destiny' of the foreign measure. Again, from the perspective of preserving equal sovereignty of the national legal systems, it would have to be concluded that national courts do not have jurisdiction to decide on the *validity* of the foreign measures on which they adjudicate, but only on their transnational *applicability*. The consequence of transnational judicial review would be then the disapplication *inter partes* of a foreign act, or the limitation of its effects, without *erga omnes* effect.

Another related problem is linked to the duplication of rulings (with possibly contradictory results): while transnational judicial review is indeed a possibility on the basis of *Berlioz*, national courts remain competent to review their own national preparatory measures. Such a solution may, at first sight, look like providing for several avenues of judicial review for applicants; however, it also bears a significant risk of potential contradictions between the assessments of various national courts.[47]

2.5 CONCLUSIONS

The analysis carried out above has sought to present the regulatory mechanism of exchange of information laid out in the DAC as generating composite procedures and transnational administrative acts. Indeed, the decision-making process sees the involvement of administrative authorities stemming from various legal systems, and the adoption of acts which are based on foreign factual or legal elements or are capable of – actually or potentially – producing effects in a foreign legal system. While not peculiar to the field of tax cooperation, the DAC is undoubtedly a privileged playground in which to study the ways in which horizontal cooperation mechanisms unfold in the EU administrative space. The analysis further zoomed in on the possible gaps in judicial protection generated by such horizontal composite procedures, because of the limitations created by the principle of territoriality and the separation of jurisdictions, which render the judicial control of foreign acts by national courts – at best – contentious. The CJEU case law has contributed to shed some light on this issue, by introducing a system of 'transnational judicial review' in exchange of information procedures; however, further case law is still needed to shed light on the details of how transnational judicial review ought to work in practice.

---

[47] Chevalier and Dubos (n 1) 343.

3. Availability and proportionality of taxpayers' information in a digitalised environment: knowledge is power

Marina Serrat Romaní

3.1 INTRODUCTION

This chapter aims, on the one hand, to discuss how the exponential development of communications technology, combined with the progressive digitalisation in all fields within our society, impacts tax administrations' ability to implement methods of information exchange that allow massive data transfers. On the other hand, it discusses how the combination of the accessible collection and exchange of information, combined with the significant amounts of data that can be processed, give rise to the question of whether the rights, guarantees and obligations surrounding the procedures of exchange of information that were considered suitable a few decades ago are possibly no longer suitable within the current context. Thus, the chapter explores whether the requirement of proportionality is still respected in the automatic exchange of information procedures or whether it is necessary to find a new balance between the rights of taxpayers and the principles and duties of tax administrations.

To this end, the chapter is structured as follows: first, it presents the philosophy behind the datafication of tax administrations and explains how the accumulation of data has reached its maximum extension, linking this sociological 'devotion' to data with the explosion of tax transparency policies. These policies, accompanied by the rapid development of information and communication technologies, have paved the way for the availability of significant amounts of data relevant for tax purposes, changing the scenario in which tax administrations enforce the duty of the taxpayer to contribute and to provide information. Second, in light of the principle of proportionality, it examines whether the impact of these new circumstances surrounding the exchanges of information necessitates an update for the way in which taxpayers' rights are protected.

3.2 DIGITALISATION AS A PARADIGM CHANGER FOR TAX ADMINISTRATIONS

3.2.1 Simplification of Data Collection

Digitalisation and new technologies have considerably simplified and accelerated the process of data collection and analysis, not only for private entities, but also for public administrations.[1] The combination of the internet with the integration of 'automated data collection and compliance mechanisms [...] can substantially lower costs of enforcement for government and costs of compliance for individuals and businesses',[2] and allow for quicker access to information. A few decades ago, obtaining information from citizens was a sizeable effort for public administrations. New technologies have simplified the process considerably, even (or especially) in the field of taxation. As Owens, Lazarov and Oliveira Costa state, 'while in the past, little information was available to fight offshore non-compliance; nowadays governments have access to a range of databases and the technology to process the high quantity of data'.[3]

Digital technologies facilitate data collection and allow – often – for the provision of information on a real-time basis. For this reason, technology has been a critical element in enforcing the new tax transparency standards. Transparency laws are fundamental norms to guarantee public accountability of institutional activities, as transparency is considered an indicator of administrative quality.[4] However, transparency – together with data[5] – is also the

---

1 Heather Broomfield and Lisa Reutter, 'In search of the citizen in the datafication of public administration' (2022) 9(1) Big Data & Society 1, <https://doi.org/10.1177/20539517221089302> accessed 5 December 2023.

2 OECD, 'Using digital technologies to improve the design and enforcement of Public Policies' (2019) *OECD Digital Economy Papers* 274, 169 accessed 11 May 2023.

3 Jeffrey Owens, Ivan Lazarov and Nathalia Oliveira Costa, *Exploring the Opportunities and Challenges of New Technologies for EU Tax Administration and Policy* (Publication for the committee on Economic and Monetary Affairs' Sub Committee on Tax Matters (FISC), Policy Department for Economic, Scientific and Quality of Life Policies 2021) 16.

4 See Alberto Alemanno, 'Unpacking the Principle of Openness in EU Law Transparency, Participation and Democracy' (2013) 39(1) European Law Review 72.

5 See Evelyn Ruppert, Engin Isin and Didier Bigo, 'Data politics' (2017) 4(2) Big Data & Society 1.

best weapon of control and surveillance currently available for post-modern States.[6]

3.2.2 The Sociological Perspective for the Need to Collect Massive Amounts of Data: Dataism

New technologies have changed the classic instrument of control and violence, replacing it with information and data. The mechanism of State power remains the same: control/surveillance; what has changed is how this power is obtained and applied, as it is now exercised through the collection of information. As Broomfield et al argue, 'the production and recirculation of data interests those who exercise power. It is therefore irresistible to the modern State and its executive powers of public administration. The modern State and data are already inseparably interwoven, as the availability of statistical information is a condition and necessity for any democracy'.[7]

Foucault, in his work *Discipline and Punish*, equated the pervasive power of the State[8] to a panopticon.[9] According to Foucault, a panopticon represents the perfect surveillance because it induces the detainees into a conscious and permanent state of visibility that guarantees the automatic functioning of power, making surveillance permanent in its effects, even if it is not so in its actions, which means the detainees find themselves in a situation of being subject to a power which they effectively wield against themselves.[10] From a sociological perspective, a correlation can be established between this and the phenomenon of the digitalisation of today's society. There has indeed been a shift from an institutionally centralised power exercising unidirectional control/surveillance based on the monopoly of violence, to a new, post-modern scenario, where

---

[6] To understand the conception of the post-modern world as that one in which there is 'rejection of the use of force in dispute resolutions, the increasing irrelevance of borders and where security is based on transparency, openness, interdependence and mutual vulnerability', Robert Cooper, 'The Postmodern State' (2005) 1 Revista Académica de Relaciones Internacionales 4.

[7] Broomfield and Reutter (n 1).

[8] Raúl Zamorano Farías and Rosario Rogel-Salazar, 'El dispositivo de poder como medio de comunicación: Foucault - Luhmann' (2013) 50(3) Política y Sociedad 970.

[9] In the 18th century, Jeremy Bentham designed a model of an institutional building – it was intended for a penitentiary, although other possible uses are also attributed to it – which he called the Panopticon. Based on a circular structure, it has a guard house in the centre so that the guards, who exercise the power of control, can observe all the subjects at any point in the building. Jeremy Bentham, *The Panopticon Writings* (Verso 1995) 7–21.

[10] Alan Sheridan, *Discipline and Punish: The Birth of the Prison* (2nd edn, Michel Foucault (tr), Vintage Books 1995).

the technological revolution has resulted in an imperceptible and transparent controlling action of the state over the subjects/citizens.

As Han has rightly posited, 'digital surveillance is more efficient precisely because it is a-perspectival. It does not have the limitation of analogue optics. Digital optics enables surveillance from all angles. It eliminates blind spots'.[11] The internet and the digitalisation of communication are transparent, which means that they are a-perspectival, allowing States to access any data on citizens to check their conduct for the 'purposes of categorisation, assessment and prediction at both individual and population level',[12] eliminating violence or coercion as a means to obtain the desired information. In turn, this empowers the State and provide the public administrations with a 'golden view' of their citizens, according to Dencik et al. This necessity of datafication of public administrations is a direct consequence of the 'ever-growing utilisation of advanced methods to analyse and recirculate data'.[13] The IT/data revolution has ushered in what has come to be known as the data and information age.[14] David Brooks prophetically coined the philosophy that reigns in the digital society: Dataism.[15] Data can be defined as a philosophy whereby reality is converted into data. Everything has to be properly recorded, so Dataism seeks to know absolutely everything.[16]

From this perspective, as data is regarded as an empirical and verifiable truth, any reality that is not adequately datafied is susceptible to doubt and mistrust, because it will not reflect an empirical knowledge of the truth. What the data show is therefore an absolute truth, which can only be verified with more data, and this is because the data are a 'transparent and reliable lens that allows us to filter out emotionalism and ideology'.[17] Therefore, in order to have absolute knowledge of the truth about any reality, everything must be converted into data and information.[18] This need for absolute knowledge means that data must be made available as quickly as possible, making immediacy

---

[11] Byung-Chul Han, *La sociedad de la transparencia* (Herder 2013) 86.

[12] Lina Dencik, Joanna Redden, Arne Hintz et al, 'The "golden view": Data-driven governance in the scoring society' (2019) 8(2) Internet Policy Review 24.

[13] See Broomfield and Reutter (n 1).

[14] See Rob Kitchin, The Data Revolution: Big Data, Open Data, Data Infrastructures & Their Consequences (Sage Publications 2014).

[15] David Brooks, 'The Philosophy of Data' *New York Times* (New York, 4 February 2013), <http://www.nytimes.com/2013/02/05/opinion/brooks-the-philosophy-of-data.html?_r=0&module=ArrowsNav&contentCollection=Opinion&action=keypress&region=FixedLeft&pgtype=article> accessed 5 December 2023.

[16] Alexander Pschera, *Dataismo: Verso I Big Data. Critica della morale anónima* (goWare 2014) 347.

[17] See Broomfield and Lisa (n 1).

[18] Han (n 11) 88.

the main characteristic of today's communication society.[19] In this light, the automatic exchange of information is recognised as the most efficient method of achieving transparency, because it guarantees immediate access to data.

However, Dataism works both ways, and affects not only citizens' behaviour, but also governmental praxis.[20] States also have to get used to giving up their data. They would otherwise have no credibility when promulgating transparency regulations to obtain more and more data from the population. These ever-growing transparency requirements must be reciprocated.

Dataism does not come without risks. This post-modern devotion that States hold for data and transparency, together with the disposition of *Big Data* and other automated data exchange, collection and analysis mechanisms, can lead to a dangerous situation of 'digital totalitarianism'.[21] This is where the Foucauldian schema presented above is reflected. Digitalisation has led to a false sense of decentralisation of power and a two-way sharing of control/oversight, from the state to the citizen and from the citizen to the state. Both the sharing of power and the bi-directionality of control/surveillance are, however, fictitious, as neither is entirely reciprocal. The vast amount of personal information released by citizens (either voluntarily or by legal requirement), collected and conveniently archived by the state, is incomparable to the strictly institutional information released by the State.[22] There is no doubt that the

---

19 Before the digitalisation of society, Vattimo sensed that in a post-modern society the mass media would be an indispensable element because they make possible 'truly timely' information about everything that happens in the world (Gianni Vattimo, 'Posmoderno: ¿Una sociedad transparente?' in Benjamín Arditi, *El reverso de la diferencia: identidad y política* (Editorial Nueva Sociedad 2000) 19). However, the 'traditional' mass media have been overtaken by digital media, as an element that goes beyond space and time as limits to communication (Jesper Taekke and Michael Paulsen, 'Luhmann and the media' (2010) 26(49) MediaKultur 5).

20 See Jun Liu, 'Social data governance: Towards a definition and model' (2022) 9(2) Big Data & Society, <https:// doi .org/ 10 .1177/ 20539517221111352> accessed 5 December 2023. Also see John Danaher, Michael J. Hogan, Chris Noone et al, 'Algorithmic governance: Developing a research agenda through the power of collective intelligence' (2017) 4(2) Big Data & Society, <https:// doi .org/ 10 .1177/ 2053951717726554> accessed 5 December 2023.

21 A totalitarian state is characterised by a desire for total control over the life and mind of human beings (Hannah Arendt, *Origins of Totalitarianism* (5th edn, Harcourt Brace Jovanovich 1973) 460–79). Therefore, its purpose will be to build a system structured around intending total control of individuals (William Ebenstein, *El totalitarismo. Nuevas perspectivas* (Editorial Paidós 1965) 20).

22 Veronic Barassi, 'Datafied citizens in the age of coerced digital participation' (2019) 24(3) Sociological Research Online 414; Arne Hintz, Lina Dencik and Karin Wahl-Jorgensen, Digital Citizenship in a Datafied Society (Polity Press 2019).

digital network is a double-edged sword that can either become an instrument of progress or a glass cage, depending on how one looks at it.

For this reason, on the one hand, it is an indispensable requirement that citizens are 'entitled to know what data is being collected about them, what data is being archived about them and how data about them is being used – and by whom',[23] especially when it comes to personal information. On the other hand, it is crucial to establish transparent criteria for the selection of truly relevant data and its use by State structures, so that it is are used objectively to identify targets, and this data is used for strictly necessary purposes. The risk of misuse of power in this respect is immense. To sum up, in an information society in which the exchange and accumulation of data are vital to its functioning, it is essential to consult whether any modifications on the status of certain rights and guarantees for citizens have accompanied the wide transparency measures implemented by States, so as to also grant the required levels of protection that taxpayers' data deserve.

3.2.3 The Right to a Good Administration in the Digital Era

There is no better way to address Dataism than through the example of the datafication of tax administrations and developments concerning tax transparency. The main objective of tax transparency has traditionally been that of achieving the maximum openness of all fiscally relevant information systematically in order to improve tax practices.[24] For that purpose, a standard of transparency is required by public authorities. This standard of transparency for tax purposes that has set the agenda of international tax policy has evolved over the last two decades and has mainly been designed by the OECD.[25] The standard mainly consists of three general elements: availability of information, adequate access to information and the existence of mechanisms to exchange information with other authorities.[26] This standard – initially designed to give effect to transpar-

---

23 Bruce Schneier, *Data and Goliath. The hidden battle to collect your data and control your world* (W.W. Norton & Company 2015) 159.

24 OECD, *OECD Best Practices for Budget Transparency* (Paris, OECD 2002) 7. <https:// www .oecd .org/ gov/ budgeting/ Best %20Practices %20Budget %20Transparency %20 - %20complete %20with %20cover %20page .pdf> accessed 5 December 2023.

25 The first transparency standard was designed for the 2002 Model Agreement on Exchange of Information in Tax Matters and the amendment of Article 26 in 2005, specifically for the exchange of information upon request.

26 'In other words, the information must be available, the tax authorities must have access to the information, and there must be a basis for exchange. If any of these elements are missing, information Exchange will not be effective' (OECD, *Implementing the Tax Transparency Standards* (OECD 2011) 23).

ency in the exchange of information upon request, as provided for in Article 26 of the DTC, and to extend it to as many States as possible – has been amended over time to increase the amount of exchangeable information.[27]

Tax transparency requirements have adapted in parallel to the changes that information and communication technologies have brought about in society, also taking advantage of the use of ICT and the Internet to support the automatic and multilateral exchanges of financial and tax information. As Oberson already foresaw, the amount of data exchanged through automatic exchange of information is more significant than with the exchange of information upon request,[28] and it allows the authorities to have free access to the bulk of the information received, thus allowing them to be able to select the information they consider relevant for their purposes.[29] The automatic exchange of information relies more than ever upon technology to be effectively implemented, as the European Court of Auditors has already admitted.[30] Furthermore, tax administrations, apart from relying on technology to allow regular automatic exchanges of information, also use *Big Data* and machine learning tools that

---

[27] It is good to remind the change in the standard of foreseeable relevance done in 2012, when there was an update in the wording and commentaries of Article 26 of the OECD Model Convention (OECD, *Update to Article 26 of the OECD Model Tax Convention, Approved by the OECD Council on 17 July 2012* (OECD 2012) <https://web-archive.oecd.org/2012-07-20/205841-120718_Article%2026-ENG_no%20cover%20(2).pdf> accessed 5 December 2023 and the 2016 Terms of Reference of the OECD (OECD, *2016 Terms of reference to monitor and review progress towards transparency and exchange of information on request for tax purposes* (OECD 2016) <https://www.oecd.org/tax/transparency/documents/terms-of-reference.pdf> accessed 5 December 2023. Both updates expanded the amount of information to the broadest possible extent, allowing the possibility to use the information exchanged for other purposes besides the ones it was exchanged for.

[28] Xavier Oberson, 'Exchange of information and cross-border cooperation between tax authorities' (2013) 98 Cahiers de Droit Fiscal International 30.

[29] According to the criteria developed by the OECD, the new automatic exchange of information contemplates using the exchanged data for purposes beyond taxation. However, as the new standard specifies, this use is limited by the domestic and supranational legal instruments that regulate it to fit appropriate purposes. The Multilateral Competent Authority Agreement confidentiality clause in section 5 leaves the protection and usage of the information in the hands of the signing State's domestic legislation. In the case of a bilateral agreement, art 26 of the OECD MC is the term of reference. If it is a multilateral agreement, art 22 of the Convention on Mutual Administrative Assistance in Tax Matters is the term of reference. Both clauses allow the use of the collected information for other purposes when said purposes are provided in the legal framework of the signing States.

[30] 'Technological advances also mean that the widespread automatic exchange of information (AEOI) has become increasingly viable as a tool to complement and reinforce EOIR' (European Court of Auditors, *Audit preview: exchange of information in the EU* (European Court of Auditors 2019, 4).

enable them to analyse – in unprecedented amounts[31] – outstanding amounts of accumulated data coming from many different channels, including exchanges of information.[32]

To sum up, there has been a constant widening of transparency requirements that, together with the powerful capacity of analytical tools, have multiplied the amount of information available to tax administrations.[33] This situation cannot but have an impact on taxpayers' rights.

The increased regulation of transparency demands must indeed be accompanied by the measures to guarantee that taxpayers' rights are still protected in such a paradigm change. In this context, the right to a good administration can play a pivotal role. The EU recognises good administration as a fundamental right,[34] and not only a principle for the functioning of the EU legal system.[35] This principle is characterised by its heterogeneous dimension that intends to guarantee the protection of different rights and principles. In other words, it derives from the existence of basic rights, as it has been shaped by them, and for them.[36] Therefore, within this heterogeneous dimension, the right to good

---

[31] Also, the last 2021 and 2022 OECD reports: Tax Administration 2021 and Tax Administration 2022, demonstrate how the pandemic has accelerated the digitalisation of ax Administrations and how approximately 80–90% of the tax administrations worldwide use data science and analytical tools (OECD, *Tax Administration 2022: Comparative Information on OECD and other Advanced and Emerging Economies* (OECD Publishing 2022) and OECD, *Tax Administration 2021: Comparative Information on OECD and other Advanced and Emerging Economies* (OECD Publishing 2021).

[32] Mark Pijnenburg, *Data Science for Tax Administration* (Universiteit Leiden 2020); OECD, 'Using big data in tax administrations' in OECD, *Technologies for Better Tax Administration: A Practical Guide for Revenue Bodies* (OECD Publishing 2016).

[33] Particularly within the EU framework, this broadening of the transparency requirements has ended up in a consecutive series of amendments that happened almost year after year on the Council Directive 2011/16/EU on administrative cooperation in tax matters in order to exchange information automatically every year.

[34] See art 41 of the Charter of Fundamental Rights which develops the regulation of the Right to a Good Administration.

[35] See the primordial jurisprudence that helped shaping the principle of Good Administration within the EU: Case C-222/86 *Unectef v Heylens* [1987] ECLI:EU:C:1987:442, para 15; Case C-347/87 *Orkem v Commission of the European Communities* [1989] ECLI:EU:C:1989:387; Case C-269/90 *Technische Universität München v Hauptzollamt München-Mitte* [1991] ECLI:EU:C:1991:438. See also Tobias Lock, 'Article 41 CFR Right to good administration' in Manuel Kellerbauer, Marcus Klamert and Jonathan Tomkin (eds), The EU Treaties and the Charter of Fundamental Rights: A Commentary (Online edn, Oxford Academic 2019).

[36] 'The Right to a good administration, as defined in art 41 Charter of Fundamental Rights, essentially codifies and summarizes rights and principles found either in other Treaty provisions of the TEU and TFEU in case law of the ECJ.' (Herwig C.H.

administration is not just a subjective right, but also an obligation to ensure the preservation of the subjective rights of citizens.[37] When referring to 'good administration', we refer, therefore, simultaneously to a fundamental right,[38] a principle of administrative action and an inherent obligation of the public authorities, who must not only look after the general interest of the State but the common good of the citizens.[39]

The right to good administration is furthermore linked to public ethics and is especially relevant when dealing with the use of information of taxpayers. In the context of the exchange of information between tax authorities, the common good should not only be seen in the exchange of information as a mechanism to curb fraud and tax evasion to increase public resources that benefits society, but also as a system equipped with guarantees that ensure respect for the subjective rights of citizens surrounding those exchanges of information and data collection. It is therefore an obligation – a duty – of the administration to undertake the guarantees that protect taxpayers by granting the protection of the subjective rights related to the data without having to resort to justice to enforce them.[40]

A guarantee is a means of protection to ensure that subjective rights recognised are fulfilled. Therefore, guarantees provide an *ex ante* protection, and it becomes a duty of any – good – tax administration to provide them within any type of tax procedure. The omission of guarantees – i.e., the failure to provide them – can lead to the infringement of subjective rights. Guarantees, thus, act as a counterweight. They are an element of balance in the interrelation between

---

Hofmann, Gerard C. Rowe and Alexander H. Türk, *Administrative Law and Policy of the European Union* (Oxford University Press 2011) 193.

37 See Ani Matei and Răzvan Băieşiu, 'Good Administration and Performance of Local Public Administration' (2014) 109 Procedia – Social and Behavioral Sciences 684; Juli Ponce 'Good Administration and Administrative Procedures' (2005) 12(2) Indiana Journal of Global Legal Studies 551.

38 Also, within the EU framework, art 41 of the EU Charter of Fundamental Rights contemplates such a fundamental right.

39 Jaime Rodríguez-Arana Muñoz, *Derecho Administrativo y Derechos sociales fundamentales* (Global Law Press-Editorial Derecho 2015).

40 See the development of the legal theory surrounding the guarantees of taxpayers and the duties of the tax administrations in Eduardo García de Enterría and Tomás-Ramón Ferandez, *Curso de Derecho Administrativo II* (Editorial Aranzadi 2011) 31; Juan Martín Queralt, Carmelo Lozano Serrano, José Tejerizo López and Gabriel Casado Ollero, *Curso de derecho financiero y tributario* (Editorial Tecnos 2014) 498; Also Elisa de la Nuez Sáchez-Casad and Modesto Ogea Martínez-Orozco, 'Derechos y garantías en los procedimientos tributarios' in Elisa De la Nuez Sánchez-Casado, Alejandro Fernández Cuevas and Modesto Ogea Martínez-Orozco, *El Estatuto del contribuyente: comentarios a la Ley 1/1998, de derechos y garantías de los contribuyentes* (Aranzadi 1998) 92.

rights of taxpayers and the powers of tax administrations. Nonetheless, the protection will be genuinely adequate if it is operated both *ex ante* before any of the rights are violated,[41] and *ex post* through the right to a fair trial. However, both types of protection need to be adapted to the current context in which we live to be effective. Where to strike a balance is a matter of proportionality in the setting up of information exchange systems.

3.3 PROPORTIONALITY IN THE NEW ERA OF AUTOMATIC EXCHANGE OF INFORMATION

3.3.1 The Principle of Proportionality According to Robert Alexy

Proportionality can be defined as the principle whereby a fair balance is sought between the public interests persuaded by public action and the restriction deriving therefrom for individuals. The concept of proportionality as the rule of law appears in the theories of self-defence of classical philosophers such as Cicero, Justinian, Augustine and Aquinas.[42] While Aristotle conceived proportionality in terms of distributive Justice,[43] Grotius turned the general principle of proportionality into a general principle of law to solve conflicts between norms.[44] The principle of proportionality, used for legal argumentation as

---

41 In this vein, Peter Häberle put forward a guarantee-oriented theory of fundamental rights. What he tried to convey is that fundamental rights should not only be understood as material rights, but also as procedural guarantees so that citizens themselves can have the power to determine the material right's content and thus adjust the material content of the fundamental right itself. Strictly speaking, the protection process of subjective rights stems from effective judicial protection, i.e., protection first requires a violation or perceived violation. However, citizens' interests can be protected in complementary ways to effective judicial protection through administrative procedures that force the state and citizens to engage in dialogue to ensure the protection of their rights. Thus, as part of the welfare state, the administration has duties of protection *ex ante*. See Peter Häberle, *Grundrechte im Leistungsstaat. Die Dogmatik des Verwaltungsrechts vor den Gegenwartsaufgaben der Verwaltung* (De Gruyter 1971); also see Peter Häberle, 'Recientes desarrollos sobre Derechos Fundamentales en Alemania', Derechos y Libertades (1993) 1 Revista del Instituto Bartolomé de las Casas 157.

42 cf Eric Engle, 'The History of the General Principle of Proportionality: An Overview' (2012) 10(1) The Dartmouth Law Journal 4.

43 cf Gerhard Michael Ambrosi, *Aristotle's geometrical model of distributive justice* (Paper prepared for the 11th ESHET Conference 'Justice in Economic Thought' 5–7 July 2007, Louis Pasteur University 2009) <https://www.academia.edu/70740409/Aristotle_s_geometrical_model_of_distributive_justice> accessed 5 December 2023.

44 Eric Engle, 'The General Principle of Proportionality and Aristotle' in Liesbeth Huppes-Cluysenaer and Nuno MMS Coelho (eds), *Aristotle and The Philosophy of Law: Theory, Practice and Justice* (Springer 2013) 270.

a test of a fair balance of interests, intends to 'safeguard of fairness whereby it controls States' freedom to restrict the non-derogable fundamental rights. As such, it functions as a tool to prevent the States' abuse of rights'.[45]

The principle of proportionality in the EU tax law framework is deeply anchored in the EU legal traditions. It is one of the core principles of EU Law,[46] currently enshrined within primary EU law,[47] but has been part of the EU legal tradition since practically the origins of the current EU,[48] as a crucial tool to grant Justice.[49] However, as García Antón and Marzal argue, 'proportionality should not be viewed as a one-size-fits-all doctrine'.[50] In that sense, Robert Alexy's theory of proportionality seems a suitable starting point.[51]

In his words:

> The core of balancing is constituted by a relation that might be termed the 'Law of Balancing', which can be formulated as follows: The greater the degree of non-satisfaction of, or detriment to, one principle, the greater must be the importance of satisfying the other. The Law of Balancing shows that balancing can be broken down into three stages. The first stage involves establishing the degree of non-satisfaction of, or detriment to, the first principle. Afterward, a second stage follows, establishing the importance of satisfying the competing principle. Finally, at the third stage, it is established whether or not the importance of satisfying the latter principle justifies the detriment to, or non-satisfaction of, the former principle.[52]

---

[45] Talya Ucaryilmaz, 'The Principle of Proportionality in Modern Ius Gentium' (2021) 36(1) Utrecht Journal of International and European Law 25.

[46] See W. Sauter, 'Proportionality in EU Law: A Balancing Act?' (2013) Cambridge Yearbook of European Legal Studies 15, 439.

[47] See Consolidated Version of the Treaty on European Union [2012] OJ C326/13, art 5(4). However, the function of proportionality is reflected in Charter of Fundamental Rights of the European Union [2000] OJ C 364/1, art 52(1).

[48] See the early cases of the CJEU, Case 11/70 *Internationale Handelsgesellschaft, bHv Einfuhr- und Vorratsstelle für Getreide und Futtermitte* [1970] ECLI:EU:C1970:114, Case 120/78 *Rewe-Zentral AG v Bundesmonopolverwaltung für Branntwein* [1979] ECLI:EU:C:1979:42, as the most well-known first cases that helped define the principle of proportionality. We can find indices of the principle of proportionality already in the *Meroni* case, Case 9/58 *Meroni & Co., Industrie Metallurgiche, SpA v High Authority of the European Coal and Steel Community* [1958] ECLI:EU:C:1958:7.

[49] See also Erik Bjorge and Jan Zglinski, 'Chapter 11: The principle of proportionality in EU law and its domestic application: ni tout à fait le même, ni tout à fait un autre' in Jatja S. Zeigler, Päivi J. Neuvone, and Violeta Morena-Lax (eds), *Research Handbook on General Principles in EU Law* (Edward Elgar Publishing 2022).

[50] R. García Antón and T. Marzal, 'Proportionality and the fight against international tax abuse: comparative analysis of judicial review in EU, international investment and WTO law' (2022) 30 Asia Pacific Law Review 5.

[51] Robert Alexy and Julian Rivers, *A Theory of Constitutional Rights* (1st edn 1985, Oxford University Press 2002).

[52] ibid 155.

Therefore, when two interests collide, both of them are in principle worthy of protection. Nevertheless, depending on the specific facts of the case, one might prevail over the other. Alexy's 'Law of Balancing' gives paramount importance to the *circumstances* surrounding each case as elements of the determination of the prevalent interest.[53] Starting from this simplified explanation of the 'Law of Balancing',[54] some reflections can be offered regarding the current rules on the automatic exchange of information within the EU.

3.3.2 The Law of Balancing Within the EU

In the EU, the extension of the mandatory automatic exchange of information obligations within the scope of the DAC seems not to find an end.[55] The question is whether constantly extending transparency measures aiming to safeguard the interest of the States in enforcing the duty of the taxpayers to provide information and contribute should prevail before the interest of the taxpayers in protecting their privacy and personal data. Considering the circumstances surrounding these exchanges of information, a balance between these two interests needs to be struck. First, the continuous changes in tax legislation towards enhancing transparency, and the fact that tax administrations count on powerful analytical tools, have multiplied the amount of information being collected from taxpayers. Second, all these large amounts of data must be exchanged regularly among the Member States, granting them free access to other tax administrations.

However, at the EU level, taxpayers continue having the same rights despite a context that has legally, sociologically and technologically changed. For instance, according to the General Data Protection Regulation (GDPR),[56] the data processing provisions provided for within the DAC 'have the sole objec-

---

[53] ibid 54; Robert Alexy, 'The Weight Formula' in Robert Alexy, *Law's Ideal Dimension* (online edn, Oxford Academic 2021) 154–74.

[54] For more details on how to elaborate on the operations of evaluation and balancing, see the referred literature in nn 43–45.

[55] See Section 3.1 above.

[56] Regulation (EU) 2016/679 of the European Parliament and of the Council of 27 April 2016 on the protection of natural persons about the processing of personal data and on the free movement of such data, and repealing Directive 95/46/EC (GDPR) [2016] OJ L 119/1; Regulation (EU) 2018/1725 of the European Parliament and of the Council of 23 October 2018 on the protection of natural persons concerning the processing of personal data by the Union institutions, bodies, offices and agencies and the free movement of such data, and repealing Regulation (EC) No 45/2001 [2018] OJ L 295/39; Decision No 1247/2002/EC of the European Parliament, of the Council and of the Commission of 1 July 2002 on the regulations and general conditions governing the performance of the European Data Protection Supervisor's duties [2002] OJ L 183/1.

tive of serving the general public interest in the field of taxation in the Member States, namely curbing tax fraud, tax avoidance and tax evasion, safeguarding tax revenues, and promoting fair taxation'.[57] Therefore, no special treatment or protection is given to taxpayers – primarily companies – whose data has been collected and exchanged automatically and multilaterally. On the contrary, it is expressly stressed in the GDPR that restrictions to fundamental rights are justified under reasons of necessity and proportionality when they try to safeguard objectives of general public interest, such as financial and taxation matters.[58]

In this context, the significant risks for taxpayers are, on the one hand, the reasonableness of each of the amendments to the transparency requirement,[59] the transfer of unnecessary information for tax purposes[60] or even false information,[61] and the risks linked to technology,[62] such as hacking or leakages of information, that can no longer guarantee the total security of data.[63] Before the automatic exchange of information, it would have made no sense to grant

---

[57] European Parliament resolution of 16 September 2021 on the implementation of the EU requirements for the exchange of tax information: progress, lessons learned and obstacles to overcome (2020/2046(INI) [2021] OJ C 117/20, para 49).

[58] Regulation (EU) 2016/679 (n 56) art 23(1)(e) and Regulation 2018/1725 (n 56) art 25(1)(c) refer specifically to taxation matters.

[59] As Pistone argues, there are serious doubts regarding the reasonableness behind the 'indicators of reportable transactions, known as "hallmarks", within the mandatory disclosure of aggressive tax planning schemes that DAC6 aims for' (Pasquale Pistone, '"Foreseeable relevance" and the impact on Taxpayers' rights in the EU' (*Review of European Administrative Law Blog*, 18 March 2022), <https://realaw.blog/2022/03/18/foreseeable-relevance-and-the-impact-on-taxpayers-rights-in-the-eu-by-pasquale-pistone/> accessed 5 December 2023.

[60] Philip Baker, 'CRS/DAC, FATCA and the GDPR' (2016) 16(3) British Tax Review 250.

[61] See *Aloe Vera of America et al. v United States*, 128 F. Supp. 2d 1235 (D. Ariz. 2000). Also see literature on the matter, Viktoria Wöhrer, *Data Protection and Taxpayers' Rights: Challenges Created by Automatic Exchange of Information* 10 European and International Tax Law and Policy Series (IBFD 2018), 176–80; Filip Develva and Irma Johanna Mosquera Valderrama, 'Privacy and Confidentiality in Exchange of Information Procedures: Some Uncertainties, Many Issues, but Few Solutions' (2017) 45(5) Intertax 362, 376–77.

[62] Lyn E. Pleger, Katharina Guirguis and Alexander Mertes, 'Making public concerns tangible: An empirical study of German and UK citizens' perception of data protection and data security' (2021) 122 Computers in Human Behavior, <https://doi.org/10.1016/j.chb.2021.106830> accessed 5 December 2023.

[63] See Shuman Ghosemajumder, 'You Can't Secure 100% of Your Data 100% of the Time' (*Harvard Business Review*, 4 December 2017), <https://hbr.org/2017/12/you-cant-secure-100-of-your-data-100-of-the-time> accessed 5 December 2023. This is the main reason why the GDPR demands to comply with the principle of accountability, in order to guarantee a pro-active responsibility to demonstrate compliance with the principles relating to processing personal data, as it is stated in the arts 5(2), 24 and 74.

taxpayers access to all the data held by the tax administrations, taking into account that, due to narrower standards of transparency, and because analogous technology did not allow for the immediacy of current digital technology in transferring information, only limited amounts of data were exchanged.[64] Nonetheless, it is to be questioned whether the same restrictions are justified today, at least within the EU, where all Member States participate in regular automatic exchanges of information.

Following the three steps of Alexy's 'Law of Balancing', there are reasons to consider that the current framework does not adequately account for the rights to privacy or data protection. Even though it is crucial to satisfy the general interest of States in enforcing the duty of the taxpayers to provide information and to contribute to the public coffers, the current measures have to ensure that this legal framework is accompanied by a corresponding update, to ensure the same level of protection is given to the right to privacy.[65] The question thus arises as to whether it is proportionate to continue restricting the right of taxpayers to privacy and data protection while continuously expanding exchange of information scenarios.

3.3.3 ARCO Rights as Guarantees to Restore Proportionality

From a proportionality point of view, the significant amount of information available to tax administrations and the technology that allows such automatic exchanges of information justify the need to change the rules regarding access to the bulk of information that is regularly automatically exchanged. In this context, the doctrine has advanced the notion of 'reciprocal safeguarding of information'.[66] From this perspective, the rights to access, rectification,

---

[64] The automatic exchange was already introduced in 2003 by Council Directive 2003/48/EC of 3 June 2003 on taxation of savings income in interest payments. However, it was built as an automatic exchange of information limited to interest payments. The lack of technological structure is one of the major concerns of developing countries to effectively apply the standards of automatic exchange of information (Adrian J. Sawyer and Kerrie Sadiq, 'Developing Countries and the automatic exchange of information standard – a "one-size-fits-all" solution?' (2016) 31(1) Australian Tax Forum 99, 102.

[65] See Maryte Somare and Viktoria Wöhrer, 'Automatic Exchange of Financial Information under the Directive on Administrative Cooperation in the Light of the Global Movement towards Transparency' (2015) 43(12) Intertax 804, 812; Saturnina Moreno González, 'The Automatic Exchange of Tax Information and the Protection of Personal Data in the European Union: Reflections on the Latest Jurisprudential and Normative Advances' (2016) 25(3) EC Tax Review 146, 153.

[66] Jeffrey Owens argued almost ten years ago that 'It is important to reconcile the need for more transparency with the need to protect the confidentiality, particularly of commercially sensitive information. Greater transparency between the taxpayer

cancellation and opposition (ARCO) should not only be seen as fundamental rights but also as procedural guarantees to safeguard the right to privacy and to data protection.[67]

Taxpayers' interests can, in this manner, be protected in a number of ways, including through administrative procedures that require a dialogue between the State and citizens and that ensure that their rights to data protection and privacy are upheld.[68] Current EU legislation, however, still fails to address the question of taxpayers' ARCO rights. In the framework of the exchange of information upon request, the Court of Justice of the European Union (CJEU) has ruled that there is the possibility for persons requested by the tax authorities to provide certain information to access some documentation related to the process to challenge the foreseeable relevance of the data request action.[69] Even though this would not be enough for automatic information exchanges, the CJEU case law proves that granting access to data being exchanged fulfils a proportionality requirement. Thinking about the ARCO rights not only as substantive rights, but also as guarantees to be included within the right to effective judicial protection as an *ex ante* measure,[70] could re-balance the rights of taxpayers in a digitalised context.

3.4 CONCLUSIONS

Any administration must pursue the common good of the citizens. This 'common good' entails that administrations ensure compliance with the duty of taxpayers to contribute and provide information to the tax administrations. The need to enhance the amount of information considered relevant for tax purposes is the ultimate reason behind the reforms of tax transparency stand-

---

and the tax authorities is good as it will lead to fewer disputes, greater mutual understanding and a relationship based on cooperative compliance.' (Jeffrey Owens, 'Tax Transparency: The "Full Monty"' (2014) 68(9) Bulletin for International Taxation 512).

[67] Philip Baker and Pasquale Pistone, 'BEPS Action 16: The Taxpayers' Right to an Effective Legal Remedy Under European Law in Cross-Border Situations' (2016) 5–6 EC Tax Review 335.

[68] Häberle (n 41) 157.

[69] See Case C-682/15 *Berlioz Inv. Fund S.A. v Directeur de l'administration des contributions directes* [2017] ECLI:EU:C:2017:373 and Joined Cases C-245/19 & C-246/19 *Etat de Luxembourg v B. and others* [2020] ECLI:EU:C:2020:795; Case C-437/19 *État du Grand-duché de Luxembourg v L* [2021] ECLI:EU:C:2021:953 and Case C-175/20 *SIA 'SS' v Valsts ieņēmumu dienests* [2022] ECLI:EU:C:2022:124.

[70] See Juliane Kokott, Pasquale Pistone and Robin Miller, 'Public International Law and Tax Law Taxpayers' Rights: The International Law Association's Project on International Tax Law Phase 1' (2021) 52(2) Georgetown Journal of International Law 381.

ards. Nevertheless, any good administration must also preserve the rights of citizens and endeavour to the respect the principle of proportionality in administrative action. Therefore, any good administration must accompany the introduction of paradigm-shifting legal measures with appropriate measures to restore the balance with citizens' rights. However, this rebalancing has yet to happen concerning taxpayers' rights vis-à-vis the expansion of the standard of transparency in the context of the automatic exchange of information mechanisms among the EU Member States.

In a context where tax administrations count on powerful technological tools that allow them not only to obtain but also to process enormous bulks of data, together with amendments in EU legislation to ensure greater tax transparency, there have been no parallel amendments to the legislation protecting taxpayers' rights in this highly digitalised and datafied environment. Digitalisation and datafication presuppose a change of paradigm in the way the protection of taxpayers' rights is to be conceived. The new risks caused by the expansion of the automatic exchange of information, such as the transfer of excessive amounts of data, together with the risk entailed by the digitalisation, such as the lack of guarantee of total security of data, need complementary methods to ensure the respect for fundamental rights, such as the right to privacy or to data protection. A potential solution would be relaxing the limits of the ARCO rights in case of the data exchanged in the automatic exchange of information procedures. Conceiving ARCO rights as not only subjective rights, but also as guarantees, would help restore balance to such mentioned rights, as they would be able to act as a complementary tool to grant *ex ante* protection.

4. The impact of the right to privacy and nemo tenetur on tax information exchange

Filip Debelva

4.1 INTRODUCTION

From the perspective of tax authorities, increasing international data flow unquestionably has positive effects on compliance and income. However, as various observers have previously noted, greater accessibility to information and increasing flows of information also pose difficulties for taxpayers' rights. This chapter aims to discuss two specific rights: the right to privacy (Section 4.2) and the prevention of self-incrimination (Section 4.3).

Several instruments on the international level contain references to taxpayers' rights, notably the right to privacy and related safeguards. In this respect, we can, for example, refer to the confidentiality requirements contained in the OECD and UN Model Tax Conventions.[1] The commentaries on these models also mention concerns relating to the right to privacy with regard to the automatic processing of data.[2] Similar rights and concerns have been expressed in other international instruments and in national legislation (including national constitutions).[3] As will be demonstrated, consecutive changes to the DAC and

---

1 OECD, *OECD Model Tax Convention on Income and on Capital* (OECD Publishing 2017), art 26(2) and United Nations (UN), *UN Model Double Taxation Convention between Developed and Developing Countries* (UN Economic and Social Affairs 2017), art 26(2) contain references to confidentiality requirements.

2 OECD, *OECD Model Tax Convention on Income and on Capital* (OECD Publishing 2017), para 10 commentary on art 26(1); UN, *UN Model Double Taxation Convention between Developed and Developing Countries* (UN Economic and Social Affairs 2017), para 5.2 commentary on art 26.

3 See for an overview: Filip Debelva and Irma Johanna Mosquera Valderrama, 'Privacy and Confidentiality in Exchange of Information for Tax Purposes: Some Uncertainties, Many Issues, but Few Solutions' (2017) 45 Intertax 362, 371–73; Viktoria Wöhrer, 'Data Protection and Taxpayers' Rights: Challenges created by Automatic Exchange of Information' (2018) 10 European and International Tax Law

the adoption of specific EU law instruments have their merit in this respect. The current position of taxpayers in the exchange of information procedure is, however, still unsatisfactory and should not be seen as an endpoint.

Given the scope of the present chapter, the focus will be placed on the specific rights as contained within the DAC and specific instruments (notably the GDPR as regards the right to privacy).[4] Reference will also be made to the rights as contained in the EU Charter[5] and the European Convention on Human Rights, given that specific legislation should be read in the light of general requirements of fundamental rights.

4.2 THE RIGHT TO PRIVACY

4.2.1 Conceptual Framework and Relevance when Exchanging Tax Information

In legal literature, it has been argued that one of the reasons why the right to privacy was, in the past, not thoroughly discussed, resulted from semantic confusion surrounding concepts such as privacy, confidentiality, and related

---

Policy Series 199–204; Xiaoqing Huang, 'Ensuring Taxpayer Rights in the Era of Automatic Exchange of Information: EU Data Protection Rules and Cases' (2018) 46 Intertax 225, 227–28; Belisa Ferreira Liotti, 'Taxpayers' Data Protection: Do International, Regional and Domestic Instruments Guarantee Adequate Rights in Tax (A)EoI?' (2022) 50 Intertax 138, 143–45.

[4] It has been submitted that relying on more generic privacy rights (e.g., under art 8 ECHR) might not be sufficient in case of EoI, a.o. because the ECtHR has recognised that national authorities enjoy a wide margin of appreciation. See: Marcel Schaper, 'Data Protection Rights and Tax Information in the European Union: An Uneasy Combination' (2016) 23 Maastricht Journal of European and Comparative Law 514, 518; Julianne Kokott and Pasquale Pistone, *Taxpayers in International Law* (Hart Publishing 2022) 393. Relevant case law includes: *F.S. v Germany* App no 30128/96 (ECtHR, 27 November 1997); *Othymia Investments BV v the Netherlands* App no 75292/10 (ECtHR, 16 June 2015); *G.S.B. v Switzerland* App no 28601/11 (ECtHR, 22 December 2015); *Big Brother Watch and Others v The United Kingdom* App nos 58170/13, 62322/15 and 24960/15 (ECtHR, 25 May 2021). See also Wöhrer (n 3) 256.

[5] The CJEU has recognised that the Charter is applicable when applying the provisions of the DAC, see Case C-682/15 *Berlioz Investment Fund v Directeur de l'administration des contributions directes* [2017] ECLI:EU:C:2017:373, para 42. It should be noted that at the time of writing a case is pending before the CJEU on the compatibility of certain provisions of DAC6 with arts 7 and 47 of the Charter. The case concerns the question whether provisions of DAC6 applicable in case of legal professional privilege (LPP) may infringe the right to a fair trial and the right to privacy. In his Opinion, Advocate General Rantos concluded that the right to privacy may indeed be violated in certain specific circumstances (Case C-694/20 *Orde van Vlaamse Balies and Others* [2022] ECLI:EU:C:2022:259, Opinion of AG Rantos).

notions such as data protection.[6] Privacy (*stricto sensu*) should be defined as the right to keep one's affairs secret, while the right to confidentiality means that information that was disclosed to a person should not be disclosed to an unrelated third party whether intentionally or by accident. Both privacy and confidentiality can also be considered to form part of a wider right to data protection.[7] However, it is clear that these notions are intertwined and also often used interchangeably.[8] This may be illustrated by an example in which we apply, for sake of simplicity, the EoIR procedure based on DAC1.[9]

Let us imagine that the tax authorities of EU Member State A are interested in learning more about allegedly undeclared bank accounts owned by one of its citizens at a financial institution in EU Member State B: (1) a request for information is sent by the state A's competent authorities to state B's equivalent; (2) state B carries out the administrative enquiries necessary to obtain the information from a financial institution located in its territory; (3) the financial institution provides the information not the state B authorities who subsequently transmit the information (4) to state A (Figure 4.1).

Even this 'plain vanilla' EoIR procedure interferes with several privacy-related rights.[10] First, if a financial institution in state B receives a request from state B for information about a particular taxpayer, the financial institution must violate their confidentiality agreement with the taxpayer (which usually takes the form of banking privilege). The taxpayer has confidence in the financial institution with regard to its personal affairs, and

6 Debelva and Mosquera Valderrama (n 3) 363.

7 Compare Eleonor Kristoffersson and Pasquale Pistone, 'General Report' in Eleonor Kristofferson, Pasquale Pistone, Michael Lang et al (eds), *Tax Secrecy and Tax Transparency: The Relevance of Confidentiality in Tax Law* (Part 1) (Peter Lang 2013) 3–6; Juliane Kokott and Christoph Sobotto, 'The distinction between privacy and data protection in the jurisprudence of the CJEU and the ECtHR' (2013) 3 International Data Privacy Law 222–28.

8 OECD, *OECD Agreement on Exchange of Information in Tax Matters* (OECD Publishing 2002), para 94 commentary on art 8. This view was also shared by the CJEU in the *Digital Rights Ireland* case: 'It should be noted that the protection of personal data resulting from the explicit obligation laid down in Article 8(1) of the Charter is especially important for the right to respect for private life enshrined in Article 7 of the Charter' (Joined Cases C-293/12 and C-594/12 *Digital Rights Ireland v Minister for Communications, Marine and Natural Resources and Others and Kärntner Landesregierung and Other* [2014] ECLI:EU:C:2014:238, para 53).

9 DAC art 5.

10 Compare Case C-175/20 *Valsts ieņēmum u dienests (Traitement des données personnelles à des fins fiscales)* [2022] ECLI:EU:C:2022:124, para 60. The Court confirmed that personal data is processed twice in the situation where first personal data is requested by the tax authority from a service provider and this information is subsequently sent to tax authorities.

presumes that information about them is kept private. Second, the financial institution trusts the state's responsible authorities to keep the information private and not divulge it to anybody without their consent or make it publicly available after they have acquired it. Third, following the transmission of the information from the state B tax authorities to the state A tax authorities, the state A authorities have a duty to both the state B tax authorities and the tax-payer himself. In each of these relations, concerns can arise regarding privacy, confidentiality and, more broadly, data protection. Generally speaking, it can be argued that the collection of tax information,[11] the information exchange as such,[12] the use of the exchanged information,[13] and the storage thereof in the hands of recipient[14] can fall within the scope of data protection rights.[15]

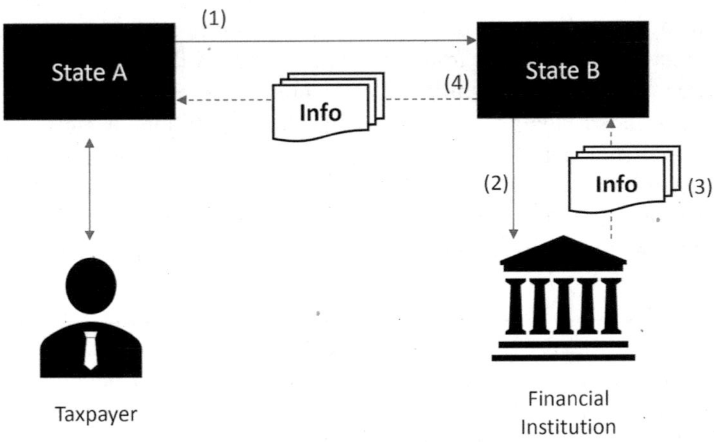

Figure 4.1 *Exchange of information upon request*

[11] Joined Cases C-465/00, C-138/01 and C-139/01 *Österreichischer Rundfunk and Others* [2003] ECLI:EU:C:2003:294.

[12] Case C-201/14 *Bara and Others v Casa Naţională de Asigurări de Sănătate and Others* [2015] ECLI:EU:C:2015:638.

[13] Case C-73/16 *Peter Puškár v Finančné riaditeľstvo Slovenskej republiky and Kriminálny úrad finančnej správy* [2017] ECLI:EU:C:2017:725.

[14] Joined Cases C-293/12 and C-594/12 (n 8).

[15] Wöhrer (n 3) 348.

4.2.2 Specific Rights and Obligations under the DAC

4.2.2.1 Secrecy and equivalent protection

The DAC itself contains a limited number of provisions dealing with disclosure of information and documents. Information communicated between Member States on the basis of the directive is covered by the 'obligation of secrecy' and enjoys the protection extended to similar information under the national law of the Member State which received it.[16] This 'relative' obligation to secrecy (due to its referral to the laws of the receiving state) is similar to the requirements contained in Article 26(2) of the OECD Model Convention. Such a relative duty of secrecy therefore does not provide for an absolute guarantee of secrecy, irrespective of domestic guarantees in this respect. In case information is communicated to the European Commission, analogous safeguards are in place.[17]

The information may be used for the assessment and enforcement of the domestic laws of the Member States concerned for the taxes referred to in Article 2 DAC. This provision (Article 16(2) DAC) was amended by DAC7 and now allows the information to be used for VAT purposes (and other indirect taxes).[18] Similar provisions already existed for other taxes and duties and compulsory social security contributions.[19] Prior to DAC7, the information could be used for 'other purposes', provided the state communicating the information gave its permission, and only insofar as this was allowed under the receiving state's legislation.[20] DAC7, however, introduced the possibility for Member States to communicate a list of such 'other purposes'. In those cases, the receiving Member State may use the information for the purposes listed without obtaining prior permission from the communicating Member State.[21] Evidently, this amendment facilitates the use of the information for the aforementioned other purposes.

Lastly, the directive contains specific rules for transmission of the information to third Member States.[22] Again, analogous provisions are in place for information shared with the European Commission.[23]

---

16 DAC art 16(1).
17 DAC art 23a.
18 DAC7 art 1(13)(a).
19 DAC art 16(1) subparas 2 and 3.
20 DAC art 16(2).
21 DAC art 16(2) subpara 2, as inserted by DAC7 art 1(13)(b).
22 DAC art 16(3)–(4).
23 DAC art 23a(2).

4.2.2.2 Interplay with other secondary legislation

When the DAC was first adopted, Article 25 contained specific provisions on data protection.[24] Currently, the first paragraph of Article 25 DAC still broadly contains the same content.[25] According to this provision, all exchange of information shall be subject to the provisions of the Data Protection Directive (Directive 95/46/EC; 'DPD').[26] It should be noted that the DPD has been repealed with effect from 25 May 2018 and has since been replaced by the General Data Protection Regulation (GDPR).[27] When this provision was last amended (when DAC7 was adopted), the references to the DPD were replaced with references to the GDPR.[28]

In essence, the GDPR imposes certain obligations upon Member States. When the GDPR is applicable, the 'data controller' – which includes public authorities[29] – shall, under the principle of accountability, be responsible for and be able to demonstrate compliance with a set of safeguards in relation to personal data:[30] (a) lawfulness, fairness and transparency; (b) purpose limitation; (c) data minimisation; (d) accuracy; (e) storage limitation; and (f) integrity and confidentiality.[31] These safeguards apply to the processing of

---

[24] Similar provisions were not yet included in the currently repealed Mutual Assistance Directive.

[25] All exchange of information pursuant to this Directive shall be subject to the provisions implementing Directive 95/46/EC. However, Member States shall, for the purpose of the correct application of this Directive, restrict the scope of the obligations and rights provided for in Articles 10, 11(1), 12 and 21 of Directive 95/46/EC to the extent required in order to safeguard the interests referred to in Article 13(1)(e) of that Directive.

[26] See for a discussion of Directive 95/46/EC of the European Parliament and of the Council of 24 October 1995 on the protection of individuals with regard to the processing of personal data and on the free movement of such data (DPD) [1995] OJ L281/31 in the area of (A)EoI: Tony Schenk-Geers, *International Exchange of Information and the Protection of Taxpayers* (Kluwer Law International 2009) 248–65; Saturnina Moreno González, 'The Automatic Exchange of Tax Information and the Protection of Personal Data in the European Union: Reflections on the Latest Jurisprudential and Normative Advances' (2016) 25 EC Tax Review 146.

[27] Regulation (EU) 2016/679 of the European Parliament and of the Council of 27 April 2016 on the protection of natural persons with regard to the processing of personal data and on the free movement of such data, and repealing Directive 95/46/EC (General Data Protection Regulation (GDPR)) [2016] OJ L119/1.

[28] Several preambles of directives amending the original DAC also mention concerns relating to personal data. See for example recital 6 to DAC5 and recital 17 to DAC6.

[29] GDPR (n 27) art 4(7).

[30] ibid art 5(2).

[31] All of these safeguards are defined in GDPR art 5(1). The number and content of these safeguards was extended as compared to DPD (n 26) art 6(A).

personal data in the context of the activities of an establishment of a controller or a processor in the Union,[32] regardless of where the processing takes place.[33] Transfer of information to a third country or an international organisation is possible in the case that an 'adequate level of protection' is ensured.[34] Aside from these 'principles',[35] the GDPR contains a specific chapter on 'rights of the data subject', including: (i) transparency; (ii) information and access to personal data; (iii) rectification and erasure ('right to be forgotten');[36] and (iv) right to object.[37] The material scope is, however, restricted in a number of ways, as the GDPR does not apply to the processing of personal data, inter alia, in the course of an activity which falls outside the scope of Union law and by a natural person in the course of a purely personal or household activity.[38]

A novelty that was introduced by DAC3 was Article 25(1a), which refers to Regulation (EC) No 45/2001, which, in turn, imposes certain rights and obligations upon Union institutions and bodies when processing personal information. These rights and obligations are similar to those imposed upon Member States under the GDPR – and similar restrictions also apply (see Section 4.2.2.3). DAC7 has renumbered this paragraph to paragraph 2 of Article 25 and has extended its scope to Union offices and agencies.

The current Articles 25(3)–(5) DAC, which were first inserted when DAC2 was adopted (as Articles 25(2)–(4)), provide a number of specifications.[39]

---

32 These notions are defined in GDPR (n 27) arts 4(7) and 4(8).

33 ibid art 3(1).

34 ibid arts 44–50. See on this notion of 'adequate level of protection' Case C-362/14 *Data Protection Commissioner v Facebook Ireland Limited and Maximilian Schrems (Schrems (I))* [2015] ECLI:EU:C:2015:650 (regarding the EU–US Safe Harbour Agreement) and Case C-311/18 *Data Protection Commissioner v Facebook Ireland Limited and Maximillian Schrems (Schrems (II))* [2020] ECLI:EU:C:2020:559 (regarding the EU-US Privacy Shield). For a detailed discussion see Gianmaria AC Favaloro, 'The exchange of tax information between EU Member States and third countries: privacy and data protection concerns' (2021) 61 European Taxation 133–38.

35 GDPR (n 27) arts 5–11.

36 Case C-131/12 *Google Spain SL and Google Inc. v Agencia Española de Protección de Datos (AEPD) and Mario Costeja González* [2014] ECLI:EU:C:2014:317, paras 93–99. The right to be forgotten shall not apply to the extent that processing is necessary for compliance with a legal obligation which requires processing by Union or Member State law to which the controller is subject or for the performance of a task carried out in the public interest or in the exercise of official authority vested in the controller (GDPR art 17(3)(b)). It seems obvious that this restriction could apply to tax-related information.

37 GDPR (n 27) arts 12–22.

38 ibid art 2(2).

39 It has been submitted that these amendments resulted from criticism that was raised by 'Working Party 29 as established by DPD' (n 26) art 29. See: Martyre Somare and Viktoria Wöhrer, 'Automatic Exchange of Financial Information under the

First, according to Article 25(3), Reporting Financial Institutions (RFI)[40] and the competent authorities of each Member State shall be considered as 'data controllers'.[41] A recent change by DAC7 extended that qualification to intermediaries (cf. DAC6) and Reporting Platform Operators (cf. DAC7). In addition, it was clarified that they shall be considered data controllers when, acting alone or jointly, they determine the purposes and means of processing of personal data within the meaning of the GDPR. Article 25(4) provides Reportable Persons with the right to be informed that information will be collected and transferred, and the aforementioned data controllers[42] will provide them with all information that they are entitled to under the domestic (implementing) legislation in sufficient time to exercise his data protection rights and in any case before the information is reported. CJEU case law has already shown that the right to be informed is key in achieving data protection,[43] even though under the EU Charter only addressees of an information order have a right to judicial protection (and hence not the taxpayer nor third parties).[44]

Article 25(5) GDPR states that information processed shall be retained for no longer than necessary to achieve the purposes of the directive and in any case in accordance with data controller's domestic rules on statute of limitations. It should be noted that this article does not provide a maximum retention limit, which might be considered undesirable from the perspective of taxpayer

---

Directive on Administrative Cooperation in the Light of the Global Movement towards Transparency' (2015) 43 Intertax 804, 812–13.

[40] The term 'Reporting Financial Institution' is defined in section VIII of Annex I as 'any Member State Financial Institution that is not a Non-Reporting Financial Institution'. The term 'Member State Financial Institution' means: (i) any Financial Institution that is resident in a Member State, but excludes any branch of that Financial Institution that is located outside that Member State; and (ii) any branch of a Financial Institution that is not resident in a Member State, if that branch is located in that Member State.

[41] It has been argued that such joint responsibility might lead to ambiguity, see Huang (n 3) 232.

[42] GDPR (n 27) art 25(4), after the update resulting from DAC7, specifies that each Member State shall lay down rules obliging Reporting Platform Operators to inform Reportable Sellers of the reported Consideration.

[43] Case C-298/16 *Teodor Ispas and Anduța Ispas v Direcția Generală a Finanțelor Publice Cluj* [2017] ECLI:EU:C:2017:843, para 39.

[44] Kokott and Pistone (n 4) 396, referring to Joined Cases C-245/19 and C-246/19 *État luxembourgeois v B and Others* [2020] ECLI:EU:C:2020:795. See similarly *Othymia Investments BV v the Netherlands* App no 75292/10 (ECtHR, 16 June 2015). The latter case refers to inter alia Case C-276/12 *Jiří Sabou v Finanční ředitelství pro hlavní město Prahu* [2013] ECLI:EU:C:2013:678, paras 41–43.

protection and might not be in line with the principle of proportionality as required by the CJEU.[45]

In response to a growing threat of data breaches, DAC7 has inserted specific procedures in this respect. Where a data breach occurs, the relevant Member State shall report the data breach and any subsequent remedial action to the Commission without delay.[46] The latter will inform all Member States, who can in turn decide to suspend the exchange of information.[47] Member States, assisted by the Commission, shall agree on the practical arrangements necessary for the implementation of Article 25, including data breach management processes.[48]

Even though the link between the DAC and secondary EU legislation on privacy should be applauded, one should also be wary of the scope of the GDPR (and, previously, the DPD). The regulation lays down rules relating to the protection of *natural persons* with regard to the processing of personal data and rules relating to the free movement of personal data,[49] thereby explicitly excluding protection for *legal persons* from its scope.[50] In the context of the DAC, information exchanges arising from DAC3[51] and DAC4[52] only apply to legal persons, hence, the GDPR will in principle not apply in that context. It has been submitted that in the absence of specific rules on data protection for legal persons, one could fall back on the generic privacy rights such as those embodied in Article 7 of the Charter.[53] As regards the right to data protec-

---

45 See, inter alia, Joined Cases C-293/12 and C-594/12 (n 8) paras 56–69; Case C-203/15 *Tele2 Sverige, AB v Post- och telestyrelsen and Secretary of State for the Home Department v Tom Watson and Others* [2016] ECLI:EU:C:2016:970, paras 95–96.

46 DAC art 25(6). A similar procedure is in place when a data breach occurs to the central directory or the CCN (Common Communication Network).

47 Other measures are listed, such as the possibility to request the suspension of the CCN access.

48 DAC art 25(7). See also DAC7 recital 32.

49 GDPR (n 27) art 1(1). DPD (n 26) art 2(a) contained similar rules, given that it applied to personal data, which was defined as "information relating to an identified or identifiable natural person".

50 See also ibid preamble 14.

51 For DAC3, this limitation results from DAC art 8a(4). It should be noted that DAC3 only does not apply where an advance cross-border ruling *exclusively* concerns and involves the tax affairs of one or more natural person. Rulings whereby natural persons are also involved therefore still fall within the scope of the GDPR.

52 This limitation results from DAC art 8aa read together with Annex III to the directive, which refers to DAC art 3(11)(b), (c) and (d).

53 Case C-450/06 *Varec SA v Belgian State* [2008] ECLI:EU:C:2008:91. A recent development is the judgment of 8 December 2022, concerning the waiver for intermediaries subject to legal professional privilege. According to the CJEU, the obligation that

tion (cf. Article 8 EU Charter), the CJEU (insofar as the data also identifies a natural person)[54] and the ECtHR[55] have in a number of more recent cases also been willing to (cautiously) extend those principles to legal persons. However, due to the courts' reluctant stance,[56] authors have concluded that chances of successfully challenging breaches of privacy rights (or data protection rights) for legal persons are slim.[57]

4.2.2.3 Restrictions on taxpayers' rights

From the above, one may conclude that the competent entities are, in principle, subject to the various obligations laid down in the GDPR, and that the addressees of the rights include taxpayers insofar as they are natural persons.[58] However, on the basis of the second sentence of Article 25(1) DAC, restrictions can be imposed on certain rights and obligations in order to ensure the application of the DAC.[59]

These restrictions refer to the rights and obligations contained in specific articles of the GDPR, such as the right to information in cases of collection of data from the data subject or from other parties, the right of access to the information, and the rectification, erasure or blocking of data subject to processing that does not comply with the provisions of the DAC, in particular because of the incomplete or inaccurate nature of the data. The DAC clarifies that such restrictions are possible to the extent required in order to safeguard 'an important economic or financial interest of a Member State or of the European Union, including monetary, budgetary and *taxation matters*' (own emphasis).[60]

---

is imposed on a lawyer acting as an intermediary to notify another intermediary who is not his client infringes Article 7 of the Charter (Case C-694/20 (n 5)).

54 Joined Cases C-92/09 and C-93/09 *Volker und Markus Schecke GbR and Hartmut Eifert v Land Hessen* [2010] ECLI:EU:C:2010:662; Case C-419/14 *WebMindLicenses kft v Nemzeti Adó- és Vámhivatal Kiemelt Adó- és Vám Főigazgatóság* [2015] ECLI:EU:C:2015:832, para 79.

55 *Bern Larsen Holding AS and Others v Norway* App no 24117/08 (ECtHR, 14 March 2013).

56 See also the arguments raised in n 10.

57 Nevia Čičin-Šain, 'New Mandatory Disclosure Rules for Tax Intermediaries and Taxpayers in the European Union – Another "Bite" into the Rights of the Taxpayer?' (2019) 11 World Tax Journal 77, 112–13.

58 Juliane Kokott, *EU Tax Law: A Handbook* (Nomos 2022) 754.

59 DAC art 25(1), second sentence: 'However, Member States shall, for the purpose of the correct application of this Directive, restrict the scope of the obligations and rights provided for in Article 10, Article 11(1), Articles 12 and 21 of Directive 95/46/EC to the extent required in order to safeguard the interests referred to in Article 13(1)(e) of that Directive'.

60 As mentioned, the DAC still refers to the provision of the DPD, in this case DPD art 13(1)(e) (n 26). A similar provision is included in GDPR art 23(1)(e) (n 27).

The recitals of both the DAC[61] and the GDPR[62] refer to possibility to apply restrictions for information exchanges between tax administrations and the need to prevent loss of revenue. For example, in the case that an information request is urgent or if notifying the taxpayer jeopardises the tax collection, the DAC deems it justifiable to not give notice of the request to the taxpayer.[63] It is important to point out that the GDPR mentions that such restrictions are a possibility,[64] while the DAC seems to contain an obligation to restrict the scope of these rights ('Member States *shall* [...] restrict' (own emphasis)).[65] This restriction has been called a significant loophole that will compromise taxpayers' rights to be informed of the ongoing exchange of information, as well as their right to rectify the information.[66]

The entry into force of the GDPR has somewhat improved this situation. The DPD merely stated that a restriction should 'constitute a necessary measure' to safeguard a number of enumerated interests.[67] The GDPR more cautiously states that restrictions should be inserted by way of a legislative measure and should 'respect the essence of the fundamental rights and freedoms and is a necessary and proportionate measure in a democratic society to safeguard'.[68] This provision introduces a threefold requirement, whereby the restriction: (1) needs to be adopted through a legislative measure; (2) should respect the essence of the fundamental rights and freedoms; and (3) needs to be necessary and proportionate. In addition, the legislative measure should contain specific provisions including information as to the scope of the restrictions introduced, safeguards to prevent abuse, storage periods, etc.[69] The European Data Protection Supervisor has published a toolkit in order to assess the necessity of

---

[61] DAC recital 27 states that limitations are necessary and proportionate in view of the potential loss of revenue for Member States and the crucial importance of information covered by the directive for the effectiveness of the fight against fraud.

[62] GDPR (n 27) recital 112 states that 'derogations should in particular apply to data transfers required and necessary for important reasons of public interest, for example in cases of international data exchange between competition authorities, tax or customs administrations [...]'.

[63] Alexander Rust, 'Data Protection as a Fundamental Right' in Alexander Rust and Eric Fort (eds), *Exchange of Information and Bank Secrecy* (Kluwer Law International 2012) 191.

[64] The CJEU has made it clear that adopting restrictions (under the DPD) indeed constitutes a possibility and does not an obligation (Case C-473/12 *Institut professionnel des agents immobiliers (IPI) v Geoffrey Englebert and Others* [2013] ECLI:EU:C:2013:715 32).

[65] DAC art 25(1).

[66] Huang (n 3) 231.

[67] DPD (n 26) art 13(1).

[68] GDPR (n 27) art 23(1).

[69] ibid art 23(2).

such restrictive measures.[70] The DAC arguably lacks clear and precise rules,[71] which may lead to the conclusion that interference on taxpayers' rights might not be justified as being strictly necessary.[72] It has, in my view, rightly been submitted that in this regard, the GDPR offers detailed guidance for future amendments to the DAC.[73]

4.3 PRIVILEGE AGAINST SELF-INCRIMINATION

4.3.1 Introduction

In stark contrast to the abundance of literature and case law on the right to privacy (Section 4.2), the privilege against self-incrimination[74] was, until recently, rarely mentioned in the context of the exchange of information.[75] This can partly be explained by the fact that the prevention of self-incrimination is mostly linked to criminal law and arguably it only became a more visible issue due to the introduction of mandatory disclosure rules (MDR) in 2018 (DAC6).[76]

4.3.2 Scope and Content of the Nemo Tenetur Principle

The ECtHR has decided that the right to remain silent and the privilege against self-incrimination (*nemo tenetur*) are generally recognised international standards that lie at the heart of the notion of a fair procedure under Article 6

---

[70] European Data Protection Supervisor, *Assessing the necessity of measures that limit the fundamental right to the protection of personal data: A Toolkit* (EDPS, 11 April 2017).

[71] Schaper (n 4) 521.

[72] B. Ferreira Liotti (n 3) 148. Compare Case C-175/20 *SIA 'SS' v Valsts ieņēmumu dienests* [2022] ECLI:EU:C:2022:124.

[73] Huang (n 3) 238–39.

[74] The privilege against self-incrimination is also known as the *nemo tenetur* principle.

[75] See for prior research on the relation of the right to remain silent and tax measures: Ana Paula Dourado and Augusto Silva Dias, 'Information Duties, Aggressive Tax Planning and nemo tenetur se ipsum accusare in the light of Art. 6(1) of ECHR' in Georg Kofler, Miguel Poiares Maduro and Pasquale Pistone (eds), *Human Rights and Taxation in Europe and the World* (IBFD 2011); Raymond Luja, 'Accounting Disclosure of Tax Liabilities, Fair Trial and Self-incrimination: Should the European Commission endorse IFRS in the light of European Human Rights?' in Georg Kofler, Miguel Poiares Maduro and Pasquale Pistone (eds), *Human Rights and Taxation in Europe and the World* (IBFD 2011).

[76] Nevertheless, see the *Van Weerelt* case involving the old Mutual Assistance Directive: *Van Weerelt v The Netherlands* App no 784/14 (ECtHR, 16 June 2015).

ECHR,[77] and more specifically Article 6(2) ECHR, providing for the presumption of innocence.[78] Similar guarantees are provided by Article 48 of the EU Charter ('Presumption of innocence and right of defence'). The Charter is addressed to institutions, bodies, offices and agencies of the Union and to EU Member States when they are implementing EU law.[79] The CJEU has already ruled that this is the case when applying provisions of the DAC.[80] Insofar as the EU Charter contains rights that correspond to rights guaranteed by the ECHR, the meaning and scope of those rights should be the same as those laid down by the said Convention.[81] Despite these similarities, it should be noted that the ECtHR's case law is more advanced at this stage.

The privilege against self-incrimination generally means that anyone accused of a criminal offence has the right to remain silent and not contribute to incriminating himself.[82] The privilege against self-incrimination does not protect against the making of an incriminating statement per se, but rather against the obtaining of evidence by coercion or oppression (i.e. evidence that has an existence depending on the will of the taxpayer).[83] For example, in cases where a suspect is obliged to testify under threat of sanctions and either testifies as a result of these sanctions[84] or is sanctioned for refusing to testify.[85]

---

77 *John Murray v The United Kingdom* App no 18731/91 (ECtHR, 8 February 1996), para 45.

78 'Everyone charged with a criminal offence shall be presumed innocent until proved guilty according to law.'

79 Charter of Fundamental Rights of the European Union (Charter) [2000] OJ C364/1, art 51(1).

80 Case C-682/15 (n 5) para 42.

81 Charter (n 79) 52(3).

82 *O'Halloran and Francis v The United Kingdom* App nos 15809/02 and 25624/02 (ECtHR, 29 June 2007), para 45.

83 It has been argued that mandatory disclosure of information does not infringe the privilege against self-incrimination because the information exchanged concerns tax information that has an existence independent on the will of the person concerned and is not, therefore, obtained by means of coercion and in defiance of the will of that person (see Andrea Ballancin and Francesco Cannas, 'The "DAC 6" and Its Compatibility with Some of the Founding Principles of the European Legal System(s)' (2020) 29 EC Tax Review 117, 123). Elsewhere, and in our opinion rightly, the opposite was argued by stating that the information under mandatory disclosure rules (including a summary of the transactions) would not have been drafted in the absence of these rules (see Esther Huiskers-Stoop, Mark Nieuweboer and Almut Breuer, 'De Mandatory Disclosure Richtlijn: beschrijving en kritische analyse' (2020) 167 Tijdschrift Fiscaal Ondernemingsrecht 29, 54–55); Florian Haase, *EU Tax Disclosure Rules* (Edward Elgar 2021) 212–13.

84 *Saunders v United Kingdom* App no 19187/91 (ECtHR, 17 December 1996).

85 *Weh v Austria* App no 38544/97 (ECtHR, 8 April 2004).

Article 6 ECHR is only applicable 'in the determination of [...] civil rights and obligations' (civil limb) or in case of a criminal charge (criminal limb). The nature of protection granted under each limb differs. Under the civil limb, only Article 6(1) ECHR is applicable, which grants the affected person with the (general) right to a fair trial, a trial within a reasonable time, etc. Where there is a criminal charge,[86] Articles 6(2) and 6(3) are also applicable, which provide for additional guarantees, such as the presumption of innocence (see above).

Although the Court's position may be criticised, it is well-known that Article 6 ECHR, under its civil limb, does not apply to ordinary tax proceedings, which do not have a criminal connotation.[87] Therefore, tax cases should be assessed under the criminal limb of Article 6 ECHR, which provides access to the aforementioned additional guarantees. This not only includes tax cases involving *criminal* penalties. Tax cases involving *administrative* penalties can qualify as criminal proceedings, provided these penalties qualify as 'criminal penalties'.[88] This involves a case-by-case analysis taking into account the so-called '*Engel*-criteria'. The criminal nature of the offence may suffice to render Article 6 applicable, notwithstanding the low amount of the tax surcharge (e.g., 10% of the reassessed tax liability).[89] However, the international exchange of information merely for purposes of correctly assessing taxes, without the intention of filing a criminal complaint or imposing fines of tax increases of a punitive nature, will render Article 6 ECHR inapplicable.[90]

---

[86] A 'criminal charge' can be defined as 'the official notification given to an individual by the competent authority of an allegation that he has committed a criminal offence' (*Deweer v Belgium* App no 6903/75 (ECtHR, 27 February 1980), paras 42–46). This can also result from another act which also substantially impacts the suspect's position, e.g., when there are plausible reasons to suspect that said person is involved in a punitive case (*Bandaletov v Ukraine* App no 23180/06 (ECtHR, 31 October 2013), para 56). This notion has been interpreted quite broadly. For example, a sufficient link between a prior administrative procedure and subsequent criminal proceedings might call for an extension of the criminal guarantees to the prior administrative procedure (*Chambaz v Switzerland* App no 11663/04 (ECtHR, 5 April 2012), para 48). In legal literature, it is argued that a taxpayer placed in a substantially similar situation as another taxpayer who is prosecuted could also consider himself to be subject to a criminal charge. In the framework of DAC6, this could have an impact in case a 'marketable arrangement' is involved (see Čičin-Šain (n 57) 105–106).

[87] *Ferrazzini v Italy* App no 44759/98 (ECtHR, 12 July 2001), paras 20–31.

[88] *Engels and Others v The Netherlands* App nos 5100/71; 5101/71; 5102/71; 5354/72; 5370/72 (ECtHR, 8 June 1976), paras 82–83.

[89] *Jussila v Finland* App no 73053/01 (ECtHR, 23 November 2006), para 38.

[90] See for a recent case in Luxembourg confirming this approach: Administrative Tribunal of Luxembourg (*Tribunal Administratif*), 4 July 2022, nos 41983–41984, discussed in Stijn Lamberigts, 'The right to silence and privilege against self-incrimination

4.3.3 Application to Reporting Obligations under DAC6

Given that DAC6 is precisely aimed at *obtaining* information on tax structures, cases where a criminal investigation is ongoing are likely to be rare (but not impossible).[91] This does not, however, exclude the application of Article 6 ECHR. As already indicated, a criminal charge can include administrative (tax) procedures, provided a penalty is imposed that complies with certain criteria. In this respect, it should be noted that the DAC itself provides for an obligation towards Member States to lay down the rules on penalties applicable in case of non-compliance.[92] The Directive does not contain specific amounts or guidelines, but merely requires that these be 'effective, proportionate and dissuasive'. In practice, there is a large variety of domestic penalties, including substantial pecuniary sanctions, which could indeed trigger protection under Article 6 ECHR.

Even though the DAC itself remains silent on the privilege against self-incrimination, the issue has received attention in the OECD/G20 BEPS Final Report on Action 12, which states that the reportable information under MDR 'is generally no greater than the information that the tax administration could require under an investigation or audit into a tax return'.[93] It was argued that the types of transactions targeted for disclosure will not generally be the types of transactions that will give rise to criminal liabilities.[94] In Annex B to the report, it was acknowledged that cases of 'illegal tax fraud' (or evasion) include false claims to exemption or deductions, unreported income, organised failure to withhold taxes, etc., that may result in criminal charges.[95]

It should be noted that a 'reportable cross-border arrangement' under DAC6 means any cross-border arrangement that contains at least one of the listed hallmarks.[96] A hallmark is defined as a characteristic or feature of a cross-border arrangement that presents an indication of a potential risk of tax avoidance.[97] It is therefore rightly submitted in legal literature that DAC6 targets the disclosure of abusive schemes that arguably fall under the national qualifications

---

and administrative cooperation in tax matters' (2022) 2 Cahiers de fiscalité luxembourgeoise et européenne, 173–77.

91 Čičin-Šain (n 57) 104.

92 DAC art 25a.

93 OECD, *Mandatory Disclosure Rules, Action 12: 2015 Final Report* (OECD/G20 Base Erosion and Profit Shifting Project, OECD Publishing 2015) 56.

94 ibid 57.

95 ibid 85.

96 DAC art 3(19).

97 DAC art 3(20).

of both tax avoidance and tax fraud.[98] This could fall in the ambit of Article 6 ECHR, given that the ECtHR has, in the past, decided that the privilege against self-incrimination applies when 'the applicant could not exclude that, if it transpired from [the information disclosed] that he had received additional income which had not been taxed, he might be charged with the offence of tax evasion'.[99] Therefore, the distinction between an ordinary tax assessment and criminal proceedings may be blurred. It has been submitted that the privilege against self-incrimination may become relevant with regard to tax offences if there is no clear separation between tax and criminal proceedings.[100]

Under DAC6, the obligation *ratione personae* to disclose information lies with two categories of persons. First, the obligation lies with an 'intermediary'[101] that has a link with the EU.[102] Second, generally speaking, situations may arise where no intermediary was involved (e.g. when an arrangement was developed 'in-house') and/or when an intermediary was involved in the arrangement, but that person enjoys an exemption from the obligation to disclose on the basis of legal professional privilege.[103] In those cases, in subsidiary order, the obligation to disclose the arrangement lies with the taxpayer themself.[104] In both situations, penalties can be imposed in the case of non-compliance.[105] In addition, depending on the domestic laws of EU Member States, intermediaries could be implicated as 'accomplices' to tax fraud.[106] Therefore, the possibility cannot be dismissed that both the taxpayer and the intermediary could be entitled to refuse to disclose information based on the privilege against self-incrimination.[107]

The OECD report itself makes a distinction between two situations. First, a situation where a person can be required to disclose information prior to the implementation of a scheme. This can be considered to be a part of the ordinary information collecting activity undertaken for tax assessment purposes. If such information is merely used for tax assessment purposes, taxpayers may

---

98 Bart Peeters and Lars Vanneste, 'DAC 6: an additional common EU reporting standard?' (2020) 12 World Tax Journal 499, 549.

99 *J.B. v Switzerland* App no 31827/96 (ECtHR, 3 May 2001), para 66. See, however, *Allen v United Kingdom* App no 76574/01 (ECtHR, 10 September 2002).

100 Kokott and Pistone (n 4) 274.

101 DAC art 3(21).

102 DAC art 3(21).

103 DAC art 8ab(5).

104 DAC art 8ab(6).

105 DAC art 25a.

106 See also OECD (n 93) 86.

107 Daniel W. Blum and Andreas Langer, 'At a crossroads: Mandatory Disclosure under DAC-6 and EU Primary Law – Part 2' (2019) 59 European taxation 313, 317.

not be able to invoke privilege against self-incrimination.[108] Second, the report acknowledges that self-incrimination may arise if it is the case that a taxpayer is required to disclose information while criminal proceedings are pending.[109] The latter statement seems to pertain to situations where a scheme already was implemented.

Several solutions to ensure compliance with the principle of self-incrimination have been advanced: (1) the OECD/G20 submit that the privilege against self-incrimination would be a 'reasonable excuse' not to disclose.[110] This would arguably undermine the efficiency of mandatory disclosure rules.[111] (2) Alternatively, countries that impose criminal penalties on taxpayers for undertaking certain tax avoidance transactions may choose to could exclude such transactions from the scope. Currently, the DAC does not provide for an explicit option for a carve-out. (3) It has been suggested that the DAC should exclude the possibility of imposing criminal sanctions or proceedings against a taxpayer based on the information obtained.[112] While this would indeed solve the issue altogether,[113] such an escape could also be abused by taxpayers by (over-)disclosing in order to avoid the possibility of imposing criminal sanctions or proceedings at a later stage.[114]

4.4 CONCLUSION

In legal literature, the impact of the right to privacy on the exchange of tax information has been extensively discussed. Several shortcomings have been identified in this respect as regards taxpayer protection, and these can be extended to the DAC. The update of Article 25 DAC resulting from the introduction of DAC2 and DAC7 together with the adoption of the GDPR, has arguably enhanced the overall legal protection of taxpayers. The latter instrument is, however, not designed, as such, to specifically deal with tax issues (hence the absence of detailed rules for tax administrations) and provides for escape routes under the form of restrictions. Legal persons are, however,

---

108 OECD (n 93) 85.

109 ibid.

110 ibid.

111 Čičin-Šain (n 57) 100–106.

112 Jasha Voje, 'EU Implementation of BEPS Action 12 in Light of Human Rights Requirements' (2017) 57 European Taxation 199.

113 Support for this position can be found in *Van Weerelt*, where the Court was of the opinion that Article 6 ECHR was not applicable due to the presence of an additional safeguard for the taxpayer in question, i.e. the information exchanged could not be used by the recipient state for criminal proceedings or in order to impose tax penalties. See: *Van Weerelt v The Netherlands* (n 76) 60.

114 Čičin-Šain (n 57) 106–107.

still (mostly) bound to rely on general (and hence vaguer) privacy and data protection rights. As argued above, it is also doubtful whether the DAC ticks all GDPR's boxes.

In stark contrast to the abundance of literature and case law on the right to privacy, the privilege against self-incrimination (or *nemo tenetur*) was until recent rarely mentioned in the context of exchange of information. The introduction of DAC6 has changed this by introducing the obligation for intermediaries (or even the taxpayer themself) to disclosure information. In my opinion, both categories of persons could refuse to disclose information based on the privilege against self-incrimination, depending on the facts and circumstances.

5. The right to be heard and other taxpayers' rights during the exchange of information procedure

Stefano Dorigo and Chiara Cinotti[1]

5.1 INTRODUCTION

Nowadays the international community largely agrees that, in order to prevent and counteract international tax evasion, tax cooperation between states and, in particular, exchange of information procedures cannot be ignored. Nevertheless, as will be shown below, what emerges from the analysis of the measures issued is that both the international community and the EU seem to have overlooked the fact that, although the exchange takes place between the administrative authorities of the states, it primarily involves the taxpayer, who should be guaranteed the possibility of exercising, already at the time of the request, the fundamental rights proclaimed by the international and supranational human rights charters, in particular those rights relating to the knowledge of and participation in the exchange procedure:[2]

(a) *Notification rights*, i.e., the right of the taxpayer to be informed of the initiation of an information exchange procedure with another state;
(b) *Consultation rights*, i.e., the right of the taxpayer to be heard before the requested information is transmitted to the requesting state;

---

[1] Although the topics discussed in this chapter are the result of a shared reflection, Sections 5.1, 5.2 and 5.3 were written by Chiara Cinotti, while Sections 5.4, 5.5 and 5.6 are the work of Stefano Dorigo.

[2] On the lack of protection of taxpayers' rights during exchange of information procedures, see Pietro Mastellone, 'Taxpayers' procedural rights during exchange of information procedures' in Eva Andres Aucejo (ed), *International Administrative Cooperation in Fiscal Matters and International Tax Governance* (Thomson Reuters 2018) 291 ff.; Roberto Cordeiro Guerra and Stefano Dorigo, 'Taxpayers' Rights as Human Rights During Tax Procedures' in Georg Kofler, Miguel Poiares Maduro and Pasquale Pistone (eds), *Human Rights and Taxation in Europe and the World* (IBFD 2011) 427.

(c) *Intervention rights*, i.e., the right of the taxpayer to request that a third and impartial body judges the legality of the request for exchange of information and verifies the correctness of the information exchanged.

However, none of the rules governing the exchange of information is currently concerned with ensuring the taxpayer any of the rights listed above. What prevails, instead, is the interest in correct and efficient cooperation between the tax administrations of the states, which is perceived as expression of a value – the value of the correct reconstruction of tax bases and thus of the timely collection of taxes due – that in the era of the global crisis is also imposed against the interests of the persons involved. The advent of the automatic exchange of information amplifies these concerns, since the ways through which the exchange is carried out seem to radically exclude the possibility of the taxpayer's involvement in the exchange procedure.[3]

In this chapter, we will analyse the main international (Section 5.2) and supranational (Section 5.3) instruments for exchanging information on tax matters with specific regard to the protection of the taxpayer's rights provided. More specifically, two main areas will be examined regarding taxpayers' participatory rights within exchange of information procedures linked to granting an effective exercise of their fair trial, which ECtHR case law also extends to the decision-making phase (Section 5.4); and data protection (Section 5.5).

5.2 THE INTERNATIONAL INSTRUMENTS

5.2.1 Taxpayers' Unsatisfactory Protection in Article 26 of the OECD Model

Among the tools that the tax administration of a state has at its disposal to obtain tax information on a taxpayer with foreign sources of income or, in any case, with elements of connection with foreign countries, are the provisions on the exchange of information provided for in double taxation treaties that are based on Article 26 of the OECD Model. As shown in the previous chapters,[4] Article 26 allows the tax authorities of a state to request the other contracting states to provide information in their possession that is 'foreseeably relevant' for tax purposes. In providing for this, however, the rule does not expressly mention any rights that states should grant to the taxpayer during the administrative procedure in which they are involved. However, it would be unreason-

[3] See in this sense the position of Philip Baker and Pasquale Pistone, 'General Report' in *The Practical Protection of Taxpayers' Rights* (Cahiers de droit fiscal international 2015) 52.

[4] See Part I, Chapter 1 in this book.

able to infer, from the mere absence of an express provision, that under Article 26 states are entitled to exchange tax information without having to guarantee taxpayers any procedural rights. This, indeed, would be in clear contrast with the fundamental principles of international law which, also by virtue of the contribution of the ECHR, now recognise to all individuals the right to a so-called fair trial – Article 6 of the ECHR – not only in judicial proceedings, but also in administrative ones.[5] On this basis, it should be ascertained whether Article 26 grants taxpayers certain procedural rights, albeit implicitly.

On closer inspection, some safeguards do seem to be apparent from the limits which the rule imposes on the exchange of information between states. First of all, the provision requires the requesting state to request only information that is 'foreseeably relevant', thus obliging the state to circumscribe its request and not to undertake 'fishing expeditions'.[6] This limitation represents a first form of procedural guarantee for the taxpayer, since the requesting state will never be able to have access to every piece of tax information in the other state's possession, but only to those pieces of information specifically identified by reason of their relevance to the tax investigation undertaken. Second, the provision limits the disclosure of exchanged tax information only to persons who are involved in the assessment, liquidation, collection or enforcement of taxes, as indicated in Article 26.2. In this respect, it is interesting to note that the OECD Commentary on Article 26 points out that such disclosure *may* also concern the taxpayer.[7] Although it is only an option, this provision represents an opening towards the recognition of the possibility that, in certain cases, some form of involvement of the taxpayer in the procedure may be foreseen. Third, Article 26.2 prevents the requesting state from using the information obtained for purposes other than taxation. This limitation is not absolute, since the wording of Article 26.2 openly allows the use of the information received for other purposes when the laws of both states and their competent authorities authorise this. Here again, therefore, international law takes a step back, leaving it to the states – requesting and requested – to identify the boundaries of the legitimate use of the information exchanged which would seem to be in potential conflict with the criterion of 'foreseeable relevance'. Finally, Article 26.3 sets out three limits to the exchange of information.

---

5 For an examination of the subject see Cordeiro Guerra and Dorigo (n 2) 425; Stefano Dorigo, 'La tutela internazionale dei diritti del contribuente' in Roberto Cordeiro Guerra (ed), *Diritto tributario internazionale. Istituzioni* (Kluwer 2016).

6 See Part I, Chapter 1 in this book.

7 OECD Model Tax Convention, Commentary on art 26, para 12: '[…] This means that the information may also be communicated to the taxpayer, his proxy or to the witness'.

Thus, although it does not affirm the procedural rights that all states are bound to guarantee to the taxpayer, Article 26 does expressly refer to the protection provided by the laws of the contracting states by preventing exchanges carried out by circumventing the laws and administrative practice of the requested state. This is, on closer inspection, a completely ineffective and even discriminatory guarantee, because in this way the taxpayers' rights are left at the mercy of the level of protection that each state, in the full exercise of its sovereign power, decides to ensure, creating, ultimately, an uneven level of protection among states. Indeed, as the Commentary points out, there are states that guarantee a right to taxpayers to receive notification of the commencement of an exchange of information procedure before it begins (*right of notification*),[8] granting the taxpayers a very high level of protection, compared to those states, like Italy,[9] whose domestic law does not recognise such a right. On the other hand, for the purposes of Article 26, any procedural guarantees ensured by a state internally may nevertheless be waived – and thus lose their effectiveness – since 'they should not prevent or unduly delay effective exchange of information'.[10]

5.2.2 Taxpayers' Rights in the Model Agreement on Exchange of Information on Tax Matters

Even in the Model Agreement on Exchange of Information on Tax Matters of 2002, on the basis of which states have stipulated the so-called TIEAs, i.e., Tax Information Exchange Agreements, there is no trace of any rules dedicated to the rights of the taxpayer involved in the exchange of information. However, an indirect protection could perhaps be found again in the establishment of the criterion of the 'foreseeable relevance' of the information exchanged.[11] However, Article 1, in its last paragraph, addresses the issue of the protection of the rights of the taxpayer involved in the procedure, by expressly referring to the level guaranteed by each state, with the same limitation already encountered in the Commentary on Article 26 of the OECD Model '[not to] unduly,

---

8 OECD Model Tax Convention, Commentary on art 26, para 14.1.

9 Italy's position could move in a more guarantee-oriented direction with the implementation of the tax delegation bill no. 111 of 9 August 2023, which, inter alia, in art 3, para 1, lett. A), delegates the Government to 'ensure the adaptation of national tax law to the principles of the tax system and to the levels of protection of rights established by the European Union system, also taking into account the development of the case law of the Court of Justice of the European Union on tax matters' (translation from Italian by the authors).

10 OECD Model Tax Convention, Commentary on art 26, para 14.1.

11 OECD Agreement on Exchange of Information on Tax Matters (2002), art 1.

prevent or delay effective exchange of information'.[12] Therefore, even the 2002 Model Agreement would seem to confirm, on a first reading, that in the area of the exchange of tax information there are no taxpayer rights recognised in a general way, but the rights – if any – are of variable protection, i.e., they depend on the system of guarantees set up by the states involved in the procedure each time.

However, the Model Agreement seems to make a further – albeit still unsatisfactory – effort to protect the taxpayer when compared to the OECD Model. Paragraph 5 of the Commentary to Article 1 lists certain procedural rights and safeguards 'that may flow from relevant international agreement on human rights',[13] which may be granted to the taxpayer by the individual national legal systems – besides the right to notification of the initiation of the procedure – and points out that 'the expression 'unduly prevent or delay' indicates that such rights may take precedence over the Agreement'.[14] In short, with this international instrument, the taxpayer is recognised human rights (and specifically the right to a fair trial) provided by the relevant international treaties, as long as such recognition does not unduly impede or delay the exchange of information. In the authors' opinion, such limitation significantly reduces the effectiveness of the protection, in addition to being completely unreasonable, given that the speed of the procedure should not prevail over the protection of human rights.

5.2.3 The Weak Protection of Taxpayers under the MAAT Convention

Although in the MAAT Convention there is no provision either that is expressly dedicated to recognising and protecting the participatory rights of taxpayers, this instrument contains some interesting statements of principle that, while extremely general in scope, suggest the possibility that greater awareness on the subject is emerging. First, Recital 6 of the Preamble acknowledges that a 'proper legal procedure' must be guaranteed in tax matters and, again, among

---

[12] OECD Agreement on Exchange of Information on Tax Matters (2002), art 1, last paragraph: 'The rights and safeguards secured to persons by the laws or administrative practice of the requested Party remain applicable to the extent that they do not unduly prevent or delay effective exchange of information'.

[13] OECD Agreement on Exchange of Information on Tax Matters (2002), Commentary on art 1, para 5.

[14] ibid.

the rights to be recognised to the taxpayer it lists 'the right to a proper procedure in the determination of their rights and obligations in tax matters'.[15]

However, this instrument too ends up entrusting the individual states with the task of giving effective protection to the taxpayers' rights,[16] as can be derived from Article 21 where it is provided that 'nothing in this Convention shall affect the rights and safeguards secured to persons by the laws or administrative practice of the requested State'.[17] Following the line of Article 26 of the OECD MC, the taxpayer may only be granted rights of participation in the procedure as long as the law and administrative practice of the states involved in the exchange allow it and always to the extent that this does not unduly delay or impede the procedure. Nevetheless, the Explanatory Report of the MAAT Convention goes further than the Commentary on the OECD MC and clarifies the obligation of states that grant the right to notification to inform the other state involved in the exchange of information procedure about it and its consequences.[18]

5.3 THE SUPRANATIONAL INSTRUMENTS

5.3.1 EU Law and Protection of Taxpayers' Rights in EoI Procedures

Turning now to the European legislation on the exchange of information, beyond the criterion of the 'foreseeable relevance' of the information exchanged provided for in Article 1 of the DAC – which recalls the criterion also established at international level – the only provision that is concerned with taxpayer's rights is Recital no. 28 of the Preamble of the DAC, which proclaims the respect for fundamental rights and principles recognised by the Charter.[19] For the rest, the Directive defers to the domestic legislation of the Member States with the result that not even EU taxpayers are granted, in a direct way, a uniform protection of their rights to information and participation. Meanwhile some states recognise all the procedural rights attributable to the taxpayer (e.g., Germany), others provide only the minimum level of protec-

[15] Explanatory Report to the Convention on Mutual Administrative Assistance in Tax Matters as amended by the 2010 Protocol (2011), introduction, para 7.

[16] Convention on Mutual Administrative Assistance in Tax Matters as amended by the 2010 Protocol (1988) Preamble at 6.

[17] Explanatory Report to the Convention on Mutual Administrative Assistance in Tax Matters as amended by the 2010 Protocol (2011) art 21, paras 179 and 181.

[18] Explanatory Report to the Convention on Mutual Administrative Assistance in Tax Matters as amended by the 2010 Protocol (2011) art 21, para 180, last sentence.

[19] DAC1 recital 28.

tion (i.e., notification rights, see Spain), and others do not even guarantee these basic rights (and among the latter is Italy).[20]

The direct consequence of the fact that the effectiveness of the protection of taxpayers' rights is left up to individual states is the emergence of discriminatory phenomena among taxpayers, which stands in sharp contrast with a system of exchange of information that, form the point of view of the effectiveness and speed of the procedure, has instead reached levels of harmonisation that were unthinkable a few years ago.[21]

5.3.2 The Case Law of the CJEU

The issue of the level of protection of taxpayer's rights granted by EU law during exchange of information procedures[22] was first addressed by the Court of Justice of the European Union in the well-known *Sabou* judgment (which concerned the MAD, still applicable, *ratione temporis*, to the present case).[23] The CJEU, after emphasising that respect for the rights of the defence constitutes a general principle of EU law that applies whenever the administration takes an act adversely affecting an individual,[24] even if EU law does not expressly provide for this right, nevertheless held that that right was not applicable to the taxpayer under investigation in the context of a procedure for the exchange of tax information concerning them. The court, in particular, pointed out, first, that in tax proceedings a distinction must be made between the investigation phase, comprising the activity of requesting and exchanging information, and the adversarial phase, which begins when the tax authorities

---

20 See again the interesting comparative analysis by Mastellone (n 2) 299 ff. As previously noted, Italy's position in this respect seems to be about to change thanks to a recent legislative intervention (n 9).

21 On the topic Pietro Mastellone, 'Exchange of information versus protection of taxpayers' rights: the evident imbalance impedes achieving a fair international tax environment' (2017) 24 Journal of International Tax, Trust and Corporate Planning 77.

22 For an in-depth analysis of taxpayer's rights in the European information exchange procedure in light of the CJEU case law, see Stefano Dorigo, 'Administrative transnationality in tax matters: from non-cooperation to shared administration' (2023) 20 Diretto e Pratica Tributaria Internatzionale 13; Stefano Dorigo, 'The Rights of Persons Involved in the Exchange of Tax Information: Recent Openings of the Court of Justice and Persisting Doubts on the Respect of EU Fundamental Rights' (2021) 13 Italian Journal of Public Law 84; Mastellone (n 2) 303; Pietro Mastellone, 'L'Unione europea non riconosce participation rights al contribuente sottoposto a procedure di mutua assistenza amministrativa tra autorità fiscali' (2013) 23 Rivista di Diritto Tributario 349.

23 Case C-276/12 *Jiří Sabou v Finanční ředitelství pro hlavní město Prahu* [2013] ECLI:EU:C:2013:678.

24 ibid para 28.

formulate the proposal to amend the tax return. Second, it stated that only in this second phase must the right of defence of the taxpayer under investigation be considered applicable.[25] The extension of participation rights to the first phase (i.e., the investigation phase) is not entirely excluded, but is left to the discretion of each Member State.[26] This position was also confirmed by the CJEU in the subsequent *Berlioz* judgment.[27]

After pointing out that the Directive does not confer specific rights on the taxpayer under investigation as regards their participation in the information exchange procedure, nevertheless, under Article 47 of the Charter, the Court acknowledged third parties the right to challenge the lawfulness of a decision that penalises them for not complying with an administrative order requiring them to provide information about a taxpayer subject to investigation in the context of an exchange of information procedure under the DAC.[28]

This is because, according to the Court, the *Berlioz* case is different to *Sabou*. In the latter case, the taxpayer's right of defence in the form of participation in the administrative procedure of exchange of information was correctly disregarded, because the procedure concerned requests for information between financial administrations, which did not directly involve the taxpayer under investigation. However, the situation was deemed different in *Berlioz*, where the Luxembourg tax authorities, at the request of the French ones, asked Berlioz to provide information in its possession concerning a taxpayer under investigation, the refusal of which resulted in the imposition of a penalty.[29] In other words, according to the CJEU, the taxpayer under investigation had no participatory rights, because they were not the addressee of the requests for exchange of information. Such rights are instead to be granted to the subject involved in the procedure because of the possession of relevant tax information on the taxpayer under investigation, who might be subject to administrative penalty if not compliant with the request of information.

---

25 ibid paras 40–44.

26 ibid para 45.

27 Case C-682/15 *Berlioz Investment Fund SA v Directeur de l'administration des contributions directes* [2017] ECLI:EU:C:2017:373. For a commentary on the judgment see Paolo Mazzotti and Mariolina Eliantonio, 'Transnational Judicial Review in Horizontal Composite Procedures: Berlioz, Donnellan and the Constitutional Law of the Union' (2020) 5 European Papers 41; Bob Michel, 'Exchange of Information on Request: Whenever, Wherever? Shakira's (and Berlioz's) Right to Judicial Review of the Foreseeable Relevance Standard' (2019) 73 Bulletin for International Taxation 98; Pietro Mastellone, 'Una nuova alba per i diritti fondamentali del contribuente europeo: alcuni spunti sistematici a margine della sentenza Berlioz della Corte di Giustizia' (2017) 14 Diritto e Pratica Tributaria Internazionale 591.

28 ibid para 73.

29 ibid para 58.

The position upheld in *Berlioz* was also confirmed in the subsequent cases, concerning a procedure of exchange of information between the Spanish administration (requesting) and the Luxembourg administration (requested).[30] The Court reaffirmed that persons requested to disclose information concerning a specific taxpayer must be granted the right to an effective remedy under Article 47 of the Charter against that decision, if considered to be arbitrary or disproportionate, because refusing to comply with it exposes the requested person to the penalty connected with that decision.[31]

However, the Court expressly denied such right to taxpayers, merely because they are the subjects of the investigation.[32] Taxpayers are not the addressees of any decision. Therefore, they are neither subject to any legal obligation nor exposed to the risk of having a penalty imposed on them for non-compliance. As already stated in the *Sabou* judgment, the CJEU reiterated that the preliminary phase of the investigation against the taxpayer is not adversarial in nature and does not entitle the taxpayer to participate in the procedure. That right arises only in the phase following the closure of the investigation, when, on the basis of the information gathered, the requesting administration sends a proposal for rectification or correction to the taxpayer, thus enabling them to exercise their right to be heard against that decision addressed to them.[33]

Hence, the Court admits for taxpayers only a form of deferred protection, enforceable in the state of residence. That type of protection, however, is not effective, since it does not allow the taxpayer to intervene immediately to suspend the information exchange procedures that are conducted unlawfully, and is thus incapable of protecting the taxpayer from any harm that might occur in the medium term.

---

30 Joined Cases C-245/19 and C-246/19 *État luxembourgeois v B and Others* [2020] ECLI:EU:C:2020:795. For a commentary on the judgment see Saturnina Moreno González, 'Cross-border exchange of tax information upon request and fundamental rights – Can the right balance be struck?: Joined Cases C-245/19 and C-246/19, Etat luxembourgeois contre B' (2021) 28(5) Maastricht Journal of European and Comparative Law 13; Chiara Francioso, 'Tutela giurisdizionale e 'prevedibile pertinenza' delle informazioni nella cooperazione amministrativa fiscale europea' (2021) 2 Tax News 423; Luca Costanzo, 'La tutela dei diritti del contribuente al crocevia tra cooperazione amministrativa e integrazione eurotributaria' (2020) 5 Rivista telematica di Diritto Tributario 988.

31 ibid para 59.

32 ibid para 93.

33 ibid paras 80–83.

5.4 LOOKING FOR TAXPAYERS' PROCEDURAL RIGHTS IN EXISTING INTERNATIONAL LAW: THE ROLE OF THE PROTECTION OF HUMAN RIGHTS THROUGH ARTICLE 6 OF ECTHR

As the section above has shown, the international and supranational regulatory landscape on the protection of taxpayers' rights in the specific context of exchange of information procedures is not reassuring. While hoping for the rules on the exchange of information, especially at the European level, to provide adequate protection for the taxpayer at the procedural stage, it is necessary to try to identify remedies on the basis of existing law. A first area of investigation is that of international human rights law, especially the European Convention on Human Rights, with reference to the extension of the principles of due process to the pre-trial phase as well.

Article 6(1) of the ECHR establishes that 'in the determination of his civil rights and obligations or of any criminal charge against him, everyone is entitled to a fair and public hearing within a reasonable time by an independent and impartial tribunal established by law'. Differently from the American Convention on Human Rights,[34] the ECHR makes no reference to tax trials. Therefore, tax procedures have traditionally been considered outside the protection afforded by Article 6.

In a first stage, the ECtHR itself supported this interpretation. In *Ferrazzini v Italy*,[35] the court clearly acknowledged that 'tax matters still form part of the hard core of public-authority prerogatives, with the public nature of the relationship between the taxpayer and the community remaining predominant'.[36]

The preparatory works do not confirm this kind of interpretation; on the contrary, they show that the drafters intended to extend the rights now enshrined in Article 6 to all the cases of judicial proceedings taking place before a court established by law, regardless of the nature of the involved individual positions and, consequently, also in cases where a taxpayer contests a tax assessment issued by the tax authorities.[37]

---

[34] Article 8(1) of the American Convention on Human Rights, adopted on 22 November 1969, establishes the right for any individual to have at their disposal an independent and impartial judicial body to address 'in the substantiation of any accusation of a criminal nature made against him or for the determination of his rights and obligations of a civil, labour, fiscal, or any other nature'. It seems important that tax issues are mentioned, with no ambiguity, among those the rule aims to protect.

[35] *Ferrazzini v Italy* App no 44759/98 (ECtHR, 12 July 2001).

[36] ibid para 29.

[37] For an analysis of the preparatory works of art 6 refer to Stefano Dorigo, 'Considerazioni storico-sistematiche sull'applicabilità dell'art. 6 della CEDU alle con-

Recently, however, the ECtHR, although in a still cautious way, seems willing to make some inroads in the conceptual foundation, apparently so rock-hard, of the interpretation followed so far. To this end, the Court has frequently made reference to the criminal head of Article 6(1), i.e., where the norm recalls the hearings concerning any 'criminal charge' against the taxpayer. In particular, the ECtHR acknowledged that those tax judicial procedures having as their object not only the amount of tax due, but also the legality of tax penalties resulting from the latter, should be regarded as falling within the scope of Article 6.[38] According to the Strasbourg court, those penalties, despite their administrative nature, show a purpose – deterrent and punitive at the same time – which is generally criminal in nature and therefore allow the application of the right to fair trial.

These conclusions can be clearly inferred in the *Jussila* judgment.[39] The ECtHR stated that 'it is […] not uncommon for procedures to combine the varying elements and it may not be possible to separate those parts of the proceedings which determine a "criminal charge" from those parts which do not'.[40] Therefore, and this is the main innovation of the judgment under consideration, the Strasbourg Court suggested that all tax proceedings, which involve the assessment of the legality of penalties stemming from a tax recovery, fall within the scope of Article 6 ECHR. As a consequence, the hard core of state sovereignty, while not being denied, cannot exclude the compliance with some minimum procedural guarantees in favour of the taxpayer.

After *Jussila*, this innovative interpretation has been further developed. The ECtHR, in a series of judgments concerning Finnish tax legislation, clearly stated that certain guarantees, which until now have been limited to the context of criminal proceedings, are applicable to tax disputes as well, wherever the substance of an administrative sanction is such to equate it to a criminal penalty.[41]

With respect to the subject matter of this chapter, i.e., the existence of participatory rights of the taxpayer in the course of the exchange of information procedure, it is necessary to understand whether the subjective situations envisaged by Article 6 can also be invoked outside the judicial process, i.e., in

---

troversie fiscali' in Francesco Bilancia, Christian Califano, Lorenzo Del Federico and Paola Puoti (eds), *Convenzione Europea dei Diritti dell'Uomo e giustizia tributaria italiana* (Giappichelli 2014) 94.

38 *Janosevic v Sweden* App no 34619/97 (ECtHR, 23 July 2002), and *Västberga Taxi Aktiebolag and Vulic v Sweden* App no 36985/97 (ECtHR, 23 July 2002).

39 *Jussila v Finland* App no 73053/01 (ECtHR, 23 November 2006).

40 ibid para 45.

41 *Hannu Lehtinen v Finland* App no 32993/02 (ECtHR, 22 July 2008), and *Kallio v Finland* App no 40199/02 (ECtHR, 22 July 2008).

the administrative phase preceding the formulation of a recovery by means of an assessment notice.

ECtHR case law has shown its readiness to also extend *fair trial* protection during the administrative phase which precedes the judicial one. In *Ravon*,[42] the Court of Strasbourg acknowledged that the guarantees mentioned in Article 6 do not concern the trial only, but must also be respected during a tax audit. In that specific case, it was the taxpayer's right to obtain suitable protection during a tax inspection which was endangered by means of a home access and the consequent document seizure in order to check their tax liability. The Court, though referring once again to the principles expressed in *Ferrazzini*, nevertheless stated that the case did not entirely regard a tax issue, since 'in its essence it includes the issue for the authorities to acknowledge or not the right to domicile'.[43] Consequently, the civil character of this right was 'evident'.

In *Kozinets v Ukraine*,[44] the ECtHR declared that the guarantee of Article 3 of ECHR, forbidding torture and inhuman or degrading treatment, was applicable to a tax audit. In this specific case, the taxpayer was the victim of threats and physical violence by officers of the tax administration, when he went to their offices to collect some of the documents which were seized during a house search.

In *Funke v France*, then, the ECtHR declared that the behaviour of French customs authorities was against Article 6 of ECHR when – during an inspection and since the taxpayer refused to show the documentation they were looking for – they summoned him, trying to oblige him to submit said documents if he wanted to prevent the imposition of serious penalties. According to the judgment, '[T]he special features of customs law [...] cannot justify such an infringement of the right of anyone "charged with a criminal offence", within the autonomous meaning of this expression in Article 6, to remain silent and not to contribute to incriminating himself'.[45]

Finally, in *Chambaz v Switzerland*,[46] the Court censored the behaviour of the Swiss tax authorities which, at the time of the audit, imposed severe penalties on the taxpayer because of his choice not to submit the documents the officers in charge asked for, in order to avoid being subject to a criminal incrimination. In particular, the Court acknowledged that such a penalty infringed Article 6(1) ECHR, being in contrast to the taxpayer's right to remain silent during the preliminary investigation: the right against self-incrimination represents therefore an addition to the set of rights connected with the fair trial principle.

---

42 *Ravon and others v France* App no 18497/03 (ECtHR, 2 February 2008).

43 *Ferrazzini v Italy* (n 35).

44 *Kozinets v Ukraine* App no 75520/01 (ECtHR, 6 December 2007).

45 *Funke v France* App no 10828/84 (ECtHR, 25 February 1993), para 44.

46 *Chambaz v Switzerland* App no 11663/04 (ECtHR, 5 April 2012).

It can cross over the limits of the *stricto sensu* criminal proceedings and be acknowledged in all those audits involving the tax authorities.[47]

The Strasbourg Court's case law thus seems to overcome the limits of the unclear wording of Article 6, bringing the protection of taxpayers during tax proceedings to the same level as that provided by the American Convention on Human Rights. Also in the European system the time is coming (even if belatedly) when the position of the taxpayer is considered equal to that of the tax administration, in the light of the equivalence between the individual's rights and the public interest in the correct application of fiscal rules.

It is therefore to be hoped that the evolution underway with regard to Article 6 ECHR may also concern the protection of the taxpayer during the administrative procedure of exchange of information, with the consequence that the rights listed therein – and in particular the right to be informed in advance of the procedure underway so as to have access to the information gathered and to be able to exercise their rights of defence from that stage – may also be activated and protected in that context.[48] This interpretative position, supported by a part of international doctrine,[49] has not yet been expressly endorsed by the European Court of Human Rights, although in some cases it has apparently taken for granted the application of Article 6 to exchange of information procedures, while denying in the cases in question that the rule had been violated.[50]

5.5 THE PROTECTION OF PERSONAL DATA AND ITS (POTENTIAL) IMPACT ON THE TAXPAYER'S PROCEDURAL RIGHTS IN THE EXCHANGE OF INFORMATION

The exchange of information, whatever method is used, involves the collection, storage and circulation of data concerning the taxpayer (as well as third parties). It is therefore obvious that, in the course of these activities, the question arises as to the application of the rights that international and European

---

47 Philip Baker, 'Recent tax cases of the European Court of Human Rights' (2012) 52 European Taxation 585 points out that 'it was clear that forcing a taxpayer to answer questions or create new documents giving information interfered with the right of silence'.

48 The extension of art 6 ECHR rights to the administrative phase of information gathering as well is supported by Cordeiro Guerra and Dorigo (n 2) 425.

49 Xavier Oberson, *International Exchange of Information in Tax Matters. Towards Global Transparency* (Edward Elgar 2018) 227.

50 See *Miahile v France* App no 18978/91 (ECtHR, 26 September 1996) where the Court held that the right under art 6 ECHR had not been violated in the course of an exchange of information procedure on the basis of the relevant double taxation convention, since the taxpayer had had access to the relevant information that was exchanged.

law recognises in favour of the owner of such data.[51] These rights include the right to be informed about the modalities and purposes of data processing; the right to intervene in order to correct incorrect processing; and finally the right to an effective judicial protection. Leaving aside this last, which does not pertain to the procedural phase, it may be observed that the first two types of right coincide with the protection that doctrine has long invoked for the taxpayer subject to an information exchange procedure, namely that of being informed and of being heard in the course of the procedure itself.[52]

Despite these similarities, in the international context of information exchange, the absence of procedural rights is accompanied by a lack of interest in the protection of personal data. The OECD Model merely states that the data exchanged shall be treated confidentially in the receiving state, whereas the Convention on Mutual Administrative Assistance in Tax Matters, while mentioning the need for adequate protection of personal data, leaves it to national legislation to define the relevant forms of protection.[53] Therefore, there is no room for personal data protection on the basis of international law.[54]

European data protection law offers more interesting insights. Article 8 of the Charter of Fundamental Rights lays down the right of anyone to have access to and obtain rectification of the data collected concerning them, which implies the possibility for the data subject to be heard by the data controller. The data protection rules, which find their legal basis in Article 16 TFEU,[55] provides for several rights of the data subject, which can be activated during the collection and processing phase: the right to be informed, the right of access and rectification, the right to object to data processing, and the right to the notification of unlawful processing. The European Information Exchange Directive, in Recital 27 of its preamble, subjects the activity of information exchange to the safeguards provided for in European instruments on the protection of personal data.[56]

---

51 More extensively, see Part I, Chapter 4 in this book.

52 OECD, *Taxpayers' Rights and Obligations: Practice Note* (2003).

53 Article 22, para 1, of the Convention on Mutual Administrative Assistance in Tax Matters, developed jointly by the OECD and the Council of Europe in 1988 and amended by Protocol in 2010.

54 Belisa Ferreira Liotti, 'Taxpayers' data Protection: Do International, Regional, and Domestic Instruments Guarantee Adequate Rights in Tax (A)EoI?' (2022) 50 Intertax 138, 144.

55 'Everyone has the right to the protection of personal data concerning them'.

56 DAC1, recital 27. The reference to the 1995 directive in that recital is now to be replaced by that to Regulation (EU) 2016/679 of the European Parliament and of the Council of 27 April 2016 on the protection of natural persons with regard to the processing of personal data and on the free movement of such data, and repealing Directive

However, Article 25 of DAC gives Member States the possibility to restrict the rights of information, access and publicity with regard to the processing of exchanged data where this is deemed necessary in order to protect 'an important economic or financial interest of a Member State or of the European Union, including monetary, budgetary and taxation matters'. According to Recital 27 to the Preamble of DAC1, mentioned above, this limitation is 'necessary and proportionate in view of the potential loss of revenue for Member States and the crucial importance of information covered by this Directive for the effectiveness of the fight against fraud'.

The European system, therefore, also seems to subordinate taxpayers' rights to the protection of their personal data exchanged between financial administrations to the revenue protection requirements of the Member States. Although the system of the GDPR provides that limitations to personal data rights can only take place in the presence of a legislative measure that respects the essence of the fundamental rights of the individual and is necessary and proportionate in a democratic system,[57] the tendency is to let the interest of the tax system prevail in any case, since it is linked to rights, individual and collective, that only the proper collection of taxes can guarantee. In this sense, Recital 112 of the Preamble to the GDPR seems to automatically recognise that the exchange of information in tax matters is a transfer of data that is necessary for reasons of public interest, thus justifying limitations to the rights of the data owner. This arrangement raised the concern of the European Data Protection Supervisor, who, in their opinion on the proposed DAC1, noted that 'the current proposal is a clear example of a lack of data protection awareness since the issue of data protection has almost completely been ignored' and called for the system of administrative cooperation between Member States to be 'developed in a way which respects the right to data protection of the European citizens'.[58]

However, a significant opening in the direction of rights protection was realised with the 2014 directive that introduced the common reporting standard into European law, i.e., the obligation for certain financial intermediaries to periodically transmit data on non-resident financial investment holders to their financial administrations with a view to a subsequent automatic exchange with

---

95/46/EC [2016] OJ L 119/1 (General Data Protection Regulation); it came into force in 2018.

[57] Xiaoqing Huang, 'Ensuring Taxpayer Rights in the Era of Automatic Exchange of Information: EU Data Protection Rules and Cases' (2018) 46 Intertax 225, 238.

[58] Opinion of the European Data Protection Supervisor on the proposal for a Council Directive on administrative cooperation in the field of taxation (2010/C 101/01), paras 7 and 8.

the authorities of the state of residence.[59] This directive introduced paragraph 3 to Article 25, stipulating that each financial institution subject to the obligation must inform the data subject in advance of the collection and subsequent transfer of data pursuant to the DAC, in sufficient time to enable them to exercise their data protection rights.

This is an important innovation. Although limited to only one form of exchange of information, that based on the Common Reporting Standard, it shows that there is in principle no incompatibility between the efficient conduct of international tax cooperation procedures and the participation of the taxpayer in them in order to enable them to exercise their rights, at least those related to the processing of personal data. At the same time, the importance of the latter rights, especially in the context of the automatic exchange of information, may justify a relaxation of the strict limits on the participation of the persons involved in the phase of collecting and sharing the data subject to exchange.

Moreover, European case law has long accepted that, through the exercise of the protections associated with the processing of personal data, the taxpayer may participate in the administrative proceedings through which those data are exchanged from one national authority to another. In *Bara and Others*, for example, the CJEU ruled that the GDPR prevents national legislation from allowing information collected by the tax administration to be made available to the social security administration without adequate notice to the individual concerned.[60] In *Ispas*, similarly, the EU Court affirmed the right of the taxpayer, subject to a tax audit, to be informed about the documents collected before the tax assessment notice is issued, unless public interest reasons preclude this.[61]

Also in the light of the openness achieved, with reference to transnational procedures, by DAC2, it seems reasonable to argue that the same interpretative solutions adopted by the CJEU in the context of domestic procedures remain valid also in the context of the exchange of information at international level. Moreover, the need to protect taxpayers' rights in relation to the processing of

---

59 DAC2.

60 Case C-201/14 *Smaranda Bara and Others v Casa Națională de Asigurări de Sănătate and Others* [2015] ECLI:EU:C:2015:638. See Juliane Kokott, Pasquale Pistone and Robin Miller, 'Diritto internazionale pubblico e diritto tributario: i diritti del contribuente. La fase I del Progetto dell'International Law Association sul diritto tributario internazionale' (2020) 17 Diritto e Pratica Tributaria Internazionale 454, 492.

61 Case C-298/16 *Teodor Ispas and Anduța Ispas v Direcția Generală a Finanțelor Publice Cluj* [2017] ECLI:EU:C:2017:843.

personal data seems even more pressing in the international context than in the domestic one.[62]

It is true that the ECtHR has always appeared very cautious towards such openness in the few cases where it has dealt with taxpayer rights in the context of information exchange procedures. However, as has been observed in doctrine, the Court always recognises the existence of taxpayers' procedural rights in such procedures and reserves the right to assess the legality of their limitation on a case-by-case basis.[63]

5.6 CONCLUSIONS

The procedural rights of the taxpayer in the course of information exchange procedures do not find adequate protection in tax law. The prevailing view is that international cooperation procedures concern relations between states and aim at achieving the correct application of tax rules. The evolution of taxpayers' rights in the international and European context now renders this position obsolete. The openings in the recent case law of the European Court of Justice, starting with the *Berlioz* case, appear comforting, although they do not yet concern the taxpayer concerned, but only third-party holders of information.

It is therefore necessary to look outside the tax field to see whether it is possible to find procedural protection in the exchange of information indirectly from other areas. The analysis carried out with reference to the ECHR system and European data protection law offers interesting insights, but a certain timidity still prevails with regard to the full recognition of such protection. The academic reflection becomes, therefore, important in order to urge a change of course, consistent with the awareness that more often than not deferred protection is not able to offer the taxpayer adequate protection of their rights.

---

62 In the abovementioned opinion of 2010, the European Data Protection Supervisor noted that 'situations which involve the trans-border exchange of personal data within the EU deserve special attention since they imply an increase in scale of the data processing which necessarily leads to bigger risks for the rights and interests of natural persons involved, since – in any event – the same personal data are processed in more than one jurisdiction' (para 5).

63 Philip Baker, 'Some Recent Decisions of the European Court of Human Rights on Tax Matters (and Related Decisions of the European Court of Justice)' (2016) 56 European Taxation 342, 348.

6. Judicial protection in exchange for tax information procedures: why ex post protection is not 'effective' protection

Aikaterini Antoniou[1]

6.1 INTRODUCTION

Tax transparency has risen to the very top of the international political agenda. Over the last decade, the EU and the OECD focused – and did make great progress – on strengthening and facilitating exchange of information (EoI) among states as a means to combat tax evasion and avoidance. Especially in the aftermath of the 2008 financial crisis, it has become clear that these phenomena cannot be tolerated anymore.[2] This is partly due to the significant loss of public revenues they cause and partly because they contribute to inequality,[3] particularly as offshore tax evasion is highly concentrated among the rich.[4]

Despite its many virtues, EoI also raises serious concerns relating to taxpayers' protection. In fact, personal data of a big number of taxpayers cross borders every year without taxpayers, on most occasions, being aware of the exchange and, thus, not being able to hold tax authorities accountable for their actions and/or omissions.

---

[1] DPhil in Law candidate, Keble College, University of Oxford. This paper builds on my DPhil research, which is funded by the Arts and Humanities Research Council in association with Keble College (Oxford), the Alexander S Onassis Foundation, and the Chartered Institute of Taxation PhD Grant. I am very grateful to Stephen Weatherill, John Vella, Filip Debelva, Olivier Dubos, Maria Teresa Martinez Escribano Serrano and the editors of the book for their comments on earlier drafts. An earlier draft was presented at the UK EU Lawyers Assembly PhD Workshop, the SLS Conference 2023, and The Lisbon International and European Tax Law Seminars 2023.

[2] See e.g. G8, *Lough Erne Declaration* (Summit Communiqué, G8 2013) para 1, in which they referred to the need to fight the 'scourge of tax evasion'.

[3] Institute for Fiscal Studies, 'Inequality: The IFS Deaton Review' (*Institute for Fiscal Studies*, 2023) <https://ifs.org.uk/inequality> accessed 6 December 2023.

[4] Annetter Alstadsæter, Niels Johannesen and Gabriel Zucman, 'Tax evasion and inequality' (2019) 109(6) The American Economic Review 2073.

Surprisingly, the EU Directive 2011/16 (DAC1) contains very little on taxpayers' rights.[5] Some rights, e.g., the right to be heard, the right to privacy, and the right against self-incrimination, are discussed in previous chapters. This chapter focuses on the right to effective judicial protection. It examines specifically taxpayers' (and third parties') right to access to court and to get effective judicial protection in the context of EoI upon request (EoIR) procedures. In fact, EoIR remains important and relevant,[6] despite the growing importance of Automatic Exchange of Information (AEoI) over the last decade.[7] As the OECD states, the two forms of EoI are complementary, namely, AEoI aims to

---

[5] See Council Directive 2011/16/EU of 15 February 2011 on administrative cooperation in the field of taxation and repealing Directive 77/799/EEC [2011] OJ L 64/1. Indeed, many scholars have criticised the EU Directive for not paying adequate attention to taxpayers' rights. See e.g. ECJ Task Force, 'Opinion Statement ECJ-TF 2/2014 of the CFE on the Decision of the European Court of Justice in Sabou (Case C-276/12), Concerning Taxpayer Rights in Respect of Exchange of Information upon Request' (2014) 54(7) European Taxation 318, 321; Niels Diepvens and Filip Debelva, 'The Evolution of the Exchange of Information in Direct Tax Matters: The Taxpayer's Rights under Pressure' (2015) 24(4) EC Tax Review 210, 216 and 218; Marcel Schaper, 'Data Protection Rights and Tax Information Exchange in the European Union: An Uneasy Combination' (2016) 23(3) Maastricht Journal of European and Comparative Law, 514, 518; Menita Giusy De Flora, 'Protection of the Taxpayer in the Information Exchange Procedure' (2017) 45(6/7) Intertax 447, 457; Filip Debelva and Irma Mosquera Valderrama, 'Privacy and Confidentiality in Exchange of Information Procedures: Some Uncertainties, Many Issues, but Few Solutions' (2017) 45(5) Intertax 362, 372 (although their criticism is mainly directed towards the Data Protection Directive/General Data Protection Regulation which – according to Article 25 of DAC1 – is applicable also to EoI among Member States in tax matters); Xiaoqing Huang, 'Ensuring Taxpayer Rights in the Era of Automatic Exchange of Information: EU Data Protection Rules and Cases' (2018) 46(3) Intertax 225, 231; Saturnina Moreno González, 'Cross-border exchange of tax information upon request and fundamental rights – Can the right balance be struck?: Joined cases C-245/19 and C-246/2019 État luxembourgeois contre B.' (2021) 28(5) Maastricht Journal of European and Comparative Law 714, 717.

[6] According to the OECD, in the period between 2009–2017, over 250,000 requests for information have been received by Global Forum members, and the EoIR alone has enabled the recovery of nearly EUR 7.5 billion of additional tax revenue. The Global Forum declares that it will continue to promote EoIR. See, OECD Global Forum, *Transparency and Exchange of Information for Tax Purposes. Multilateral Co-operation Changing the World. 10th anniversary report* (OECD, 2019) 35 <https://www.oecd.org/tax/transparency/global-forum-10-years-report.pdf> accessed 6 December 2023.

[7] AEoI was first regulated in DAC1. Ever since, the Directive has constantly been amended to broaden the scope of AEoI. It covers: employment income, pension income, directors fees, income and ownership of immovable property and life insurance products (DAC1), financial account information (Directive 2014/107), advance cross-border rulings and advance pricing arrangements (Directive 2015/2376),

draw states' attention to suspicious cases for tax purposes, which can then be investigated more deeply through EoIR.[8] Thus, it is reasonable to expect that the number of requests for information will only increase in the coming years (grounded on the information received automatically).

The CJEU has only recently discussed the issue of access to court. It ruled in favour of *ex post facto* review, i.e., after the exchange.[9] As to the type of review, the CJEU decided that, if protection is to be truly effective, national courts must be able to review the legality of all previous acts, including the ones performed in a foreign State.[10]

This chapter claims that the existing regime, in particular the concept of *ex post facto* judicial protection, and the ensuing reviewability of foreign decisions, fails to guarantee adequate protection to taxpayers and to affected third parties. It identifies three main reasons for this. First, the requesting authority, which is also the recipient of the exchanged information, may decide to not issue a tax adjustment act at the end of the investigation. Yet, it can make use of the exchanged data for other purposes. In this case, taxpayers may not learn about the EoI, and thus all illegalities that took place in previous stages of the procedure will also remain without review. Second, compensation, at least when it is the only remedy available, is not an effective remedy. This is demonstrated by comparing the ECtHR with the CJEU case law. Third, EU law and/or ECHR law – as they currently stand – *do not* guarantee that: (1) information about the source and methods of collection of data will be exchanged, or that information of 'unknown source' will be excluded; (2) the requesting State will make use of the EoI procedure to obtain also exculpatory evidence, and/or that all data relevant to the case will be passed on; and (3) illegally obtained information will be excluded from the proceedings. Without these rights, however, it is impossible to talk about adequate and effective protection in the requesting State. In other words, these rights are essential for taxpayers' protection when we deal with a composite administrative procedure, such as the one of EoIR in tax matters.

The chapter is structured as follows: first, it presents the state of affected persons' judicial protection under the current law. This covers two different

---

country-by-country reports (Directive 2016/881) and reportable cross-border arrangements (Directive 2018/822).

8 Global Forum on Transparency and Exchange of Information for Tax Purposes, 'Automatic Exchange of Information' <https:// www .oecd .org/ tax/ transparency/ > accessed 6 December 2023.

9 Joined Cases C-245/19 and C-246/19 *État du Grand-duché de Luxembourg v B (and Others)* [2020] ECLI:EU:C:2020:795, paras 92 and 104.

10 ibid para 83.

sources of law, namely, EU law and ECHR[11] law. Then, it identifies inconsistencies between them. In fact, the chapter discusses both 'internal' inconsistencies, i.e., within the ECtHR case law, and 'external' inconsistencies, i.e., between the ECtHR and the CJEU case law. Finally, the chapter discusses why *ex post facto* protection does not amount to effective protection.

6.2 RIGHT TO ACCESS TO COURT IN EOIR UNDER EU LAW

The CJEU discussed the right to access to court for both taxpayers under investigation and affected third parties in two – relatively recent – cases: *Berlioz*[12] and *Luxembourg v B*.[13] Given that it issued different judgments depending on who is the source of information, I will distinguish between the right to appeal when the information is collected from the taxpayer under investigation (Section 6.2.1), and when the information is collected from a third party (Section 6.2.2).

6.2.1 Information Collected from the Taxpayer(s) under Investigation

EU law confers on taxpayers under investigation the right to appeal directly against *the collection order addressed to them* (*Luxembourg v B*), as well as against *the penalty imposed on them* in case they refuse to comply with the collection order (*Berlioz*).[14] A clarification is necessary at this point: in both *Berlioz* and *Luxembourg v B*, the collection orders (and the penalties imposed for non-compliance with them) were addressed to third parties (i.e., another person than the taxpayers under investigation). However, the CJEU ruled that this case law can be extended to taxpayers under investigation in case their circumstances are similar to those of third parties in the cases discussed, namely, when the requested authority addresses the order for information to the taxpayer, and exposes him/her to risks of penalties in case of non-compliance.[15]

To be more specific, in *Berlioz*, the tax authorities of Luxembourg (requested State) imposed on Berlioz a pecuniary administrative sanction because the company refused to comply fully with the collection order. In fact, Berlioz handed over only part of the requested information because it

---

[11] Convention for the Protection of Human Rights and Fundamental Freedoms (signed 4 November 1950, entered into force 3 September 1953) CETS 5.

[12] Case C-682/15 *Berlioz Investment Fund SA v Directeur de l'administration des contributions directes* [2018] ECLI:EU:C:2017:373.

[13] *Luxembourg v B* (n 9).

[14] ibid paras 68–69; *Berlioz* (n 12) para 52.

[15] *Luxembourg v B* (n 9) para 80.

thought the rest went beyond the 'foreseeable relevance' standard required by DAC1.[16] The CJEU ruled that the person on whom a pecuniary penalty has been imposed for failure to comply with an administrative decision directing that person to provide information has the right – based on Article 47 of the Charter[17] (right to effective judicial protection), in conjunction with the EU general principle of protection against arbitrary or disproportionate intervention by public authorities in the sphere of the private activities of any natural or legal person – to challenge that penalty.[18]

In *Luxembourg v B*, the CJEU took an additional step. Relying again on Article 47 of the Charter and the same EU general principle, it ruled that addressees of collection orders have the right to appeal against them directly.[19] Although the CJEU acknowledged that Member States can restrict the exercise of rights,[20] it concluded that national legislation which totally *excludes* direct actions against decisions which order the provision of information to the tax administration violates the essence of the right to effective judicial protection (which is a requirement for restrictions to be lawful under Article 52(1) of the Charter), and thus is incompatible with EU law.[21] In fact, an exclusion of the right to appeal against the collection order would mean that addressees of such orders have only one way left to access courts. They have to refuse to comply with the order and wait until a penalty is imposed on them for their non-compliance, which they can then challenge.[22] The CJEU found, however, that a structure which requires affected persons to break the law in order to get access to a court does not satisfy the standard of 'effective judicial protection'.[23]

6.2.2 Information Collected from Third Parties

When the requested information is collected from third parties (e.g., a bank), the CJEU distinguishes between the right of *taxpayers under investigation* (Section 6.2.2.1) and the right of *third parties who are concerned by the information* (Section 6.2.2.2) to access to court.

---

16 DAC1 art 1(1) and recital 9 of the preamble.
17 Charter of Fundamental Rights of the European Union [2012] OJ C 326/391.
18 *Berlioz* (n 12) paras 44, 51–52.
19 *Luxembourg v B* (n 9) paras 57 and 59.
20 ibid paras 61 and 64.
21 ibid paras 60 and 69.
22 ibid para 67.
23 ibid para 68.

6.2.2.1 Right of taxpayer(s) under investigation to challenge the collection order addressed to third parties

In *Luxembourg v B*, the CJEU ruled that national legislation which *excludes* taxpayers under investigation from challenging the collection order addressed to third parties is compatible with EU law. To reach this conclusion, the Court first found that the decision ordering third parties to disclose information relating to the taxpayer under investigation constitutes an interference with that person's right to privacy (Article 7) and data protection (Article 8).[24] Accordingly, the taxpayer has – in principle – the right to appeal against it, this right derived from the combined reading of Articles 7, 8(1) and Article 47 of the Charter.[25]

Then, the CJEU examined whether national legislation which contains an absolute prohibition to appeal fulfils the conditions of Article 52(1) of the Charter, in particular, whether it is necessary and genuinely meets an objective of general interest recognised by the EU in compliance with the principle of proportionality, and whether it respects the essence of the right.[26] In relation to the first requirement, the CJEU found that legislation with this content is necessary to fulfil the aims of the Directive, namely, to enable States to cooperate efficiently and quickly, and thus to help them combat international tax fraud and tax evasion.[27] As to the essence of the right, the CJEU found that this is also respected given that taxpayers can challenge the tax correction or adjustment act issued by the authorities of the State which receives the information.[28] In fact, the CJEU ruled that the taxpayer, in the context of his/her action against the tax adjustment/correction act, has the possibility of challenging, indirectly, the decisions of the requested State, namely, the decision ordering that information be provided and the conditions under which the evidence gathered as a result of that investigation was obtained and used, in particular whether the information has been obtained in line with EU law.[29] Thus, the rights to effective judicial protection and data protection, which have been restricted in the requested State, are ultimately protected.

6.2.2.2 Right of third parties concerned by the information to appeal against the collection order addressed to another person

Third parties concerned by the information collected from another person receive the same treatment as the taxpayers under investigation. More specif-

---

24 ibid paras 72 and 73.
25 ibid para 75.
26 ibid paras 76, 78 and 85.
27 ibid paras 90–91.
28 ibid para 82.
29 ibid paras 82–83.

ically, in *Luxembourg v B*, the CJEU found that third parties whose personal data is being processed have, in principle, the right to challenge the collection order pursuant to Article 47 of the Charter in conjunction with the EU general principle of protection against arbitrary or disproportionate intervention by the public authorities in the sphere of their private activities.[30]

However, given that Member States can restrict the exercise of rights subject to compliance with Article 52(1) of the Charter,[31] the CJEU ruled that national legislation which *prohibits* third parties from challenging the collection order addressed to another person constitutes a necessary and proportionate restriction to ensure a speedy and efficient EoI.[32] It also found that legislation with this content does not violate the essence of third parties' rights either, as long as national law offers them the opportunity to bring proceedings before a court which is competent to decide whether there has been an infringement and can award compensation for the harm suffered as a result of that infringement.[33] In other words, the standard is only met if the court hearing the compensation dispute is also competent to review the act which has given rise to the infringement and the harm.[34]

6.3 RIGHT TO ACCESS TO COURT IN EOIR PROCEDURES UNDER ECHR LAW

This section examines the level of protection of taxpayers under investigation and affected third parties under the ECHR. ECHR law is relevant because, similarly to EU law, it binds all EU Member States. There are two reasons for this. First, all EU Member States are signatories to the ECHR. Second, the CJEU, in its early case law, ruled that international treaties for the protection of human rights of which the Member States are signatories, i.e. the ECHR, are a 'source of inspiration' for the general principles of EU law.[35] This case law is now codified in Article 6(3) TEU. In addition, Article 52(3) of the Charter states that, '[i]n so far as this Charter contains rights which correspond to rights guaranteed by the ECHR, the meaning and scope of those rights shall be the same as those laid down by the said Convention. This provision shall not prevent Union law providing more extensive protection'.

The ECtHR has discussed – on few occasions so far – taxpayers' and affected third parties' right to appeal in exchange of tax information proce-

30 ibid paras 96–97.
31 ibid para 105.
32 ibid paras 103–104.
33 ibid paras 101 and 104.
34 ibid.
35 See e.g. Case 4/73 *Nold v Commission* [1974] ECLI:EU:C:1974:51, para 13.

dures. A conclusion drawn from this case law is that the ECtHR takes a 'holistic' approach towards the right to an effective remedy, this meaning that it examines all national remedies available in a Member State before concluding whether national law satisfies the requirements of the right to fair trial (Article 6 ECHR), or of the right to privacy and data protection (Article 8 ECHR).

6.3.1 Right of Taxpayers under Investigation to Appeal against the Search and Seizure Orders Addressed to Them

In *Ravon v France*, the ECtHR decided that taxpayers, whose private and business premises are searched, must – pursuant to Article 6 ECHR – be given access before an independent and impartial tribunal which has jurisdiction to rule on all issues of law and of fact in order to question the validity of these inspection orders.[36] In order to decide whether this standard was met in the case at hand, the ECtHR examined all means available under French national law to taxpayers to get protection, but found them to be inadequate.

More specifically, the ECtHR first found that the national court responsible to decide the appeal against the search and seizure orders did not meet Article 6(1) ECHR criteria since its review was limited to issues of law (i.e., not factual review).[37] Second, the requirement to get judicial authorisation prior to the inspection was found insufficient to fill the gap in protection, simply because the persons against which the planned search was to be carried out were unaware at that stage of the proceedings against them and they were not heard.[38]

Similarly, all other legal routes available to taxpayers for challenging the validity of the order were found to be 'more theoretical than effective'.[39] For example, the fact that taxpayers were able to challenge the specific search and seizure operations, while they were still in progress, was found inadequate because the agents who carried out the searches were not legally obliged to inform the persons concerned of their right to submit any difficulty to the judge, the judge was also not obliged to mention this possibility in the authorisation order, the presence of the interested parties during the inspection was not required, the law did not provide for the possibility to call on a lawyer or to have contacts with the outside world during the search, etc.[40] As for the possibility to ask for compensation for the damages caused during a home search,

---

[36] *Ravon and Others v France* App no 18497/03 (ECtHR 21 February 2008), paras 27 and 34.

[37] ibid para 29.

[38] ibid para 30.

[39] ibid para 31.

[40] ibid.

this was also seen as an ineffective remedy, because compensation proceedings did not allow for a review of the lawfulness of the decision ordering the search and of the measures taken on the basis of that decision.[41]

6.3.2 Right of Affected Third Parties to Appeal against the Collection Order Addressed to Another Person

In *M.N. and Others v San Marino*, the ECtHR decided that third parties concerned by the collected information (i.e., other persons than the taxpayer under investigation and the addressee(s) of the collection order) have – pursuant to Article 8 ECHR – the right to challenge directly the collection order addressed to another party.[42] In this case, the third party was excluded from challenging the collection order. To decide whether Article 8 ECHR was violated, the ECtHR took into account the overall circumstances of the case, including the availability of alternative remedies under national law.

More specifically, the ECtHR first found that the collection orders were very broad and affected the applicant, despite the fact that he was not subject to the ongoing investigation, and there were no suspicions in relation to him.[43] The ECtHR also found that the judicial authorities 'could not, or in any event, had failed to make any assessment as to the need for such a wide-ranging order, or its impact on the multiple third parties'.[44]

Second, the ECtHR found that all remedies available to the applicant for reviewing the collection orders subsequent to their implementation, these being an ordinary civil remedy and action for damages, did not offer sufficient protection.[45] In relation to the civil remedy, the ECtHR was not convinced that it allowed for an examination of the applicant's challenges to the exequatur decision in a timely procedure, nor that it could have, if necessary, annulled the said order or its consequences.[46] As for the action for damages, the ECtHR found that its aim is 'distinct from, and should not be confused with, an application for judicial review'.[47] More specifically, the ECtHR underlined

---

[41] ibid para 33.

[42] *M.N. and Others v San Marino* App no 28005/12 (ECtHR 7 July 2015), paras 78, 85. However, the right to appeal against the collection order does not follow from the general rule of the right to data protection, but it is part of what counts as a proportionate restriction to the right, i.e. it follows from the restrictions. See e.g. *M.N. and Others v San Marino,* paras 75, 76 and 83; *G.S.B. v Switzerland* App no. 28601/11 (ECtHR, 22 December 2015), para 96.

[43] *M.N. and Others v San Marino* (n 42) para 77.

[44] ibid.

[45] ibid para 81.

[46] ibid.

[47] ibid.

that compensation is not a 'remedy capable of achieving the aim sought by the applicant of having the impugned search and seizure, or its consequences, annulled and could therefore not be regarded as an "effective review" for the purposes of Article 8'.[48]

Third, the ECtHR took into account the difference in treatment between, on the one hand, the applicant, who was not an accused person in the original criminal procedure, and, on the other hand, both the taxpayer-accused person and the owners of the banking or fiduciary institute, who were the addressees of the collection order.[49] In fact, the applicant was only notified of the collection of information, whereas the other two were also given the opportunity to challenge the collection order.[50] Accordingly, the applicant 'was at a significant disadvantage in the protection of his rights'.[51]

6.3.3 Right of Affected Third Parties to Appeal against the Exchange of Information Decision

In *Othymia Investments v the Netherlands*, the ECtHR decided that it cannot be a requirement of Article 8 ECHR that third parties, whose personal data is subject to exchange, will always get notified about it before the EoI. In particular, the ECtHR found that 'in the context of the "interests of national security", "public safety" and the "prevention of crime"', investigative methods may have to be used covertly'.[52] In this case, the information, which formed the subject-matter of the request sent by the Spanish authorities, was already in the files of the Dutch tax authorities. Although Dutch law provided that 'interested parties' will be notified about the processing of their personal data, it also included exceptions to prior notification for 'urgent grounds', including when there are suspicions of 'serious tax fraud'.[53] The ECtHR thought this is a valid justification for not notifying affected third parties and, thus, for depriving them of the opportunity to challenge the EoI decision. To reach this conclusion, the ECtHR took into account that Othymia Investments had the possibility to get some type of *ex post facto* protection since Dutch law offered interested parties the opportunity to claim compensation if they suffered damage due to the exchange, e.g., in case of exchange of inaccurate information.[54]

---

48 ibid.
49 ibid para 83.
50 ibid.
51 ibid.
52 *Othymia Investments BV v the Netherlands* App no 75292/10 (ECtHR, 16 June 2015), para 44.
53 ibid para 24.
54 ibid paras 25 and 47.

6.4 'INTERNAL' AND 'EXTERNAL' INCONSISTENCIES

The ECtHR case law is inconsistent in relation to the nature of compensation as an 'effective alternative remedy' ('internal' inconsistency). In particular, in *MN and Others,* the ECtHR decided that (ex post) compensation for the damage suffered cannot substitute (ex ante) judicial review because an action for damages cannot achieve the aim of annulling the act and its consequences. On the contrary, in *Othymia Investments,* compensation is treated as an effective *ex post facto* remedy, which can compensate for the absence of review before the exchange.

The different outcomes of the cases can (perhaps) be attributed to the different structure/content of national laws. More specifically, in *MN and Others,* San Marino law *totally excluded* third parties affected by the (collected and exchanged) information from challenging the collection orders. Accordingly, *ex post facto* compensation was the only remedy available to them. On the contrary, in *Othymia Investments*, *ex post facto* compensation is an exceptional remedy, while the prime remedy remains *ex ante* notification and appeal against the decision to exchange information. In fact, as mentioned previously, Dutch law simply allowed for exceptions to prior notification in case there were some 'urgent grounds' which justified investigations to be carried out covertly. Of course, if this requirement is satisfied and, therefore, interested parties are not notified before the EoI, they also lose the opportunity to appeal against the EoI decision and thus to prevent the damage.

If this reading of the case law is advanced, the 'internal' inconsistency within the ECtHR case law is remedied. On the other hand, the fragmentation between the CJEU and the ECtHR case law remains ('external' inconsistency). As a reminder, in *Luxembourg v B*, the CJEU found that national legislation which excludes affected third parties from challenging the collection order addressed to another party is compatible with EU law. It based this conclusion on the fact that affected third parties can still get compensation for the damage suffered due to the exchange. From this it follows that the CJEU treats compensation as an effective *ex post facto* remedy (subject to the condition that national courts can review both the act that led to the infringement and the harm), despite being the only remedy available to affected third parties. On the contrary, if the above reading of the ECtHR case law is advanced, compensation is an effective *ex post facto* remedy only if it is exceptional in nature.

AG Kokott (partly) shares this view. In *Luxembourg v B*, she disagreed with compensation being treated as an effective remedy. She argued that 'State liability proceedings is not an effective remedy within the meaning of Article 47 of the Charter […] such a legal remedy, which is also subject to further conditions, cannot prevent a violation of fundamental rights, but can at most provide compensation for any damage suffered'.[55] And then, by citing *M.N v San Marino*, she concluded that 'secondary means of redress alone do not constitute an effective remedy'.[56]

6.5 *EX POST FACTO* PROTECTION IS NOT 'EFFECTIVE' PROTECTION?

As mentioned previously, in inter-state tax cooperation proceedings, EU law guarantees that taxpayers under investigation will get the right to appeal in the final stage of the procedure by challenging the tax adjustment or correction act. In order for protection to be effective, national courts are competent to review illegalities that occurred in previous stages of the procedure, i.e., in the requested State. At first sight, this structure seems ideal. It enables taxpayers' protection without compromising the effectiveness of the investigation (which could be undermined if taxpayers participated in the procedure before the EoI). However, a closer look at the existing legislation and case law of the European Courts casts doubt on the true 'effectiveness' of taxpayers' protection in the final stage of the procedure.

6.5.1 No Tax Adjustment/Correction Act Issued at the End of the EoI Procedure

Taxpayers subject to cross-border investigations will be left without protection in case the requesting State does not issue a tax adjustment/correction act at the end of the EoIR (unless, of course, the requested State offers them the right to appeal before the exchange). Indeed, the tax adjustment act is the only act in relation to which EU law confers on taxpayers the right to be heard and to appeal. More specifically, in *Sabou*, the CJEU distinguished between the investigation and the contentious stage of the EoI procedure, and concluded that taxpayers have, based on the EU general principle of the right of defence, the right to be heard only in the latter stage, which begins when the taxpayer is sent the proposed tax correction or adjustment act.[57] Later on, in *Luxembourg v B*, the CJEU ruled that 'a correction or adjustment decision constitutes an act in relation to which the taxpayer concerned must have a right to an effective remedy'.[58]

---

55 Joined Cases C-245/19 and C-246/19 *État du Grand-duché de Luxembourg v B (and Others)* [2020] ECLI:EU:C:2020:516, Opinion of AG Kokott, para 102.

56 ibid.

57 Case C-276/12 *Sabou* [2013] ECLI:EU:C:2013:678, paras 40–44.

58 *Luxembourg v B* (n 9) para 82.

Accordingly, in case the inter-state tax investigation does not lead to a tax adjustment act, taxpayers will – in all likelihood – never get informed about the EoI and, therefore, they will not be able to challenge the unlawfulness of collection of information by the requested State. AG Kokott is aware of this risk. She thinks there is a gap in protection, not only when the requesting State decides, based on the data collected, that it does not have a tax claim, and thus does not issue a tax adjustment act, but also in case it does issue a tax assessment notice, but it is not based on the exchanged data since they proved to be irrelevant for tax purposes.[59] For this reason, AG Kokott – contrary to the CJEU – argued that taxpayers under investigation must be given the right to appeal in the requested State, and not wait until (and *if*) a tax adjustment act is issued.[60]

On the other hand, it is true that if a tax adjustment act is not issued at the end of the EoIR procedure the interference with taxpayers' right to data protection, which initially took place in the requested State, is not perpetuated any further. It could be argued, therefore, that taxpayers are ultimately protected. This argument is not valid for two reasons. First, as AG Kokott argues, a defence against the interference itself is different from a defence against the perpetuation of the interference because the first aims to prevent the interference.[61] Therefore, offering taxpayers the right to directly challenge the interference with their personal data remains important even if the requesting State decides to not use the information at the end. Second, even if the requesting State does not issue a tax adjustment act at the end of the EoIR procedure, this does not mean it cannot use the exchanged information for a different purpose, e.g., in order to initiate a new investigation against the taxpayer. Indeed, Article 16(2) of DAC1 allows the requesting State to use the exchanged information for non-tax related purposes subject to the conditions that this is allowed under the requesting State's national law and that the requested State will first consent to such use. It is obvious that – under current EU law – the consent, or at least the notification or some other type of participation of the taxpayer under investigation before any further use of the exchanged information is not required. Such a requirement can only be imposed by national law and, thus, if not regulated,

59 *Luxembourg v B* (n 55), Opinion of AG Kokott, para 73.

60 ibid para 82.

61 *Luxembourg v B* (n 55), Opinion of AG Kokott, para 74. Pantazatou is also critical of the CJEU's understanding of the essence of the right to effective judicial protection for taxpayers. See Katerina Pantazatou, 'The Evolution of the Right to an Effective Remedy and to a Fair Trial in Direct and Indirect Taxation: Are We There Yet?' in Matteo Bonelli, Mariolina Eliantonio and Giulia Gentile (eds.), *Article 47 of the EU Charter and Effective Judicial Protection, Volume 1: The Court of Justice's Perspective* (Hart Publishing 2022) 269–271.

taxpayers lose their last opportunity to learn about and control the interference with their personal data.

6.5.2 No Obligation to Exchange Information about the Source and Methods of Collection of Data

DAC1 states that information obtained by the requested authority 'may be invoked as evidence by the competent bodies of the requesting Member State on the same basis as similar information, reports, statements and any other documents provided by an authority of that Member State'.[62] From this it follows that the requesting State will treat the exchanged information in accordance with its national evidentiary standards. For example, if the requesting State does not accept witness statements as proof of tax violations, the same will apply to witness statements obtained from another Member State.

Based on the above, it seems essential for the requesting State to get informed about the sources and methods of collection of information in the requested State. Otherwise, it will not be able to assess the accuracy, admissibility and probative value of the evidence transferred from the cooperating State and, accordingly, the taxpayer under investigation will not get a 'real' right of defence and 'effective' judicial protection in the final stage of the procedure.[63] Despite this, the CJEU decided that EU law, in particular the Directive 77/799 (the predecessor of DAC1),[64] does not impose obligations on Member States with regard to the content of the information conveyed.[65] In other words, the requested State is totally autonomous to decide what information will be disclosed.[66]

Given that national (procedural) autonomy is the guiding principle here, it is essential to distinguish between the case the requested State conveys information about the collection conditions and the case it does not. In the first scenario, and contrary to what Article 16(5) of the DAC1 suggests, the requesting State is not anymore – fully – autonomous to decide on the admissibility of the information conveyed. For example, Article 6 ECHR, which guarantees the

---

[62] DAC1 art 16(5).

[63] José Manuel Calderón Carrero and Alberto Quintas Seara, 'The Taxpayer's Right of Defence in Cross-Border Exchange-of-Information Procedures' (2014) 68(9) Bulletin For International Taxation 498, 501–503, 507. See also CFE ECJ Task Force (n 5) 321.

[64] Council Directive 77/799/EEC of 19 December 1977 concerning mutual assistance by the competent authorities of the Member States in the field of direct taxation [1977] OJ L 336/15.

[65] *Sabou* (n 57) para 48.

[66] ibid para 49.

right to fair trial, obliges States to not decide the case on the basis of witness statements when this is the sole evidence available, unless the suspected person has the opportunity to examine the witness(es). This was decided in *Janyr v the Czech Republic*, in which the applicant claimed that his right to fair trial was violated because his request to summon and examine a witness, G., was refused, despite the fact that he was the source of the information exchanged by the requested state.[67] The ECtHR, however, found that the Convention does not require national courts to accede to all requests from accused persons to call witnesses, and concluded that Article 6 ECHR was not violated.[68] In doing so, the ECtHR put emphasis on the fact that the conviction was not based on G's testimony, in the sense that G's statements were superfluous in view of the amount of other evidence in the hands of the Czech Republic's authorities which proved against the applicant's allegations.[69] Also, the ECtHR was not convinced that the hearing of G could have brought new and relevant elements to the examination of Janyr's case.[70]

Turning to the second scenario, namely, when the requested State does not disclose how it collected the information, there is still a scenario taxpayers will get adequate protection. This happens in case the requesting State treats 'evidence of an unknown source' as inadmissible or less reliable/having limited probative value. This seems to be also AG Kokott's argument, who supported that 'to convey information without disclosing the methods through which it was acquired severely restricts its probative value and, thus, it is not of particular use for the requesting State'.[71] However, it remains unclear whether AG Kokott thinks that States will not rely on evidence whose source or methods of collection is not known because they are obliged to do so under EU law, or this is simply a practice that many States are expected to apply following their national law. In any case, as long as the CJEU or the ECtHR have not given a definitive answer to the question of admissibility/probative value of evidence of 'unknown source', it remains a matter for national law. Therefore, there will

---

67 *Janyr v the Czech Republic* App no 42937/08 (ECtHR 31 October 2013).

68 ibid paras 82–83. Baker is very critical of this judgment because the taxpayer is placed 'in a position where he is unable to challenge the evidence obtained by exchange and consequently is unable to obtain a fair trial'. See Philip Baker, 'Some Recent Decisions of the European Court of Human Rights on Tax Matters' (2014) 54(6) European Taxation 250, 251–52.

69 *Janyr* (n 67) para 81.

70 ibid para 82.

71 Case C-276/12 *Sabou* [2013] ECLI:EU:C:2013:370, Opinion of AG Kokott, para 80. AG Kokott – contrary to the CJEU – argued that the requested State is obliged – pursuant to Articles 1(1) and 2 of Directive 77/799, which require the information conveyed to be useful as far as possible – to provide information about the inquiries on which the notified findings are based (paras 79, 82).

definitely be occasions where taxpayers are left unprotected against the use of unreliable evidence.

6.5.3 No Obligation to Exclude Illegally Obtained Information

In *Luxembourg v B,* the CJEU ruled that the courts of the requesting State hearing the dispute over the tax adjustment/correction act can indirectly review the decisions of the requested State.[72] In particular, they can verify whether the evidence on which that act is based has been obtained or used in breach of the rights and freedoms guaranteed to the person concerned by EU law.[73] However, this does not say anything about the potential use of this information. In other words, it does not necessarily follow from *Luxembourg v B* that the requesting State must abstain from using the exchanged evidence in case they have been acquired illegally in the requested State.[74]

Indeed, as AG Kokott argues in *Luxembourg v B.*, EU law does not contain an absolute prohibition on the use of data unlawfully collected.[75] Some scholars disagree though. For example, Panayi and Perrou argue that the obligation to disregard unlawfully obtained information and to annul any decision based on such evidence derives from the *WebMindLicenses* case-law.[76] However, a close look at *WebMindLicenses* shows that this interpretation simply misreads the CJEU judgment. In fact, as AG Kokott argued in *IN JM v Belgische Staat*, the *WebMindLicenses* case simply established that national courts must be able to verify whether the evidence has been obtained and used in line with EU law.[77] In other words, in *WebMindLicenses*, the CJEU aimed to empower

---

[72] *Luxembourg v B* (n 9) para 83.

[73] ibid para 82.

[74] On the contrary, Zagá reads the *Luxembourg v B* case law as introducing an obligation on States to prohibit their authorities from using, during a trial, evidence acquired *contra legem* in the cooperating State. He thinks that only if illegally obtained information is excluded from being used, ex post protection will be effective judicial protection. See Stefano Zagà, 'The Protection of Individual Taxpayer Rights Regarding Exchange of Information on Request in the European Union' (2022) 62(2/3) European Taxation 105, 112.

[75] *Luxembourg v B* (n 55), Opinion of AG Kokott, para 72. See also Juliane Kokott and Pasquale Pistone, *Taxpayers in international law: International minimum standards for the protection of taxpayers' rights* (Hart Publishing 2022) 270 and 308.

[76] Case C-419/14 *WebMindLicenses kft v Nemzeti Adó* [2016] ECLI:EU:2015:606, paras 87–88; Christiana HJI Panayi and Katerina Perrou, 'Tax Justice in the Post-BEPS Era: Enhanced Cooperation Among Tax Authorities and the Protection of Taxpayer Rights in the EU' in Dominic de Cogan and Peter Harris (eds), *Tax Justice and Tax Law: Understanding Unfairness in Tax Systems* (Hart Publishing 2020) 212–213.

[77] Joined cases C-469/18 and C-470/19 *IN JM v Belgische Staat* [2019] ECLI:EU:C:2019:597, Opinion of AG Kokott, paras 69–72.

national courts to review the lawfulness of collection of evidence. It did not aim to establish that the finding of an infringement in the gathering of evidence should automatically result in their use being prohibited.

From this it follows that Member States can decide freely on the admissibility of unlawfully obtained information.[78] There is only one restriction to Member States' autonomy: the proceedings as a whole, taking also in account the way the evidence was obtained, must not be rendered unfair.[79] According to AG Kokott, some of the considerations national courts can take into account when deciding on the 'overall' fairness of the proceedings are the provision that has been infringed and the nature of that infringement.[80]

ECHR law takes a very similar approach towards illegally obtained information. It does not oblige States to disregard such information, subject to the condition that the illegality is not such that renders the proceedings 'as a whole' unfair.[81] To assess the overall fairness of the proceedings, the ECtHR takes into account the overall circumstances of the case, including whether the applicant's rights of defence have been respected (e.g., whether the applicant is aware of the unlawfulness; whether he is given the opportunity of challenging the authenticity of evidence and opposing their use, etc.), and the quality and importance of the evidence in question for the outcome of the proceedings (e.g., whether the unlawfully obtained evidence is the only evidence on which the conviction was based; whether the evidence is so strong that there is no risk of it being unreliable; etc.).[82]

It is clear that States are left with a great degree of autonomy to decide on the admissibility of illegally obtained information. This becomes particularly problematic in the context of inter-state cooperation procedures, in which the illegally obtained information will ultimately be used in a State different from the one that collected it.[83] In fact, due to the differences between national rules

---

78 For a discussion of the different approaches of states towards the use of illegally obtained information, see Calderón Carrero and Quintas Seara (n 63) 502–503; Michael Dirkis, 'The "Lion's Mouth" postbox: A comparative review of the limitations on the use by revenue authorities of leaked and stolen information' (2016 Tax Research Conference, Sydney, November 2016) <https://www.sydney.edu.au/law/news-and-events/news/2016/12/02/ross-parsons-2016-taxation-conference.html> accessed 6 December 2023; Tatiana Falcão and Armando Lara Yaffar, 'General Report' in *International Fiscal Association, Exchange of Information: issues, use and collaboration* (Cahiers de droit fiscal international, 105(B), International Fiscal Association 2020) 55–56.

79 Case C-276/01 *Steffensen* [2003] ECLI:EU:C:2003:228, paras 75–76.

80 *IN JM v Belgische Staat* (n 77) Opinion of AG Kokott, para 79.

81 See e.g. *Schenk v Switzerland* App no 10862/84 (ECtHR, 12 July 1988), para 46.

82 ibid paras 47–48. See also Kokott and Pistone (n 75) 270, 273.

83 Calderón Carrero and Quintas Seara (n 63) 502–503.

as to the admissibility of illegally obtained information, which – as discussed – are to a great extent accepted by EU and ECHR law, a scenario may arise in which the requesting State allows the use of information collected illegally abroad, whereas the requested State – which is the source of the information – could not have used it (because of its stricter rules on admissibility of evidence). In this case, taxpayers find themselves in a disadvantaged position due to the cross-border character of the investigation. A solution could be to require the requesting State to not rely on illegally obtained information no matter whether it is its own domestic law or the domestic law of the requested State which prohibits such use. In other words, the issue of admissibility of illegally obtained information should be governed by the domestic rules on evidence of the State which provides higher protection to the taxpayer (subject to the additional condition that the proceedings are not rendered as a whole unfair).[84]

6.5.4 No Obligation to Request and/or Exchange Exculpatory Evidence

Taxpayers are adequately protected only if they are given access to all evidence relevant to their case, meaning both to incriminating and to exculpatory evidence.[85] This generates three types of obligations for tax authorities and courts. The first one is that taxpayers subject to a tax adjustment/correction act must get access to all information in the tax authorities' possession, whether for or against them.[86] The second one is that the requested State must pass on all information relevant to the case under investigation, including exculpatory evidence. And the third one is that tax authorities of States must make use of

---

[84] Dourado goes a step further and argues that the use of illegally obtained data should always be prohibited (i.e., independently of whether the cooperating State allows or prohibits it). Otherwise, EoI will contribute to 'a global market where those data can be sold and bought, and where the confidentiality rules will not be observed'. See Ana Paula Dourado, 'Exchange of Information and Validity of Global Standards in Tax Law: Abstractionism and Expressionism or Where the Truth Lies' (2013) EUI Working Paper RSCAS 2013/11, 9 <https:// cadmus .eui .eu/ bitstream/ handle/ 1814/ 26059/RSCAS_2013_11.pdf?sequence=1&isAllowed= y> accessed 6 December 2023.

[85] Kokott and Pistone (n 75) 207, 218.

[86] ibid 218–19. See also Baker (n 68) 252; Juliane Kokott, Pasquale Pistone and Robin Miller, 'Public International Law and Tax Law: Taxpayers' Rights: The International Law Association's Project on International Tax Law – Phase 1' (2021) 52(2) Georgetown Journal of International Law 381, 399.

inter-state cooperation procedures not only to obtain evidence that harms the taxpayers, but also evidence that exonerates them.[87]

The ECtHR, although given the opportunity to decide on the first issue, ie the right of taxpayers to get access to all information in the file, hesitated to take a clear position on the content of the ECHR right to fair trial. More specifically, in *Miailhe v France no 2*, the applicant argued that the tax authorities of the requesting State infringed his right to fair trial under Article 6 ECHR by not giving him access to all documents supplied by the cooperating state, but producing only those documents that supported their submissions.[88] In this case, the French tax authorities had not included all of the documents provided by the Philippine authorities in the file. These were only added to the file, at the request of the investigating judge, during the judicial investigation.[89] Still, the applicant objected that a key document, i.e., the letter in which the Philippines authorities recognised his status as a Philippine resident, was withheld by the French Revenue.[90] Although he had been able to procure some documents from the Philippines authorities himself, he could not obtain that one.[91]

The ECtHR found that irregularities that took place before the case was brought before the courts of trial and appeal do not necessarily render the proceedings as a whole unfair as long as those courts are able to remedy them.[92] As a result, it found that the failure of the tax administration to produce all documents in the pre-trial stages did not infringe Mr Miailhe's defence rights or the principle of equality of arms, given that this irregularity was remedied in the trial stage.[93] It concluded that tax rulings were based solely on the documents in the case file, on which the parties had presented argument at hearings before them, thereby ensuring that the applicant had a fair trial.[94]

---

[87] See e.g. Baker (n 68) 252; Philip Baker and Pasquale Pistone, 'General Report' in IFA, *The practical protection of taxpayers fundamental rights* (IFA Cahiers 100B, International Bureau For Fiscal Documentation 2015) 60; International Fiscal Association, *Exchange of Information: issues, use and collaboration* (Cahiers de droit fiscal international, 105(B), International Fiscal Association 2020). IBFD Observatory on the Protection of Taxpayers' Rights (OPTR), *2015–2017 General Report on the Protection of Taxpayers' Rights* (IBFD 2018) 68–69 <https:// www .ibfd .org/ sites/ default/ files/ 2022 -05/ OPTR %202017 %20General %20Report.pdf> accessed 6 December 2023.

[88] *Miailhe v France (No 2)* App no 18978/91 (ECtHR, 26 September 1996).

[89] ibid para 38.

[90] ibid.

[91] ibid.

[92] ibid para 43.

[93] ibid para 44.

[94] ibid.

In the author's view, the ECtHR judgment is not satisfactory. The ECtHR simply found that the decision of tax authorities was based on the information in the case file. But it did not discuss at all the applicant's specific complaint that there was some exculpatory evidence among the information exchanged to which he was not given access, or that this exculpatory evidence was not exchanged in the first place (given that he could not obtain it after liaising with the Philippines authorities himself). In a way the ECtHR deferred to national court's jurisdiction, by saying that 'the ordinary courts did, within the limits of their jurisdiction, consider the objections of nullity raised by Mr Miailhe and dismissed them'.[95]

Recent CJEU case law strengthens taxpayers' position in relation to their right to access all evidence in the file. In *Glencore*, the CJEU clarified that the EU general principle of respect for the rights of defence is only satisfied when the taxable person is given access to *all evidence, including evidence which may be useful for his or her defence*.[96] This means that taxpayers must be given access not only to those evidence on which the tax authorities intend to base their decision against them,[97] but also to the documents which are potentially beneficial for the taxpayer.[98] However, the CJEU ruled that this protection is not absolute. In fact, national law can impose restrictions to the right to access to documents in order to, for example, protect requirements of confidentiality or business secrets, as well as the private life of third parties, the personal data relating to them or the effectiveness of the criminal action, which may be harmed if access to certain documents is given.[99] In this case, tax authorities should consider whether to provide partial access.[100]

Glencore is definitely a step in the right direction but still leaves some issues open. For example, Kokott and Pistone point out that the grounds/justifications for restricting taxpayers' access to documents are so broad that actually the decision as to what information will be disclosed and what will remain secret can become arbitrary, without taxpayers being able to hold tax authorities accountable.[101] Chaouche and Haslehner make a step further. They argue that denying taxpayers the right to access all documents on which the tax ruling is based, no matter whether it is justified or not, restricts their basic right to

95 ibid.

96 Case C-189/18 *Glencore Agriculture Hungary Kft. v Nemzeti Adó-és Vámhivatal Fellebbviteli Igazgatósága*, [2019] ECLI:EU:C:2019:861, para 57 (emphasis added).

97 ibid para 53.

98 ibid para 54.

99 ibid para 55.

100 ibid para 56.

101 Kokott and Pistone (n 75) 219.

defend themselves.[102] For this reason, they support that 'taxpayers' private interest in accessing the relevant documents and information exchanged should outweigh any other secrecy considerations'.[103]

In any case, contrary to the right to access exculpatory evidence in tax authorities' files, the other two issues discussed in this section, namely whether evidence that exonerates the taxpayer will be requested, or whether the requested State will pass on exculpatory evidence even when the main purpose for the request is to collect incriminating evidence, are left to be decided by national law. More specifically, in *Twoh International*, the CJEU decided that Directive 77/799 (the predecessor of DAC1) was simply adopted to offer tax authorities *the possibility* to obtain information from other States for the purpose of the correct assessment of taxes, without in any way making such cooperation necessary, e.g., when the taxpayer is not himself able to provide the necessary evidence.[104]

Since *Twoh International,* the legislation has changed. Still, DAC1 does not add much to taxpayers' protection since it does not include a clear obligation for States to request information that assist taxpayers' defence.

Not everyone, however, shares this view. Lejeune and Vermeire, for example, argue that States' obligation to request exculpatory evidence can derive from DAC1's recital 29, which very broadly defines the aim of tax cooperation to be about overcoming the negative effects of the increasing globalization on the internal market.[105] To strengthen their argument, they point to the *WebMindLicenses* case law, where the CJEU decided that a request for information is required when the Member State 'knows or should reasonably know that the tax authorities of another Member State have information which is useful, or even essential, for determining whether VAT is chargeable in the first Member State'.[106] The author believes, however, that more attention should be paid to the specifics of *WebMindLicenses*, in particular to the fact that this case concerns VAT, and thus the CJEU was asked to interpret Regulation 904/2010, which governs cooperation on indirect taxes, and not the DAC1. As long as the CJEU has not extended its *WebMindLicenses* case law

---

[102] Fatima Chaouche and Werner Haslehner, 'Cross-Border Exchange of Tax Information and Fundamental Rights' in Werner Haslehner, Georg Köfler, and Alexander Rust (eds), *EU Tax Law and Policy in the 21st Century* (Eucotax Series on European Taxation vol 55, Kluwer 2017) 179, 200.

[103] ibid.

[104] Case C-184/05 *Twoh International BV v Staatssecretaris van Financiën* [2007] ECLI:EU:C:2007:550, paras 32–34.

[105] Ine Lejeune and Liesbeth Vermeire, 'The Influence of the EU Charter of Fundamental Rights on ECJ Case Law on the International Exchange of Information' (2017) 57(4) European Taxation 157, 161.

[106] *WebMindLicenses* (n 76) paras 55–60.

to cover direct taxes, it comes as no surprise that Member States' practices still differ in relation to this issue.[107]

Similarly, DAC1 does not contain a concrete obligation for States to pass on all evidence relevant to the case, including exculpatory ones. This may not be a problem in case the exculpatory evidence forms the subject-matter of the request for information. In fact, when the request itself aims at collecting data that confirm taxpayers' nil or reduced liability, the requested State has an obligation, pursuant to Article 5 DAC1, to exchange them. The problem arises, however, in case the requesting State resorts to inter-state cooperation to obtain information that incriminates the taxpayer. In this case, the requested State may simply collect the incriminating information requested without making any effort to gather also exculpatory evidence, or – perhaps – without paying attention to some exculpatory evidence found during the searches. Thus, taxpayers will be left unprotected, unless the requested State has an obligation *under national law* to search for, collect and exchange exculpatory information as well.

6.6 CONCLUDING REMARKS

In the attempt to increase tax transparency and combat phenomena of tax evasion and tax avoidance taxpayers' rights have taken a backseat. This chapter shows that the current regime, which accepts *ex post facto* appeal to be an effective remedy, does not strike the balance between effectiveness of cooperation and taxpayers' protection in a satisfactory way. The reason is that *ex post facto* appeal, especially when it is the only remedy available, deprives taxpayers under investigation and affected third parties of the opportunity to prevent the interference with their right to data protection. Additionally, other rights that are essential to ensure effective exercise of the right to judicial protection in the final stage of the procedure are not guaranteed by EU law or ECHR law. These rights include: the right of taxpayers to be informed about the EoIR even when the requesting State has no intention to use the exchanged information or intends to use the exchanged information for purposes other than tax reassessment; the right that illegally obtained information will not be used by the requesting State (at least in case its use is prohibited either by the requesting or the requested State's national law); the right that information whose source and/or methods of collection are unknown will be treated as

---

[107] IBFD OPTR, *2019 General Report on the Protection of Taxpayers' Rights* (IBFD 2020) 134 <https://www.ibfd.org/sites/default/files/2021-06/2019%20IBFD%20Yearbook%20on%20Taxpayers%27%20Rights%20%28final%29_0.pdf> accessed 6 December 2023. The Report finds that some states, including EU Member States, have shifted away from the practice of asking for exculpatory evidence.

inadmissible or having less probative value; the right that all information relevant to the case under investigation, including exculpatory evidence, will be requested (by the requesting State) and passed on (by the requested State). Unless these rights are regulated, *ex post facto* protection is not adequate. For this reason, it is urgent and important that the EU legislature steps in and harmonises these rights.[108]

---

[108] Of course, the requirement of unanimity will continue to block attempts for further harmonization on the part of the EU. Many scholars have put forward similar proposals for the adoption of universal (soft or hard law) minimum standards of protection of taxpayers' rights (although the discussion is not limited to the specific rights discussed in this section). See, indicatively, Philip Baker and Pasquale Pistone, 'BEPS Action 16: The Taxpayers' Right to an Effective Legal Remedy Under European Law in Cross-Border Situations' (2016) 25(5/6) EC Tax Review 335, 343–44; Perrou and Panayi (n 76) 220; Moreno González (n 5) 728–730; Kokott and Pistone (n 75) chapters 10 and 11.

7. Exchange of information: effectiveness and efficiency

Willem Boei and Sjoerd Douma

7.1 INTRODUCTION

This chapter discusses whether the DAC (Directive on Administrative Cooperation) is fit for purpose. The DAC has caused – and is causing – a considerable compliance burden for companies and individuals. This burden needs to be balanced against the intended effects of the DAC. In this context, the chapter discusses the need for effective exchange of information in Section 7.2. Section 7.3 analyses how the former Mutual Assistance Directive (MAD) addressed the situation and why it was desirable to repeal that directive and replace it with the DAC. The various amendments to the DAC are examined in Section 7.4, which focuses on the relationship between the stated objectives of each amendment and their practical effects. Section 7.5 provides a conclusion.

7.2 THE NEED FOR AN EFFECTIVE EXCHANGE OF INFORMATION

States cannot exist without taxation. As a consequence, the right to levy taxes is at the core of state sovereignty. The traditional approach of establishing tax jurisdiction is founded on the territorial and personal bases of jurisdiction.[1] Nationality and incorporation are widely accepted as a valid jurisdictional basis for the assertion of a state jurisdiction over individuals and legal entities, leading to worldwide tax liability. The principle of fiscal territoriality refers to jurisdiction over persons, matters and things within the geographical boundaries of a state. A state may tax a person residing in its territory or income arising therein. The scope of jurisdiction of persons or income is by its nature different. A state has unlimited fiscal jurisdiction over individuals and companies residing within its territory. Consequently, a state is competent

1 See Sjoerd Douma, *Optimization of Direct Tax Sovereignty and Free Movement* (IBFD Doctoral Series No. 21, 2011) para 2.2.2, and the literature referred to therein.

to tax the worldwide income of individuals and companies. A state may also tax non-resident aliens, individuals and companies, but only with regard to the particular sources of income within its territory. Accordingly, the fiscal jurisdiction of a state in respect of non-resident aliens is limited to the sources of income within the state.

The extent of a state tax jurisdiction as described above means that a state needs information regarding facts taking place outside its physical boundaries to establish a taxpayer's tax liability: both the source of the income and the residence of the taxpayer may be located elsewhere. Oberson has pointed out an important development which took place in parallel:

> Sophisticated taxpayers, such as multinational companies, could try to use the international legal framework, typically double taxation treaties (DTT), in order to ensure double non-taxation. Other taxpayers, including individuals, were developing schemes of tax evasion or aggressive tax planning through the use of offshore, hybrid or complex structures. Transfer of the place of residence to tax-favourable countries also started to develop.[2]

It is thus clear that an effective international exchange of information framework is necessary for a state to enforce its tax sovereignty.

7.3 MAD AND DAC

In the 1970s, the European Economic Community realised that the problem described above needed to be addressed. This led to the Council Resolution of 10 February 1975 on the measures to be taken by the Community in order to combat international tax evasion and avoidance. This resolution emphasised that tax evasion and tax avoidance reach beyond national borders of Member States, lead to budget losses, violations of the principle of fiscal justice, and distortions of capital movements and of conditions of competition.

To this end, the MAD contained not only provisions for exchange of information on request (EOIR), but also on automatic and spontaneous exchanges of information (AEOI and SEOI). The problem was, however, that the Member States did not really fulfil the commitments they had undertaken with the MAD. The DAC thus repealed the MAD, building on its achievements, but providing clearer and more precise rules governing administrative cooperation between Member States where necessary, in order to establish, especially as regards the exchange of information, a wider scope of administrative coopera-

---

[2] Xavier Oberson, *International Exchange of Information in Tax Matters. Towards Global Transparency* (3rd edn, Elgar Tax Law and Practice series 2023) 1–2.

tion between Member States.[3] As the European Court of Auditors has shown, the DAC pursues three specific objectives:

1. to improve Member States' ability to prevent cross-border tax fraud, evasion and avoidance;
2. to reduce the scope for incentives and advantages leading to harmful tax competition, including counteracting tax avoidance and aggressive tax planning; and
3. to promote spontaneous tax compliance by making it easier to detect cross-border income and assets.[4]

The next section will discuss the DAC and its subsequent amendments, specifically with a view to effective rule design and implementation.

7.4 EFFECTIVENESS ANALYSIS

7.4.1 Introduction

In this section, we will analyse, for each DAC amendment, whether the reason and objectives behind each successive amendment align with the type of exchange of information introduced. We will start by describing in general the exchange of information mechanisms introduced with each amendment of the DAC.[5] Subsequently, the reasons behind each exchange of information will be set out, followed by our analysis of whether the objectives of the newly introduced exchange and the exchange itself align. We will conclude with the

---

[3] DAC1 preamble at (7). More extensively, see Part II, Chapters 10 and 11 in this book.

[4] European Court of Auditors, Exchange of information in the EU: solid foundation, cracks in the implementation' Special Report 3 (2021) (hereinafter: ECA Report).

[5] For a more exhaustive discussion of each DAC, we refer to the specific DAC chapters in Part II in this book.

results of the evaluations carried out by the EC in 2017[6], 2018[7] and 2019[8] and the 2020 report of the European Court of Auditors.[9]

7.4.2 DAC1

7.4.2.1 What/how

DAC1 introduced a new approach to the exchange of information. Compared to the MAD, DAC1 provides for a clearer and more precise set of rules governing administrative cooperation.[10] One of the most fundamental changes is the wider scope of taxes that are covered by DAC1 compared to the MAD. The MAD only covered information regarding the taxation of income or capital. DAC1 broadened the scope of taxes for which information should be exchanged to all taxes of any kind on both a national level and more local level that are not VAT, customs and excise duties. These latter taxes have their own system for exchanging information.

Just like the MAD, DAC1 consists of three types of exchange of information: EOIR, AEOI and SEOI. However, in contrast to the Mutual Assistance Directive, DAC1 foresees a stricter regime.

As for the introduction of the DAC, the procedures for EOIR as SEOI are bound to a specific time limit, varying from no later than one month after the information becomes available (with regards to SEOI) to no later than six months from the date of receipt of a request for EOIR. The MAD, on the other hand, stated that the information should be forwarded as swiftly as possible and did not contain a specific time limit. Furthermore, a procedure has been introduced from the moment a Member State receives a request for information (EOIR) up and until the actual exchange itself.

The largest steps have been taken from an AEOI perspective. This developed from a bilateral approach, where two Member States had to agree which information they wanted to automatically exchange between each other, into

---

6 European Commission, Report from the commission to the European Parliament and the Council on the application of Council Directive (EU) 2011/16/EU on administrative cooperation in the field of direct taxation COM(2017) 781 final (hereinafter: Report 2017).

7 European Commission, Report from the Commission to the European Parliament and the Council on overview and assessment of the statistics and information on the automatic exchanges in the field of direct taxation COM(2018) 844 final (hereinafter: Report 2018).

8 Commission Staff Working Document, Evaluation of the council directive 2011/16/EU on administrative cooperation in the field of taxation and repealing Directive 77/799/ECC SWD(2019) 327 (hereinafter: SWD 2019).

9 ECA Report (n 4).

10 DAC1 preamble at (7).

a multilateral one where Member States are obliged to exchange information regarding five categories of income and capital to all other Member States. The DAC therefore introduced separate rules for this type of exchange without the need for individual Member States to bilaterally agree which information they wish to exchange. Article 19 of the DAC contains a most-favoured-nation clause: when a Member State foresees in wider cooperation with a third country, then that Member State may not refuse to also provide such wider cooperation to any other Member State.

From a practical point of view, the exchange has to be carried out through standard forms, formats and channels of communication. The channel being used for the exchange is the Common Communication Network (CCN).[11] All exchanges of information based on the DAC should be carried out using this network. The European Commission has been made owner of the network, but may only access the information contained in it insofar as it is necessary for the care, maintenance and development of the network.

7.4.2.2 Why

The reason for replacing the MAD with the DAC was that the state of play in 2011 (i.e., the year of the introduction of DAC1) was very different compared to 1977, when the MAD was introduced. The ever-increasing globalisation of the internal market required a new approach to efficiently cooperate on an international level.[12] The methods of exchange are similar, but there was a greater need for a binding, clearer and precise set of rules on how and when information had to be exchanged.[13] There was also a need to cover the expanding array of legal arrangements and new instruments which were being set up by taxpayers.[14] DAC1 contains minimum rules and therefore does not affect the rights of Member States to enter into wider cooperation with other Member States.

7.4.2.3 Alignment

The main objective of DAC1 was to foster cooperation between Member States because of ever expanding cross-border transactions and arrangements. The MAD did not contain a binding set of rules and gave plenty of freedom to Member States to bilaterally agree which information they wished to exchange as well as how and when. A binding set of more precise rules, but still with a limited freedom for Member States to deviate from them, is – in our

---

11 DAC arts 20 and 21.
12 DAC1 preamble at (3).
13 DAC1 preamble at (7).
14 DAC1 preamble at (8).

view – required to tackle the lack of information Member States suffer from in respect of what is happening in the jurisdiction of another Member State. Using the CCN and standard templates also makes it easier for both the sender and receiver of information to understand what type of information is being exchanged. The choice to start with a clean slate by replacing the MAD with the DAC also seems more appropriate than dramatically altering the MAD. Our conclusion, therefore, is that DAC1 contains an effective set of rules.

7.4.3 DAC2

7.4.3.1 What/how

After just three years, in 2014, the first amendment of the DAC occurred. DAC2 introduced the Common Reporting Standard (CRS), developed by the OECD, into the DAC. The new rules had to be applied as of 1 January 2016. DAC2 introduced a new reporting obligation regarding bank statements. Financial institutions are required to perform reporting and due diligence activities, such as verifying the account holder and collecting personal information such as their date of birth, residential address, TIN, bank account number, account balance and, if applicable, the amount of interest paid. Where the account holder is part of an intermediary structure, financial institutions need to look through that structure and identify and report on its beneficial owners. Financial institutions need to report information on their non-resident account holders and their accounts to the tax authorities in the Member State where the financial institution is residing. This Member State must subsequently exchange the information with other Member States via the CCN. Since the already existing Savings Directive[15] had thus become redundant, it was repealed in 2016.

7.4.3.2 Why

The objective of DAC2 was, unlike DAC1, not primarily to rearrange an already existing practice of exchange between Member States, but to combat cross-border tax fraud and tax evasion using bank accounts. This objective was not restricted to the borders of the EU internal market, but also focused on evasion on a more global level. Its primary focus was on unreported and, therefore, untaxed income. The CRS follows the Foreign Account Tax Compliance Act (FATCA) which was introduced by the United States of America. Following the FATCA regulations, Member States were concluding agreements with the United States of America and therefore providing wider

---

[15] Council Directive 2003/48/EC of 3 June 2003 on taxation of savings income in interest payments [2003] OJ L 157/38.

cooperation within the meaning of the Article 19 DAC.[16] The EU feared parallel and uncoordinated agreements that could lead to distortions of the smooth functioning of the internal market and therefore adopted the CRS.[17]

7.4.3.3 Alignment

To have a coordinated approach regarding the exchange of information on bank accounts of non-residents is a positive development. Following the possible fear of bilateral FATCA agreements in connection with the most-favoured-nation clause in DAC1, an EU-wide approach was required. DAC2 introduced the obligation to outsource the collection of information. Instead of the Member States themselves, financial institutions need to collect information and report about their account holders. Discussions may arise in respect of the place of residence of a person. Why is a financial institution the right party to make a statement about the place of residence of a person? Narrowing the scope of exchanging information to non-resident account holders is both the strength and weakness of DAC2. It is a strength, because information about accounts of resident is not of use for other Member States. They most likely do not wish to tax either the capital or income derived from it. However, if a financial institution concludes that an account holder is a resident of the Member State where the institution is based, but another Member State does not share this conclusion, no information is exchanged. The latter Member State then still has no information as to any 'foreign' held bank accounts. This is, in our opinion, a substantial weakness of DAC2. The need to share information about a non-resident account with all other Member States is also questionable. The financial institution needs to conclude in which Member State the account holder is a resident. Exchanging only information with this latter Member State may have been a more proportionate solution.

7.4.4 DAC3

7.4.4.1 What/how

Within a year following the introduction of DAC2, in 2015, and even before the expiration of the implementation deadline of DAC2, DAC3 was adopted. DAC3 introduced the AEOI of (unilateral) Advance Pricing Agreements (APAs) and Advance Tax Rulings (ATRs). DAC3 introduced definitions for both APAs and ATRs. Only rulings that a person may rely on fall within the scope of the exchange rules.

---

16 DAC2 preamble at (7).

17 DAC2 preamble at (8).

Member States must exchange basic information about the ruling using a standard form that has to be uploaded to the CCN and is, therefore, accessible to all Member States. If a Member State wishes to receive additional information and for example the full text of the ruling, it can send a general request for information (EOIR) based on Article 5 of the DAC to the Member State that issued the ruling. The European Commission also receives a limited amount of information in order for it to be able to monitor and evaluate the effective application of the exchange of information. The received information may not be used for state aid investigations.

7.4.4.2 Why

The exchange of rulings has been introduced for increasing the transparency of agreements concluded by the Members States with one or more of their taxpayers. In the preamble, rulings are referred to as a method to provide certainty for business, to clarify tax law for taxpayers and to encourage investment and compliance with the law.[18] They are therefore conducive to the further development of the EU single market. Rulings that are based on tax-driven structures may however lead to less effective or ineffective taxation or artificially high amounts of income in the Member State issuing the ruling, leaving low amounts of income being taxed in any other country involved. DAC1 already stated that Member States should inform each other if they have grounds for supposing that there may be a loss of tax in another Member State (as part of the SEOI through Article 9 DAC). This obligation is also applicable to tax rulings. This exchange possibility was, however, hindered by important practical difficulties, such as the margin of discretion allowed to the issuing Member State to decide which other Member States should be informed.[19] Therefore, there was a need for information about rulings to be accessible for all other Member States and therefore to be exchanged automatically.

7.4.4.3 Alignment

DAC3 is the first of the DAC amendments which does not attempt to fix the lack of data available to Member States, but the lack of the knowledge about the tax treatment of companies or other business activities in other Member States. DAC1 and DAC2 (re)-arranged the exchange of information which can be used as a starting point for a Member State to determine whether a person should pay tax and for what amount. DAC3, however, does not introduce an additional exchange of information, but sets rules concerning information on the application of the tax law of a Member State. Member States are not bound

---

18 DAC3 preamble at (1).

19 DAC3 preamble at (4).

by foreign rulings, so it is not immediately clear why this exchange would be useful. Transparency is the recurring theme in the preamble of DAC3; however, it does not become clear why transparency in respect of cross-border rulings is of particular interest for another Member State. If an APA is agreed between a Member State and a taxpayer, another Member State may still disagree with the pricing agreed and levy tax using the pricing that the latter Member State considers appropriate according to its own tax law. The same applies when a taxpayer agrees with a Member State that the taxpayer has a permanent establishment in this state. The Member State of residence of the taxpayer/'head office' is not bound to the agreement and in the situation that it does not agree that there is a permanent establishment (according to its national law), it can still levy tax on the income of this – to its opinion non-existent – 'permanent establishment'.

Furthermore, basic information on all cross-border rulings is exchanged, despite the scope of the problem being rulings concerning tax-driven structures. We understand that it is nearly impossible to formulate a general definition of tax-driven structures in the light of tax rulings, but to exchange all cross-border rulings does appear somewhat disproportionate.

An advantage of exchanging cross-border rulings with other Member States could be that the latter are informed about a specific tax treatment of a taxpayer in a different jurisdiction and try to respond to possible mismatches, both in terms of the pricing of cross-border transactions between affiliated parties and the treatment of the cross-border activities of one and the same taxpayer (e.g., the existence of a permanent establishment which is being taxed or not). This, however, is not mentioned in the preamble of DAC3. It is interesting to note that its preamble states (at 15) that:

> [F]eedback by the receiving Member State to the Member State sending the information is a necessary element of the operation of an effective system of automatic information exchange. It is therefore appropriate to underline that Member States' competent authorities should send, once a year, feedback on the automatic exchange of information to the other Member States concerned. In practice, this mandatory feedback should be done by arrangements agreed upon bilaterally.

Such feedback seems very helpful for an effective application of the directive, but Member States seem to have been sloppy in this respect.[20]

---

[20] See Report 2017 (n 6) 15; SWD 2019 (n 8) 53 and the results from the audit performed by the ECA discussed in Section 7.4.9 of this chapter.

7.4.5 DAC4

7.4.5.1 What/how

The CbCR rules of DAC4 were introduced in the first quarter of 2016. Multinational Enterprises (MNEs) with a total consolidated group revenue of €750 million or more, are obliged to file a country-by-country report (CbCR). Subsequently, the Member State of which the ultimate parent entity is a resident should exchange the CbCR report with any other Member State in which, based on the information in the report, one or more entities of the MNE group is either resident for tax purposes or subject to tax with respect to the business carried out through a permanent establishment. The report must contain aggregated financial information such as amount of revenue, profit, income tax paid but also information like the number of employees and tangible assets regarding each jurisdiction in which the MNE group operates. Furthermore, each entity within the MNE group must be identified and the nature of the main business activity/activities of that entity described. Standard forms have to be used and the channel of exchange is the CCN.

7.4.5.2 Why

According to the preamble, the increase of transparency towards tax authorities could lead to an incentive for MNE groups to abandon certain practices and pay their fair share of tax where profits are made and is, therefore, an essential part of tackling base erosion and profit shifting.[21] Knowledge about the structure of MNE groups, their transfer-pricing policy and international transactions will enable tax authorities to react to harmful tax practices, for example by changing legislation and/or tax audits. By requiring MNE groups to make a CbCR, tax authorities could also identify whether these groups have engaged in practices that have the effect of artificially shifting substantial amount of income into a tax-advantaged environment.[22]

7.4.5.3 Alignment

The exact purpose of this amendment of DAC4 does not become clear. The main objective seems to be prevention. MNE groups that need to report that they have activities in tax haven jurisdictions might, by being obliged to report these activities, be inclined to restructure their activities to prevent (tax) audits by other market jurisdictions. Knowing how many people work in other jurisdictions combined with the activities and assets of the companies active there can be quite informative. In the example of a tax haven entity, a market juris-

---

21 DAC4 preamble at (4).

22 DAC4 preamble at (3).

diction might indeed be inclined to conduct a thorough investigation when one entity has almost no employees, but a huge amount of earnings. It is, however, a bit odd that the report only covers tangible assets and not also intangible assets. Intangible assets are very mobile and often owned by companies in low- to non-taxing jurisdictions. Having to report on whether the company has intangible assets could, therefore, also be of great use of market jurisdictions.

The downside of CbCR especially for the reporting MNE groups is the high amount of compliance costs. The group needs to draw up a report which covers every jurisdiction it is active in.[23] If the main purpose is prevention, it would be interesting to know whether an actual change of behaviour on the part of MNEs has taken place.

7.4.6 DAC5

7.4.6.1 What/how

DAC5 was adopted in December 2016. Member States received via DAC5 access to the anti-money-laundering (AML) information already obtained pursuant to Directive (EU) 2015/849 (the so-called AML Directive).[24] This Directive was introduced to identify the beneficial owner(s) of a company or group of companies with respect to anti-money-laundering in the financial market. With the introduction of DAC5, tax authorities of the Member States received access to the AML information in possession of financial institutions to ensure the functioning of the DAC.

7.4.6.2 Why

In order for Member States to be able to check whether financial institutions send a complete and correct set of information about their account holders which they are required to do under DAC2, Member States received access to the same AML information financial institutions are required to gather when someone wants to, for example, open a bank account. By having this extra

---

[23] In December 2021 the EU introduced a separate Directive introducing public CbCR rules. This Directive is not part of the DAC and will therefore not be considered in this chapter. The focus on this Directive is – other than the DAC – not to stimulate the exchange of information between Member States but for MNEs to be more transparent to the public. See for an overview, S. Verloove et al., 'EU Public Country-by-Country Reporting' (2022) 29(3) International Transfer Pricing Journal 1.

[24] Directive (EU) 2015/849 of the European Parliament and of the Council of 20 May 2015 on the prevention of the use of the financial system for the purposes of money laundering or terrorist financing, amending Regulation (EU) No 648/2012 of the European Parliament and of the Council, and repealing Directive 2005/60/EC of the European Parliament and of the Council and Commission Directive 2006/70/EC [2015] OJ L 141/73.

control mechanism through accessing the data, Member States could check whether the information exchanged pursuant to DAC2 was complete and correct.

7.4.6.3 Alignment

Since financial institutions already had the obligation to perform due diligence procedures such as the identification of the beneficial owner of an account holder of a financial product, and information about the account holder was already exchanged between Member States, it is in our opinion more than logical that tax authorities received access to the financial institutions' AML information for verification purposes. This additional control mechanism does not result in additional compliance costs, because DAC5 only introduced an access facility to data that already exists and must be kept for a specific amount of time pursuant to the AML Directive.

7.4.7 DAC6

7.4.7.1 What/how

DAC6 introduced mandatory disclosure rules (MDR) for potentially aggressive cross-border tax-planning arrangements. Intermediaries and other providers of tax advice need to file information that is within their knowledge, possession or control on reportable cross-border arrangements with the tax authorities within 30 days. This reporting needs to be carried out already on the day after the arrangement is made available for implementation, is ready for implementation or the first step in the implementation of the arrangement has been taken, whichever occurs first. If the intermediary has, for example, a legal professional privilege and could therefore ignore the reporting obligation, the obligation to report shifts to another intermediary involved or, ultimately, to the taxpayer himself.

A vast framework of definitions has been introduced to determine whether an arrangement is reportable or not. One of the key questions for an arrangement to be reportable is whether one of the five hallmarks is met. The hallmarks have been formulated through a list of features and elements of transactions that would present a strong indication of tax avoidance or abuse rather than through the introduction of a definition of aggressive tax planning.[25] Some hallmarks also require the fulfilment of a main benefit test (if the main benefit or one of the main benefits which a person may reasonably expect to derive from an arrangement is the obtaining of a tax advantage).

---

[25] DAC6 preamble at (9).

After the reporting by the intermediary to the tax authorities, the tax authorities will subsequently exchange the information with all other Member States through the CCN. Member States must lay down effective, proportionate and dissuasive penalties against the violation reported.

7.4.7.2 Why

According to the preamble, the reason for introducing the MDR is primarily to provide Member States with comprehensive information about potentially aggressive tax arrangements.[26] This is because of the increased mobility of capital and persons within the internal market. The main objective is again to protect the national tax base of Member States from erosion and tax planning. By receiving information about tax structures, Member States would be able to react promptly against harmful tax practices and close loopholes or undertake audits.[27] The preamble refers to how certain financial intermediaries and other providers of tax advice seem to have actively assisted their clients in concealing money offshore. Getting the information from the intermediaries at an early stage would lead to a possible deterrent effect.[28] Furthermore, it is mentioned that, in order to develop a more comprehensive policy, it is necessary that following the reporting by the intermediary, the tax authorities of Member States share information with their peers in other Member States.[29]

7.4.7.3 Alignment

It is questionable whether the MDR is really fit for purpose. We would expect that Member States are aware of many of the possible arrangements. If they are not aware of the arrangement and the arrangement is reported at an early stage, a tax audit may take place, possibly followed by a correction of the tax assessment. If the arrangement is not contrary to the law, however, the Member State is not able to counter the arrangement on short notice. It can change its national law, but this takes time. In our view, the real aim of DAC6 may be to deter intermediaries from advising aggressive tax planning structures by compelling them to report such arrangements proactively on pain of penalties. Alternatively, intermediaries who have advised aggressively, but have not reported can be put under pressure during tax audits. DAC6 provides the tax authorities with an instrument to pursue aggressive tax planners. The fact that the hallmarks are not overly specific may help to attain this objective.

---

26 DAC6 preamble at (2).
27 DAC6 preamble at (2).
28 DAC6 preamble at (7).
29 DAC6 preamble at (6).

Another effect of the vague hallmarks is that intermediaries are reporting all kinds of arrangements, whereas they may have made sure that the truly aggressive ones are no longer being implemented. Penalties in some Member States, such as in the Netherlands, are very high (up to €900,000). Due to the vagueness of the hallmarks and the fear of penalties, intermediaries might overreport or report about an arrangement if they are not totally sure whether it is defined by a hallmark. Overreporting leads to too much data and, therefore, to inefficiency.

Overreporting may also take place in respect of 'off-the-shelf' arrangements. Why is there a need to report the same structure hundreds of times, but for a different taxpayer? The answer might relate to the need to provide the tax authorities with a tool to go after the intermediaries who advised the structure.

In summary, we see shortcomings both in the formulation of DAC6's objectives and in the massive overreporting it may lead to. The first cracks in DAC6 are already becoming visible. The Belgian Constitutional Court has raised questions with the CJEU on, among other things, whether the definitions being used in the Directive are specific and clear enough so that penalties may be invoked for intermediaries who, according to the Member State, failed to report.[30] The Belgian court refers to the principle of legal certainty. If the CJEU indeed rules that the definitions are not specific and clear enough and, therefore, the imposition of a penalty will be in breach of the principle of legal certainty, the whole basis of the reporting obligation under MDR will be undermined. It is the fear of a penalty that makes intermediaries report as much as they do.

7.4.8 DAC7

7.4.8.1 What/how

The foundation of DAC7 is comparable to DAC2. (Digital) platform operators are, under DAC7, obliged to report information about sellers conducting commercial activities on their platforms, irrespective of the legal nature of the seller. Examples of commercial activities are rental of immovable property, personal services, sale of goods and rental of any mode of transport.[31] There is a threshold in place for, for example, hotels or tour operators above which the reporting obligation does not apply. Non-resident platforms ('foreign platform operators') are also required to report. Foreign platforms need to register in one single Member State and report to this state. Following the report of the platform operator, the Member State where the platform operator is based/reg-

---

30 Cour constitutionnelle, 15 September 2022, ECLI:BE:GHCC:2022:ARR.103.
31 DAC7 preamble at (18).

istered exchanges the reported information within one month with the Member State where the seller is located and, if the seller is renting out immovable property, with the Member State where the immovable property is located.

Apart from a newly introduced exchange of information, DAC7 also contains a clearer and codified definition of 'foreseeable relevance' (which is a condition when filing a request for information by a Member State to another Member State).[32] This codification was also partly undertaken because of CJEU case law. In several rulings, questions were raised as to how the condition should be interpretated when a Member State filed a group-oriented request for information to another Member State (for example, a request to receive information on who the ultimate beneficial owners or shareholders of an entity being resident in the requested Member State are).[33] Furthermore, DAC7 urged Member States to include the tax identification number (TIN) issued by the Member State of residence in the communication of the categories of income and capital subject to the mandatory automatic exchange of information set out in DAC1.

7.4.8.2 Why

DAC7 is comparable to DAC2 in its foundation and tries to fill the gap originating from the insufficient information that Member States have. It therefore tries to counter tax fraud, evasion and avoidance. In our opinion is it primarily tax fraud that is being targeted by DAC7, for example by sellers who do not state the income derived via the platform in their income tax return. DAC7, in particular, targets income derived from commercial activities by taxpayers via a digital platform. This is, according to the preamble, particularly problematic if the digital platform is established in another jurisdiction.[34] Furthermore, the preamble states that Member States frequently request information from platform operators and/or introduced unilateral reporting obligations which cause these operators to incur significant administrative and compliance costs.[35] Making one reporting framework for the whole EU internal market results in less compliance costs for these operators.

7.4.8.3 Alignment

Having information about the income of sellers using digital platforms while not declaring the income in their annual tax return is in our opinion an effective measure to combat tax fraud. Digital platforms having to report the informa-

---

[32] DAC art 5a. More extensively, see Part I, Chapter 1 in this book.

[33] For example, Case C-437/19 *État du Grand-duché de Luxembourg v L* [2021] ECLI:EU:C:2021:953.

[34] DAC7 preamble at (6).

[35] DAC7 preamble at (7).

tion does result in compliance costs for them, but it is probably difficult to reduce these costs.

The additional rules about the interpretation of the 'foreseeable relevance' criterion are most welcome. Member States and persons that are asked to cooperate in an investigation for their Member State to exchange information now have more guidance on how this condition needs to be interpreted. It is a welcome development that the EU legislator has taken recent case law into account when introducing these additional rules.

7.4.9 EU Evaluation Reports

7.4.9.1 Regulatory evaluation framework

Besides regulation about exchange obligations and procedures, the DAC also contains an article on feedback and best practice sharing. Article 14(1) DAC contains the possibility for Member States to request feedback from the receiving entity for the information exchanged under Articles 5 (EOIR) and 9 (SEOI). With regard to the AEOI, Member States are, according to Article 14(2) DAC, required to send feedback to the other Member States once a year in accordance with bilateral agreements.

Article 15 DAC states that Member States shall, together with the European Commission, examine and evaluate administrative cooperation pursuant to the DAC and share their experience with a view to improving such cooperation and, where appropriate, draw up rules in the fields concerned. Member States may, together with the European Commission, produce guidelines for sharing experiences and best practices.

In addition to Article 15 DAC, the DAC contains two evaluation (reporting) obligations, of which one was only temporary. The temporary obligation was introduced in Article 8b DAC and required that Member States provide to the European Commission, before 1 January 2018 and on an annual basis, statistics on the volume of the automatic exchanges and information on the administrative and other relevant costs and benefits relating to exchanges for both tax administrations and third parties. Before 1 January 2019, the European Commission had to file a report following the information received from the Member States. As of 1 January 2018, Member States are no longer required to send the information.

Article 23 DAC contains a more general evaluation obligation. Member States and the Commission must examine and evaluate the functioning of the administrative cooperation provided for in the DAC. For the Commission to be able to do this, Member States must communicate any relevant information necessary for the evaluation of the effectiveness of the DAC in combating tax evasion and tax avoidance. Member States must also communicate a yearly assessment of the effectiveness of the AEOI based on DAC1, DAC2, DAC3, DAC4 and DAC6.

According to Article 27 DAC, as of 1 January 2013, the Commission must submit every five years a report on the application of the DAC to the European Parliament and to the European Council.

Until now, three reports have been made public on the functioning of the DAC: one report based on Article 27 DAC in December 2017,[36] one report based on Article 8b DAC in December 2018[37] and one 'special report' following an audit by the European Court of Auditors (ECA).[38] In 2019, the EC also published a stand-alone Staff Working Document (SWD).[39,40]

7.4.9.2 General evaluation by the European Commission (2017)

The first report from December 2017 is based on Article 27 DAC and is a report on the overall application of the DAC. The report only covers the exchange mechanisms introduced with DAC1 and is accompanied by a Commission SWD.[41] According to the report, the exchanges based on DAC2 and DAC3 were too recent to be evaluated.

The report and the SWD do not reach hard conclusions and contain a lot of data on the number of exchanges (on an automatic, requested and spontaneous basis). The SWD mentions that it is difficult to evaluate whether additional tax revenue has been raised because of the exchange of information. This is because Member States are not able to provide statistical data on the accrued tax benefits.[42] It is also mentioned that the exchange of information is only one of many sources of information about a taxpayer under tax audit. This sounds logical, but tax authorities should in our opinion be able to assess whether the exchanged information under the DAC played an important role in, for example, successfully ending a tax audit with an additional amount of tax payable. The Member States are obliged to send information based on Article 23 DAC.

---

36 Report 2017 (n 6).
37 Report 2018 (n 7).
38 ECA Report (n 4).
39 SWD 2019 (n 8).
40 There is another study published in February 2021 for the European Parliament's Committee on Economic and Monetary Affairs (ECON) by the European Parliamentary Research Service (EPRS): Implementation of the EU requirements for tax information exchange, PE 662.60, that we do not discuss in this chapter.
41 Commission Staff Working Document on the application of Council Directive (EU) no. 2011/16/EU on administrative cooperation in the field of direct taxation, SWD(2017) 462 (hereinafter: SWD 2017).
42 SWD 2017 (n 41) 1.

Furthermore, the SWD notes that Member States are in general satisfied with the overall quality and completeness of the information received through the exchange on request procedure, but have reported that, in some instances, they have been unable to respond within the time limits.[43] Regarding the AEOI, it is stated that the information received is not always useable, because of the information being incomplete or more accurate information being required, such as the (correct) TIN and full name.[44] The SWD contains an odd conclusion about the SEOI. It mentions that, in general, all information provided spontaneously is effective, as it is selected by tax officials relying on their own practical experience and expertise.[45] In our opinion, this argument is perhaps too enthusiastic.

The report contains three main findings:

1. DAC provisions have been implemented, but not all of them effectively;
2. The application of the DAC exchange of information has resulted in a great increase in the amount of data tax administrations have to handle – but on average their capacity to do so has not increased at the same rate;
3. The assessment of the benefits of the DAC is being carried out at a very early stage.[46]

The second finding is in our view alarming. We can have a vast system of exchange of information, but if there is nobody to further process the exchanged information, there is no point in exchanging at all. The report states that on average the Central Liaison Offices (the office of each individual Member State responsible for the coordination of the exchange of information, 'CLO') ranges from one to five officials.[47] Until the date of the report, no significant increase of CLO staff has been reported, while the mechanisms of administrative cooperation have expanded in scope and evolved greatly in a very short period.[48] Another problem mentioned is that the IT work required to process the information in an automated manner is only just starting. This problem is linked with the problem mentioned in the SWD regarding the difficulties Member States have in matching the information received with the information on taxpayers in their own local tax database (among other reasons because of the national TIN or full name of taxpayers are missing in information received).

---

[43] SWD 2017 (n 41) 3 and 5.
[44] SWD 2017 (n 41) 7.
[45] SWD 2017 (n 41) 8.
[46] Report 2017 (n 6) 3.
[47] Report 2017 (n 6) 4.
[48] Report 2017 (n 6) 4.

In the report, the European Commission states that, beyond the number of exchanges, the DAC has had a significant deterrent effect, which is a key tool in the fight against tax evasion.[49]

7.4.9.3 Statistical information on AOEI by the European Commission (2018)

The report based on the former Article 8b DAC provides an overview and assessment of the AEOI under DAC1, DAC2 and DAC3. The report has been drafted mainly based on information collected from Member States through an annual survey and annually collected sets of statistical data. It covers the period from 2015 until mid-2018 as regards DAC1 and from 2017 until mid-2018 as regards DAC2 and DAC3. It is important to note that Member States only had to share the information with the Commission which was available in their national tax databases.

In this report, the same conclusion is drawn about the importance of the TIN. Including the TIN in the exchanged information would by-pass several problems connected to the use of the name for identification, such as misspelling or translation/transliterations.[50] With regard to DAC1, only 2% of the taxpayers on which information was exchanged were associated with a TIN issued by the recipient Member State.[51]

In 2017, 23 Member States reported opening received files with information exchanged on the basis of DAC1 during the year of reception.[52] As of 2017, only three Member States (Bulgaria, Malta and Slovakia) appear to not have worked with the files received either during the year they received them or in the following years. Other Member States not using the files in 2017 were Germany and Luxembourg.

In 2017, information exchanged under DAC2 was not used by nine Member States.[53] Italy is a limited user of the DAC1 information and only uses DAC2 data for awareness campaigns. It was too early to report on the actual usage by Member States of the DAC3 information.[54] Almost 18,000 rulings were recorded in the central directory in 2017 compared to hardly any exchanged spontaneously in the years up to 2015 (before the introduction of DAC3).

The report also depicts the costs incurred through the exchange of information. Particularly interesting are the costs incurred for financial institutions with the introduction of DAC2 and CRS. The costs for DAC2 and CRS for

---

[49] Report 2017 (n 6) 7.
[50] Report 2018 (n 8) 6.
[51] Report 2018 (n 7) 6 (particularly figure 5).
[52] Report 2018 (n 7) 7.
[53] Report 2018 (n 7) 10–11.
[54] Report 2018 (n 7) 11.

financial institutions in Austria, France, Germany, Luxembourg and the UK are estimated at €340 million in one-off costs, while yearly costs are estimated at €120 million.[55] The costs for implementing DAC3 were €2.1 million.[56] This is, according to the report, lower than the costs for DAC1 and DAC2. Because DAC3 information is not exchanged on a bilateral basis but uploaded to the CCN, the number of pieces of information is much lower and less complex systems and procedures are required to be put in place by Member States.

Regarding the benefits of the exchange, the report reminds us that it is difficult for Member States to quantify the additional tax revenues.[57] Tax correctness (i.e., the correct filling of tax returns by taxpayers) is also a benefit, but that does not necessarily mean additional tax revenues. Another important benefit according to the report is the deterrent effect for taxpayers due to the expected increasing use of information exchanged. Some Member States have been able to quantity the benefits in added tax revenues because of DAC1. The amounts are not immense, the highest being €3.5 million additional tax revenue for Slovenia in 2017.[58] In the case of DAC2 and DAC3, no information is available on the benefits due to the short period of time between the report and the first exchanges in 2017.

Three conclusions are mentioned in the report:

1. The exchanged information on an automatic basis can be used for different purposes, such as risk assessments and personal income tax assessments. However, several Member States still make very limited, if any, use of the information they receive.
2. The AEOI requires significant development investments by Member State and there are annual costs to maintain the exchange activities. As regards the benefits, it appears that the main benefits lie in increased tax compliance and the deterrent effect for taxpayers. However, is it very difficult to quantify the benefits in terms of additional tax revenues.
3. The information being sent by Member States often does not include all the necessary identification elements to permit an automated matching of this information with the national tax database.[59]

Following these conclusions two main areas of improvement are identified in the report: Member States should: (1) improve the quality of information, and (2) make better use of data. The quality of data should be improved by

[55] Report 2018 (n 7) 12.
[56] Report 2018 (n 7) 12.
[57] Report 2018 (n 7) 13.
[58] Report 2018 (n 7) 14 (particularly table 12).
[59] Report 2018 (n 7) 15.

reviewing the quality of the information Member States collect before they send it. Beyond this, Member States receiving the information should give timely and constructive feedback to those sending it, so that the quality of the information sent can be improved. Member States should provide feedback to the entities (e.g., financial institutions) which supply information for the automatic exchange of information.

Making a better use of data is to be achieved by: (1) developing a common methodology to estimate the benefits, (2) ensuring the information is part of the tax risk management cycle and that it is used more for awareness campaigns to improve voluntary compliance, and (3) sharing knowledge of best practices for full and efficient use of the data.[60]

7.4.9.4 Staff Working Document by the EC (2019)

In 2019, another Commission SWD was published regarding the performance of the DAC. The report in our opinion does not contain new key observations. It is worth mentioning that it seems that the Commission is pulling back from its stance that the DAC has a major deterrent effect on taxpayers (as mentioned in its evaluation report in 2017). In its 2019 SWD, the Commission states that there is limited evidence of this effect.[61] Some Member States reported an increase in the voluntary disclosure of foreign proceedings, but a substantial part of them only after being contacted by the tax authorities. A direct connection between the DAC and additional tax revenues cannot be drawn. The Commission thus still concludes that there is little information as to whether the DAC leads to a positive cost-benefit ratio.[62]

7.4.9.5 Audit by the ECA (2021)

In 2021, the ECA has performed an audit on the exchange of tax information system based on the DAC. The audit covered the period between 2014 and 2019, where the ECA assessed the legislative framework that the Commission proposed and put in place and examined how well the Commission was monitoring the implementation and performance of the system of information exchange (according to DAC1 through DAC5). The ECA visited five Member States (Cyprus, Italy, the Netherlands, Poland and Spain) to assess how they use the exchanged information and how they measure the effectiveness of the system.

---

60 Report 2018 (n 7) 15.

61 SWD 2019 (n 8) 30.

62 SWD 2019 (n 8) 32.

According to the ECA, the DAC is based on a clear demarcation of tasks and responsibilities and has well-defined objectives. The ECA makes a few general observations:

1. While ahead of international developments, the EU legislative framework presents gaps;
2. Member States make only limited use of the information exchanged automatically;
3. EOIR, SEOI and simultaneous controls work well;
4. Information necessary for measuring effectiveness is largely unavailable.

The first observation primarily concerns categories of information which were not being exchanged until 2019. The ECA however also found a number of gaps with regard to the role of the Commission. The latter sufficiently monitors the transposition of the DAC into national legislation, but the scope of monitoring the implementation of legislation is not broad enough.[63] The Commission performs high-level monitoring based only on the information provided by Member States[64] and bilateral feedback between Member States. It does not monitor the taking of direct and effective actions to address the lack of quality of the data sent as identified in its 2018 evaluation. Furthermore, the Commission does not carry out visits to Member States to assess progress and to identify good practices and issues. The Commission has developed a program called Fiscalis 2020, the main role of which is to provide IT support enabling the exchange of information. It finances the exchange of best practices and experience through workshops, workings visits and project groups.[65] Member States found the project groups and the technical support valuable.[66] Furthermore, they appreciated the Commission guidelines for the implementation of DAC1 and DAC2. However, due to the complexity and the constant evolution of the DAC, it has become increasingly difficult for Member States to address all discussion points during their meetings.[67] The Commission has not produced further guidelines on the use of information. The five Member States the ECA visited expressed the wish for more exchange of good practices (through the project groups, workshops and working visits) and guidelines, especially in the field of data analysis and data use.[68]

---

63 ECA Report (n 4) 22, number 37.
64 That Member States are obliged to do so based on DAC art 23.
65 ECA Report (n 4) 23 number 40.
66 ECA Report (n 4) 23, number 42.
67 ECA Report (n 4) 23, number 43.
68 ECA Report (n 4) 23, number 44.

With respect to the second observation, the ECA comes to the same conclusions as the Commission: Member States make only limited use of the information exchanged.[69] One of the problems arising in this field is the lack of quality control on the data exchanged. Only one of the Member States visited by the ECA carried out checks on data quality, but only on a limited data sample and not based on systematic process. Information sent based on DAC1 and DAC2 is generally on time, but lacks quality and completeness. Specifically, for the DAC2 exchange, the ECA concludes that only one of the five Member States visited performed quality checks on the data submitted by financial institutions.[70] Three of the five had no specific procedures for auditing the financial institutions regarding the quality and completeness of the data sent, and four of the five visited kept no register of the financial institutions subject to the DAC2 reporting requirement. Another problem is linked to the reporting format of DAC2. It does not allow for the identification of multiple ownership accounts.[71] As a result, tax authorities allocate the full amount to several owners resulting in the duplication of account records.

Member States give, according to the ECA, very little feedback based on Article 14(2) DAC on data quality, completeness and timelines, and no feedback on other quantitative or qualitative aspects.

The ECA also mentions corresponding problems arising with the exchanged information and the relevant taxpayer. Where the five Member States were able to match the information, DAC1 and DAC2 information was not rigorously used. One Member State highlighted certain data fields in tax returns, but without pre-filling amounts.[72] Another Member State notified taxpayers that information was available, and that they should complete the corresponding fields in the tax return. The strategy of both Member States was to produce a deterrent effect on the non-declaration and therefore increased taxpayer compliance. The other three Member States did not provide pre-filled tax declarations. Risk analysis based on the incoming data were only performed by two of the five Member States. Specifically for DAC1, the ECA sampled a total of 75 items of information received during 2016.[73] 51 of the items were matched and 40 were of these were uploaded to the tax authority's database. There was evidence that 13 items were used to review tax returns and or perform tax audits. For DAC2, the ECA also sampled 75 items.[74] 55 were matched to taxpayers while 20 were neither matched nor analysed further. Of these 55 items, 39 were

69 ECA Report (n 4) 23 number 46.
70 ECA Report (n 4) 28, number 52.
71 ECA Report (n 4) 29, number 55.
72 ECA Report (n 4) 32, number 64.
73 ECA Report (n 4) 32, number 69.
74 ECA Report (n 4) 32, number 70.

uploaded to central databases. There was evidence that 32 items were used to pre-fill tax returns and perform audits. Central and local offices did not give much feedback on the use of the incoming information, though this is essential to measure performance of the use of the information and its benefits.

The exchange under DAC3 was also analysed. The ECA took in total 50 data items, of which 36 were matched to taxpayers.[75] In total only 4% of the 50 items was used. With respect to DAC4, the Member States performed insufficient checks on whether all the entities falling within its scope had reported.[76] Four of the five Member States limited their checks to verifications against technical criteria provided by the OECD and the Commission. Only one ran additional risk analysis on the data it was exchanging with other Member States. Very little use of incoming DAC4 information was made by the Member States visited.[77] One Member State had a rigorous system of risk analysis, while two were planning to introduce a risk analysis mechanism and two had not used the information they received. The ECA took 50 CbCRs related to fiscal year 2016–2017. 20 of those were matched to taxpayers, of which 10 had been subjected to risk analysis. Only two reports had been used in taxation follow-up and no feedback had been received so far on their use.

The third observation made by the ECA was that the EOIR and SEOI work reasonably well, despite delayed replies and poor feedback. Given the volume of the EOIR and SEOI the feedback on information quality is not sufficient.[78] Providing feedback is not only important for improving the quality of the information and, thus, increasing the effectiveness of the exchange, it is also a way of showing recognition for the tax officials who put in so much work collecting the requested information. The Member States visited had no system for feedback to demonstrate how and where the information is most useful. Feedback was usually only provided by regional tax offices when requested for by the sending Member State and was not always given.

The overall conclusions of the ECA were that the Commission did not pro-actively monitor the implementation of the legislation and provide sufficient guidance, nor did it measure the outcomes and impact of the system.[79] Based on the five Member States they visited, the ECA concluded that the information being exchanged was of limited quality and underused. There was also minimal action being taken to monitor the system's effectiveness.

75 ECA Report (n 4) 35, number 78.
76 ECA Report (n 4) 38, number 81.
77 ECA Report (n 4) 38, number 82.
78 ECA Report (n 4) 43 number 91.
79 ECA Report (n 4) 48, number 106–108.

The ECA produced clear recommendations.[80] The Commission should take direct and effective actions to address the lack of quality of data sent by Member States and further develop guidance for Member States on implementing the DAC, performing risk analysis and using the tax information received. Member States should perform quality checks on data and ensure the completeness of the data before sending it to other Member States. Member States should also use all incoming information as extensively as possible. The Commission should establish, together with Member States, a reliable common framework for measuring the benefits of the system for exchange of tax information.

7.4.9.6 Resolution by the European Parliament (2021)

In 2021, the European Parliament adopted a resolution which provides a brief reflection on tax evasion and the DAC.[81] It contains many calls and suggestions, from among which we summarise the most vital for the effectiveness of the DAC. The Parliament urged the Commission to take direct action to address the quality and completeness of the data, further develop guidance for Member States on implementing the DAC legislation and perform risk analysis using the tax information received.[82] The scope of the DAC framework has been steadily increased (including already plans for DAC8), but too little attention was paid to improving data quality and completeness.[83] The lack of information publicly available on the quantitative data of the exchange of information under DAC1 to DAC4 makes democratic scrutiny by national parliaments and the European Parliament significantly difficult.[84] Furthermore, the Parliament invited the Commission and the Member States to take the report of the ECA into account in terms of monitoring, ensuring data quality and using the information received in order to make the exchange of tax information more effective.[85]

Importantly, the Parliament stressed that the 2019 SWD evaluation carried out by the Commission demonstrated the need for consistent monitoring of the effectiveness of the DAC framework.[86] The Parliament called on the Member States to communicate statistics, tax revenue gains and all other relevant

---

[80] ECA Report (n 4) 48-52, number 109–120.

[81] European Parliament resolution of 16 September 2021 on the implementation of the EU requirements for exchange of tax information: progress, lessons learnt and obstacles to overcome, 2020/2046(INI).

[82] ibid 11, number 25.

[83] ibid 7, number 1.

[84] ibid 6, letter W.

[85] ibid 14, number 38.

[86] ibid 16, number 44.

information needed to properly assess the effectiveness of all exchanges to the Commission on an annual basis; and it called on the Commission to continue to properly monitor and evaluate the effectiveness of the exchange of information. Finally, the Parliament requested a new comprehensive evaluation by January 2023.

Since a report based on and according to Article 27 DAC needs to be submitted to the Parliament and to the European Council every five years after 1 January 2013, the following evaluation report should already have been published before 1 January 2023. We, however, have not been able to find this report.

7.5 CONCLUDING REMARKS AND OUTLOOK

This chapter has shown that the DAC is a necessary instrument. At the same time, the objectives pursued have not always been stated with sufficient precision and the design of the rules does not always attain the objectives pursued in a proportionate manner. More crucially, however, the information exchanged is often of insufficient quality and underused. It may be expected from the EU and its Member States that they show clearly why the considerable compliance burden placed on companies leads to concrete results. Without any proof of effectiveness, the legitimacy of this burden becomes questionable. With DAC8 adopted in the meantime and the Unshell directive[87] on the way, this observation has become even more pressing.

---

[87] Proposal for a Council Directive laying down rules to prevent the misuse of shell entities for tax purposes and amending Directive 2011/16/EU [2021] COM(2021) 565 final

8. Exchange of information, national tax havens regimes and EU/EEA law

Andrés Báez Moreno and Martin Wenz

8.1 INTRODUCTION

Many EU Member States employ tax haven or non-cooperative jurisdictions[1] regimes (TH/NCJ regimes).[2] These regimes involve, in essence, the creation of a national list of taxwise 'suspicious' jurisdictions or territories to which a set of disadvantageous tax rules is linked (defensive TH/NCJ measures). These special rules apply to taxpayers resident in those TH/NCJ (inbound TH/NCJ regime) or residents of the listing country performing transactions in or through those countries or territories (outbound TH/NCJ regime). It is less common, however, for the national lists of TH/NCJs upon which the application of the corresponding national defensive measures is based to be identical to the European list of non-cooperative jurisdictions for tax purposes (the 'EU-List').[3] This asymmetry between the Member States' 'national lists' and

[1] The term 'Tax Haven' has been much discussed from a purely semantic point of view. On the other hand, the use of the term 'Tax Haven' or 'Non-Cooperative Jurisdiction' may not be neutral as to the foundations and objectives of the regime. As these are minor issues, we prefer to leave these terminological discussions aside and use the broad term referred to in the text.

[2] This chapter does not provide a detailed analysis of these regimes. However, a comprehensive overview is given e. g. by Susan Adriaans, Loes van Hulten and Jasper Korving, 'Cooperation with Non-Cooperative Jurisdictions' (2021) 61(8) European Taxation 349, para 6.2.

[3] The authors refer to the official uniform EU-List that was published as Annex I to the Council conclusions on the EU list of non-cooperative jurisdictions for tax purposes on 5 December 2017 (Council Conclusions on the EU list of non-cooperative jurisdictions for tax purposes [2017] OJ 15429/17). At the time this chapter went to press, the list is composed of 16 jurisdictions (American Samoa, Anguilla, Bahamas, British Virgin Islands, Costa Rica, Fiji, Guam, Marshall Islands, Palau, Panama, Russian Federation, Samoa, Trinidad and Tobago, Turks and Caicos Islands, US Virgin Islands and Vanuatu) according to the conclusions on the revised EU-List of non-cooperative jurisdictions for tax purposes, approved by the Council at its meeting held on 14

the ‘EU-List’ should not come as a surprise, considering the latter’s inclusion in the Council conclusions and not in a binding EU legal instrument.[4] Indeed, even after the official adoption of the EU-List, Member States remain free, in principle, to apply national TH/NCJ regimes and, if they have them, to link (or not) the application of their defensive TH/NCJ measures to the European list. Thus, unless a Member State refers solely to the EU-List with respect to the jurisdictions or territories to which its defensive measures apply,[5] its national TH/NCJ regime will necessarily apply to jurisdictions and territories other than those listed in successive versions of the EU-List.

In principle, these asymmetries would be of no legal significance, considering that the EU authorities have deliberately decided for the EU-List not to be a legally binding instrument. However, this chapter demonstrates that the above conclusion may be too hasty and perhaps erroneous, particularly with regard to the consistency of national listings of jurisdictions or territories that are not on the EU-List with EU/EEA law. In order to reach this conclusion, the remainder of this contribution is organised as follows. First, Section 8.2 explores the general circumstances under which national TH/NCJ regimes should be analysed under EU/EEA law. Second, Section 8.3 discusses why the application of defensive TH/NCJ measures might infringe on the fundamental freedoms of the Treaty on the Functioning of the European Union (TFEU), in particular concerning third countries, but also regarding EEA Member States under the Agreement on the European Economic Area (EEA Agreement). Section 8.4 concludes by indicating the effect that the non-inclusion of a jurisdiction in the EU-List should have on the fundamental freedoms’ compatibility analysis referred to above.

8.2 THE SIGNIFICANCE OF EU/EEA LAW FOR NATIONAL TH/NCJ REGIMES

As already mentioned, TH/NCJ regimes consist, in essence, in the application of disadvantageous tax rules to certain transactions carried out in or from the jurisdictions or territories that the regime has decided to classify as TH/NCJ. Although, in principle, there is no obligation to do so, the fact is that most of the domestic TH/NCJ defensive rules refer to direct taxes and, in particular, to

---

February 2023 (Council conclusions on the revised EU list of non-cooperative jurisdictions for tax purposes [2023] 6375/23 FISC 29, <https://data.consilium.europa.eu/doc/document/ST-6375-2023-INIT/en/pdf> accessed 6 December 2023).

4 Ana Paula Dourado, ‘The EU Black List of Third-Country Jurisdictions’ (2018) 46(3) Intertax 178, 180.

5 Something that is not very common in practice (see Adriaans, van Hulten and Korving (n 2) section 6.2).

those levied on the foreign-sourced income of residents and domestic-sourced income of non-residents.[6] Although there are no specific EU competencies in the area of direct taxation, it is almost a truism, at this stage of EU law development, that Member States must exercise their competencies in this field consistently with (primary) EU law and, particularly with the fundamental freedoms laid down in the TFEU. Thus, the disadvantageous tax rules that make up the core of national TH/NCJ regimes must not result in unequal treatment that, according to the fundamental freedoms, proves unjustified or disproportionate.

Notwithstanding the above, it is uncommon, if not unheard of, for EU Member States to include other Member States in their TH/NCJ blacklists.[7] Consequently, one might conclude that an analysis of the compatibility of the national TH/NCJ regimes with EU law would be utterly unnecessary, since there would be no case in which Member States' defensive TH/NCJ measures would infringe on fundamental freedoms. This point of view would, however, be overly reductionist because it would lose sight of the following facts.

First, apart from the so-called 'grandfathering clause' contained in Article 64(1) TFEU and the special clauses contained in Articles 64(3), 65(4), and 66

---

[6] For example, the defensive rules that the OECD recommended introducing or improving to face the phenomena of Harmful Tax Competition mainly referred to corporate income taxation (see OECD, *Harmful Tax Competition. An Emerging Global Issue* (OECD 1998) 37–62). The same applies to the recommendations for defensive measures at the European Union level (see Adriaans, van Hulten and Korving (n 2) section 4.3). The few comparative law studies on this issue have led to the conclusion that most, if not all, national defensive measures relate to direct taxation: Brian Arnold and Patrick Dibout, *Limits on the use of low-tax regimes by multinational businesses: current measures and emerging trends* in (55th congress of the International Fiscal Association, San Francisco, 2001) 21–89.

[7] However, Greece regards several EU Member States (Bulgaria, Cyprus, Hungary, and Ireland) as jurisdictions with a preferential tax regime as they impose a corporate income tax equal or lower than 13,2%, i.e., equal or lower than 60% of the Greek corporate income tax rate of 22% (see the updated list of the Greek Government regarding jurisdictions with a preferential tax regime in Decision A 1027/2023 ('Government's Gazette Bulletin B' 1539/13.3.2023). Moreover, and with significant doubts of legality according to Belgian practitioners' recent statements by the Belgian tax administration allow the inclusion in the corresponding blacklist of jurisdictions qualified by the Global Forum as 'Partially Compliant' with the EOIR, which has facilitated the recent inclusion of Malta (see Nikolaas Van Robbroek, 'Belgium adopts multiple defensive tax measures towards EU blacklisted jurisdictions' (*Risk and Compliance Blog*, 4 January 2021), <https:// riskandcompliance .freshfields .com/ post/ 102gny8/ belgium-adopts-multiple-defensive-tax-measures-towards-eu-blacklisted-jurisdiction> accessed 6 December 2023).

TFEU,[8] the free movement of capital covers not only transactions between Member States, but also transactions between Member States and third countries. For that reason, the free movement of capital can be relied upon when judging the conformity with EU law of defensive measures that affect this freedom[9] and relate to transactions carried out by residents of Member States in TH/NCJs which are not Member States or by residents of those same TH/NCJs carrying out transactions in EU Member States.[10]

Second, the fundamental freedoms, or some of them, have been extended, under reciprocity, to certain non-EU jurisdictions on the basis of international treaties. In this context, mention is usually made to the Free Movement Agreement with Switzerland[11] and several Association Agreements with different jurisdictions,[12] although the EEA Agreement deserves special attention.[13]

---

8 None of these three modulations of the scope of application of the free movement of capital has had any practical effect as they have so far not been used; see Karoline Spies, 'The external dimension of the fundamental freedoms and taxation' in Christiana HJI Panayi, Werner Haslehner and Edoardo Traversa (eds), *Research Handbook on European Taxation Law* (Edward Elgar 2020) 568.

9 Some of the most common defensive rules affect or may affect the free movement of capital. Among them, special mention should be made of CFC rules. In a work of this nature, we cannot dwell, in detail, on the thorough analysis of the fundamental freedom applicable to each defensive rule and, in particular, on the problematic question of whether the freedom of establishment or the free movement of capital applies to a specific case. For a brief analysis of the various defensive measures in the Spanish regime and the fundamental freedom(s) affected, see José Manuel Calderón Carrero and Adolfo J. Martín Jiménez, 'Las normas antiparaíso fiscal españolas y su compatibilidad con el Derecho Comunitario: el caso específico de Malta y Chipre tras la adhesión a la Unión Europea' (2004) 11 Documentos de Trabajo del Instituto de Estudios Fiscales 31.

10 According to CJEU case law, the free movement of capital applies to the relations of a Member State with the overseas countries and territories of another Member State (Case C-384/09 *Prunus SARL and Polonium SA v Directeur des services fiscaux* [2011] ECLI:EU:C:2011:276, para 20). Although the Court has not addressed this additional question, it would be reasonable to understand that the free movement of capital does not apply to movements between a Member State and its own overseas countries and territories as this is a purely internal situation (in this vein: Ben J.M. Terra and Peter J. Wattel, *European Tax Law* (6th edn, Wolters Kluwers 2012) 83).

11 Agreement between the European Community and its Member States, of the one part, and the Swiss Confederation, of the other, on the free movement of persons [2002] OJ L 114/6, art 6.

12 On these Agreements: Daniël S. Smit, 'Company taxation aspects of investment liberalization provisions under EU Association Agreements' in Christina H.J.I. Panayi, Werner Haslehner and Edoardo Traversa (eds), *Research Handbook on European Union Taxation Law* (Edward Elgar Publishing 2020) 611–31.

13 Agreement on the European Economic Area [1994] OJ No L001 (EEA Agreement) 3.

This agreement is of significance for the analysis at stake here, as it implies the application of the fundamental freedoms to transactions carried out in or from the jurisdictions party to the Agreement.[14] This has been compounded by both the Court of Justice of the European Union (CJEU)[15] and the EFTA Court,[16] which have held emphatically that the provisions of the EEA Agreement, insofar as they are identical in substance to corresponding rules in the EEC or the ECSC Treaties,[17] shall be interpreted in conformity with the relevant rulings of the CJEU. In these circumstances, the fundamental freedoms and their possible infringements also affect operations carried out in or from certain EEA Member States which some EU Member States still – in a questionable manner – include in their national lists of TH/NCJs.[18]

8.3 WHEN COULD THE APPLICATION OF DEFENSIVE TH/NCJ MEASURES INFRINGE ON THE FUNDAMENTAL FREEDOMS OF THE TREATY?

National TH/NCJ regimes always follow the same logic: the imposition of a series of burdensome tax measures on transactions carried out by residents of the listing jurisdictions in the TH/NCJ or by residents of TH/NCJ in the listing jurisdictions. Naturally, these measures are not imposed either on purely domestic transactions or on cross-border transactions carried out in

---

14 ibid art 1(2).

15 Case C-471/04 *Finanzamt Offenbach am Main-Land v Keller Holding GmbH* [2006] ECLI:EU:C:2006:143, paras 47–50.

16 Case E-1/03, *EFTA Surveillance Authority vs. The Republic of Iceland* [2003] para 27.

17 There is practically unanimous agreement that the EEA Agreement incorporates a regulation of the fundamental freedoms almost identical to that contained in its day in the Treaty on the Functioning of the European Union (see Thor Leegard, 'Impact of the European Economic Area Agreement on Direct Taxation: A Norwegian Perspective' in Xavier Oberson, Reitan Tonie and Frederik Zimmer (eds), *Chapter VI – The impact of prohibition of discrimination and restriction granted under the EC Treaty in non-EU States (Switzerland and Norway)* (for the EU Freedoms and Taxation EATLP Congress, Paris 3–5 June 2004, IBFD 2006 234).

18 See the respective lists of Belgium, Greece and Slovenia that also include Liechtenstein regarding its corporate income tax rate of 12,5% that is lower or equal than the respective threshold of 15% (Belgium), 13,2% (Greece) and 12,5% (Slovenia), but higher than the corporate income tax rate of Bulgaria (10%) and Hungary (9%), which are both EU Member States. Vice versa, Spain has consequently resigned to include Liechtenstein from its list of NCJ in 2023 (see Ministerio de Hacienda y Funcion Publica, *BOE-A-2023-3508* (2023). Portugal still lists Liechtenstein, although it fulfils all so-called guidelines Portugal is referring to.

or from jurisdictions or territories not classified as TH/NCJ. Such disparate treatment(s) need not necessarily involve discrimination that is forbidden under EU/EEA law. However, in line with the consistent case law of the CJEU, different treatment of comparable situations that is either not justified, or justified but not proportional, may result in an infringement of the fundamental freedoms enshrined in the TFEU. The following is a brief analysis of these structural elements (i.e. comparability, justification and proportionality) based essentially on the case law of the CJEU, which may eventually determine the infringement of fundamental freedoms by domestic TH/NCJ measures or regimes affecting EEA Member States or any other state (in the case of measures affecting the free movement of capital). As the free movement of capital and the other fundamental freedoms share many elements, the analysis will be carried out jointly.[19]

8.3.1 Comparability

The fundamental freedoms do not prohibit all types of different treatment between domestic and cross-border taxpayers or transactions, but only those concerning comparable situations. In this respect, defensive TH/NCJ measures imply four basic types of unequal treatment, which correspond to the possible four dimensions of comparability: unequal treatment of resident and non-resident taxpayers and more burdensome for the latter (inbound vertical comparability); unequal treatment for transactions carried out by a resident in his state of residence and outside that state which is more burdensome for the latter (outbound vertical comparability); unequal treatment of taxpayers who are non-residents but reside in different jurisdictions (inbound horizontal comparability); and finally, unequal treatment of cross-border transactions by residents in different jurisdictions (horizontal outbound comparability). The authors have already examined the different facets of comparability in previous works, where the interested reader is directed: in summary, some of these different treatments do not refer to comparable situations, and are therefore immune to an analysis of discrimination based on fundamental freedoms.[20] However, the particular features of this work do not allow us to explore this issue further. For this reason, we shall take comparability for granted, particularly taking into account two main factors. First, the CJEU's response to

[19] Only when some peculiarity affects the free movement of capital the corresponding exception will be made.

[20] Particularly regarding inbound vertical comparability, limited cases of outbound vertical comparability and horizontal comparability; see: Andrés Báez, 'El negro futuro de la lista negra española de paraísos fiscales' (2019) 439 Estudios Financieros Revista de Contabilidad y Tributación 37, 65–69 and 74–77.

the issue of whether the fundamental freedoms only prohibit discrimination, or any restriction applied without distinction of domestic and cross-border situations, has been rather vague. This means that the importance of the very concept of comparability is at risk of being several downplayed,[21] to the point that there is a growing body of academic and professional opinion that suggests giving up the very concept of comparability altogether.[22] Second, the CJEU has traditionally been reluctant to recognise 'horizontal comparability' and, therefore, many of the different treatments enshrined in domestic TH/NCJ defensive measures would prove immune to an EU/EEA law discrimination analysis.[23] However, this case law must be put into the context of the problem at stake here. These cases analyse different treatments originating from a Double Taxation Convention and, by denying comparability between two non-residents of different Member States, attempt to not compromise the principle of reciprocity in public international law.[24]

Nevertheless, different treatments originating in the domestic law of Member States – among them domestic TH/NCJ defensive measures – should be screened out of these pronouncements, as the risks associated with a 'Most -Favoured-Nation-Treatment' in a treaty context simply do not exist. This is exactly the idea defended more recently by the CJEU when stating: '… [the free movement of workers] also prohibits discrimination between non-resident workers if such discrimination leads to nationals of certain Member States being unduly favoured in comparison with others'.[25] We are faced, in fact,

---

[21] José Manuel Calderón Carrero and Adolfo Martín Jiménez, *Derecho tributario de la Unión Europea* (Wolter Kluwers CISS 2019) 102–108.

[22] Juliane Kokott, *EU Tax Law. A Handbook* (Beck-Hart-Nomos 2022) 166.

[23] Case C-376/03 *D. v Inspecteur van de Belastingdienst/Particulieren/ Ondernemingen buitenland te Heerlen* [2005] ECLI:EU:C:2005:424, paras 53–63; Case C-374/04 *Test Claimants in Class IV of the ACT Group Litigation v Commissioners of Inland Revenue* [2006] ECLI:EU:C:2006:773; Case C-194/06 *Staatssecretaris van Financiën v Orange European Smallcup Fund* [2008] ECLI:EU:C:2008:289, paras 61-63; Case C-176/15 *Guy Riskin and Geneviève Timmermans v État belge* [2016] ECLI:EU:C:2016:488, paras 82–93.

[24] The fear that horizontal comparability may open the door to a 'most-favoured nation treatment' that would overturn the bilateral paradigm that still governs such treaties has always been present in the Court of Justice Case Law. Critical on this phenomenon: Andrés Báez Moreno and José Manuel Calderón Carrero, 'The Columbus Container Services ECJ Case and Its Consequences: A Lost Opportunity to Shed Light on the Scope of the Non-discrimination Principle' (2009), 37(4) Intertax 212, 216–17.

[25] Case C-512/13 *Sopora v Staatssecretaris van Financiën* [2015] ECLI:EU:C:2015:108, para 25. This approach to horizontal comparability might prove consistent with the aforementioned case law if, as rightly stated by Kokott, the reciprocity and overall balance of double taxation conventions is a true ground of justification

with an unambiguous recognition of the EU/EEA law relevance for 'horizontal discrimination'.[26]

8.3.2 Justification

Three main objectives are often alleged to support different treatments inherent to national TH/NCJ regimes: the prevention of abnormally low taxation, the effectiveness of fiscal supervision, and the need to prevent abuse of the law.[27] The effectiveness of fiscal supervision is one of the most common reasons (sometimes even the only reason)[28] for listing jurisdictions and is linked to the lack of proper exchange of information in the corresponding jurisdiction. In this context, it seems clear, in principle, that the different treatments inherent to national TH/NCJ regimes might be justified, from an EU/EEA law perspective, by the need to preserve the effectiveness of fiscal supervision,[29] which the CJEU has repeatedly recognised as a mandatory requirement of public interest[30] and has linked to the existence of administrative cooperation instruments.[31]

8.3.3 Proportionality

The practical importance of the effectiveness of fiscal supervision as a mandatory requirement of public interest and, therefore, as a justification for intra-EU unequal treatment has extraordinarily dropped. Indeed, the existence of an EU

---

even though the ECJ has examined it under the heading of comparability (Kokott (n 22) 344).

[26] Eric Kemmeren, 'Sopora: A Welcome Landmark Decision on Horizontal Comparison' (2015) 24(4) EC Tax Review 178, 179–82; Michael Lang, 'Totgesagte leben länger: Horizontale Vergleichbarkeit und die Verwirklichung des Binnenmarkts' (2016) 26(3) Steuer und Wirtschaft International 118, 128; Georg Kofler, 'Chapter 11 "Horizontal Discrimination" in European Tax Law' in Heike Jochum, Peter Essers, Michael Lang, Norbert Winkeljohann and Bertil Wiman (eds), *Practical Problems in European and International Tax Law: Essays in Honor of Manfred Mössner* (IBFD 2017) chapter 11.5; Smit (n 12) 623. On the relevance of this decision for an EU-Law analysis of TH/NCJ regimes: Adriaans, van Hulten and Korving (n 2) 4.2.

[27] These justifications typically coincide with the abstract legal criteria upon which the inclusion of jurisdictions in TH/NCJ lists is based. All these criteria (justifications) appeared in the OECD Harmful Tax Competition Report 1998 (OECD (n 6) 22–25).

[28] This criterion became in fact the only one handled by the OECD since the 2001 progress report (OECD, *The OECD's project on harmful tax practices: the 2001 progress report* (OECD 2001) 7 and 10.

[29] Calderón Carrero and Martín Jiménez (n 9) 34; Báez (n 20) 76.

[30] Kokott (n 22) 315–16.

[31] ibid 320–21.

administrative cooperation legal framework[32] has made it more difficult for EU Member States to defend the proportionality of those national measures – among them domestic TH/NCJ defensive measures – imposing burdensome tax treatments for cross-border transactions on the pretext that the facts underlying these transactions are more difficult to monitor than pure domestic constellations.[33] However, the diminished importance of the effectiveness of fiscal supervision as an overriding requirement of general interest might prove immaterial in the context here at stake, as EU Member States do not include other Member States in their respective TH/NCJ blacklists. Nevertheless, it should be borne in mind again that the free movement of capital also covers transactions between Member States and third countries and that all fundamental freedoms have been extended to transactions between EU Member States and states party to the EEA Agreement. This has not gone unnoticed by the CJEU, which has, on many occasions, expressed its views on the effectiveness of fiscal supervision as a mandatory requirement of public interest concerning the free movement of capital with third countries.

The CJEU has repeatedly claimed that the reduced importance of the effectiveness of aforementioned fiscal supervision cannot be transferred immediately to movements of capital between Member States and third Countries. The legal contexts of intra-European and extra-European movements – particularly concerning the tax cooperation framework – are too different to draw such a parallel.[34] Beyond this general statement, this case law contains an extremely relevant nuance: when exchange of information mechanisms do exist with the corresponding jurisdiction, enabling the tax authorities to verify the information submitted by taxpayers, the situation parallels that of intra-European movements and, therefore, burdensome tax treatments for cross-border transactions might prove disproportionate and thus be in breach

---

[32] Essentially, the Directives 77/799/EEC (Mutual Assistance Directive) and DAC1 but also Directive 2003/48/EC (Savings Directive).

[33] The case law of the Court of Justice on this lack of proportionality is abundant. See: Calderón Carrero and Martín Jiménez (n 21) 113; Kokott, (n 22) 320–21.

[34] Case C-101/05 *Skatteverket v A* [2007] ECLI:EU:C:2007:804, para 60; Case C-540/07, *Commission v Italy* [2009] ECLI:EU:C:2009:717, para 82; Joined Cases C-436/08 and C-437/08, *Haribo Lakritzen, Österreichische Salinen v Finanzamt Linz* [2011] ECLI:EU:C:2011:61, para 65; Case C-72/09, *Établissements Rimbaud SA v Directeur général des impôts and Directeur des services fiscaux d'Aix-en-Provence* [2010] ECLI:EU:C:2010:645, para 40; Case C-267/09 *Commission v Portugal* [2011] ECLI:EU:C:2011:273, para 54; Case C-190/12 *Emerging Markets Series of DFA Investment Trust Company* [2014] ECLI:EU:C:2014:249, para 82; Case C-135/17, *X GmbH v Finanzamt Stuttgart – Körperschaften* [2016] ECLI:EU:C:2019:136), para 90; Case C-572/20 *ACC Silicones Ltd v Bundeszentralamt für Steuern* [2022] ECLI:EU:C:2022:469, para 27.

of the free movement of capital (third countries) or the fundamental freedoms (EEA Member States).

The oldest decisions of the CJEU in this respect seemed to suggest that the mere existence of a tax convention providing for the exchange of information could be enough to minimise the differences between EU and EEA Member States and third countries.[35] In more recent times, the CJEU[36] has indicated that national courts should examine whether the undertakings of mutual assistance between a Member State and the concerned jurisdiction provide mechanisms for the exchange of information capable of enabling the Member State tax authorities to verify, where necessary, the information provided by the taxpayers, in order to determine that they operate within a regulatory framework equivalent to that of the European Union.[37] Hence, it may appear at first glance that the proportionality analysis of domestic TH/NCJ defensive measures, in those cases in which mutual assistance legal instruments do exist with listed jurisdictions, is left to the discretion of the national courts or the Commission when carrying out the equivalence analysis described above. In our view, the EU list of non-cooperative jurisdictions for tax purposes can significantly limit this discretion, as will be shown in the next concluding section.

8.4 THE EU-LIST SCREENING PROCESS AS A GUIDE AND A LEGAL LIMIT FOR NATIONAL DEFENSIVE MEASURES RESTRICTING FREE MOVEMENTS OF CAPITALS TO THIRD COUNTRIES TH/NCJ

The non-inclusion or the exclusion of a particular jurisdiction from the EU-List depends on the cumulative compliance with several tax good governance criteria,[38] among which so-called tax transparency merits particular attention in this context. In this respect, a jurisdiction could avoid being listed only by meeting the following requisites cumulatively: (1) Possessing

[35] Case C-101/05 *Skatteverket v A* [2007] ECLI:EU:C:2007:804, para 67; Case C-540/07 (n 34) para 71; Case C-436/08 and C-437/08 (n 34) para 66 (referring to any undertaking of mutual assistance); Case C-72/09 (n 34) para 41; Case C-267/09 (n 34) para 55.

[36] Case C-190/12 (n 34), para 88; Case C-135/17 (n 34) para 94 (less categorical).

[37] Kokott suggests that the responsibility of the national courts (in preliminary references) and the Commission (in infringement procedures) to assess the sufficiency of these international agreements to verify the information submitted by the taxpayers has been present throughout the case law of the Court (Kokott (n 22) 322).

[38] See Annex to the Council Conclusions on the criteria and process leading to the establishment of the EU list of non-cooperative jurisdictions for tax purposes [2016] OJ 14166/16, 4.

at least a 'Largely Compliant' rating by the Global Forum with respect to the Automatic Exchange of Information (AEOI) standard (the Common Reporting Standard – CRS); (2) Possessing at least a 'Largely Compliant' rating by the Global Forum with respect to the OECD Exchange of Information on Request (EOIR) standard; and (3) Having ratified, agreed to ratify, be in the process of ratifying, or committed to the entry into force, within a reasonable time frame, of the OECD Multilateral Convention on Mutual Administrative Assistance (MCMAA) in Tax Matters or having a network of exchange arrangements in force by 31 December 2018 which is sufficiently broad to cover all Member States, effectively allowing both EOIR and AEOI.[39]

Despite the strong criticism it has attracted,[40] it cannot be denied that the tax transparency requirements imposed by the screening and listing process of the EU-List are precise and demanding. Despite its lack of legally binding nature, the transparency analysis that provides the foundation of the EU-List may be helpful for national courts or the Commission in assessing the equivalence of the EU and the extra-EU tax cooperation frameworks upon which, according to relevant case law, the proportionality of unequal treatments affecting the free movement of capital must be based. In a nutshell, what greater proof of this equivalence can one reasonably ask for than the fact that the Council has excluded or delisted a jurisdiction precisely because it meets a set of (very demanding) criteria? And, to take it a step further, could national courts, the Commission, or even the CJEU not be asked, as a requirement of the principle of legal certainty, to automatically conclude on the equivalence between the EU and the non-EU mutual assistance framework based upon the criteria decided by the Council when screening and (de)listing jurisdictions? A minimum degree of (legal) coherence would oblige that this question be answered in the affirmative.

8.5 CONCLUSION

Many EU Member States focus on the fight against the use of tax havens or non-cooperative jurisdictions by multinational enterprises, for instance by elaborating national lists of taxwise 'suspicious' jurisdictions to which a set

39 ibid section I, para 1.1.

40 Ana Paula Dourado (n 4) 179–80; Alexandra Koutsouva 'The European Union's List of Non-Cooperative Jurisdictions for Tax Purposes' (2020) 29(4) EC Tax Review 178, 193–94; Adriaans, van Hulten and Korving (n 2) 4.2 and 4.3. In less academic terms see IFC, 'Is the EU tax blacklist more political than technical?' (*IFC Articles*, 8 February 2023), <https://www.ifcreview.com/articles/2023/february/is-the-eu-tax-blacklist-more-political-than-technical/> accessed 6 December 2023, in particular the contributions by Cobham, Kenney, Dukharam, Dwyer, Hoor and Traversa.

of disadvantageous tax rules is linked. The respective national lists are usually not identical to the EU-List of non-cooperative jurisdictions for tax purposes, generating an asymmetry between the Member States' national lists and the EU-List.

The EU Member States remain free to apply disadvantageous tax rules and to link these to a list of jurisdictions, either a national list or the EU-List. However, this chapter has shown that the use of different types of lists might be ambiguous and perhaps erroneous. It is questionable whether it is in line with EU/EEA law to list jurisdictions or territories on a national list that are not on the EU-List. The EU listing process, after all, depends on the cumulative compliance with several tax good governance criteria, among which are the so-called tax transparency conditions. As such, these tax transparency requirements imposed by the screening and listing process of the EU-List are precise and demanding and, therefore, the application of different criteria for national lists, which leads to the asymmetries, should be carefully reasoned for.

Thus, even though the EU-List is not a legally binding instrument, the transparency analysis behind the EU-List might be a helpful tool in order to achieve lists that are in line with the free movement of capital principles. If a national court or the Commission is to determine whether there is a sufficient level of transparency in an extra-EU relation, it can use the transparency criteria in its assessment. What greater proof of this equivalence can one reasonably ask than the fact that the Council has excluded or delisted a jurisdiction precisely because it meets a set of (very demanding) criteria? Besides that, it would be a welcome addition if the national courts, the Commission, or even the CJEU were to be requested, as a requirement of the principle of legal certainty, to automatically conclude on the equivalence between the EU and the non-EU mutual assistance framework, based upon the criteria decided by the Council when screening and (de)listing jurisdictions. This can only be achieved if a minimum degree of (legal) coherence is achieved.

9. Exchange of information and transparency and the NCJ listing process: exchange of information and the level playing field of taxation

Martin Wenz, Tobias Koegl and Kasem Zotkaj

9.1 EXCHANGE OF INFORMATION AS AN INTEGRAL PART OF THE LEVEL PLAYING FIELD OF TAXATION

International and European tax transparency standards regarding the various concepts and forms of exchange of information (EoI) for tax purposes are an important part of the so-called Level Playing Field of Taxation (LPFT). Among other functions and applications, the exchange of information constitutes one of the criteria to identify non-cooperative jurisdictions (NCJs) for tax purposes. This contribution examines the inclusion of exchange of information as a listing criterion applied by an extensive group of institutions and organisations and, furthermore, analyses the application of such criterion to derive non-cooperative jurisdictions lists. In addition, other listing criteria are identified and used. Different lists of non-cooperative jurisdictions may be biased or misleading if the listing criteria do not reflect current tax and legal dispositions from a national and international perspective. Therefore, a reliable and coherent international level playing field of taxation and an inclusive process for listing non-cooperative jurisdictions is needed to achieve the objectives of such lists; former non-cooperative jurisdictions complying with the listing criteria of different institutions and organisations have to be recognised as cooperative jurisdictions for tax purposes and should participate equally in the international level playing field of taxation.

There are different mechanisms for exchanging information for tax purposes upon request, including group requests, spontaneous or even automatic. They all aim to increase tax transparency and create a broad information exchange network to combat tax evasion and help governments to secure a higher proportion of tax revenues.[1] Among several other aspects, the lack of information exchange has been widely used as a criterion to identify so-called tax havens and tax haven regimes. International governmental and non-governmental organisations, national authorities and academic institutions and scholars deliberately rely on the lack of information exchange to identify and list certain jurisdictions as non-cooperative or so-called tax haven. Thus, for the purpose of this contribution, the terms non-cooperative jurisdiction and tax haven will be used synonymously.

There is an extensive group of institutions and organisations that have shaped the overall perception of NCJs over the years, from the definition to the listing criteria and lists. Major intergovernmental organisations such as the OECD[2] and the EU,[3] play an active and significant role in this field. Non-governmental organisations (NGOs) such as Tax Justice Network (TJN),[4] Oxfam[5] and The South Centre[6] should be mentioned, particularly regarding their research studies and publications in this area in recent years. In addition, national tax and financial authorities[7] as well as academic studies and publications[8] are seen as further influential components in the context of so-called NCJ. The above-mentioned organisations have at least one element in common

---

1 OECD, *Model Agreement on Exchange of Information on Tax Matters* (OECD 2002).

2 OECD, *Harmful Tax Competition: An Emerging Global Issue* (OECD 1998).

3 Council Conclusions on the EU list of non-cooperative jurisdictions for tax purposes [2017] OJ 15429/17.

4 Tax Justice Network, 'Identifying Tax Havens and Offshore Finance Centers' (2007).

5 Oxfam, *Assessing Jurisdictions against EU Listing Criteria: Oxfam Methodology* (Oxfam 2017).

6 Jahanzeb Akhtar and Verónica Grondona, 'Tax Haven Listing in Multiple Hues: Blind, Winking or Conniving?' (2019) South Centre Research Paper 94, <https://www.southcentre.int/wp-content/uploads/2019/04/RP94_Tax-Haven-Listing-in-Multiple-Hues-Blind-Winking-or-Conniving_EN.pdf> accessed 6 December 2023.

7 Order HFP/115/2023 of 9 February determining the countries and territories, as well as harmful tax regimes, that are considered to be non-cooperative jurisdictions (2023), Appendix IV. Non-cooperative jurisdictions.

8 Mihir Desai, Fritz Foley and James Hines, 'The Demand for Tax Haven Operations' (2006) 90(3) Journal of Public Economics 513; Dhammika Dharmapala and James Hines, 'Which Countries become Tax Havens?' (2009) 93(9–10) Journal of Public Economics 1058; James Hines and Eric Rice, 'Fiscal Paradise: Foreign Tax Havens and American Business' (1994) 109(1) Quarterly Journal of Economics 149; Gabriel Zucman, 'The Missing Wealth of Nations: Are Europe and the U.S. net Debtors or net Creditors' (2013) 128(3) Quarterly Journal of Economics 1321–64; Martin Wenz, Tobias Kögl and Kasem Zotkaj, *A Meta-Analysis of Studies on Tax Havens* (University of Liechtenstein 2020).

in qualifying jurisdictions as non-cooperative for tax purposes: a lack of EoI. However, when considering the key factors and criteria for identifying NCJs, there are other tax factors besides tax transparency and exchange of information that are used as proxies as well.[9]

It is observed that specific forms of EoI have been used as criteria, among others, to name a jurisdiction a tax haven, non-cooperative or even non-compliant. Commonly used in the 1970s, 1980s or even 1990s, various international institutions, governmental organisations and academic publications referred to banking secrecy as an instrument utilised by tax havens.[10] Banking secrecy embodied by the lack of EoI was therefore accused to help individuals and legal entities to evade taxes. Only in the late 1990s did the concept of retrieving and sharing information replace banking secrecy with an EoI. Accordingly, in the 1998 OECD report 'Harmful Tax Competition: An Emerging Global Issue',[11] the concept of EoI for tax purposes was used as an instrument to 'record' jurisdictions as being tax havens. However, the principles of EoI gained significance with the establishment in 2000 and the restructuring in 2009 of the Global Forum on Transparency and Exchange of Information for tax purposes and the request for agreements on EoI for tax purposes.[12] Seemingly pushed by the financial crisis, the G20 and in particularly the Global Forum recognised the necessity to address tax evasion and the implementation of internationally agreed tax standards on transparency and exchange of information. Thus, in April 2009, the G20 issued an 'Action Plan for Recovery and Reform'[13] at their London Summit and agreed on strengthening financial supervision and regulation and on taking action against NCJs, including tax havens, thus putting an end to the era of banking secrecy.[14] Accordingly, regarding the meeting of the Global Forum in Mexico in September 2009, when the Global Forum was restructured, it published its annual review 'Towards a Level Playing Field', an annual assessment of jurisdictions on matters closely linked to exchange of information upon request on tax matters.[15] These events mark a tone setting moment for tax transparency, followed by the decision of the G20 Finance Ministers and Central Bank

---

[9] Harmful and/or preferential tax regimes, no or low taxation, unfair taxation.

[10] Milton Grundy, *Grundy's tax havens: A world survey* (3rd edn, Sweet & Maxwell Ltd 1974); Hines and Rice (n 8); André Beauchamp, *Guide mondial des paradis fiscaux* (Bernard Grasset 1983).

[11] OECD (n 2).

[12] OECD, *Tax co-operation 2009: Towards a level playing field: 2009 assessment by the Global Forum on Transparency and Exchange of Information* (OECD 2009).

[13] OECD/G20, *G20 Action Plan for Recovery and Reform: London Summit – Leaders' Statement* (OECD 2009).

[14] ibid.

[15] OECD (n 12).

Governors in April 2013, to endorse automatic EoI as the expected new international standard.[16] In addition, the Base Erosion and Profit Shifting (BEPS) project was initiated in 2013.[17] The goals of the BEPS Action Plan, consisting of 15 actions and standards, with currently only four minimum standards, are explicitly to tackle tax avoidance, to improve the coherence of international taxation and to increase tax transparency.[18] In addition to the comprehensive development towards a global LPFT focusing on EoI for tax purposes, the EU institutionalised matters of EoI regarding the LPFT as a criterion in order to generate a list of NCJ in December 2017 as well. In order to fully understand the listing criteria, the creation of a list, and its consequences, a closer look at the EU NCJ listing process is outlined in the following sections.

9.2 THE EU LIST OF NON-COOPERATIVE JURISDICTIONS FOR TAX PURPOSES

9.2.1 Listing Process

The EU has been intensively addressing and regularly reporting on the issue of NCJs since December 2017. However, the thematic debate began as early as 1997 with the establishment of the Code of Conduct Group for Business Taxation (CoCG)[19] with a package of measures to tackle harmful tax competition to help reducing distortions within the Single Market. Moreover, in 2016, a report by the Council of the EU was published with specific identification criteria for NCJs and instructions for the establishment of an EU list of NCJs for tax purposes.[20] The result of the report was the precise definition of rather objective and comprehensible criteria for identifying NCJs for tax purposes, which can be interpreted as the establishment of identification criteria for qualifying tax jurisdictions as NCJs.[21]

The criteria of the EU list of NCJs follow a rule-based approach. In this approach, the identification criteria – i.e., 'Tax transparency, Fair taxation, and Implementation of anti-BEPS measures' – are used *a priori* and applied to all

---

[16] OECD, *A step change in tax transparency: OECD Report for the G8 Summit* (OECD 2013).

[17] OECD, *Addressing Base Erosion and Profit Shifting* (OECD 2013).

[18] See OECD, *BEPS Actions* <https:// www .oecd .org/ tax/ beps/ beps -actions/ > accessed 6 December 2023.

[19] Conclusions of The Ecofin Council Meeting on 1 December 1997 concerning taxation policy (98/C 2/01) [1997] OJ C 2.

[20] Council Conclusions on the criteria for and process leading to the establishment of the EU list of noncooperative jurisdictions for tax purposes [2016] OJ 14166/16 Annex.

[21] ibid.

jurisdictions by means of a screening procedure[22] to evaluate so-called 'tax good governance'.[23] The resulting list is then used to distinguish 'cooperative' and 'non-cooperative' jurisdictions. The methodology for compiling the list of NCJs is thus based on a three-step process: scoreboard, screening and listing.[24] However, the EU does not disclose the exact way the screening methodology is conducted.[25] The CoCG is responsible for the listing process within the EU. When a jurisdiction is placed on the EU list, it is notified by the CoCG. The reasons for the inclusion of a jurisdiction and the measures that need to be taken for its removal are communicated bilaterally.[26] Thus, bilateral dialogues between the CoCG and the respective jurisdiction should help to identify measures proposed by the CoCG and to support the latter in being delisted.[27] Subsequently, the jurisdictions concerned should make formal commitments to eliminate their harmful tax practices. The CoCG assesses whether the commitments have been implemented and comply with the identification criteria, and the EU updates the list of NCJs accordingly from time to time.[28]

The criteria 'Tax transparency, Fair Taxation, and Implementation of anti-BEPS measures' are used to evaluate tax good governance and to generate the EU list of NCJ, which are line for line laid out below:[29]

1. Tax transparency criteria:
   a. The jurisdiction should possess at least a 'Largely Compliant' rating by the Global Forum with respect to the Automatic Exchange of Information (AEOI).
   b. The jurisdiction should possess at least a 'Largely Compliant' rating by the Global Forum with respect to the Exchange of Information on Request (EOIR).
   c. Ratification of the OECD Multilateral Convention on Mutual Administrative Assistance in Tax Matters (MCMAA) or have

22 General Secretariat of the Council of the European Union, *Code of Conduct Group (Business Taxation): Report to the Council – Endorsement* (OJ 14114/19, Council of the European Union 2019).

23 Council Conclusions on the criteria for and process leading to the establishment of the EU list of noncooperative jurisdictions for tax purposes (n 20).

24 Ana P. Dourado, 'The EU Black List of Third-Country Jurisdictions' (2018) 46(3) Intertax 178.

25 Oxfam (n 5).

26 Council Conclusions on the criteria for and process leading to the establishment of the EU list of noncooperative jurisdictions for tax purposes (n 20).

27 Council Conclusions on the EU list of non-cooperative jurisdictions for tax purposes (n 3).

28 ibid.

29 Council Conclusions on the criteria for and process leading to the establishment of the EU list of noncooperative jurisdictions for tax purposes (n 20).

a network of exchange arrangements in place that covers all EU member states. Exchange of information regarding beneficial ownership is to be incorporated as a criterion at a later stage. Initially, the EU only required jurisdictions to comply with two criteria to avoid being placed on the list, but since June 2019, a jurisdiction is considered compliant only if it meets all three tax transparency criteria.[30]

2. Fair taxation:
   a. No regulations on special tax treatments in accordance with the Code of Conduct for Business Taxation.
   b. No regulations on the creation of offshore structures with the aim of attracting foreign profits.
3. Implementation of anti-BEPS measures:
   a. Commitment to implement BEPS minimum standards (harmful tax measures, treaty shopping, country-by-country reporting, and dispute resolution).
   b. Positive peer-review assessments for the effective implementation of the anti-BEPS minimum standard.

In 2017, the EU published its first list of NCJs. This list included 72 tax jurisdictions. The distinctive feature of the list was that only 17 jurisdictions qualified directly as 'non-cooperative' and were thus placed on Annex I, whereas the remaining 55 jurisdictions sufficiently committed to reform their tax laws and to implement the international tax standards in a timely manner and thus were placed on Annex II and remained subject to a close monitoring until their commitments sufficiently executed.[31] During the first few years that the EU list came into existence, updates and revisions of the list took place irregularly. In 2018, the list was updated twice, whereas in 2019 it was updated five times, meaning insufficient time was given to the EU Member States to amend domestic legislation when needed. In order to consider future developments in 'Tax transparency', 'Fair taxation', and 'Implementation of anti-BEPS measures', the CoCG has committed to limit updates of the list to twice a year starting from 2020.[32]

9.2.2 Counter Measures

Once a jurisdiction is listed as an NCJ, i.e., within Annex I, the consequences are evident. In the conclusions of the Council of the EU of December 2017, it

[30] Council Conclusions on the EU list of non-cooperative jurisdictions for tax purposes (n 3).

[31] ibid.

[32] General Secretariat of the Council (n 22).

is stated that sanctions or defensive measures should be implemented against jurisdictions that are listed. In a summary statement adopted by the Council of the EU in December 2019, on the guidelines developed by the CoCG on the coordination of defensive measures against NCJ, Member States agreed that such defensive tax measures should be implemented nationally as of January 2021.[33] As a result, Member States agreed to implement at least one of the following four legislative measures:[34]

1. Non-deductibility of costs: Member states are to deny the deductibility of costs and payments to the extent that they are directed to companies or individuals that are on the list of NCJs. The measure is intended to cover, for example, interest, royalties, and other payments for intellectual property (IP) and service fees.
2. Rules for Controlled Foreign Companies (CFC): Member States are to include in the taxpayer's tax base income derived from companies that are resident or have a permanent establishment in a jurisdiction included in the list of NCJs. Member States may apply these measures in accordance with the provisions of Articles 7 and 8 of the Anti-Tax Avoidance Directive (ATAD).
3. Withholding tax measures: Member States should apply a higher withholding tax rate on payments of interest, royalties, service fees or remuneration if these payments are made to jurisdictions on the list of NCJs. Alternatively, or in combination with this measure, Member States may also consider applying a specific withholding tax on such payments.
4. Limitation of participation exemption on shareholder dividends: Member States that have national participation exemption rules may deny or limit such participation exemptions if dividends originate from jurisdictions that are on the list of NCJs.

Despite the high expectations for Member States to implement these tax defensive measures, it remains unclear how strong the call in this regard exactly is. Neither the CoCG nor the Council of the EU made it completely clear whether Member States are obliged to implement national legislative measures on the listed jurisdictions or are simply invited to do so.[35] Nevertheless, as of

---

[33] ibid.
[34] ibid.
[35] Susan Adriaans, Loes van Hulten and Jasper Korving, 'Cooperation with Non-Cooperative Jurisdictions' (2021) 61(8) European Taxation 349, 352–353.

November 2021, 26 Member States apply or are committed to apply at least one of the four tax defensive measures (Table 9.1).[36]

Table 9.1 *Legislative defensive measures adopted by each Member State*

Member States	Non-deductibility of costs	CFC rules	Participation exemption	Withholding tax measures
Austria	–	x	–	–
Belgium	x	x	x	–
Bulgaria	x	–	x	x
Croatia	–	x	–	x
Cyprus	–	–	–	x
Czech Republic	–	x	–	–
Denmark	x	–	–	x
Estonia	x	–	x	x
Finland	–	x	–	–
France	x	x	x	x
Germany	x	x	x	x
Greece	x	–	–	–
Hungary	–	x	–	–
Ireland	–	x	–	–
Italy	–	–	–	–
Latvia	x	x	x	x
Lithuania	x	x	x	x
Luxembourg	x	–	–	–
Malta	–	–	x	–
Netherlands	–	x	–	x
Poland	–	x	–	–
Portugal	x	x	x	x
Romania	x	–	–	–
Slovakia	x	–	x	x
Slovenia	x	–	x	–
Spain	x	x	–	x
Sweden	x	x	–	–

Source: Council of the European Union, 'Code of Conduct Group (Business Taxation) – Report to the Council' (OJ 14230/21, November 2021).

[36] General Secretariat of the Council, 'Code of Conduct Group (Business Taxation) – Report to the Council' (OJ 14230/21, Council of the European Union 2021). For an

In addition to the four tax defensive measures, at least one of the following three administrative measures should also be applied:[37]

1. Increased monitoring of transactions;
2. Increased risk audits for taxpayers benefiting from arrangements of listed jurisdictions; or
3. Increased risk audits for taxpayers using tax schemes involving listed jurisdictions.

The aim of these guidelines is to implement a holistic coordination of defensive measures for all Member States applicable to NCJs for as long as they are on the EU list. The EU list of NCJs, together with the defensive measures, is intended to bring a positive change in tax fairness, as both instruments are preventive in nature and yet send a strong signal to the countries concerned.[38] The Council of the EU emphasises that regardless of the defensive measure chosen, each Member State should ensure that the measure(s) bring a positive change leading to the removal of jurisdictions from the list of NCJs.

9.3 LISTING CRITERIA AND PROCESSES BY OTHER ORGANISATIONS AND INSTITUTIONS

Besides the EU, other organisations and institutions have also addressed the issue of so-called tax havens as well as developed criteria for their classification. Below, the respective criteria of the OECD and TJN are outlined.

With its 1998 report 'Harmful Tax Competition: An Emerging Global Issue',[39] the OECD played a pioneering role worldwide in creating a level playing field for fair taxation. The term 'Harmful Tax Practices' (a synonym for tax practices that are considered to be unfair and therefore harmful) was defined by the following criteria:[40] Low taxes on income, lack of information exchange, lack of transparency and no substantial economic activities. Since

update see also KPMG, *EU Defensive measures against non-cooperative jurisdictions for tax purposes* (2023) 6.

[37] General Secretariat of the Council (n 22).

[38] ibid.

[39] OECD (n 2).

[40] ibid.

2009, the OECD has focused on EoI for tax purposes and the adjusted classification criteria are the following:[41]

1. Status 'largely compliant' in the peer review process of the 'Global Forum on Transparency and Exchange of Information for Tax Purposes' on the exchange of information on request (EOIR).
2. Issuance of a declaration of commitment to implement the 'Common Reporting Standard' (CRS) for the automatic exchange of information.
3. Participation in the Multilateral Convention on Mutual Administrative Assistance in Tax Matters.

In addition, TJN (a major NGO) deals with the issue of tax avoidance, tax evasion and the identification of tax havens.[42] In a report published in 2019, TJN created a 'Corporate Tax Haven Index' (CTHI) with the aim of providing a statistically valid measure of how intensively all tax jurisdictions worldwide provide opportunities for tax avoidance and thus qualify as a tax haven. The five main indicators used to qualify jurisdictions as tax haven are:[43]

1. Lowest Available Corporate Income Tax Rate: Determines the lowest available corporate tax rate for all companies domiciled in a jurisdiction.
2. Loopholes and Gaps: Examines whether significant tax exemptions exist (e.g., sectoral exemptions, tax holidays, economic zones, patent boxes, etc.).
3. Transparency: Assesses the effectiveness of a national implementation of various unilateral, bilateral and multilateral transparency regulations.
4. Anti-Avoidance: Analysis the effectiveness of rules to prevent tax evasion and profit shifting (e.g., CFC-regimes, interest deduction limitations, withholding taxes, etc.).
5. Double Tax Treaties Aggressiveness: Shows the impact of a double tax treaty agreement network on the taxation of interest, dividends and royalties with respect to a reduction of withholding taxes vis-à-vis another jurisdiction.

Out of the five indictors, only one is related to the exchange of information and transparency. Nevertheless, TJN defines exchange of information and transparency as a necessary criterion for the international LPFT.

---

[41] OECD, Brief on the State of Play on the international tax transparency standards (OECD 2017).

[42] Tax Justice Network, 'The Corporate Tax Haven Index (CTHI)' (*Corporate Tax Haven Index*, 2021) <https://cthi.taxjustice.net/en/> accessed 6 December 2023.

[43] ibid.

9.4 ANALYSIS OF LISTING OUTCOMES

After prudently observing and perceiving the emerge of EoI as an instrument to derive an International LPFT, various drawbacks such as the fragmentation of the LPFT and inconsistencies of the different Peer Reviews and listings can be identified. The fragmentation of the LPFT from the national to the European and then to the international level causes irrefutable confusion. At the international level, the G7/G20 mandates the OECD and different institutions such as the Global Forum, the Inclusive Framework (IF), and the Forum on Harmful Tax Practices (FHTP) to develop and lead initiatives that include EoI for tax purposes as well as to include certain tax principles into the respective (different) International LPFT. The reason why this is regarded as a fragmentation of the LPFT is the fact, that at the level of the EU and TJN, different criteria regarding: (1) EoI for tax purposes, and (2) tax principles are connected, whereas, at the level of the OECD, different criteria and Peer Reviews focusing either on the former or the latter are distinguished and treated separately. To address the fragmentation of the LPFT and specific inconsistencies, certain examples of measures applied differently by the OECD, the EU and national lists are elaborated upon below.

As the EU listing criteria rely heavily on OECD data, it is necessary to delve into the OECD tax data sources and peer review publications to justify some listing behaviours. The below-listed examples attempt to point out inconsistencies referring to the EU list of NCJs.

1. AEOI as a tax transparency criterion: It is observed that regarding the EU NCJ listing criterion 1.a on tax transparency, the Global Forum determines two different scores: one on the AEOI legal framework and another on the effectiveness in practice of AEOI. However, from the interpretation of the EU, there is only one score of being compliant ('largely compliant') or not. In fact, the Global Forum sees the matter in a broader spectrum and the judgement of the EU may sound incomplete. Chile and Croatia (an EU Member State) seem to be 'non-compliant' regarding the effectiveness in practice of AEOI but receive a rating of 'in place but needs improvements' concerning the AEOI legal framework[44] of the Global Forum. Israel receives a 'not in place' on the AEOI legal framework but has a 'partially compliant' regarding the effectiveness in practice of AEOI[45] of the Global Forum. It is rather unclear how the EU converts these two opposing scores

---

[44] OECD, *Peer Review of the Automatic Exchange of Financial Account Information* (OECD 2022).

[45] ibid.

into their compliance sphere as none of the above-mentioned countries are on the EU list of NCJ.[46]

2. Harmful tax practices: An additional interesting case is displayed to understand the reasoning behind the inclusion of the Bahamas in the EU NCJ list. According to the current EU NCJ list,[47] the Bahamas facilitate offshore structures that attract profits without real economic substance, therefore failing to ensure the effective implementation of substance requirements, one of the two criteria on fair taxation. Being classified as harmful tax practice, the status of the Bahamas in the latest report on 'Harmful Tax Practices-Peer Review Results',[48] a report based on BEPS Action 5 from the FHTP, is classified as 'not harmful' regarding economic substance requirements; therefore it should not be included in the EU list, at least not for that criterion.
3. EU Membership: Another case about the EU NCJ list throughout the years is the listing of the Cayman Islands in February 2020, and its subsequent delisting only eight months later. The Cayman Islands, as a British Overseas Territory, could not have been included in the EU NCJ until BREXIT was effectuated, as of 1 February 1 2020. By definition, a Member State will not be part of any screening, monitoring, and NCJ listing processes simply because of their membership to the EU. Therefore, the list is only for non-EU Member States and once the United Kingdom (UK) exited the EU, the CoCG screened the UK including British Overseas Territories, whereas EU Member States have still been excluded.[49] Moreover, Malta represents a captivating case as a 'partially compliant' jurisdiction assessed by Global Forum on both EOIR and AEOI (1.a and 1.b EU criteria). Failure to meet two Tax Transparency criteria would have resulted in Malta being placed on the EU NCJ list; however, EU membership prevents the potential inclusion of Malta on the list.
4. National Peculiarities: Besides European and international institutions, also national tax authorities anticipate the LPFT with their own manners.[50] An illustrative example is the curious case of Panama as a cooperative and non-cooperative jurisdiction at the same time. Panama, considered

---

46 Council conclusions on the revised EU list of non-cooperative jurisdictions for tax purposes [2023] OJ 13879/23.

47 ibid.

48 OECD, *Harmful Tax Practices – Peer Review Results: Inclusive Framework on BEPS: Action 5* (OECD 2023).

49 Oxfam, 'Briefing Note: Blacklist or Whitewash? What a real EU Blacklist of Tax Havens should look like' (*Oxfam Policy and Practice*, November 2017).

50 For a comprehensive overview of varieties of relationships between EU Member States national NCJ lists and the EU NCJ list see Adriaans, van Hulten and Korving (n 35) 354–55.

and listed as an NCJ by the Spanish Tax Agency under the blessing of the Finance Ministry in 1991,[51] managed to exit the list in 2011 after the double tax treaty between Panama and Spain was signed and entered into force.[52] This is a strong reason for the Spanish tax authorities to consider a jurisdiction as cooperative and therefore not harmful for tax purposes. The Spanish position towards Panama's tax-cooperation has not changed since then.[53] On the other hand, the EU decided to include Panama in the EU NCJ list in 2020 due to Panama's downgrade from 'largely compliant' to 'partially compliant' after the second peer reviewing process conducted by the Global Forum on tax transparency and exchange of information on request.[54] Thus, from the perspective of the EU and the OECD, Panama is seen as a NCJ, but from the perspective of Spain (an EU and OECD Member State), Panama is a fair 'tax partner' and a compliant jurisdiction, although there is a clear European obligation for Spain to apply counter measures towards Panama.

9.5 CONCLUSIONS

The various forms of EoI for tax purposes play a major role in what is referred to the LPFT. Their embodiment as key factors in determining NCJs for tax purposes has been evident for at least two decades, and the several forms of EoI are used as a rating tool to construct respective lists. Despite the broad application of EoI as a NCJ listing criterion, other tax aspects and approaches are also used to thoroughly screen and classify jurisdictions as non-cooperative for tax purposes. Although it may be regarded as desirable to evaluate jurisdictions as NCJs according to a comprehensive set of criteria, taking into consideration aspects of both EoI and tax principles to determine an individual score for each jurisdiction, e.g., according to the Corporate Tax Haven Index by the TJN or the EU list of NCJs, a reliable and coherent realisation of an inclusive International LPFT and the inclusive process of listing NCJ should rather follow a differentiated rule-based approach as both perspectives follow different approaches. This is even more important when it is taken into account that the realisation of a genuine International LPFT needs both: former NCJs to be entirely compliant with the respective criteria, but organisations and institutions like the OECD, the Global Forum, the IF and the FHTP, as well as the EU and the respective Member States, to acknowledge former NCJ as equivalent within the International LPFT.

---

51 Ministerio de Economía y Hacienda, *Real Decreto 1080/1991* (1991).

52 Ministerio de Asuntos Exteriores y de Cooperación, *BOE-A-2011-11425* (2011).

53 ibid.

54 Council conclusions on the revised EU list of non-cooperative jurisdictions for tax purposes' [2020] OJ 6129/20.

PART II

EU Council Directive on administrative cooperation: analysis of its origin and evolution

10. The evolution of the exchange of information standards from a global perspective: the influence of the OECD on EU legislation

Stefanie Geringer

10.1 INTRODUCTION

In a book on the exchange of information for tax purposes and administrative cooperation within the European Union (EU), a chapter describing the developments in this area at the level of the Organisation for Economic Co-operation and Development (OECD) might seem odd at first glance. However, it ought to be borne in mind that 22 of the 27 EU Member States are currently members of the OECD.[1] Accordingly, they are politically obliged to adopt decisions made in OECD-based fora.[2] While this could be done solely at the national level, it was obviously considered preferable to fulfil many of these obligations through appropriate action at EU level, so as to ensure a harmonised legal framework and level playing field within the EU. Exploring the evolution of exchange of information standards in the OECD thus appears as a useful complement to the chapters devoted to examining related EU rules and initiatives.

Against this background, this chapter sets out to investigate the development of exchange of information standards at the OECD level from the early beginnings to the present day. The actions taken are contextualised with their political, economic, social and legal environment to offer explanations for the

---

1 OECD, 'Our Global Reach' (OECD About 2023) <https://www.oecd.org/about/> accessed 6 December 2023.

2 Agreements at the OECD level are not legally binding. This notwithstanding, the member countries may still feel obliged to act accordingly for political reasons, particularly in light of the consensus-based decision-making processes, e.g. Thomas Dubut, 'The Court of Justice and the OECD Model Tax Conventions or the Uncertainties of the Distinction between Hard Law, Soft Law, and No Law in the European Case Law' (2012) 40(1) Intertax 3–4.

status quo and to illustrate their implications and significance for exchange of information within the EU territory, thereby bridging the gap to the following chapters. In order to provide for a well-structured and easily accessible overview, the assessment is divided in terms of the type of information exchange (information exchange upon request, spontaneous exchange of information or automatic exchange of information, respectively) and the legal quality of the underlying instrument (bilateral, multilateral or unilateral measures, respectively). This analysis will show that the OECD standards for information exchange have proven to be highly influential and can indeed be seen as the main driver of the corresponding initiatives at the EU level.

10.2 EXCHANGE OF INFORMATION UPON REQUEST FROM THE EARLY BEGINNINGS TO THE ESTABLISHMENT OF THE 'OECD STANDARD'

Access to information is critical to the accurate assessment and collection of taxes. For purely domestic matters, national lawmakers are free to introduce the necessary procedural rules which oblige taxpayers to submit the relevant documents (and sanction non-compliance). However, in cross-border situations, jurisdictions face significant difficulties, since international law disallows the unilateral collection of tax information and conduct of tax investigations in foreign territories.[3]

It is therefore not surprising that the setting of standards for information exchange has formed part of the drafting of model provisions for double tax conventions (DTCs) at the OECD level ever since. A related provision was already included in the 1963 draft of the OECD Model Tax Convention (OECD MTC).[4] The basic rules, which were largely adopted in Article 26 of the first OECD MTC from 1977,[5] were characterised in particular by the following features:

1. They enabled the contractual partners to request information relevant for the carrying out of the respective DTC or further for the application of

---

[3] See e.g. Ana P. Dourado, in Ekkehart Reimer and Alexander Rust (eds), *Klaus Vogel on Double Taxation Conventions* (Vol. II, 5th edn, Wolters Kluwer 2022) art 26(2).

[4] OECD Draft Double Taxation Convention on Income and Capital (1963).

[5] OECD Model Double Taxation Convention on Income and Capital (OECD MTC) (1977). Apart from linguistic (rather than substantive) differences, Art 26 OECD MTC 1977 stipulated that, in contrast to Article 26 of the 1963 draft, information exchange shall not be limited to residents of the contracting states.

the domestic laws of the contracting states regarding taxes covered by the respective DTC (depending on whether they agreed on a minor or major information exchange clause).[6]

2. Accordingly, the scope was narrowed to the taxes on income and/or capital as defined in the provisions of the relevant treaty (typically Article 2).
3. Necessity of the information at issue was a condition for an information request to be admissible.
4. In the absence of statements to the contrary,[7] bank secrecy, among other types of secrecy, was a valid (or at least arguable) reason for refusing requests of information.

Apart from an expansion of the scope regarding the taxes for which an information request can be validly made,[8] these standards remained unchanged until the mid-2000s.

In the economic reality existing at the time of adoption of the 1963 draft and the 1977 OECD MTC – hence, when brick-and-mortar companies were the only dominant, and business, trade and financial relations were usually restricted to the domestic areas – the deficiencies of the early exchange of information clauses were not yet capable of having such a serious impact. However, as part of the extensive liberalisation of national regulatory regimes and growing globalisation, further fuelled by the digitalisation of business models, the circumstances have changed significantly.[9] The augmentation of cross-border trade and new opportunities for cross-border investment simultaneously increased the need for tax-related information in the countries of residence (especially industrialised countries).[10] Both the relatively high threshold

---

6 Filip Debelva and Niels Diepvens, 'Exchange of Information. An Analysis of the Scope of Article 26 OECD Model and Its Requirements: In Search for an Efficient but Balanced Procedure' (2016) 44(4) Intertax 299; Roman Seer, 'Exchange of Information between Tax Authorities: Structures and Recent Developments' in Heike Jochum, Peter Essers, Michael Lang, Norbert Winkeljohann and Bertil Wiman (eds), *Practical Problems in European and International Tax Law: Essays in Honor of Manfred Mössner* (IBFD 2017 454).

7 See Section 10.3.

8 I.e. taxes of every kind and description imposed on behalf of the Contracting States, or of their political subdivisions or local authorities. These amendments to OECD MTC art 26(1) were introduced with the 2000 update: OECD Model Double Taxation Convention on Income and Capital (OECD MTC) (2000).

9 See e.g. Miranda Stewart, 'Transnational Tax Information Exchange Networks: Steps towards a Globalized, Legitimate Tax Administration' (2012) 4(2) World Tax Journal 153–54; Yariv Brauner, 'What the BEPS' (2014) 16(2) Florida Tax Review 57.

10 See also OECD, *Manual on the Implementation of Exchange of Information Provisions for Tax Purposes* (2006), paras 6 and 7, <https://www.oecd.org/ctp/exchange-of-tax-information/36647823.pdf> accessed 6 December 2023: 'The contin-

of necessity of the requested information and bank secrecy as a possible reason for refusal to provide information yet rendered information requests to a considerable extent an ineffective means. The situation proved to be even more problematic in relation to so-called tax havens, which, according to the OECD's 1998 Report on Harmful Tax Competition,[11] were defined by a zero or only nominal taxation of income from geographically mobile activities, a lack of effective exchange of information and transparency, and the absence of a requirement that the activity at issue be substantial.[12]

The initiative against harmful tax competition led to the creation of the Global Forum on Taxation, an OECD-based body to discuss related issues and work out possible solutions to the problems identified by its members.[13] For the purpose of effective exchange of information,[14] the respective Global Forum Working Group developed a model for tax information exchange agreements (TIEAs), hence a bilateral agreement which exclusively concerns the exchange of tax information upon request. The source of inspiration for this approach is likely to be found in a corresponding initiative by the United States of America (US) in the 1980s.[15]

The OECD TIEA model was introduced in 2002[16] and can be seen as pioneering for two reasons in particular: Departing from the strict necessity criterion, Article 1 of the TIEA model has merely required a foreseeable relevance of the requested information, in order to ensure exchange of information

---

ued viability of an open world economy depends on international co-operation, including co-operation in tax matters. A key element of international co-operation in tax matters is exchange of information.'

[11] OECD, *Harmful Tax Competition: An Emerging Global Issue* (OECD Publishing 1998).

[12] ibid paras 52–56.

[13] Reuven S. Avi-Yonah, 'The OECD Harmful Tax Competition Report: A Tenth Anniversary Retrospective' (2009) 34(3) Brooklyn Journal of International Law 786; Stefanie Geringer, 'Dissemination of tax good governance standards by the EU and the OECD: A comparative analysis of changes in treatment and tone' (2023) 77(4) Bulletin for International Taxation 153.

[14] The narrative of the OECD campaign was changed in the early 2000s to focus specifically on transparency and effective exchange of information, probably due to a loss of support by the US government, with notable influence from actions of the Black Caucus; Steven A. Dean, 'FATCA, the U.S. Congressional Black Caucus, And the OECD Blacklist' (2020) 99 Tax Notes International 83–90.

[15] See on the US initiative in detail: Steven A. Dean, 'The Incomplete Global Market for Tax Information' (2008) 49 Boston College Law Review 650–53.

[16] OECD, Agreement on Exchange of Information on Tax Matters (2002) <https://www.oecd-ilibrary.org/taxation/agreement-on-exchange-of-information-in-tax-matters_9789264034853-en> accessed 6 December 2023.

in tax matters to the widest possible extent.[17] Furthermore, bank secrecy has been explicitly ruled out as a potential justification to refuse the provision of tax information (Article 5(4)(a) of the TIEA model).[18]

These new parameters, also referred to as the 'OECD standard on exchange of information',[19] were subsequently adopted in Article 26 of the OECD MTC through the 2005 update.[20] Since then, they have represented the 'state of the art' in the exchange of information upon request on the basis of DTCs, and also inspired the legal design of the EU's Directive on Administrative Cooperation (DAC).[21] The monitoring and peer-review of its full and effective implementation and enforcement was later transferred to the 'Global Forum on Transparency and Exchange of Information for Tax Purposes' (Global Forum), the successor to the Global Forum on Taxation.[22]

The last related changes to the OECD MTC Commentary (through the 2012 update) did not affect the fundamental ideas of the OECD standard on exchange of information, but instead mainly intended to allow the information

---

[17] The boundaries to inadmissible information requests are to be drawn along the lines of outright fishing expeditions (ibid para 3; see on the foreseeable relevance criterion in detail Part I, Chapter 1 in this book). Contrary to the view expressed in the OECD MTC Commentary (art 26 para 4.1), it is acknowledged here that the introduction of the foreseeable relevance is difficult to understand as a mere clarification. Rather, there seems to be a substantive difference between necessity and foreseeable relevance from a semantic perspective.

[18] OECD (n 16) para 46.

[19] OECD, *Terms of Reference to Monitor and Review Progress Towards Transparency and Exchange of Information for Tax Purposes* (CTPA 2010), paras 5–6 <https://web-archive.oecd.org/2012-06-14/108479-44824681.pdf> accessed 6 December 2023.

[20] See also e.g. Roman Seer, 'Recent Development in Exchange of Information within the EU for Tax Matters' (2013) 22(2) EC Tax Review 67; Roman Seer and Sascha Kargitta, 'Exchange of information and cooperation in direct taxation' in Christiana H.J.I. Panayi, Werner Haslehner and Edoardo Traversa (eds), *Research Handbook on European Union Taxation Law* (Edward Elgar Publishing 2020) 495. The introduction of the new (current) standard has made it easier to request tax information, but conversely has likely also led to an increase in data protection and privacy issues; for the related issues in detail, see Part I, Chapter 4 in this book.

[21] See e.g. Ana P. Dourado, 'The European Commission Tax Package: The Condition of Foreseeable Relevance, Group Requests and Data Breaches' (2020) 48(11) Intertax 950. See also Part II, Chapter 11 in this book.

[22] See in detail e.g. Stewart (n 9) 161–63; Geringer (n 13) 10–12; Alicja Brodzka and Sebastiano Garufi, 'The Era of Exchange of Information and Fiscal Transparency: The Use of Soft Law Instruments and the Enhancement of Good Governance in Tax Matters' (2012) 52(8) European Taxation 398–400; Leo E,C, Neve, 'The Peer Review Process of the Global Forum on Transparency and Exchange of Information for Tax Purposes: A Critical Assessment on Authority and Legitimacy' (2017) 11(2) Erasmus Law Review 95–102.

obtained to be used for other purposes as well,[23] to clarify the essence of the foreseeable relevance criterion,[24] to define criteria for the identification of the relevant taxpayer,[25] and to explicitly recognise the principal admissibility of group requests,[26] respectively. The latter has proved influential both in the interpretation of the OECD-based standards for information exchange in the DAC[27] and in EU legislative action (i.e. DAC7).

10.3 OECD WORK ON SPONTANEOUS EXCHANGE OF INFORMATION

As described above, the origins of exchange of information at the OECD level primarily lie in its most primitive form, hence the exchange of information upon request.[28] This type of information exchange has yet a decisive disadvantage: requesting information presupposes that the respective tax authorities have knowledge of the existence of tax-relevant cross-border situations relating to a particular taxpayer (or a clearly defined group of taxpayers). One of the options for addressing this issue[29] is to conclude an arrangement between two or more countries according to which tax officials ought to actively transmit foreseeably relevant information to other tax authorities without prior request, hence a spontaneous exchange of information.[30]

The broad wording of Article 26 of the OECD MTC has provided sufficient discretion to allow negotiations on all forms of information exchange, including spontaneous exchange of information, ever since.[31] In contrast, the TIEA model was deliberately designed as to only cover exchange of

---

[23] OECD MTC (n 8) art 26(2), as amended by the 2012 update.

[24] Accordingly, the information requested need not prove actually relevant in the definitive assessment. It suffices that 'at the time a request is made there is a reasonable possibility that the requested information will be relevant': OECD MTC Commentary, art 26 para 5. See also Moreno González (n 17).

[25] ibid art 26 para 5.1.

[26] ibid art 26 para 5.2.

[27] See in detail Stefanie Geringer, 'Is the OECD Able to Exert Influence on the Essence of OECD-Inspired EU Secondary Law?' in Anders Hultqvist and Johan Lindholm (eds), *The Power to Tax in Europe* (Hart Publishing 2022) 251–73.

[28] See e.g. Shimeng Lan, 'The Change of Paradigm of Tax Transparency and Its Challenges to Taxpayers' Rights to Privacy and Personal Data Protection' in Jeffrey Owens and Robert Risse (eds), *Tax Law and Digitalization: The New Frontier for Government and Business* (Wolters Kluwer, 2021) 145.

[29] The other concerns the automatic exchange of information; see Section 10.4.

[30] Compare with, for example, the description provided in OECD (n 10) para 18.

[31] *Argumento* OECD MTC art 26(1): 'The competent authorities of the Contracting States shall exchange such information.' This reading is also confirmed by OECD MTC Commentary art 26 para 9.

information upon request. However, this does not preclude contracting partners from extending the scope of their particular bilateral agreement to include spontaneous exchange of information on a negotiation basis.[32] The Convention on Mutual Administrative Assistance in Tax Matters (hereinafter: the Convention), as the most comprehensive multilateral legal framework for the purposes of information exchange,[33] instead contains a specific provision for the spontaneous exchange of information (Article 7), and even describes precisely the circumstances under which a country shall actively forward tax information, hence:

1. when a loss of tax might occur in the other country;
2. when a reduction in or an exemption from tax in its state could lead to an increase in tax or to liability to tax in the other country;
3. when cross-border dealings are conducted in such a way that a saving in tax may result in one or both of the affected countries;
4. when a tax saving might result from artificial intra-group transfers of profits;
5. when the information may be relevant in assessing the liability to tax.[34]

This definition of events triggering the need for spontaneous exchange of tax information has been adopted identically for the purposes of information exchange within the EU through the DAC.[35]

While the aforementioned instruments address the spontaneous exchange of information more broadly, this type of information exchange has recently gained particular prominence as a tool for targeted purposes under the OECD/G20 base erosion and profit shifting (BEPS) Project regarding harmful tax practices (OECD BEPS Action 5). The establishment of the OECD/G20 BEPS project grounded on the legacies of the 2007/2008 financial and economic crisis and has thus aimed to 'address tax avoidance, ensuring that profits are taxed where economic activities generating the profits are performed and where value is created.'[36] The changed zeitgeist (and corresponding public pressure) led the countries and jurisdictions engaged in the OECD/G20 BEPS

---

32 OECD (n 16) para 39. For this purpose, the OECD Committee on Fiscal Affairs approved a complementary model protocol in June 2015; <https://www.oecd.org/ctp/exchange-of-tax-information/Model-Protocol-TIEA.pdf> accessed 6 December 2023.

33 See also Section 10.5.

34 Convention on Mutual Administrative Assistance in Tax Matters (Mutual Administrative Assistance Convention) (2011), art 7(1).

35 See Pantazatou (n 21).

36 OECD, 'BEPS Actions' (BEPS: Inclusive Framework on Base Erosion and Profit Shifting, 2023) <https://www.oecd.org/tax/beps/beps-actions> accessed 6 December 2023.

Project to finally deliver on the plans of the 1998 report[37] and accordingly address actions of states which might cause BEPS in other jurisdictions.[38] As part of the BEPS minimum standard,[39] all 142 countries and jurisdictions currently participating in the OECD/G20 Inclusive Framework on BEPS[40] are obliged to implement the measures carved out in the final report,[41] among them actions to provide a spontaneous exchange of relevant information[42] on taxpayer-specific rulings which could give rise to BEPS concerns in the absence of such information exchange.[43] Such a threat has been identified in relation to five categories of rulings:

1. rulings relating to preferential regimes;[44]
2. cross-border unilateral advance pricing arrangements or other unilateral transfer pricing rulings;[45]
3. rulings giving a downward adjustment to profits (particularly where there are not directly reflected in the taxpayer's financial or commercial accounts);[46]
4. rulings concerning the existence or absence of or the allocation of profits to a permanent establishment;[47]
5. rulings which cover arrangements involving conduit companies.[48]

Further categories could be added in the future due to a respective agreement at the level of the Forum of Harmful Tax Practices (FHTP),[49] which has also been tasked with the monitoring and peer-review processes to ensure compli-

---

37 See Section 10.2.

38 Christiana H.J.I. Panayi, *Advanced Issues in International and European Tax Law* (1st edn, Hart Publishing 2018) 77.

39 These include OECD BEPS Actions 5, 6, 13 and 14, respectively: OECD (n 36).

40 OECD, Members of the OECD/G20 Inclusive Framework on BEPS (2022) <https://www.oecd.org/tax/beps/inclusive-framework-on-beps-composition.pdf> accessed 6 December 2023.

41 OECD/G20 Base Erosion and Profit Shifting Project, *Countering Harmful Tax Practices More Effectively, Taking into Account Transparency and Substance, Action 5 – 2015 Final Report* (OECD Publishing 2015).

42 Therefore, a two-step process is applied, where, under step 1, it suffices to supply a summary and some basic information, using the template in Annex C of the final report; ibid paras 130–31.

43 ibid para 126.

44 ibid paras 103–05.

45 ibid paras 107–12.

46 ibid paras 113–16.

47 ibid para 117.

48 ibid paras 118–19.

49 ibid para 120.

ance with the regulatory framework,[50] such as the three-month time limit for providing the relevant information[51] and measures to safeguard confidentiality of the information exchanged.[52] Similar to the automatic exchange of information,[53] the use of uniform standards for data transmission (and error reporting) is ensured by providing an XML schema and a corresponding user guide.[54] The OECD's efforts regarding the spontaneous exchange of information on taxpayer-specific rulings have been paralleled by actions at the EU level as far as they concern cross-border rulings and advance pricing arrangements (i.e., DAC3).[55]

10.4 THE RISE OF AUTOMATIC EXCHANGE OF INFORMATION IN THE OECD CONTEXT

Notwithstanding the above-described advantages of exchanging information spontaneously over exchanging information upon request,[56] it is recognised that this form is also case-specific and can therefore likewise represent a time-consuming and cost-inefficient practice. Furthermore, it also requires active engagement of the tax authorities.[57] These shortcomings can be overcome by way of exchanging bulk information automatically and on a routine basis.[58] Indeed, automatic exchange of information has been found to be 'crucial in bringing national tax administration in line with the globalised economy'.[59]

Although the broad wording of Article 26 of the OECD MTC principally allows the inclusion of automatic exchange of information,[60] this does not

---

50 OECD, 'BEPS Actions' (BEPS: Inclusive Framework on Base Erosion and Profit Shifting, 2023) <https://www.oecd.org/tax/beps/beps-actions/action5> accessed 6 December 2023.

51 OECD (n 41) paras 133–34.

52 ibid paras 137–140.

53 See Section 10.4.

54 OECD, *Exchange on Tax Rulings XML Schema: User Guide for Tax Administrations* (2nd edn, 2019) <https://www.oecd.org/tax/beps/exchange-on-tax-rulings-xml-schema-user-guide-for-tax-administrations.htm> accessed 6 December 2023.

55 See Part II, Chapter 12 in this book.

56 See Section 10.3.

57 See e.g. Roman Seer and Isabel Gabert, 'European and International Tax Cooperation: Legal Basis, Practice, Burden of Proof, Legal Protection and Requirements' (2011) 65(2) Bulletin for International Taxation 94.

58 Compare, for example, the description provided in OECD (n 10) para 18.

59 OECD, 'Home' (*Automatic Exchange Portal*, 2023) <https://www.oecd.org/tax/automatic-exchange> accessed 6 December 2023.

60 See, on the wide scope of this provision already, Section 10.3 (fn 31).

appear to be typically the case in DTCs based on the OECD MTC.[61] As well as for the spontaneous exchange of information, contractual partners of a TIEA can extend its scope to include the automatic exchange of information on a bilateral basis.[62] Within the legal framework of the Convention, the automatic exchange of information has similarly been dependent on the signing of a supplemental agreement by the participating jurisdictions.[63]

Instead of a broad orientation, which both the OECD MTC and the Convention have pursued, a more targeted promotion of automatic information exchange has apparently proven to be more promising. In this context, too, US tax policy can be identified as the source of inspiration for action at the OECD level.[64] When the US unilaterally enacted provisions to obtain foreign bank account information from individuals and entities subject to US tax in response to the revelations of offshore activities in the wake of the 2007/2008 financial and economic crisis, the OECD recognised and seized the opportunity to simultaneously benefit from the structures established for the purposes of the US Foreign Account Tax Compliance Act (FATCA) regime.[65] Consequently, the OECD developed and published the 'Standard for Automatic Exchange of Financial Account Information in Tax Matters' in 2014, which was immediately endorsed by the G20[66] as well as OECD member countries, non-member countries and the EU.[67] The standard is characterised by a two-pronged approach, incorporating:[68] the Multilateral Competent Authority Agreement (MCAA), which provides a legal framework for the automatic information exchange (among others, notably DTCs, TIEAs, the Convention and the DAC);[69] and the Common Reporting Standard (CRS), which thoroughly

---

61 Seer and Kargitta (n 20) 494.

62 See Section 10.3.

63 Convention on Mutual Administrative Assistance in Tax Matters (Mutual Administrative Assistance Convention) (2011), art 6.

64 Joshua D. Blank and Ruth Mason, 'Exporting FATCA' (2014) 142 Tax Notes 1245–50.

65 This was acknowledged, for example, in OECD, *Standard for Automatic Exchange of Financial Account Information in Tax Matters* (OECD Publishing, 2014) para 5.

66 G20, *Communiqué – Meeting of Finance Ministers and Central Bank Governors, Sydney, 22–23 February 2014* (2014) para 9, <https://www.mofa.go.jp/files/000059873.pdf> accessed 6 December 2023.

67 OECD Council, *Declaration on Automatic Exchange of Information in Tax Matters* (Paris, 2014) <https://www.oecd.org/mcm/documents-archive/2014/MCM-2014-Declaration-Tax.pdf> accessed 6 December 2023.

68 OECD, *Standard for Automatic Exchange of Financial Account Information in Tax Matters* (2nd edn OECD Publishing 2017) para 15 <https://doi.org/10.1787/9789264267992-en> accessed 6 December 2023.

69 OECD (n 68) para 16.

describes the reporting and due diligence standards for the affected financial institutions. These are accompanied by commentaries on the MCAA and the CRS, and the CRS XML Schema user guide.[70]

The automatic exchange of financial account information in tax matters has been a success story for the OECD from the start. More than 40 countries and jurisdictions committed to participate in the first round of information exchange under the CRS regime in 2017 ('early adopters'),[71] and more than 115 countries and jurisdictions were expected to undertake first exchanges by 2023.[72]As with the OECD standard for exchange of information upon request,[73] compliance with the OECD CRS has been subject to in-depth monitoring and peer review under the aegis of the Global Forum.[74] The adoption in the EU was made by DAC2.[75]

The structures of the automatic exchange of financial account information have meanwhile been mimicked for the purposes of Country-by-Country (CbC) reporting. The role and importance of standardised transfer pricing documentation was intensively explored in the course of the OECD/G20 BEPS project. The results of these discussions fed into the recommendations of the final report on OECD BEPS Action 13.[76] Since they also form part of the BEPS minimum standard,[77] all participating countries and jurisdictions need to adopt regulations which oblige multinational enterprises (MNEs) with an annual consolidated group revenue of at least EUR 750 million to transmit a master file, a local file and a CbC report. The master file, describing the respective MNE's global business operations and transfer pricing policies, and the local file, including detailed transfer pricing documentation for the respective country, shall be forwarded to and remains with the affected local tax authorities.[78] Conversely, the CbC report, containing aggregate data on

70 ibid Section III and Annex 3, respectively.

71 OECD, *Joint Statement by the Early Adopters Group* (2014) <https://web-archive.oecd.org/2014-10-31/257787-AEOI-early-adopters-statement.pdf> accessed 8 February 2023.

72 OECD Global Forum on Transparency and Exchange of Information for Tax Purposes, *Automatic Exchange of Information (AEOI): Status of Commitments* (2023) <https://www.oecd.org/tax/automatic-exchange/commitment-and-monitoring-process/AEOI-commitments.pdf> accessed 6 December 2023.

73 See Section 10.2.

74 OECD, 'Home' (*Automatic Exchange Portal*, 2023) <https://www.oecd.org/tax/automatic-exchange> accessed 6 December 2023.

75 See Pantazatou (n 21).

76 OECD/G20 Base Erosion and Profit Shifting Project, *Transfer Pricing Documentation and Country-by-Country Reporting, Action 13 – 2015 Final Report* (OECD Publishing 2015).

77 See Section 10,3 (n 39).

78 OECD (n 76) 14–15 and 20.

the global allocation of income, profit, taxes paid and economic activity among the tax jurisdictions in which the MNE operates, is subject to mutual exchange between the participating tax administrations on an annual basis,[79] in order to allow for 'assessing high-level transfer pricing risks and other base erosion and profit shifting related risks, as well as for economic and statistical analysis, where appropriate'.[80] The automatic information exchange may occur on the basis of the CbC MCAA,[81] bilateral agreements (e.g., DTCs and TIEAs) or other legal sources such as the DAC, which has been amended for these purposes through the DAC4.[82] Similar to the automatic information exchange under the CRS, a standardised XML schema and a corresponding user guide are available to accommodate transmission and data processing.[83] As of writing, more than 3,300 bilateral exchange relationships have been in effect for the purposes of exchanging CbC reports.[84]

While the automatic exchange of financial account information and CbC reports thus represents the status quo at the OECD level, a further expansion of this standard is on the horizon. In March 2022, the OECD released a public consultation document on a possible future automatic information exchange on transactions in crypto-assets (coined as the 'Crypto-Asset Reporting Framework' or 'CARF').[85] In particular, it was suggested therein to amend the CRS so as to bring these new financial assets as well as corresponding products and intermediaries within its scope.[86] A public consultation meeting

---

79 ibid 16 and 23.

80 Preamble to the CbC MCAA; OECD, *Multilateral Competent Authority Agreement on the Exchange of Country-by-Country Reports*, <https://web-archive.oecd.org2020-05-29/385805-cbc-mcaa.pdf> accessed 6 December 2023.

81 ibid. See in detail Section 10.5.

82 See Part II, Chapter 13 in this book.

83 OECD, *Country-by-Country Reporting XML Schema: User Guide for Tax Administration* (2nd edn, 2019) <https://www.oecd.org/tax/beps/country-by-country-reporting-xml-schema-user-guide-for-tax-administrations-june-2019.pdf> accessed 6 December 2023. An XML schema and corresponding user guide for providing structured feedback was additionally published: OECD, *Country-by-Country Reporting Status Message XML Schema: User Guide for Tax Administrations* (2nd edn, 2019) <https://www.oecd.org/tax/beps/country-by-country-reporting-status-mesage-xml-schema-user-guide-for-tax-administrations-june-2019.pdf> accessed 6 December 2023.

84 OECD, 'Activated Exchange Relationships for Country-by-Country Reporting' (*Base Erosion and Profit Shifting*, 2023) <https://www.oecd.org/tax/beps/country-by-country-exchange-relationships.htm> accessed 6 December 2023.

85 OECD, *Public Consultation Document: Crypto-Asset Reporting Framework and Amendments to the Common Reporting Standard* (OECD Publishing 2022) <https://www.oecd.org/tax/exchange-of-tax-information/crypto-asset-reporting-framework-and-amendments-to-the-common-reporting-standard.pdf> accessed 6 December 2023.

86 ibid paras 5–6.

based on the comments received was held in May 2022,[87] and a follow-up report containing the rules on the CARF, a related commentary as well as the amendments to the CRS were published in October 2022.[88] It remains to be seen how the OECD initiative – which, to some extent, parallels actions at the EU level (i.e., DAC8)[89] – will further develop from there.

10.5 THE TREND TOWARDS MULTILATERAL LEGAL FRAMEWORKS ON THE EXCHANGE OF TAX INFORMATION

The OECD's efforts in the area of information exchange have traditionally focused on developing standards for bilateral treaties.[90] However, it has become apparent that multilateral conventions could prove particularly beneficial, as they allow for agreements to be reached immediately with a large number of jurisdictions on a uniform standard for information exchange without the need to undergo negotiations with each of them separately (this is an advantageous feature that has been made fruitful in a similar way in the EU area in the context of the DAC and the corresponding amending directives).

Despite this notable advantage, it took more than 20 years for multilateral information exchange instruments (co-)initiated by the OECD to gain widespread traction. The Convention, the most comprehensive multilateral legal framework providing all types of information exchange as well as provisions on simultaneous tax examinations, examinations abroad and assistance in the recovery of tax claims (including measures of conservancy), was originally a 'slow seller'. Its growing relevance over the last 13 years may be especially traced back to two factors: First, in 2010, the Convention underwent a major overhaul,[91] to the effect that the personal scope of the Convention is no longer restricted to the members of the Council of Europe or the OECD.[92] Second,

---

87 A recording is available on the OECD's website: <https://web-archive.oecd.org/2022-10-10/630708-public-consultation-meeting-crypto-asset-reporting-framework-and-amendments-to-the-common-reporting-standard-23-may-2022.htm> accessed 6 December 2023.

88 OECD, *Crypto-Asset Reporting Framework and Amendments to the Common Reporting Standard* (OECD Publishing 2022) <https://www.oecd.org/tax/exchange-of-tax-information/crypto-asset-reporting-framework-and-amendments-to-the-common-reporting-standard.pdf> accessed 6 December 2023.

89 See Part II, Chapter 17 in this book.

90 See Section 10.2.

91 The amended text is available at <https://www.oecd.org/tax/exchange-of-tax-information/ENG-Amended-Convention.pdf> accessed 6 December 2023.

92 See on the amended admission procedure in detail Article 28(5) of the Mutual Administrative Assistance Convention art 28(5) (which further stipulates that the appli-

both the CRS and CbC MCAAs require unanimous participation in the Convention in order to be effective for a given bilateral relationship.[93] These developments arguably explain the fact that, as of writing, the Convention applies in 147 jurisdictions.[94]

Article 6 of the Convention, which authorises the conclusion of supplementary agreements on automatic information exchange,[95] thus provided the relevant legal basis for the adoption of the CRS and CbC MCAAs. These two agreements set the terms for the automatic exchange of financial account information and CbC reports,[96] and especially determine:

1. the information to be exchanged (CRS MCAA: name, address, TIN, date and place of birth, account number, name and identifying number (if any) of the financial institution and account balance or value; CbC MCAA: CbC report);[97]
2. the time (CRS MCAA: 9 months after the end of the calendar year; CbC MCAA: no later than 15 months after the last day of the fiscal year of the relevant MNE group);[98]
3. the manner (i.e., using the XML format);[99]
4. co-operation in cases of errors in data transmission or non-compliance by the reporting entities;[100]
5. confidentiality and data safeguards;[101]

---

cation of the jurisdiction wishing to accede to the Convention is to be decided upon by the co-ordinating body, which, according to Article 24(3) of the Convention, is in charge of 'monitor[ing] the implementation and development of this Convention, under the aegis of the OECD').

93 This has been clarified in the preambles to the CRS and CbC MCAAs.

94 OECD, 'The Convention' (*Convention on Mutual Administrative Assistance in Tax Matters*, March 2023) <https://www.oecd.org/tax/exchange-of-tax-information/convention-on-mutual-administrative-assistance-in-tax-matters.htm> accessed 6 December 2023.

95 See Section 10.5.

96 ibid.

97 Multilateral Competent Authority Agreement on the Exchange of Country-by-Country Reports (2016) (CbC MCAA), s. 2; Multilateral Competent Authority Agreement on Automatic Exchange of Financial Account Information (2016) (CRS MCAA), s. 2(2).

98 CbC MCAA, s. 3(3); CRS MCAA, s. 3(3).

99 CbC MCAA, s. 3(4); CRS MCAA, s. 3(5).

100 CbC MCAA, s. 4; CRS MCAA, s. 4.

101 Particularly also an obligation to report breaches of confidentiality or data protection to the co-ordinating body secretariat; CRS MCAA, s. 5; CbC MCAA, s. 5(1) and (3).

6. additionally, in the CbC MCAA: restrictions to the use of CbC reports (i.e., only for the purposes mentioned in the agreement);[102]
7. consultations due to income adjustments (only in the CbC MCAA) or difficulties in the implementation or interpretation of the agreements;[103]
8. amendments to the agreements;[104] and
9. further terms of agreement (e.g., terms for suspending or terminating information exchange under the respective MCAA).[105]

These two multilateral agreements have received wide recognition. As of writing, the CRS MCAA was applicable in 120 countries and jurisdictions.[106] Similarly, 96 countries and jurisdictions have committed to automatically exchange CbC reports under the CbC MCAA.[107]

Another MCAA, structured along the same lines as the CRS and CbC MCAAs, has been drafted for the purposes of the annual information exchange under the (extended) model rules for digital platforms[108] (the 'Multilateral Competent Authority Agreement on Automatic Exchange of Information on Income Derived through Digital Platforms,' or 'DPI MCAA').[109] Whether and when it will enter into force remains to be seen.

---

[102] CbC MCAA, s. 5(2). Any non-compliance should moreover be reported to the co-ordinating body secretariat under CbC MCAA, s. 5(3).

[103] CRS MCAA, s. 6 (1); CbC MCAA, s. 6.

[104] CRS MCAA, s. 6 (2); CbC MCAA, s. 7.

[105] CRS MCAA, s. 7; CbC MCAA, s. 8.

[106] OECD, *Signatories of The Multilateral Competent Authority Agreement on Automatic Exchange of Financial Account Information and Intended First Information Exchange Date* (2023). <https://www.oecd.org/tax/automatic-exchange/about-automatic-exchange/crs-mcaa-signatories.pdf> accessed 6 December 2023.

[107] OECD, *Signatories of The Multilateral Competent Authority Agreement on the Exchange of Country-by-Country Reports (CBC MCAA) and Signing Dates* (2023) <https:/www.oecd.org/tax/automatic-exchange/about-automatic-exchange/CbC-MCAA-Signatories.pdf> accessed 6 December 2023.

[108] See Section 10.6.

[109] OECD, *Model Reporting Rules for Digital Platforms: International Exchange Framework and Optional Module for Sale of Goods* (2021) 6–13 <https://www.oecd.org/tax/exchange-of-tax-information/model-reporting-rules-for-digital-platforms-international-exchange-framework-and-optional-module-for-sale-of-goods.pdf> accessed 6 December 2023.

10.6 RECOMMENDATIONS FOR UNILATERAL ACTION IN THE FIELD OF INFORMATION EXCHANGE

While setting standards for the exchange of tax information on a bilateral and, more recently, multilateral basis has been the focus of most OECD initiatives,[110] model regulations for transposition into domestic laws have gained importance since the establishment of the OECD/G20 BEPS project. The associated actions are consistently characterised by the fact that third parties or the taxpayers shall be obliged to actively provide the relevant information to the national tax authorities (and, if necessary, implement the necessary structures and IT systems accordingly). These features correspond to a recent trend originating in the area of automatic exchange of information[111] to outsource the (time-consuming and costly) acquisition of information. Moreover, it reflects the growing desire of countries and jurisdictions – including OECD members in particular – to get hold of tax-relevant information in a timely manner and from multiple sources in order to improve their risk management and compliance assessment systems.

OECD BEPS Action 12 was devoted to the carving-out of a modular framework for mandatory disclosure rules. This should enable the financial authorities to obtain information on 'aggressive' tax planning strategies at an early stage, so as to have 'the opportunity to quickly respond to tax risks through informed risk assessment, audits, or changes to legislation or regulations'.[112] The recommendations of the final report concern the definition of:

1. the affected persons (taxpayers and/or planners);[113]
2. the reportable schemes (using generic and specific hallmarks, potentially in conjunction with a main benefit test or other filters);[114]
3. the timing of reporting (i.e., at what stage and within which period);[115]
4. eventual other obligations (e.g., the provision of identification numbers or clients lists);[116]

---

[110] See Sections 10.2–10.5.

[111] See Section 10.5.

[112] OECD/G20 Base Erosion and Profit Shifting Project, *Mandatory Disclosure Rules, Action 12– 2015 Final Report* (OECD Publishing 2015) 9.

[113] ibid paras 61–77.

[114] ibid paras 78–137.

[115] ibid paras 138–57.

[116] ibid paras 158–73.

5. consequences of compliance (e.g., no protection of confidence) and non-compliance (especially penalties);[117] and
6. procedural and tax administration matters (e.g., the use of disclosure forms).[118]

These recommendations have been flanked by a complementary publication containing detailed rules on CRS avoidance arrangements and opaque offshore structures, hence any arrangement which leads to the CRS being circumvented or the precise identification of the beneficial owners not being made possible, respectively.[119] Implementation in the participating countries and jurisdictions is on a voluntary basis and should be made in accordance with the needs and requirements of their legal systems.[120] The most prominent adoption of these model regulations[121] was by the EU, through the DAC6.[122]

In a similar vein, the OECD's 2020 model rules on reporting obligations by digital platform operators have been aimed at providing a standardised set of provisions to collect information on transactions and revenues realised by platform sellers, in order to increase compliance and, conversely, minimise administrative and compliance burdens for tax administrations and taxpayers, respectively.[123] The material scope was narrowed to the services which appear to be the most relevant in practice; hence, the original model rules cover the rental of immovable property and personal services, including transportation and delivery.[124] However, on the basis of an optional module introduced by a supplementary publication, the material scope may be extended to the sale

---

[117] ibid paras 174–200.

[118] ibid paras 201–22. Specified recommendations for cross-border situations are made in ibid paras 223–75.

[119] OECD, *Model Mandatory Disclosure Rules for CRS Avoidance Arrangements and Opaque Offshore Structures* (2018) <https://www.oecd.org/tax/exchange-of-tax-information/model-mandatory-disclosure-rules-for-crs-avoidance-arrangements-and-opaque-offshore-structures.pdf> accessed 6 December 2023. The model rules are supplemented by a commentary.

[120] OECD/G20 Base Erosion and Profit Shifting Project (n 112) para 56.

[121] Considering that, among others, it is explicitly mentioned on the OECD's website: <https://www.oecd.org/tax/beps/beps-actions/action12> accessed 6 December 2023.

[122] See Part II, Chapter 15 in this book.

[123] OECD, *Model Rules for Reporting by Platform Operators with respect to Sellers in the Sharing and Gig Economy* (2020) 7 <https://www.oecd.org/tax/exchange-of-tax-information/model-rules-for-reporting-by-platform-operators-with-respect-to-sellers-in-the-sharing-and-gig-economy.pdf> accessed 6 December 2023. The model rules are supplemented by a commentary.

[124] ibid 10–11.

of goods and the rental of means of transportation.[125] The information to be collected and verified typically includes: the first and last name, primary address, TIN, and date of birth (for individual sellers); or the legal name, primary address, TIN, and business registration number (for entities). In the case of rental of immovable property, the address of each rented property must also be communicated.[126] These processes should be completed by the end of each calendar year and the relevant information principally reported until 31 January of the following year,[127] using the XML format.[128] The document further provides guidance on administration and enforcement, such as rules for record keeping penalties in cases of non-compliance.[129] The recommendations on the introduction of reporting requirements for digital platform operators were adopted in the EU under DAC7.[130]

10.7 CONCLUDING REMARKS

Exchange of information in the OECD has transformed significantly since its beginnings in the 1960s. The changes have manifested themselves in particular in relation to: its fundamental importance for the OECD's agenda (being at the heart of OECD policy especially since the 2007/2008 financial and economic crisis and revelations of 'aggressive' tax planning strategies by MNEs and high-net-worth individuals); the basic parameters (with the foreseeable relevance and the abolition of bank secrecy representing the current 'state of the art'); the types of exchange of information used (with automatic information exchange being on the rise since the 2010s); the character of the underlying legal frameworks (with multilateral agreements gaining importance since the 2010s); and the increasing provision of recommendations for unilateral action (feeding into the countries' and jurisdictions' growing desire for (early) access to information from multiple sources).

Changes in US tax policy can occasionally be identified as the main drivers behind the setting of new information exchange standards at the OECD level. For their part, the OECD instruments have had a noticeable influence on the

---

125 OECD (n 109) 15–18.

126 OECD (n 123) 21–22.

127 ibid 22–23 and 29–30.

128 For these purposes, and similar to data transfers under OECD BEPS Action 5 (Section 10.3) and the CRS (Section 10.4), the OECD has published a user guide for tax administrations; <https://www.oecd.org/tax/exchange-of-tax-information/model-rules-for-reporting-by-digital-platform-operators-xml-schema-user-guide-for-tax-administrations.pdf> accessed 6 December 2023.

129 ibid 35–36.

130 Part II, Chapter 16 in this book.

shaping of the EU legal system for the exchange of information (as will be demonstrated in the chapters to follow). Conversely, the OECD's current interest in regulating the exchange of information on transactions in crypto-assets may have likely been sparked by the related EU initiative. Therefore, it cannot be ruled out that the EU and its Member States will continue to use their market power – in a similar vein as they did in the context of the 'Two-Pillar Approach'[131] – to trigger a reaction from the OECD and thereby accelerate developments at the international level, the results of which will then form the basis for corresponding EU legislation. In any case, it can be expected that related OECD actions will continue to play a decisive role for the definition of exchange of information standards in the EU.

---

131 R Mason, 'The 2021 Compromise' (2021) 172 Tax Notes Federal 569–75.

11. The evolution of the exchange of information in the EU: early years, DAC1 and DAC2

Katerina Pantazatou and Arthur Bianco

11.1 INTRODUCTION: THE NEED FOR EXCHANGE OF INFORMATION

Exchange of information (EOI) has recently become a synonym for transparency and tax cooperation and one of the most useful tools in the ongoing fight against tax evasion and tax avoidance.[1] Tax transparency has become a key goal at the international and EU levels, especially after the revelations regarding multiple tax evasion and tax avoidance scandals. According to the OECD, 'tax transparency is about putting an end to bank secrecy and tax evasion through *global tax co-operation'*.[2] Transparency constitutes one of the pillars of the 15 BEPS Actions, which is especially relevant in the context of Actions 11, 12 (which is the precursor to DAC6), 13 and 14. Several other OECD actions have as their purpose the promotion of tax transparency, including the Global Forum on Transparency and Exchange of Information for Tax Purposes and the Multilateral Convention on Mutual Administrative Assistance in Tax Matters.

Furthermore, transparency at the EU level, through tax cooperation – that is, information collection, exchange and monitoring – was echoed in the EU

---

1 Gaëtan Nicodème, 'On Recent Development in Fighting Harmful Tax Practices' (2009) 62 National Tax Journal 755. See also Erwin Nijkeuter, 'Exchange of Information and the Free Movement of Capital between Member States and Third Countries' (2011) 20 EC Tax Review 235; George Gilligan, 'Whither or wither the European Union Savings Tax Directive? A case study in the political economy of taxation' (2003) 11 Journal of Financial Crimes 56.

2 OECD/G20, 'Tax Transparency' <https:// www .oecd .org/ tax/ beps/ tax -transparency/> accessed 7 December 2023).

Anti-Tax Avoidance Package.[3] With the increasing globalisation of economies, it was inevitable that tax avoidance and tax evasion would increasingly appear in a cross border context. Consequently, it came as no surprise that the EOI between Member States became fundamental in fighting such practices.[4] At the same time, technological advancements allowed (from a technical perspective) for an increase in information sharing and closer administrative cooperation in taxation,[5] but also required a revised and up-to-date legal framework. The adoption and subsequent revision of the Directive on Administrative Cooperation (DAC) constituted, thus, one of the key pillars in the EU's strategy to combat tax avoidance and evasion.[6]

While a framework for mutual assistance among Member States has been in place from the very early years (1977) of the European Communities, the need for more information exchange was exacerbated by the 2008 financial crisis,[7] and thus the first proposal for the 'new' 'DAC1' was published in COM(2009) 29. Transparency, a beacon in the fight against tax avoidance and evasion as expressed through EOI, was, however, only crystallised in the amendment of the DAC in 2014 (DAC2).[8]

The present chapter aims to provide a legal overview of the first two DACs, DAC1 and DAC2. In giving an overview of these two fundamental directives, it will also assess them from a legal perspective. In this bid, this contribution will not touch upon the interaction of DAC1 and DAC2 with taxpayers' fundamental rights and the legal issues that arise therefrom, as this is covered in a separate chapter of this volume.[9] It will, however, place the two directives in their historical and political context and will eventually show how, despite some flaws, DAC1 and DAC2 have contributed tremendously to enhancing transparency and fighting tax evasion.

---

3 European Commission, 'Anti-Tax Avoidance Package' (*Taxation and Customs Union,* January 2016), <https://eur-lex.europa.eu/legal-content/EN/TXT/PDF/?uri=CELEX:52016DC0023&from=EN> accessed 7 December 2023.

4 Marius Vascega and Servaas van Thiel, 'Assessment of Taxes in Cross-Border Situations: The New EU Directive on Administrative Cooperation in the Field of Taxation' (2011) 20 EC Tax Review 148. See also Andres Caram, 'Enhancing International Cooperation among Tax Authorities in the Assessment and the Recovery of Taxes: The Proposals for New European Directives' (2009) 37 Intertax 631.

5 Caram (n 4) 631.

6 ibid.

7 Vascega and van Thiel (n 4) 150. See also Tracy A. Kaye, 'Direct Taxation in the European Union: From Maastricht to Lisbon European Union Law' (2011) 35(5) Fordham International Law Journal 12.

8 Hanno Kube and Ekkehart Reimer, 'Tax Policy: Trends in the Allocation of Powers Between the Union and Its Member States' (2016) 25 EC Tax Review 247.

9 See Part I, Chapter 5 in this book.

11.2 DAC'S PREDECESSORS

11.2.1 The Mutual Assistance Directive of 1977

The first segments of 'mutual assistance' among Member States can be traced to the early years of the European Communities (EC) and specifically, the Mutual Assistance Directive of 1977.[10] The directive, now repealed by DAC1, has been amended several times since its adoption. Already in 1975, the Council highlighted the need to introduce legislation to further cooperation in view of combating tax evasion and avoidance.[11] The adoption of the Mutual Assistance Directive in 1977 illustrates that co-operation towards this purpose was perceived as a top priority in direct taxation.[12] Mutual Assistance was also justified, at the time, by the risk of increased tax competition that could impede the functioning of the internal market,[13] an argument that was later used also in the drafting of the DAC to justify the necessity of an Automatic EOI (AEOI) framework.

The 1977 Mutual Assistance Directive introduced all three major types of information exchange; EOI on Request (EOIR) (Article 2), AEOI (Article 3), and Spontaneous EOI (SEOI) (Article 4). Nonetheless, AEOI was limited to bilateral agreements among Member States, as opposed to the multilateral AEOI framework that was later introduced by DAC1. The 1977 Directive also included other forms of cooperation, including collaboration between Member States' authorities, as well as a number of other forms introduced in the 2004 amendment.

The Mutual Assistance Directive has been criticised as having many shortcomings,[14] including the EOIR procedure which, to be initiated, required

---

[10] Proposal for a Council Directive Concerning Mutual Assistance by the Competent Authorities of Member States in the Field of Direct Taxation [1976] COM(1976) 119 final; Council Directive 77/799/EEC of 19 December 1977 concerning mutual assistance by the competent authorities of the Member States in the field of direct taxation [1977] OJ L 336/15.

[11] Council Resolution of 10 February 1975 on the measures to be taken by the Community in order to combat international tax evasion and avoidance [1975] OJ C 35/1.

[12] Kaye (n 7) 11. See also the Council Directive 2010/24/EU of 16 March 2010 concerning mutual assistance for the recovery of claims relating to taxes, duties and other measures [2010] OJ L 84/1, recital 1 that lists tax avoidance and evasion as drivers behind the need for further cooperation.

[13] Roman Seer, 'Recent Development in Exchange of Information within the EU for Tax Matters' (2013) 22 EC Tax Review 66, 69.

[14] Vascega and van Thiel (n 4) 149.

exhaustion of all domestic possibilities for assessment,[15] as well as the number of limitations to EOI which included references to domestic laws or administrative practices, which, in turn, prevented the authorities from carrying out enquiries or collecting information, especially the ones covered by bank secrecy. The latter was pointed out as one of the main reasons for the need for an update of the Directive.[16] Furthermore, Member States could refuse to communicate the information if it could lead to the disclosure of professional, commercial or industrial secrets, if it were contrary to public policy, or if the requesting state was unable, for legal or practical reasons, to provide similar information. Other problems concerned time limits, which were not sufficiently specified to ensure the effectiveness of the cooperation procedure,[17] the limitation of the use of the information received only for the case at hand (no possibility to use it for other purposes, including tax claim, criminal procedures),[18] and the requirement that the AEOI had to be complemented further by a bilateral agreement with the Member State at issue.[19] All these variations had led to a lack of uniformity within the EU regarding mutual assistance in tax matters.

After the 1977 directive's amendment in 2003,[20] VAT was removed from its scope and the scope of the use of the information received was slightly broadened to include purposes other than tax assessments (e.g., judicial proceedings, administrative proceedings, including sanctions for infringements of tax law). In its subsequent amendments in 2004,[21] domestic investigation procedures were aligned with the EOIR investigations; simultaneous controls and assistance procedures for notification purposes were introduced and reciprocity in the ability of a Member State to provide a similar type of information (either in law or fact) was imposed. Furthermore, the 2004 amendment introduced

---

15 Council Directive 77/799/EEC (n 10) art 21.

16 Nicodème (n 1) 765.

17 Council Directive 77/799/EEC (n 10) art 5.

18 ibid art 7.

19 ibid art 5.

20 Council Directive 2003/93/EC of 7 October 2003 amending Council Directive 77/799/EEC concerning mutual assistance by the competent authorities of the Member States in the field of direct and indirect taxation [2003] OJ L 264/23.

21 Council Directive 2004/56/EC of 21 April 2004 amending Directive 77/799/EEC concerning mutual assistance by the competent authorities of the Member States in the field of direct taxation, certain excise duties and taxation of insurance premiums [2004] OJ L 127/70, and Council Directive 2004/106/EC of 16 November 2004 amending Directives 77/799/EEC concerning mutual assistance by the competent authorities of the Member States in the field of direct taxation, certain excise duties and taxation of insurance premiums and 92/12/EEC on the general arrangements for products subject to excise duty and on the holding, movement and monitoring of such products [2004] OJ L 359/30, the latter removed excise duties from the scope of the Directive.

the possibility to refuse cooperation if the requested state's legislation or administrative practices did not allow for such an enquiry. The effectiveness of the directive, even in its amended version, was questioned by the European Commission[22] and the literature as arguably not fit to achieve its intended purpose.[23]

11.2.2 Savings Directive

The Savings Directive[24] was adopted following the liberalisation of the movement of capital under the current Article 63 TFEU and the implementation of Directive 88/361/EC. The aim was to ensure the exchange of information or the minimum taxation of savings in the form of interest payments. The directive was adopted after the 'Scrivener directive', a predecessor of the Savings directive, failed in 1989. That failed project led Germany to adopt a 15% withholding tax (WHT) on dividends and interests paid to residents of other Member States.[25]

The Savings directive was adopted despite Member States' difficulties in agreeing on its content. It was the first directive that provided for a multilateral scheme of AEOI which operated initially among 24 Member States, excluding Austria, Belgium and Luxembourg, all of which decided to apply a WHT instead of an AEOI for bank secrecy reasons.[26] Although all three Member States had committed to gradually phasing out the use of the WHT and implementing the same AEOI framework by 2017,[27] the possibility to opt-out provided in the directive was heavily criticised. Belgium switched to the AEOI system in 2010, in accordance with the 'coexistence principle' that

---

[22] Communication From The Commission To The Council, The European Parliament And The European Economic And Social Committee, Exit taxation and the need for co-ordination of Member States' tax policies [2006] COM(2006) 825 final.

[23] Caram (n 4) 630.

[24] Proposal for a Council Directive to ensure effective taxation of savings income in the form of interest payments within the Community [2001] COM(2001) 400 final; Council Directive 2003/48/EC of 3 June 2003 on taxation of savings income in the form of interest payments [2003] OJ L157/38, amended by Council Directive 2014/48/EU of 24 March 2014 amending Directive 2003/48/EC on taxation of savings income in the form of interest payments [2014] OJ L 111/50, repealed by Council Directive (EU) 2015/2060 of 10 November 2015 repealing Directive 2003/48/EC on taxation of savings income in the form of interest payments [2015] OJ L 301/1 (Savings Directive).

[25] Alberto Barreix, Jeronimo Roca, Fernando Velayos, *A Brief History of Tax Transparency* (Inter-American Development Bank 2016) 3.

[26] Michel Aujean, 'Savings Taxation: Is Automatic Exchange of Information Becoming a Panacea?' (2010) 19 EC Tax Review 2.

[27] Savings Directive (n 24).

was included in the proposal of the directive.[28] At the time, the introduction of an AEOI framework in tax was seen as a huge leap forward towards better cooperation among Member States.[29]

However, the Savings Directive was (still) perceived as drawing a delicate balance between the need for EOI and the (at the time) strict banking secrecy rules.[30] Both Austria and Luxembourg agreed in 2014 to join the AEOI framework by 2017,[31] although this never happened due to the earlier repeal of the directive and the adoption of DAC2 in 2014. Interestingly, the first proposal for the Savings Directive did not envisage an AEOI framework but proposed to implement a European-wide 15% WHT on savings income, which did not meet with agreement from the Member States following the poor German experience with a similar system. Eventually, the adopted text of the directive allowed for a transitional period for Member States that did not wish to implement the AEOI system, starting initially with a 15% WHT for the first three years, followed by a 20% WHT for the following three years and finally 35% thereafter. It should be noted that 75% of the taxes levied should then go to the State of residence.[32]

Another ground of criticism was that the scope of the income covered by the directive was too narrow. According to some, the AEOI framework should have covered royalties and income derived from capital,[33] and the directive's focus on interest only was detrimental, especially since it did not cover certain types of savings.[34] Furthermore, as the directive only covered interest payments made to individuals and not legal persons, it allowed for circumventions of the EOI framework through the use of legal entities and arrangements.[35] The 2014 amendment of the Savings Directive introduced a number of workarounds in its definition to close some loopholes, but the problem was eventually solved with the adoption of DAC2, which included legal persons in its scope.

---

28 Nicodème (n 1) 766; Gilligan (n 1) 58.

29 Aujean (n 26) 1.

30 Henry Christensen and Jean-Marc Tirard, 'The amazing development of exchange of information in tax matters: from double tax treaties to FATCA and the CRS' (2016) 22 Trust & Trustees 903.

31 Lukas Hakelberg, *The Power Politics of International Tax Cooperation. Why Luxembourg and Austria Accepted Automatic Exchange of Information on Foreign Account Holders' Interest Income* (EUI Working Papers, Robert Schuman Centre for Advanced Studies 2014) 9.

32 Savings Directive (n 24) arts 10, 11 and 12.

33 Alberto Gil Soriano, 'Toward an Automatic but Asymmetric Exchange of Tax Information: the US Foreign Account Tax Compliance Act (FATCA) as Inflection Point' (2012) 40 Intertax 544.

34 Barreix, Roca and Velayos (n 25) 5.

35 Gil Soriano (n 33) 544.

Other problems, which were later rectified in DAC2, included the possibility given to Member States to restrict the amount of information to be sent through the EOI framework (e.g., exchanging information on the total amount of interest payment made to an account holder rather than singling out each payment,[36] the date of payment of income not included among the minimum information to be exchanged,[37] and the non -inclusion of paying agents located outside of the EU).

11.2.3 DAC1

The adoption of DAC1 marked the shift from Mutual Assistance to Administrative Cooperation. The change in the language, possibly, goes beyond mere semantics and represents the transition to a new legal framework (DAC1) that would be built on a system of closer cooperation and trust among Member States.[38]

The Commission underlined in the Proposal for DAC1 that the current state of tax avoidance and tax evasion required both action at the EU level and a departure from an administrative cooperation based on bilateral relationships.[39] The need for a new directive was justified, inter alia, on grounds of the increased mobility of the taxpayers, the increased number of cross-border transactions, the internationalisation of financial instruments, and the frictions between national sovereignty in tax and globalisation.[40] Unsurprisingly, the need to update the EOI framework was, further, deemed necessary, not only in light of the 1977 directive's insufficiency, but also in view of the new(er) technologies introduced.[41]

11.2.4 DAC1 in the Making: From the Proposal to the Final Text

Although the DAC was drafted to compensate for the shortcomings of the 1977 Mutual Assistance Directive, the AEOI framework delayed the adoption of the directive as Member States had difficulties in reaching an agreement.[42]

---

36 Christensen and Tirard (n 30) 904.

37 See e.g. Xavier Oberson, *International Exchange of Information in Tax Matters, Towards Global Transparency* (Edward Elgar 2018).

38 Giuseppe Marino, *New Exchange Of Information Versus Tax Solutions Of Equivalent Effect* (EATLP International Tax Series, IBFD 2014) 8.

39 Proposal for a Council Directive on administrative cooperation in the field of taxation [2009] COM(2009) 29 final (DAC1 Proposal), recitals 320 and 327.

40 ibid.

41 Caram (n 4) 630.

42 Martyre Somare and Viktoria Wöhrer, 'Automatic Exchange of Financial Information under the Directive on Administrative Cooperation in the Light of the Global Movement towards Transparency' (2015) 43 Intertax 804.

This led not only to an interval of two years between the initial proposal that was issued in 2009 and the adopted directive in 2011, but also to many discrepancies between the two texts.

According to the 2009 proposal, the scope of the cooperation between States would be broadened beyond the taxes that were covered by the 1977 Directive,[43] marking the first step towards wider harmonisation in tax cooperation among Member States[44] and solving a number of issues that were already raised before the CJEU concerning the scope of the 1977 directive.[45] The 2009 proposal extended the scope of the directive also by introducing the possibility for a cooperation not only between States but including the Commission.[46] Ex post, it remains debatable whether the European legislator really wants the Commission to still play an important role in the framework, as, for example, DAC3 expressly excluded the Commission from accessing the database for tax rulings.

Furthermore, as both the 1977 Mutual Assistance Directive and the Savings Directive were criticised for the lack of specific guidelines on time limits for exchange, the 2009 Proposal included in its preamble specific reference to the need for pre-defined time limits.[47] To ensure the effectiveness of the EOI, the 2009 Proposal introduced the concept of EOI by electronic means[48] and highlighted the fact that the development of new technologies and information systems was relevant for the development of a successful cooperation among States.[49]

Interestingly, the preamble of the proposal already dismissed the possibility for a Member State to refuse to exchange information on the basis of bank secrecy.[50] According to the literature, the main aim of the DAC was to introduce in the EU a gradually increasing AEOI framework whose scope would broaden following consecutive amendments.[51]

The final adopted text deviated on certain grounds from the 2009 proposal. Among the most notable differences, one can distinguish the reference to the concept of 'foreseeably relevant' information in Article 1, which was not included in the proposal. Arguably, it was the Member States that agreed to introduce such a limitation to avoid a very broad EOI system, but also to ensure

---

43 DAC1 Proposal (n 39) recital 130.
44 DAC1 Proposal (n 39) recital 120. See also Caram (n 4) 632.
45 ibid 631.
46 ibid.
47 DAC1 Proposal (n 39) recital 9.
48 ibid art 1.
49 Caram (n 4) 63.
50 DAC1 Proposal (n 39) recital 19.
51 Oberson (n 37).

alignment with Article 26 OECD MC that also requires that the information exchanged be foreseeably relevant to the pursued purpose. In the same vein, Article 2 was eventually adopted without including in its scope compulsory social security provisions, which were initially included in the proposal.

In contrast to the proposal that was meant to give the Commission the flexibility to determine every two years the categories of income covered by the AEOI, the content of the information exchange, the frequency of the exchanges and arrangements and conditions, the adopted text defined the five categories of income that would be covered, as well as the extent of the information exchange obligation under Article 8.[52] The published directive also included the availability clause in the AEOI procedure (today restricted to Article 8(1) – DAC1 AEOI), most likely as a mitigating factor to ensure agreement among Member States. Furthermore, a clause was added to ensure that States could refuse to receive information on certain categories of income, or if such income did not reach a certain threshold. The published directive also added a Most Favoured Nation (MFN) clause.[53]

The final text still included the possibility for the Commission to broaden the scope of the AEOI framework, and introduced the obligations for Member States to communicate statistics on AEOI exchanges for the Commission to take into consideration when proposing amendments and in preparation of its report in 2017.[54]

The spontaneous exchange of information (SEOI) was further narrowed down, in comparison to the proposal, to only five cases, potentially to ensure agreement among Member States. The published directive still included the possibility for SEOI to be extended on a voluntary basis. Specific time limits were included in DAC1 to ensure an effective SEOI.

Contrary to the proposal, which would have allowed for the information received through the EOI framework to be exchanged with any other authority in that same Member State as long as no legislation barred it, the adopted text submitted each information to the same protection of official secrecy as granted domestically. Furthermore, the adopted directive limited the use of that information in cases of judicial and administrative proceedings initiated in response to an infringement of tax law. In contrast to the proposal that did not include a similar provision, the final text allows the requesting state to use the information for other purposes, only if the information can be used in a similar way in the requested State.

---

[52] Report on the proposal for a Council directive on administrative cooperation in the field of taxation [2010] COM(2009)0029 – C6-0062/2009 – 2009/0004(CNS).

[53] ibid.

[54] ibid. Note that the Commission's report was eventually published in 2019.

While the proposal provided that EOIR could potentially be refused if the requesting state had not exhausted all sources of information and only if the volume or nature of the request did not impose a disproportionate burden on the requested authority, no such provision was included in the adopted directive. However, the final text added a grandfathering clause as a ground of refusal: if an information request related to a taxable period anterior to 1 January 2011 and such exchange could have been refused according to the 1977 Directive, then such refusal should be granted.

With regard to 'practical arrangements' as provided in Article 21 of the directive, the proposal provided for the possibility for the Commission to be able to set a minimum threshold of taxes involved triggering the need for an EOI (either EOIR, SEOI or AEOI), which was removed from the published directive. Furthermore, while the proposal set up a broad system of the evaluation of the directive at Commission level, including on AEOI, the published text inserted additional requirements of secrecy on both sides (Commission and other Member States).[55]

11.3 ASSESSMENT OF THE DIRECTIVE

11.3.1 Scope of the EOI Framework

Both the objective and subjective scopes of the directive constitute improvements over the previous EOI frameworks set up by the 1977 Directive and the Savings Directive. In terms of objective scope, the DAC not only covers direct taxation (of all kinds) but also indirect taxes, except for VAT and excise and custom duties. By reference to its subjective scope, the directive encompasses both legal persons and individuals, which has been lauded as a positive development in closing loopholes where taxpayers could hide behind entities to avoid information exchanges.[56] Indeed, the definition of the term 'Persons' included in Article 3(11) is wider than what was included in the other Directives, as it not only includes individuals and legal persons, but also associations and entities that do not have legal personalities that own or manage assets and are subject to the taxes covered.[57]

---

[55] ibid.

[56] See e.g. Fatima Chaouche and Werner Haslehner, 'Cross-Border Exchange of Tax Information and Fundamental Rights', in Werner Haslehner, Georg Kofler, Alexander Rust (eds), *EU Tax Law and Policy in the 21st Century* (Wolters Kluwer 2017); Marino (n 38) 8.

[57] DAC1 art 3(11)(c) and (d). See also Vascega and van Thiel (n 4) 152.

Despite the positive extended scope, two different issues have ensued with regard to the AEOI framework: the types of income covered by the directive and the availability clause.

As stated, the AEOI in DAC1 covers only five income types that are expressly listed in the text of the directive. The categories of income currently covered by Article 8(1) of the DAC are still those same five, although initially the DAC was drafted to be an evolutive piece of legislation that includes plans for reports and potential amendments of the AEOI provisions.[58] More specifically, the categories available for AEOI were meant to be amended following the 2017 Report from the Commission on the assessment of the AEOI framework. The first amendment, however, already took place in 2014 with the adoption of DAC2. Another six amendments that have extended the scope of the AEOI framework followed since.

Furthermore, Member States are not currently obliged to exchange information on each and every category either, which makes the framework less effective. The DAC7 amendment, however, mandates Member States to (compulsorily) exchange on at least two categories of information, and by 2024 four categories.[59] Member States are often unwilling to provide information on all categories of income, because of practical difficulties.[60] The inability of some Member States to exchange on certain categories is often explained by the difficulties these States have in gathering the requested information (e.g., if that particular category of income is not taxed in said Member State).[61] The Commission found that only ten Member States in 2018 exchanged information on all five categories, while one (Cyprus) only exchanged on one category (pensions).[62] According to the European Parliament, life insurance products in 2017 were by far the category of income made least available by Member States. Member States were required before 2014 to inform the Commission of the categories of income on which they had information available, and keep the Commission informed to any change to that list.[63]

Beyond the categories of income covered, the directive only requires Member States to automatically exchange information only if this information

---

58 ibid art 8(5).

59 DAC7 art 1(7).

60 European Court of Auditors, *Exchanging tax information – solid foundation, cracks in the implementation* (Special Report, vol 03, European Court of Auditors 2021) (ECA Report) 26; Report from the Commission to the European Parliament and the Council on overview and assessment of the statistics and information on the automatic exchanges in the field of direct taxation [2018] COM(2018) 844 final (Commission Report 2018) 6.

61 ECA Report (n 60) 27.

62 Commission Report 2018 (n 60) 5.

63 DAC1 art 8(2).

is available. Consequently, Member States are not obliged to investigate or gather information solely for AEOI purposes and must rely on other States' willingness to collect information for their own needs first in the hope that this information may be communicated to them through the AEOI framework.[64] This has led to wide discrepancies in what is being reported by the States and the amount of information exchanged for each category.[65]

In regard to the EOIR, beyond specific cases and grounds for refusal to cooperate, EOIR exchanges may be limited by the required standard of 'foreseeable relevance' of the information.[66] The subjective concept of foreseeable relevance and the assessment of whether a request meets that standard have reportedly proven to be difficult for the Member States.[67] Arguably, however, the standard of EOIR in DAC1 is wider than the OECD standard, as the latter has a wider scope concerning the information to be exchanged.[68] It is, therefore, easier to produce a valid request for information under DAC1 than under the OECD Standard.[69]

Finally, in the context of the SEOI framework, in the absence of a specific request, tax authorities find it challenging to establish whether one of the five categories of circumstances that calls for SEOI has been triggered. Similarly, SEOI exchanges are mandatory solely in case of potential tax loss or tax increase in the other Member States, other situations are subject to voluntary communications, which may limit the effectiveness of the exchange framework.[70] Article 9(2) is particularly problematic as the Directive refers to information that 'may be useful' for the Member State, a concept which remains quite vague.[71]

11.3.2 Effectiveness of the Directive

While most authors agree that the directive has achieved its goal of increasing cooperation among Member States, the effectiveness of DAC1 has been challenged. Numbers showcase that the new system established by DAC1 can

---

64 Vascega and van Thiel (n 4) 154 discusses both the issues with the availability standard and the possibility for the European Commission report to lead to an amendment that would allow for the limitation of that standard.

65 ECA Report (n 60) 20.

66 For more on the concept, see Part I, Chapter 1 in this book.

67 European Parliament, *Implementation of the EU requirements for tax information exchange, European Implementation Assessment* (European Parliamentary Research Service 2021) (EP Research Paper) 82.

68 Kaye (n 7) 13.

69 Vascega and van Thiel (n 4) 152.

70 EP Research Paper (n 67) 2.

71 Seer (n 13) 71.

be considered successful as EOI in all 'types' has been increasingly popular and the volume of exchanges has been growing steadily across each category. According to research, the number of DAC1 AEOI exchanges has increased steadily since 2015. In its first three years (2015–2017), there have been 11,000 exchanges, concerning around 16 million taxpayers for a combined value of all income covered of around 120 billion.[72] Likewise, EOIR exchanges have been increasing at a steady pace over the years.[73] SEOI exchanges have also increased exponentially since 2016,[74] almost reaching a number of exchanges of eight times higher in 2017 compared to the numbers in 2014.[75]

However, despite this success in numbers, the lack of quality of the information exchanged as well as its underuse by Member States, arguably, impede the effectiveness of the directive.[76] The information exchanged is often incomplete due to the limited income categories in DAC1, the 'freedom' of Member States to choose which category of income they are willing to include in their AEOI system and the availability clause. The fact that very few Member States have made all categories of information available for exchange creates information gaps, although the adoption of DAC7 may have provided a (partial) solution to that issue. Beyond AEOI, Member States have also raised concerns as to the quality of information being exchanged under EOIR, as a large number of requests required additional information.[77]

Beyond the quality of information, the results as to the actual use of the information exchange are also mixed: While the European Court of Auditors (ECA) concludes that both EOIR and SEOI information sent is used and dealt with,[78] the information exchanged under the DAC1 AEOI framework is apparently vastly underused as it states that little of the information received is actually sent to local tax administration offices.[79] Similarly, the Commission finds little evidence that the information collected through the AEOI system is actually being used by Member States.[80] One example of this, according to the Commission, is that, on average, the information received was only opened

[72] EP Research Paper (n 67) 91.

[73] ECA Report (n 60) 39.

[74] ibid 40.

[75] EP Research Paper (n 67) 94.

[76] ECA Report (n 60) 22.

[77] EP Research Paper (n 67) 85; European Commission, *Evaluation of Administrative Cooperation in Direct Taxation* (Final Report, 2019) (EC Report 2019) 42.

[78] ECA Report (n 60) 41–43.

[79] ibid 32.

[80] Commission Staff Working Document on the application of Council Directive (EU) no 2011/16/EU on administrative cooperation in the field of direct taxation [2017] SWD(2017) 462 final (Commission Working Document 2017) 3–4.

a year following the exchange,[81] possibly undermining the timeliness of the reaction of the receiving tax administration.

The underuse of the exchanged information can be explained by the difficulties Member States have in matching the information received with the relevant taxpayer. According to the ECA, this is most likely due to lack of technology solutions leading to substantial variations as to the matching rate across Member States.[82] The Commission found that very few Member States had automatically associated the TIN of the taxpayer with the information concerned, while many never associated it.[83] This issue may be solved by DAC7, which makes Member States automatically exchange the TIN alongside other information as of 2024.[84] Apart from improving matching in information treatment, another way to limit the underuse of information by Member States would be for them to bilaterally agree on only exchanging information on certain categories they deem relevant and provide guarantees that the exchanged information will actually be used.[85]

Other criticisms inherent to the EOI framework pertain to the increase in data that tax administrations have to deal with and the risk of infringements to the protection of personal data.[86] It has been argued that setting up a WHT system could circumvent these difficulties, as it would take into account the differences among States (e.g., access to resources or size of the State). However, such a system could disincentivise Member States from cooperating all together (e.g., as happened with Luxembourg and Austria in the context of the Savings Directive), and the successive amendments to the DAC have sufficiently increased the scope and reworked certain issues (e.g., the availability clause) to reduce limitations towards making the framework more effective.[87]

11.3.3 Technical Questions in the EOI Framework

When looking into the transposition of DAC1 into domestic laws, three main issues arise, namely the timeliness of the exchanges among Member States, the organisation of the EOI framework domestically, and the resources available to Member States to comply with their obligations.

---

81 Commission Report 2018 (n 60) 7.
82 ECA Report (n 60) 25 and 29–30.
83 Commission Report 2018 (n 60) 6.
84 DAC7 art 1(6).
85 Seer (n 13) 72.
86 Marino (n 38) 4.
87 Nicodème (n 1) 765.

Despite the positive development of including specific time limits in DAC1, Member States do not always abide by these time limits.[88] For AEOI purposes, timelines are not respected, as the exchanges usually take place one year after the information has become available to the Member States, instead of six months, as provided in DAC1.[89] The Commission also found that there were wide discrepancies across Member States with respect to time limits.[90] While the ECA found that EOIR are usually answered on time, and delays only occur if the request is not sufficiently clear,[91] the Commission states that EOIR are not as timely as they should be and that only about half of the EOIR requests were fulfilled in the six month time frame set in DAC1. According to the tax administrations, most of these delays resulted from difficulties in obtaining the information from the taxpayer or due to an ongoing investigation. There have been very few instances where Member States have agreed bilaterally on a different time limit as provided in the DAC (those cases often involved complex investigations with information held by banks).[92]

Most authors and representatives of Member States agree that the organisational structure provided in DAC1 is particularly favourable to the development of a well-functioning cooperation framework, especially in regards to the creation of a Central Liaison Office (CLO). According to literature, the designation of a CLO, the centralised authority, makes the exchange of information faster and more effective as other Member States' administrations know which authority to contact. These improvements to the framework were necessary to foster confidence between Member States and to ensure a continuous cooperation centred around a single point of contact (between Member States and between local and national tax offices)[93] which also contributes to accelerating the rate of exchange.[94] The introduction of standardised forms for EOIR and SEOI in DAC1 and computerised, standardised forms for AEOI constitute one of the most important steps forward.[95] This solution allows for language barriers to be overcome as the standardised form does not require translation.[96] In the same vein, Article 21(4) provides that any cooperation

---

88 Vascega and van Thiel (n 4) 152; Marino (n 38) 8; Christensen and Tirard (n 30) 905; Michael Schilcher and Karoline Spies, 'The Directive on Mutual Assistance in the Assessment and in the Recovery of Tax Claims in the Field of Direct Taxation' in M. Lang et al (eds), *Introduction to European Tax Law on Direct Taxation* (Linde 2018).

89 ECA Report (n 60) 27.

90 Commission Report 2018 (n 60) 7.

91 ECA Report (n 60) 41.

92 Commission Working Document 2017 (n 80) 3–5.

93 Seer (n 13) 73.

94 ibid 3.

95 ibid 70.

96 ibid.

request, including notifications and documents, can be made in any language agreed upon between the two authorities, allowing Member State to simply determine which language should be used for all exchanges, effectively eliminating language-related issues.[97]

Finally, the EOI framework in the directive is highly dependent on the resources available to Member States. For the DAC to be effective, Member States must rely on technology and sufficient staff to address the significant increase in the data they have to deal with.[98]

Despite the welcomed addition of the Fiscalis Programme 2020 (which has now been extended as the Fiscalis Programme 2027) that provides for technological support for solutions to improve the EOI framework in the DAC,[99] Member States have requested further support to introduce newer technologies to facilitate the functioning of the EOI system.[100] The reinforcement of domestic databanks appears to be one of the most pressing matters. To improve cooperation among Member States the European Commission is contemplating the idea of building a central database that would be linked to the domestic databases, when/if those comply with EU standards.[101] It is worth noting that the Directive does introduce the CCN ('Common Communication Network') to ensure the faster and more effective transmission of information via electronic means. However, according to Article 21(2), Member States are responsible to develop domestic computerised systems of EOI that would work together with the CNN. This framework should be complemented by sufficient staff resources. Currently, the personnel directly allocated to the EOI framework varies considerably among states.[102]

11.3.4 Evaluation of the Directive

One main shortcoming that risks compromising the effectiveness of DAC1 is the absence of sufficient monitoring of the actual functioning of the EOI framework at both state level and European level. While Article 23 of the Directive provides for an evaluation system of the functioning of the DAC1 (and the subsequent DACs), including a specific assessment of the AEOI framework, there is no specific national assessment on the enforcement and the

97 Isabel Gabert, 'Council Directive 2011/16/EU on Administrative Cooperation in the Field of Taxation' (2011) 51 European Taxation 342, 346.
98 Commission Working Document 2017 (n 80) 4.
99 ECA Report (n 60) 23.
100 ibid.
101 Marino (n 38) 10.
102 Commission Working Document 2017 (n 80) 2.

performance of the EOI framework.[103] Also, little to no checks are made on the quality of the data sent through the DAC1 AEOI framework, as cited earlier.[104]

Beyond AEOI, not enough feedback is sent back by requesting states on the quality of information due to the large number of SEOI and EOIR. This is to be expected, as the directive has no provision requiring feedback from the requesting state in the context of EOIR or SEOI,[105] unlike AEOI, where authorities have to send feedback once a year.[106] This lack of feedback, however, prevents the Commission from assessing the SEOI/EOIR's effectiveness and may undermine the continuous improvement of the EOI framework.[107]

Finally, as there is no evaluation of the penalties implemented by Member States and their enforcement, it is very difficult to determine whether or not they are actually useful.

11.3.5 Remaining Legal Questions

Besides the aforementioned issues, other legal issues can be identified with regard to DAC1. One of these issues is the directive's relationship with fundamental rights, which will only be explored here briefly.[108] It is obvious that the protection of personal data and privacy in the context of EOI is particularly relevant, especially in relation to the GDPR.[109] According to the literature, all information exchanged under the directive is compliant with the regime set by the GDPR that acknowledges tax information exchanges as being of utmost importance for the public interest.[110] This not only covers intra-European exchanges but also exchanges with third States according to Article 24 DAC.

---

[103] ECA Report (n 60) 45–46.

[104] ibid 24.

[105] DAC1 art 14(1): The Member State wishing to receive feedback on a EOIR or SEOI communication should first ask for it from the other State.

[106] DAC1 art 14(2).

[107] ibid; Report from the Commission to the European Parliament and the Council on the application of Council Directive (EU) 2011/16/EU on administrative cooperation in the field of direct taxation [2017] COM(2017) 781 final 3; ECA Report (n 60) 43.

[108] For more details on the relationship between EOI and fundamental rights, see Part I, Chapters 4, 5 and 6 in this book.

[109] Reference to the repealed data protection directive, currently GDPR, is made in DAC7. Subsequent amendments to the DAC reflect compliance with the GDPR, for instance, limitations were added relating to the retention of data.

[110] Regulation (EU) 2016/679 of the European Parliament and of the Council of 27 April 2016 on the protection of natural persons with regard to the processing of personal data and on the free movement of such data, and repealing Directive 95/46/EC (General Data Protection Regulation) [2016] OJ L 119/1 (GDPR), recital 112.

Other fundamental rights may also be at stake when complying with the DAC obligations, including Article 47 EU Charter of Fundamental Rights (Charter),[111] which might give rise to the right to appeal for the taxpayer and necessitate notification for every personal data disclosure made in the context of the DAC, risking of severely undermining the effectiveness and timeliness of the exchange.[112] In addition, the principle of good administration, which encompasses several rights relevant in this context, such as the rights to access to documentation and to a reasoned decision, may entail additional responsibilities and obligations on behalf of the tax authorities. Finally, commercial secrecy has remained a protected principle under the DAC (contrary to banking secrecy) as it is protected as a fundamental right under the freedom to conduct a business in Article16 Charter[113], but also because commercial secrecy does not aim at protecting income from taxation.[114]

Another legal issue that has arisen in the context of the DAC is the application of Article 24(1) DAC, according to which a Member State may provide another Member State information received from a third state, if this information is foreseeably relevant and if this is allowed pursuant to the DTC between the Member State and the third state. According to Spies, this particular issue might not be as relevant as first anticipated.[115] First, the wording of Article 24 DAC seems to only refer to information already available following an exchange between a Member State and a third State, barring the possibility to specifically initiate an exchange with the aim of then transmitting it to another Member State. Second, according to the OECD Model Convention Standard (OECD MC), exchanges are only possible if the information is foreseeably relevant for the other Contracting State, excluding all exchange initiated for the purpose of transmitting the information to another Member State. Furthermore, the OECD MC seems to prohibit the passing of information received through Article 26 to another state without express consent from the other Contracting State. Interestingly, this seems to severely limit the possibility for exchanges under Article 24 between Member States on information received through a convention with a third state.

---

111 See Part I, Chapter 6 in this book.

112 Roman Seer and Sascha Kargitta, 'Exchange of Information and cooperation in direct taxes' in Christiana H.J.I. Panayi, Werner Haslehner and Edoardo Traversa, *Research Handbook on European Union Taxation Law* (Edward Elgar Publishing 2020) 507.

113 It is also protected under Charter of Fundamental Rights of the European Union [2012] OJ C 326/391, art 17.

114 Kaye (n 7) 13 and Gabert (n 97) 345.

115 Schilcher and Spies (n 88).

Other limitations in the directive, such as Article 16 DAC, which limits the use of information exchanged only to tax purposes, unless Member States acquire authorisation first, may raise problems. This is because, first, approval is given on voluntary basis, as the requested State is not obliged to give right to the demand of the requesting State. Second, no time limits are provided for the requested State to give its authorisation,[116] thus undermining the timeliness of the use of the information.

Similarly, the grounds for refusal to cooperate foreseen in the directive have also led to much discussion, as, according to Vascega and Van Thiel, the possibility for Member State to deny exchange of information based on the justification that it is against domestic law could end up having a reciprocal effect as Member States can also refuse to exchange information based on the fact that the other Member State is legally unable to provide similar information.[117] The availability standard could lead to similar refusals by Member States due to lack of reciprocity.[118] The ground for refusal for lack of exhaustion of domestic investigation possibilities in the requesting state represents the balance between the principle of subsidiarity and the risk of jeopardising the objectives of DAC1.[119] The possibility of refusal based on the exhaustion of domestic procedures is nevertheless impossible for the requested state to verify, which must, thus, rely on the good faith of the requesting state. Nevertheless, according to the European Commission, there have been very few explicit refusals based on Article 17.[120]

11.4 DAC2

11.4.1 Background

The need for more revenue for states hard-hit by the financial crisis, together with a series of tax and financial scandals,[121] has shifted the focus at a global level to curbing tax avoidance practices in order to ensure enough revenue,

[116] ECA Report (n 60) 80.

[117] DAC1 art 17(2) and (3).

[118] Christensen and Tirard (n 30) 906.

[119] Seer (n 13) 72.

[120] Commission Working Document 2017 (n 80) 5, according to which 31 refusals between 2013 and 2016 were based on DAC1 art 17.

[121] See e.g. LuxLeaks files (2014), database available at: <https:// www .icij .org/ investigations/ luxembourg -leaks/ explore -documents -luxembourg -leaks -database/ > accessed 7 December 2023; International Consortium of Investigative Journalists, An ICIJ Investigation: The Panama Papers: Exposing the Rogue Offshore Finance Industry (ICIJ: Stories that Rock the World, 2016), available at <https://www.icij.org/ investigations/panama-papers/> accessed 7 December 2023.

but also to appease public opinion that was governed by a feeling of injustice. In order to combat tax evasion and tax avoidance, abolishing bank secrecy and solidifying and enhancing exchange of taxpayers' information became a priority.

With this purpose in mind, the OECD developed the Common Reporting Standard (CRS) in 2014, in response to the G20. According to the CRS, financial institutions have to regularly report all capital income held by non-resident individuals and entities, as well as their account balances and the different tax administrations have to automatically exchange that information with other jurisdictions on an annual basis, effectively abolishing bank secrecy, in certain cases. The general consensus is that it was the USA, as a major economic player, which deserves credit for this major regulatory breakthrough.[122] Its 'indirect contribution' materialised in 2009 through the adoption of the Foreign Account Tax Compliance Act (FATCA) that obliged foreign financial institutions to automatically report to the IRS on the income of non-resident US customers. The penalty for failing to do so would be a 30% withholding tax on the payments the institution receives from US sources. By 2014, the USA had concluded bilateral FATCA agreements with more than 100 jurisdictions, including traditionally 'non-cooperative' jurisdictions.[123] Despite this framework, which could be seen as the precursor to the CRS, it has been shown that, in fact, there was no reciprocity in the exchange of information under FATCA agreements.[124] This resulted in a situation where the USA would receive the requested information, without disclosing equivalent information on non-residents to its treaty partners.

Part of literature was of the opinion that the adoption of DAC2 was spurred from the inclusion in DAC1 of the MFN clause and the consequences of the FATCA agreements.[125] Because of the MFN, Member States that had committed under bilateral or multilateral agreements with third states to a wider cooperation than the one under the DAC had to provide the same level of cooperation also to other EU Member States, non-members to these agreements, upon their request. Therefore, the amendment of the DAC was considered pressing in

---

[122] See indicatively, Lukas Hakelberg, *The Hypocritical Hegemon – How the United States Shapes Global Rules against Tax Evasion and Avoidance* (Cornell University Press 2020); Patrick Emmenegger, 'The long arm of justice: U.S. structural power and international banking' (2015) 17 Business and Politics 473; Lukas Hakelberg, 'Coercion in international tax cooperation: identifying the prerequisites for sanction threats by a great power' (2016) 23 Rev Int'l Pol Economy 511.

[123] Hakelberg (n 122).

[124] Hakelberg (n 122); Allison Christians, 'What you give and what you get: reciprocity under a model 1 intergovernmental agreement on FATCA' (2013) Cayman Financial Rev 24.

[125] Somare and Wöhrer (n 42) 814. See also DAC2 recital 7.

order to avoid possible tensions between the Member States.[126] Others suggest that the momentum coming from and the enthusiasm for FATCA, rather than fear of the possible tensions arising from the MFN clause, were the main drivers behind the first amendment to DAC1.[127] Regardless of the underlying purpose, these political and international pressures led to a deviation from the original plan under DAC1, according to which the intended amendment would only happen at the earliest in 2017 (and not in 2014 when DAC2 was adopted).

In light of the FATCA and the many uncoordinated agreements existing between Member States,[128] the adoption of DAC2 aimed also at reducing costs and administrative burdens both for tax administrations and for economic operators, and at ensuring that the expanded scope of automatic exchange of information within the EU was in line with international developments.[129] Thus, the reporting and due diligence obligations enshrined in DAC2 had to be fully consistent with those set out in the CRS. DAC2 or the EU CRS equivalent, was adopted in 2014. Member States were obliged to apply the DAC2 measures as of 1 January 2016, and the first information exchange between national tax authorities was due by 30 September 2017.[130]

The implementation process was not an 'easy ride', as can be showcased by the high number of infringement proceedings opened by the European Commission for late implementation of the DAC2.[131] Presumably, this high number could be explained not only by the complexity of the Directive, but also by the required involvement of the financial sector in the process.

DAC2 repealed the Savings Directive, and due to DAC2's wider objective (covering all types of income from financial assets and the value of the assets) and subjective scope (covering accounts held by both individuals and legal persons, as well as interposing entities, under conditions), many of the problems identified in the context of the Savings Directive were rectified.

11.4.2 Content in Brief

The main idea behind DAC2 is identical to that of the CRS, that is, that banks and other financial institutions play a crucial role in providing information on

---

[126] ibid 814.

[127] Marino (n 38) 19.

[128] Concluded in light of and under DAC1 art 19.

[129] DAC2 recital 78.

[130] Because of existing structural differences, Austria was allowed to exchange information automatically under this Directive for the first time by 30 September 2018 instead of 30 September 2017, see DAC2 recital 7 and Section X.

[131] According to the EP Research Paper (n 67) 16, the European Commission opened 13 infringement procedures in relation to DAC2.

taxpayer's income and assets to tax authorities around the globe. The ultimate purpose, as illustrated also in the preamble of DAC2, is to limit opportunities for tax fraud and tax evasion and to increase the efficiency and effectiveness of tax collection.[132]

DAC2, as the CRS, is built on the following concepts and procedures: the Reporting Financial Institutions (FIs) in Member States must follow a list of reporting and due diligence rules, enshrined in Annex 1 of DAC2. Different due diligence procedures apply depending on the nature of the 'Reportable Account', notably whether the account belongs to an individual or an entity and whether it is pre-existing (to the implementation of the directive) or new. Thus, the FI must report to the competent authority of its Member State the requisite information with respect to each different category of financial accounts, the so-called 'Reportable Accounts'. This information is then automatically exchanged by the Member States on an annual basis through a secure IT network, the CCN system.

Section VIII of Annex 1 becomes of particular importance as it provides all defined terms for the purposes of DAC2, including what an FI is and what falls under Non-Reporting Financial Institutions.[133] In principle, according to DAC2, all financial institutions that are not Non-Reporting Financial Institutions, are considered FIs. FIs include custodial or depository institutions, investment entities, and specified insurance companies.[134]

In terms of procedure, as a first step, the FIs have to identify the Reportable Accounts. These are accounts held by individuals or entities resident for tax purposes in any other Member State. However, the FIs do not have to identify the residence of all their account holders but may rely on the due diligence procedure set out in Annex 1 to assume the Member State of residence.[135]

'Reportable Accounts' include also accounts of 'Controlling Persons' and 'Passive NFE' (non-financial institutions), where one or more controlling persons are resident for tax purposes in any other Member State. This means that FIs must also report, under conditions, on accounts held by interposed legal entities or arrangements, and therefore, FIs are effectively required to 'look through' the often complex ownership structures to find beneficial

---

[132] DAC2 recital 1.

[133] Annex 1, section VIII (B) provides a list of the Non-Reporting Financial Institution that includes primarily and in brief, financial institutions that qualify as Governmental Entities, International Organisations, Central Fund, Pension Funds, 'any other Entity that presents a low risk of being used to evade tax [and] has substantially similar characteristics to any of the Entities described [above], an Exempt Collective Investment Vehicle.

[134] DAC2 Annex 1, Section VIII (A).

[135] Somare and Wöhrer (n 42) 808.

owners.[136] However, certain financial accounts are excluded from reporting for being considered as low-risk.[137] The relevant information to be reported covers, inter alia, the account balance and value and different types of investment income (e.g., interest and dividends).

11.4.3 Progress and problems

DAC2 is a directive that – despite its many merits, adds a high degree of complexity to Member States' cooperation and their relationship with reporting institutions. In contrast, taxpayers are little affected by this complexity due to their 'passive' involvement in the reporting and AEOI.[138]

Both Member States and FIs have reported problems that relate to the high compliance costs DAC2 entails. This comes as no surprise as, in addition to the technical details of the directive, Member States and FIs must navigate the co-existence of DAC2, their relationship with the USA as established by the bilateral FATCA agreements, and a multilateral framework modelled in accordance with OECD's Global Standard.[139] Despite the obvious relationship between the CRS and DAC2, disparities still exist across the different rules and standards, especially regarding collection, storage and transmission of data that fall primarily on the FIs to solve.[140] Indicatively, the EP study indicates that complying with the procedures laid down in DAC2 costs Member States approximately twice as much as it costs them to comply with DAC1 and DAC3

---

136 Oberson (n 37) 189.

137 These include: (i) corporations listed at a recognised stock exchange and their related entities, (ii) governmental entities, (iii) international organisations, (iv) central banks, (v) and financial institutions.

138 As noted by Stjepan GadŽo and Irena Klemencic, 'Effective international information exchange as a key element of modern tax systems: promises and pitfalls of the OECD's common reporting standard' (2017) 41 Public Sector Economics 207, 218: 'In light of the mechanics of information exchange envisaged in the Global Standard, it is perfectly clear that the additional cost linked with the complexity of the new regime is not an issue for the taxpayers, since their role in the international information exchange is merely "passive"'.

139 The OECD Global Standard for AEOI constitutes the basis for the Common Reporting Standard (CRS); OECD, *Standard for Automatic Exchange of Financial Account Information: Common reporting standard* (OECD 2016).

140 Frans Vanistendael, 'The international information exchange puzzle' (2016) 75 Tax Notes International 1149, 1152; Ross McGill, 'International – GATCA: The Globalization of Anti-Tax Evasion Frameworks' Derivatives & Financial Instruments' (2016) 18 Finance and Capital Markets, section 5.1; Itai Grinberg, 'Beyond FATCA: An Evolutionary Moment for the International Tax System' (2012) Georgetown Law Faculty Working Papers, available at: <https://scholarship.law.georgetown.edu/fwps_papers/160/> accessed 7 December 2023.

together.[141] From a technical aspect, according to the European Commission, Member States have found difficulties in downloading and uploading DAC2 data.[142] These practical difficulties may even compromise the Member States' ability or incentive to comply with the provisions.[143]

Other practical difficulties that may compromise the effectiveness of the directive relate to the quality of information itself and the ability of different Member States to process such high amounts of information. The lack of resources and the consequent inability of many states to handle and process such amounts of information is a general problem in the context of AEOI in DACs and beyond, as pointed out earlier. The different capacities of different tax administrations towards this purpose is a problem that has been pointed out within and outside the EU.[144]

The last assessment made by the Commission only covered September 2017 to March 2018 and provided limited results with regard to the information exchanged in the context of DAC2.[145] Nonetheless, it found that 4 000 messages were exchanged covering 8.3 million accounts, and end-of-the-year account balances were by far the most exchanged information, with redemption or sale of financial asset coming in second, other unspecified income third, whereas information relating to interest and dividend income lagged behind.

The possible inaccuracy of the information is another element that may compromise the effectiveness of the directive towards limiting tax evasion and tax fraud. This is because under DAC2 most due diligence requirements are satisfied by simply checking that the self-certification provided by the account holder seems reasonable or by relying on Anti Money Laundering (AML) / Know Your Customer documentation. In absence of enhanced due diligence procedures, especially for lower value individual accounts, the possibility of misrepresentation by account holders becomes a real possibility.

Loopholes can also be detected with regard to FIs. Although, at first glance, the term appears to cover a broad range of institutions, DAC2 allows for several exceptions, such as certain types of pension funds and FIs that present a low risk of being used to avoid tax. Among those entities that are not obliged to report one can also find investment entities managed by an individual rather than a reporting FI. Although the expressed exempted entities may allow

---

[141] ECA Report (n 60) 86.

[142] Commission Working Document 2017 (n 80) 4.

[143] ibid; noting also the Minutes of the 18th meeting of the Sub-Group on the Automatic Exchange of Information Register, 2020.

[144] McGill (n 140) section 7.

[145] This is because information collection as per DAC2 was planned to start on 1 January 2016.

certain accounts to 'escape' reporting, DAC2 may also inadvertently allow prospective tax evaders to avoid reporting of their offshore financial assets.

For instance, while, for individuals holding accounts through the interposition of a passive NFE, the latter would have to be looked through to identify who the controlling persons are,[146] the same does not apply to accounts held through *active* entities. In the latter case, only the residence of the entity needs to be reported, and not that of controlling persons/beneficial owners.[147] In these cases, only if the entity is resident in the EU and is subject to rules under the AML Directive, will the beneficial owner be identified.[148]

The limited 'understanding' of the beneficial ownership concept under DAC2 also allows for possible overrides. While the directive refers primarily to 'account holders' and 'controlling persons' that is, individuals who exercise control over an entity, it mandates that '[t]he term [...] must be interpreted in a manner consistent with the Financial Action Task Force Recommendations', [149] which recommends setting a minimum threshold of 25% to determine beneficial ownership. Thus, anyone holding 25% or less of the ownership interest will not be identified as a beneficial owner or controlling person.

Another flaw, also common to the CRS and FATCA reporting draws, again, from the circumstances under which FIs need to report the beneficial owners of the accounts. As Noked notes, in cases where accounts and assets are held through closely-held private companies and family trusts, that qualify as FIs but are controlled and managed by the beneficial owners of those accounts/assets, then imposing a reporting obligation on these entities is in substance similar to requiring self-reporting of the beneficial owners.[150]

11.6 CONCLUSION

There is no doubt that the adoption of DAC1 and DAC2 constitutes a fundamental change in the field of direct taxation. These two directives solidify the exchange of information in the EU, and they set the legal framework for AEOI, EOIR and SEOI (DAC1), while also effectively abolishing bank secrecy in certain cases (DAC2). Thus, they have both opened up a new era in the EU's fight against tax evasion.

---

146 In this case the residence of both the entity and the controlling person(s) would have to be reported.

147 ECA Report (n 60) 73.

148 ibid.

149 DAC2 Annex 1, Section VIII, D (5).

150 Noam Noked, 'FACTA, CRS, and the Wrong Choice of Who to Regulate' (2018) 22 Florida Tax Review 77, 81.

It is common for academic scholarship, policy reports, and stakeholders to focus on the flaws of each 'new' legal framework. The present contribution has also discussed these flaws that risk compromising the effectiveness of the directives and often result in imposing heavy burdens on the different stakeholders.

Yet, the contribution of DAC1 and DAC2 to the EU's fight against tax evasion should not be overlooked. The numbers of bilateral exchanges provided above show that the coordination between Member States indeed works well and has brought to light tax evasion scandals.[151] In addition, several economic analyses show the positive impact that the CRS and FATCA had on fighting tax evasion. For instance, it has been found that the CRS introduced a reduction of 11.5% in cross-border deposits parked in tax havens,[152] and that 'household assets in tax havens that are not hidden behind corporate identities are estimated to be 67% lower than they would have been without automatic exchange of information'.[153] Given that DAC2 constitutes the implementation of the CRS in the EU, these findings could be carefully transposed in the intra-EU framework. A distinct 'success' to be credited to DAC2 is that it constitutes the first successful attempt of the EU to implement internally an OECD Global Standard.

Besides the obvious positive direct effect, the first two DACs also paved the way for the evolutionary and gradually increasing AEOI framework that followed. Had the experience with the first two directives not been so positive, it is doubtful whether we would currently count eight DACs. In addition, they opened the way for the application of the Charter and the fundamental rights enshrined therein in the exchange of information among Member States. Considering that bilateral exchanges of taxpayer's information were until then based on Article 26 OECD MC (if the given DTC included such or an equivalent), it becomes obvious that requests based on DAC1 now allow taxpayers to invoke the protection of the Charter. Despite their shortcomings, DAC1 and DAC2 laid the foundations for the EOI in the EU, and now constitute possibly the most important instrument in the EU's fight against tax evasion, tax fraud and tax avoidance. What remains, in order to increase their effectiveness, is for

---

151 See for instance Joined Cases C-245/19 and C-246/19 *État luxembourgeois v B and Others* [2020] ECLI:EU:C:2020:795.

152 Elisa Casi-Eberhard, Christoph Spengel, and Barbara MB Stage, 'Cross-border tax evasion after the common reporting standard: Game over?' (2020) 190 (C) Journal of Public Economics 104240.

153 Leo Ahrens and Fabio Bothner, 'The Big Bang: Tax Evasion After Automatic Exchange of Information Under FATCA and CRS' (2020) 25 New Political Economy 849.

Member States and the EU to work together towards improving the available resources to make full use of this framework.

12. DAC3: mandatory automatic exchange of information on advance cross-border rulings and advance pricing arrangements

Alicja Brodzka

12.1 INTRODUCTION

In recent years, one instrument of fiscal optimisation has raised certain doubts on their acceptability: individual tax rulings. The initial purpose of tax rulings is to provide legal certainty for the taxpayer and reduce financial risk in cases in which the application of tax regulations is unclear or subject to diverging interpretations.[1] Theoretically, tax rulings have particular importance in complex transactions with a cross-border element, as such arrangements to prevent future disputes between the taxpayer and the tax authority. In practice, in some EU Member States tax agreements have been commonly used to grant tax benefits arbitrarily, in isolation from the actual economic activity of international entities.

In November 2014, 'Lux Leaks' revealed the scale of Luxembourg's secret deals, featuring complex financial structures designed to obtain drastic tax reductions.[2] At the same time, the European Commission decided to launch a broader inquiry into whether the tax policies of Luxembourg and the other EU Member States are compatible with EU law or, instead, give rise to state

1 European Parliament, European Parliament Resolution of 25 November 2015 on tax rulings and other measures similar in nature or effect (2015/2066(INI)) [2015] OJ C 366.

2 Leslie Wayne, Kelly Carr, Marina Walker Guevara, Mar Cabra and Michael Hudson, 'Leaked Documents Expose Global Companies' Secret Tax Deals in Luxembourg' (date issued 05 November 2014), <https://www.icij.org/investigations/luxembourg -leaks/ leaked -documents -expose -global -companies -secret -tax -deals -luxembourg/> accessed 7 December 2023.

aid issues.[3] Moreover, the 2015 investigation of a Special Committee of the European Parliament (TAXE Committee) confirmed that Luxembourg's practices were not an isolated issue, and that tax rulings were often issued without a legal framework through informal or discretionary arrangements.[4]

These findings triggered a European initiative towards decreasing the opacity of the entire tax rulings system. As a consequence, on 8 December 2015, the EU Member States decided on the amendment of the Directive on Administrative Cooperation in the field of direct taxation. Council Directive (EU) 2015/2376 (further: DAC3) extended the scope of mandatory automatic exchange of information (AEOI) to advance cross-border rulings (ATR) and advance pricing arrangements (APA) that are provided to companies and other entities in respect of all taxes except VAT, customs duties, excise duties and compulsory social security contributions.[5] DAC3 has been in force since 1 January 2017, with the first information exchange carried out by 30 September 2017.

The main aim of this chapter is to provide an in-depth analysis of the Directive. First, it presents the concepts behind DAC3 and focuses on the discussed options with respect to the scope of the Directive, the type of information to be exchanged and the additional measures implemented in order to increase the effectiveness of the designed instrument. Next, the chapter focuses on the effectiveness of the Directive with specific reference to the issues of DAC3 transposition, followed by the analysis of the volume, the quality and the use of DAC3 information exchanges. The chapter also identifies some sensitive issues, namely potential discrepancies in international and EU standards and the loopholes that reduce the effectiveness of the AEOI on tax rulings. The analysis allows some suggestions for the future strengthening the EU's tax information exchange system.

---

[3] The first in-depth investigations, Apple in Ireland, Starbucks in the Netherlands and Fiat Finance & Trade in Luxembourg (June 2014) were followed by the case of Amazon in Luxembourg (October 2014) and the tax rulings that used Belgium's 'excess profits' tax regime (February 2015). In parallel with these formal investigations, the Commission decided to extend its inquiry into tax rulings practices in general so as to cover all Member States, see: European Commission, Report on Competition Policy 2014, Report from the Commission to the European Parliament, the Council, the European Economic and Social Committee and the Committee of the Regions COM(2015) 247 final, 15.

[4] European Parliament, Special Committee on Tax Rulings and Other Measures Similar in Nature or Effect, Report on tax rulings and other measures similar in nature or effect (2015/2066(INI)), p. 10/87.

[5] Yvonne Quirke and Anne Margaret Gormley, 'New International Requirements on the Exchange of Information on Tax Rulings' (2016) 29(3) Irish Tax Review 98.

12.2 DAC3 NEGOTIATING PROCESS

12.2.1 AEOI on Advance Cross-border Tax Rulings: the Options Discussed

The previous version of DAC already provided for the mandatory spontaneous exchange of information between EU Member States. In reality, however, countries shared little data about their cross-border tax rulings. It was the country itself that decided whether a tax ruling might be relevant to another EU Member State – for instance, in cases where one Member State had grounds for supposing that, as a result of the concluded ruling, there may be a loss of tax in another state.[6] The amended Directive removed Member States' discretion to decide what information is shared, when and with whom, as it introduced the duty to exchange information automatically on cross-border tax rulings. DAC3 established a so-called two-phase approach: the first phase, i.e., the 'push' phase, requires the automatic exchange of information (AEOI) between countries. Subsequently, as a second or 'pull' phase, the Member States receiving the information should be able to request further information where appropriate. This new initiative fitted the policy of maximum transparency and EOI that the European Commission has been following as part of the OECD Base Erosion and Profit Shifting programme (BEPS).[7]

The main issue discussed during the negotiating process while drafting the DAC3 provisions was the diversity of tax rulings applied by the EU Member States. The European Commission intended to cover the administrative practice of ATRs, APAs and all 'other advance tax arrangements'. The crucial question was whether the Member States would qualify their country-specific 'statements', 'opinions', 'decisions', 'clearances', etc., as a 'tax ruling' in the sense of this Commission proposal on AEOI.[8] In the process of drafting the Directive several options were taken into account. They were presented in a Commission staff working document.[9] The document highlighted the main doubts arising in determining the proper definition of 'tax ruling' and provided the reasons for the final choices.

---

[6] DAC3 recital 3.

[7] Frans Vanistendael, 'Automatic Exchange of Tax Rulings in the EU' (2015) 78 Tax Notes International 261.

[8] European Parliament, *Tax rulings in the EU Member States* (2015) Study for the ECON Committee IP/A/ECON/2015-08, 6–7.

[9] European Commission, Commission Staff Working Document on the technical analysis of focus and scope of the legal proposal Accompanying the document Proposal for a Council Directive amending Directive 2011/16/EU as regards exchange of information in the field of taxation, SWD(2015) 60 final, 39.

The next part of the chapter focuses on the decision-making process on the issues that provoked most debate: the type of tax agreements to be covered by the provisions of the Directive, together with the additional conditions and exclusions regarding the AEOI and the scope of information exchanged under DAC3. It also presents a new instrument chosen to enhance the efficient use of resources and facilitate the exchange of information: a secure central directory.

12.2.2 Type of Tax Rulings Covered by DAC3 – the Debate on the Objects of Reporting

Within the negotiation process on types of tax rulings to be covered by the amended Directive, three areas were identified and discussed: (1) cross-border vs. domestic tax rulings, (2) pre-return vs. post-return tax rulings, and (3) unilateral vs. bilateral and multilateral tax rulings – as the options of rulings to fall within the scope of DAC3.

12.2.2.1 Cross-border vs. domestic tax rulings

While considering whether DAC3 should be limited to cross-border aspects or also include domestic rulings, the first option prevailed. It was decided that only tax rulings potentially affecting another EU Member State or a third country should be covered as they may influence the establishment or functioning of the internal market. However, in order to avoid future problems, the Directive should offer a precise definition of cross-border rulings.

12.2.2.2 Pre-return vs. post-return tax rulings

In the discussion, the question arose as to whether DAC3 should cover only advance (e.g., pre-return) rulings, or that, additionally, post-return rulings should be taken into account as well. The extension of tax rulings to post-return ones was found to be excessive: it would lead to an unjustified administrative burden (since post-return rulings would only lead to a limited potential increase of the projected changes).[10] The chosen option was thus to remain within the initially proposed approach, enhanced by the definition of advance tax rulings. As a consequence, the definition was intended to cover tax rulings that are provided either before the relevant transaction (or series of transactions) took place, or in advance of the deadline for filing a tax return covering the period in which the transaction takes or took place. The definition should also include tax rulings given in the context of a tax audit when they apply to future years for which tax returns have not yet been received. Such a solution was expected

[10] ibid 49.

to have a positive impact on the effectiveness of the planned measure, as it would eliminate any potential ambiguity in its interpretation.[11]

12.2.2.3 Unilateral vs. bilateral and multilateral tax rulings

The considerations concerning the question of whether the proposal should include only unilateral tax rulings or also bilateral and multilateral ones, resulted in the recommendation of extending the coverage to all tax arrangements.[12] Such a move would, according to the European Commission, create a more effective measure to enhance transparency in tax practices while avoiding the creation of blind spots. It would also ensure simplification by eliminating the Member States' discretionary assessments of whether all foreseeably relevant rulings had been included in the AEOI process. This approach would also avoid potential circumvention of the information exchange by adapting aggressive tax planning strategies and tax practices in that direction. Including bi- and multilateral tax rulings into the AEOI mechanism was perceived as an extension of the current framework, but in line with the horizontal objective of fighting tax avoidance, thus having a significant impact on the overall coherence of the system. The additional administrative burden in the exchange of information was considered limited and justified.[13]

12.2.2.4 Wide vs. narrow definition of international tax ruling

As mentioned above, the Commission's work resulted in a statement that an explicit definition of cross-border tax rulings is required. A wide definition would ensure complete coverage, and contribute better to increasing overall transparency. A narrower definition of tax rulings would reduce the administrative burden of the associated restricted information exchange, but also limit the number of tax rulings subject to AEOI, thus weakening the intended increase in transparency.[14]

---

[11] On the other hand, some authors point out that tax rulings are covered only if they are considered 'advanced', but not if they are issued after filing the tax return, for instance during a tax audit. Doubts were also raised as to whether such an option would not create a loophole to circumvent the provisions of the Directive. It might be plausible for taxpayers who want to avoid AEOI of their ruling to start their activities first (at a smaller scale than ultimately anticipated) and only thereafter conclude a tax ruling, see: Andres Knobel, *Reporting Taxation: Analysing Loopholes in the EU's Automatic Exchange of Information and how to Close Them* (2018) Report Commissioned by the Greens/EFA Group in the European Parliament, 35, Rijkele Betten, 'EU Directive on Exchange of Information about Advance Rulings Implemented in Legislation' (2017) 24 International Transfer Pricing Journal 401.

[12] European Commission (n 9) 50.

[13] ibid.

[14] ibid 48–50.

In the negotiations the first option prevailed. The broad definition of 'international tax ruling' was to cover various situations, including, but not limited to:

- advance pricing arrangements and/or decisions: both unilateral and bilateral/multilateral ones;
- permanent establishment arrangements/decisions that determine: the existence (or absence) of a permanent establishment; or the existence (or absence) of facts with a potential impact on the permanent establishment's tax base;
- arrangements/decisions determining the tax status of a hybrid entity in a Member State which relates to a resident of another jurisdiction;
- arrangements/decisions on an assessment basis for the depreciation of an asset in a Member State that is acquired from a group company in another jurisdiction.[15]

12.2.3 The Scope of the AEOI Mechanism

12.2.3.1 Tax ruling

As a consequence of its design, DAC3 provides quite a wide definition of 'tax rulings', in order to capture all similar instruments and irrespective of the actual tax advantage involved, as 'any agreement, communication or other instrument or action of similar effect (including one issued in the context of tax audits), given by or on behalf of a Member State, regarding the interpretation or application of its tax laws'.[16]

The scope of the AEOI includes tax rulings of any material form, irrespective of their binding or non-binding character and how they are issued.[17]

---

[15] DAC3 recital 6.

[16] It means rulings that are issued (amended or renewed) in relation to a particular person (or a group of persons), and upon which that person is entitled to rely. The scope covers rulings issued by, or on behalf of, the government or the tax authority of a Member State, or its territorial or administrative subdivisions, including local authorities – irrespective of whether they are effectively used, see DAC3 art 3(14) and (15).

[17] In some opinions such a wide definition raises serious doubts: it could be understood that not only written, but also oral rulings are covered. The meaning of the former is not evident, given that only rulings on which the taxpayer is entitled to rely fall under the scope of DAC3. One possible interpretation could be that this covers situations where an agreement as such is not (yet) 'reliable' (i.e., able to be relied upon), but – seen together with the behaviour of tax authorities – does give rise to legitimate expectations. If so, it is not easy to determine the point in time when the ruling is granted and, thus, subject to mandatory exchange, see: D. Van Stappen, Wolfgang Oepen, Eugena Molla, 'Mandatory Automatic Exchange of Information on Tax Rulings: Political

Member States are obliged to exchange information irrespective of whether or not the taxpayer abides by the terms of the advance cross-border tax ruling.[18]

DAC3 provisions also specify how the abovementioned 'cross-border decisions' and 'advance pricing arrangements' should be understood. Both definitions are placed in the amended Article 3 of the Directive.

12.2.3.2 Advance Tax Ruling

Pursuant to Article 3(14), 'Advance Tax Ruling' (ATR) means any agreement involving the interpretation or application of a legal or administrative provision, which concerns the administration or enforcement of national laws relating to taxes in the Member State. The ruling must relate to a cross-border transaction or to the question of whether activities carried out by a person in another jurisdiction create a permanent establishment. Moreover, the arrangement should be made in advance of the transactions/activities in another jurisdiction potentially creating a permanent establishment – or in advance of the filing of a tax return covering the period in which the transaction or series of transactions or activities took place. The cross-border transaction may involve, but is not restricted to, investments, provision of goods, services, finance or the use of tangible or intangible assets and does not have to directly involve the person receiving the advance cross-border ruling. Consequently, the ATR can cover various types of taxes and income and all income types can fall under the scope of the provisions.

12.2.3.3 Advance Pricing Arrangement

The definition of 'Advance Pricing Arrangement', included in Article 3(15), is comparable with the definition for general ATR, with the addition that the ruling concerns cross-border transactions between associated enterprises and contains the criteria for the advance determination of the transfer pricing for those transactions, or determines the attribution of profits to a permanent establishment.

12.2.4 Additional Requirements and AEOI Exclusions

DAC3 foresees some additional conditions for mandatory AEOI. According to the new Article 8a, information about cross-border tax rulings issued (amended or renewed) on or after 1 January 2017 is to be exchanged within

---

Agreement Reached in ECOFIN Council' (2016) 3(1) International Transfer Pricing Journal 11.

[18] DAC3 recitals 5, 7, 8.

three months following the end of the half of the calendar year during which the cross-border pricing agreements are issued, amended or renewed.

What is important is that 'old' (but still existing) arrangements issued before this date also fall under the scope of DAC3. For the years 2012–2013, the mandatory EOI on cross-border tax rulings were to take place only if they were still valid on 1 January 2014; for the years 2014–2016, the required exchange of information on qualifying tax rulings would take place before 1 January 2018, irrespective of whether they were still valid or not.[19] For all 'old' rulings within the scope of DAC3, the information had to be communicated before 1 January 2018.

Member States were granted the possibility of excluding certain cross-border tax rulings from the AEOI obligation, if they were issued to companies with an annual net turnover of less than EUR 40 million at group level – on condition that the arrangements were issued, amended or renewed before 1 April 2016. However, this exemption did not apply to companies conducting mainly financial or investment activities.[20]

Generally, the provision of information should not have led to the disclosure of commercial, industrial or professional secrets or of commercial processes, or the disclosure of information which would be contrary to public policy.[21]

It is worth stressing that the amended Directive did not apply to domestic tax rulings with no consequences for other Member States nor to tax rulings concerning individuals. Such an exclusion seemed to be a consequence of the fact that data protection concerns could not be overcome for individuals.[22]

Moreover, DAC3 excluded some bilateral or multilateral APAs with third countries from mandatory AEOI. This paragraph was included for reasons of legal certainty, to follow the framework of existing international treaties, where their provisions do not permit the disclosure of the information received

---

[19] The Proposal for the Directive dealt with a ten-year period. However, opinions expressed in the consultation process pointed out that that the transmission of all tax rulings issued in the last ten years, including those which are not still valid, would constitute an excessive administrative burden, see: European Committee of the Regions, Opinion of the European Committee of the Regions – tax transparency package (2015/C 423/14) [2015] OJ C423/77; and, European Parliament, European Parliament legislative resolution of 27 October 2015 on the proposal for a Council Directive amending Directive 2011/16/EU as regards mandatory automatic exchange of information in the field of taxation (2017/C 355/21) [2017] OJ C355/134.

[20] DAC3 art 8a(2).

[21] DAC3 recital 9.

[22] DAC3 art 8a(4). On the other hand, according to the Opinion of European Committee, this restriction on the scope of application can be seen as a step backwards compared with Directive 2011/16/EU. At present, rulings concerning exclusively natural persons can be exchanged within the EU using the spontaneous mode.

under that treaty to a third country. Such bilateral or multilateral APAs should be exchanged with the use of spontaneous EOI on the condition that the DTA under which the arrangement was negotiated permits its disclosure, and the competent authority of the third country gives permission for the information to be disclosed.[23]

12.2.5 The Type of Information to be Exchanged under AEOI

The discussion on the scope of information to be exchanged focused on the first phase of EOI, i.e., the 'push' element, which is the mandatory and automatic information exchange by the sending Member State. The scope of information exchanged in response to a possible subsequent 'pull' request by the receiving Member States remains unaffected.

The first option of minimum information sharing covered an explicitly listed minimum number of key elements, that should enable the receiving Member States to identify whether the respective ruling might be relevant to them. Such a choice would allow for ensuring the administrative burden proportionate was to the objectives of the initiative. However, the more limited the set of key variables to be exchanged in the first 'push' phase, the more likely it is that the receiving Member States would not be able to recognise whether the tax ruling might be relevant to them or not. The consequence could be a large number of the second phase 'pull' requests for detailed information because of too limited information sent in the first, mandatory and automatic phase.

After taking into account the abovementioned elements, another option prevailed. In addition to the key elements exchanged, Member States were to provide a brief summary of the tax ruling. Such a solution should ensure greater effectiveness than the option limited to minimum information. Each receiving state would be better positioned to conclude whether the tax ruling potentially has an impact on them. Moreover, the summary could further increase transparency by providing relevant information to other, not directly affected, Member States as well. The preparation of the summary would require an additional administrative burden. Nevertheless, this would be out-weighed by the limited number of unnecessary 'pull' requests, thanks to the access to the relevant information.[24]

---

23 DAC3 art 8a(3).

24 European Commission (n 9) 52.

Based on the above, the information to be communicated by the sending Member State through AEOI shall include the following:

- the identification of the person (other than an individual), and, where appropriate, the group of persons to which it belongs;
- a summary of the content of ATR/APA, including a description of the relevant business activities or transactions or series of transactions provided in abstract terms, without leading to the disclosure of commercial, industrial or professional secrets or of commercial processes, or of information whose disclosure would be contrary to public policy;
- the dates of issuance, amendment or renewal of ATR/APA;
- the start date of the period of validity of ATR/APA, if specified;
- the end date of the period of validity of ATR/APA, if specified;
- the type of the ATR or APA;
- the amount of the transaction or series of transactions of ATR/APA if such amount is referred to in the ruling;
- the description of the set of criteria used for the determination of the transfer pricing or the transfer price itself in the case of an APA;
- the identification of the method used for the determination of the transfer pricing or the transfer price itself in the case of APA;
- the identification of the other Member States, if any, likely to be concerned by ATR/APA;
- the identification of any person (other than an individual) in the other Member States, likely to be affected by ATR/APA (indicating to which the Member States the affected persons are linked); and
- the indication whether the information communicated is based upon the APA itself or upon the request (in case of tax arrangements with third countries that do not allow for disclosure of the information received under that treaty to a third-party country).[25]

Such information exchanged in the first, automatic, phase, which consists of key elements complemented by a summary, should ensure the effectiveness of the whole EOI process. In the second phase the receiving Member States may request additional information, including the full text of the tax ruling.[26]

DAC3 also contains a clause stating that the information received by the Member States under the Directive shall be covered by the obligation of official secrecy of the applicable national law of the Member State.[27]

---

[25] DAC3 art 8a(6).

[26] DAC3 art 8a(10).

[27] DAC3 art 23a(2). Frans Vanistendael stresses that the same information, communicated to different Member States, can be protected in different ways and that only the

12.2.6 The EC Central Directory

DAC3 also foresaw the implementation of a new instrument to enhance the efficient use of resources and facilitate the EOI: a secure central directory. A central directory allows the uploading of information by the individual EU Member States and its safe storage. Such a solution should prevent the duplications of national IT systems and – more importantly – increase the security of sensitive data. The directory shall be accessible to all Member States and, to the extent required for monitoring the correct implementation of the Directive, to the Commission.[28]

Tax authorities can access the Central Directory both on a regular basis (in order to verify whether any relevant information has been added) and on a case-by-case basis when the need arises (e.g., during a tax audit). As mentioned above, if a Member State finds itself affected by a specific tax ruling described and stored in the EC Central Directory, it may request additional information from the state that issued the tax ruling. After obtaining such information, the receiving state should send feedback on the EOI to the sending state. This was considered necessary to create an effective AEOI system, as it should enhance international cooperation between EU countries and improve the quality of the information exchanged. In practice, this mandatory feedback should be provided through arrangements agreed upon bilaterally on an annual basis.[29]

---

weakest national protection rule will apply, since the information will freely cross the borders of the internal market, see: Vanistendael (n 7) 262.

[28] During the consultation process, particular emphasis was placed on the confidentiality of information and its potential use by the European Commission. Consequently, the Directive was adopted with the reservation, stating that: ‘information communicated to the EC (…) may not be used for any purposes other than those required to determine whether and to what extent Member States comply with this Directive’ (DAC3 art 23a(1)). Moreover, some key elements of information are not be communicated to the EC: the identification of the person, a summary of the content of tax ruling, the identification of the method used for the determination of the transfer pricing and an indication of whether the information communicated is based upon ATR or APA itself or upon the request (DAC3 art 8a(8)). Further reports studying the effectiveness of DAC3 point that the Commission can only extract statistical information on the activities of Member States from the Directory. As the complete information provided in the Central Directory is accessible only by the Member States, no details are available on the nature of the rulings (i.e., ATR or APA), the date of issue, the duration and the industry. Therefore, the concluded analysis must be limited to the review of key trends, see: European Commission, *Evaluation of Administrative Cooperation in Direct Taxation*, Final Report (24 April 2019) (hereinafter: EC Evaluation) 52.

[29] DAC3 recital 15.

Moreover, the European Commission stated that transparency and access to information at an early stage should allow the authorities to improve the speed and accuracy of their risk assessment and make timely and informed decisions on protecting their tax revenues. Ideally, information concerning a specific scheme could be obtained before it is implemented and used.[30]

12.3 THE EFFECTIVENESS OF DAC3 PROVISIONS

12.3.1 Reviews by Several Institutions

The European Commission intended to evaluate the objectives and the overall impacts on companies and the internal market five years after the implementation of the instrument. Meanwhile, in April 2019, the Commission released an Evaluation Study,[31] that looked at DAC as a complex system. The Commission indicated that by that time, Directive 2011/16/EU had been amended five times (DAC2 to DAC6). The evaluation analysed the Directive as a whole and posed questions about its efficiency, effectiveness, relevance and coherence. It also sought to check whether the administrative cooperation in direct taxation delivered added value for the EU. Two years later, in 2021, the European Court of Auditors (ECA) prepared their Special Report,[32] intending to assess the key aspects determining the effectiveness of the EOI system in the EU. The audit, which covered the period 2014–2019, looked at the legislative framework that the Commission proposed and put in place, and examined how well it was monitoring the implementation and performance of the EOI system. Also in 2021, the European Parliamentary Research Service (EPRS) released a complex analysis of the implementation of the EU requirements for tax information exchange.[33]

The next sections present the most critical conclusions regarding the effectiveness of DAC3 arising from the abovementioned reports, by focusing on the process of DAC3 transposition and accompanying costs, the volume and the quality of information exchanges, and the use of the exchanged information.

---

[30] This measure was perceived as very perceptive, as it would dissuade intermediaries from designing and marketing such schemes. As a consequence, the mandatory disclosure of potentially aggressive tax planning schemes was implemented with DAC6, see Part II, Chapter 15 in this book.

[31] EC Evaluation (n 28).

[32] European Court of Auditors, 'Exchanging tax information in the EU: solid foundation, cracks in the implementation' Special Report 3 (2021) (hereinafter: ECA Report).

[33] European Parliamentary Research Service, Implementation of the EU requirements for tax information exchange (2021) (hereinafter: EPRS Study). Also see Part I, Chapter 7 in this book.

They also identify obstacles to be overcome and provide some recommendations for future amendments to the AEOI system on tax agreements.

12.3.2 DAC3 Transposition, Preparation for Implementation and Compliance Costs

The provisions of DAC3 concerning the AEOI on tax rulings were to be implemented by the EU Member States by 31 December 2016. The transposition process took longer than envisaged, but was eventually completed with no outstanding issues.[34] About two-thirds of the Member States adopted the necessary measures on time and notified the Commission accordingly.

The preparatory work for implementing DAC3 was carried out at two levels, the EU and the individual MS. The Commission was responsible for the design of the Central Directory of cross-border tax rulings. The Commission presented the directory prototype in January 2016, and the system's first release became available in April 2017, shortly before the initiation of exchanges. The preparatory work at the level of the Member States involved: (1) identifying the information to be exchanged, (2) formulating summaries of tax rulings to be uploaded to the EC Central Directory, and (3) adapting the necessary IT systems. Based on the available information, Member States started sharing information in mid-June 2017, but the bulk of the information was uploaded in the second half of 2017.

The information on the costs borne by the Member States for transposing the rules and operationalising DAC3, incurred in the first year (i.e., up to the end of 2017), has been provided by 13 countries. The implementation of AEOI on the provisions of tax rulings resulted in total compliance costs of around EUR 2.2 million.[35] This modest figure – compared to the expenses of the Member States to pay for other AEOI amendments of the Directive – was mainly due to the fact that the relevant information was uploaded to the Central Directory, managed by the Commission. Moreover, the amount of information to be exchanged turned out to be much lower than in the cases of DAC1 and DAC2. Those two facts reduced the complexity of the IT systems and procedures that had to be put in place by the Member States, with obvious implications for the related costs.

---

[34] In 2017, the Commission opened infringement procedures for late transposition by issuing letters of formal notice to nine Member States. The procedures with the Czech Republic, Estonia, Greece, Hungary and Poland were closed in 2017 itself, whereas reasoned opinions were sent to Belgium, Bulgaria, Cyprus and Portugal. Finally, all of the infringement procedures were closed by 2018, see EC Evaluation (n 28) 42.

[35] EC Evaluation (n 28) 101.

12.3.3 The Volume of the Information Exchanged

As of 1 February 2018, Member States had sent information on 17,652 tax rulings. The information included data on 11,457 tax rulings in force and 6,195 tax rulings discontinued before the start of the exchanges. Since the mandatory exchange started in June 2017, these figures referred to the 2017 data of 24 countries.[36] The statistics were based on the data extracted by the Commission from the Central Directory. As a consequence, no details were provided on the nature of the rulings (i.e., ATR or APA), the date of issue, the duration nor the industry. Therefore, the analysis presented in the Evaluation was limited to the review of key trends.

The statistics, however, made it possible to determine the direction of the information flow. The country leading the ranking in terms of information exchanged was the Netherlands, with nearly 9,000 tax rulings (e.g., more than 50% of the total traffic). Luxembourg ranked second, with data disclosed on nearly 5,000 ATR/APA (accounting for over 25% of the total). The UK was a distant third, with data uploaded to the Directory on just over 1,200 tax rulings (7% of the total). All other Member States together accounted for about 2,600 ATR/APA (15% of total traffic), with only four Member States (Belgium, Ireland, Italy and Poland) accounting for at least 1% of the total. Information on the total number of ATR/APA in force in the EU Member States was not available. Still, the above ranking seems to reflect the use of this instrument by various countries.[37]

The comparison between 17,652 information exchanges of 2017 and none in 2013, 11 in 2014 and 113 in 2015, proves that, before DAC3 entered into force, the EOI on tax rulings (which would have been possible on a spontaneous basis) took place very rarely.[38] While the Netherlands was one of the few countries to send information on tax rulings even before the adoption of DAC3, Luxembourg and the UK started sending some information only in 2016. That year also Spain communicated some 220 rulings. It brought the 2016 total volume of DAC3 information exchanges to 2,529.[39]

As mentioned above, the number of exchanges peaked in 2017, soon after they became mandatory, including ATR/APAs issued before 2017 in the first

[36] Bulgaria, Croatia, Greece and Romania had not sent any DAC3 related information by this time.

[37] EC Evaluation (n 28) 52–53.

[38] European Parliament, European Parliament Resolution of 16 September 2021 on the implementation of the EU requirements for exchange of tax information: progress, lessons learnt and obstacles to overcome (2020/2046(INI)) [2021] OJ C 117, 123.

[39] EC Evaluation (n 28) 53.

reporting data set. In subsequent years, the number of exchanges dropped: in 2018 there were 4,352 exchanges on tax rulings, and the year 2019 saw 4,950.[40]

12.3.4 The Quality and Comprehensiveness of DAC3 Exchanges

Due to the recent implementation of DAC3, the 2017 Commission Evaluation could not provide a comprehensive assessment of the quality and exhaustiveness of the directive. However, during the initial period of the national implemented provisions being in force, one critical issue emerged: the insufficient level of detail in the summary of the tax ruling uploaded to the Central Directory. Member States tax authorities pointed to the limitations on the usability of this tool, as the summaries often did not include the most important information to arrive at a sufficient understanding of the ruling itself. They also declared the need for guidance on what to put in the summaries of tax rulings.[41]

Later reports examined the uploads to the Central Directory and found no significant issues with the completeness of the database. However, data quality could be deficient. The Member States sometimes did not name individual taxpayers. This would prove to be an obstacle to data matching in the target country. The additional inquiry led by the ECA confirmed the conclusions of the Commission Evaluation: some summaries lacked sufficient detail to properly understand the underlying information. As a result, it was difficult for Member States to know when to request further information and, if they did, to demonstrate its relevance for tax assessment purposes.[42]

12.3.5 The Use of DAC3 Information

In 2017 it was still too early to assess the extent to which Member States put the DAC3 information to good use. The Commission Evaluation concluded that the transparency of advanced rulings has increased, given that the introduction of the provision resulted in a significant growth in the number of tax rulings disclosed. Predictably, the information on tax rulings from AEOI was mostly used in corporate taxation (though a few respondents also mentioned individual taxation). Countries intended to use the information collected in the DAC3 process mainly for high-level risk assessment. At the same time, the Commission stated that DAC3 thus far had not affected the behaviour of tax

---

40 ECA Report (n 32) 34.
41 EC Evaluation (n 28) 77.
42 ECA Report (n 32) 35.

authorities in granting ATR/APA, nor the attitude of enterprises affected by these rulings.[43]

More recent reports showed that DAC3 information in the Central Directory was mostly complete, but not used much by the Member States. The ECA Report mentioned that those Member States which were interviewed during the review process do not have systematic procedures for the risk analysis of DAC3 data nor for the use of the information in the Central Directory. Only one of five examined Member States had analysed the DAC3 information uploaded in 2017 and selected some for further investigation. Although the country could generally match the information to taxpayers, it had no procedure for analysing and using it in its taxation follow-up.[44]

There is also one more important aspect of the EOI process: the feedback, that should finally lead to improving the quality of the information exchanged. The overall assessment of DAC revealed that in 2017 all Member States provided and received AEOI feedback, but not all of them did it in the case of DAC3 exchanges (they did so only with respect to DAC1). The lack of common practice in the DAC3 field could be explained by the different periods covered by the various clauses of DAC (i.e., DAC1, DAC2, DAC3). In this regard the Commission expressed their hope that the feedback procedure, which worked with DAC1, would become a standard practice for DAC3 in years to come.[45]

12.3.6 Discrepancies in a Worldwide EOI System: BEPS and DAC3

The Commission Evaluation also looked at the relations between two standards of EOI on tax rulings – the international standard, deriving from BEPS Action 5, and the European one, driven by the provisions of DAC3. The obligations under both initiatives are very similar. However, the different institutional setting implies that, under DAC3, the information on cross-border tax rulings is available to all Member States once uploaded to the Central Directory, while, under BEPS Action 5, the rulings need to be exchanged with the 'relevant jurisdictions' (i.e., those that may be affected by the ATR/APA). This can result in a duplication of efforts, in particular when the same ruling must be uploaded both to the Central Directory and exchanged with non-EU jurisdictions. Moreover, as the scope of the two obligations differs regarding

---

43 EC Evaluation (n 28) 83, 94.

44 See more in Part I, Chapter 7 in this book.

45 EC Evaluation (n 28) 53.

the types of ATR and APA to be exchanged, the types and number of rulings to be exchanged remain different. This can cause uncertainty and confusion.[46]

From an operational perspective, the EU solution of a centralised directory was considered more efficient. DAC3 was also perceived as superior to BEPS Action 5 at a more technical level due to exchanging the data in a single, automatically processable XML format. The conclusion stated that, as the OECD provided for several more complex formats, it meant the information was not (always) automatically processable. On the other hand, some Member States' tax authorities raised doubts about the overly restricted format of information downloaded to the Central Directory, as it could cause additional difficulties, making the Directory impossible to search and impractical for analytical purposes.[47]

12.3.7 Potential Problems Reducing the Effectiveness of DAC3 Provisions

Evaluation reports highlighted a number of loopholes in DAC3 provisions, which contributed to creating potential problems and reducing the effectiveness of AEOI on tax rulings. The most synthetic analysis was presented in the 2021 EPRS Study.[48]

With respect to the scope of the provision, some doubts were raised – especially the issue of old, pre-2012, ATR/APAs, and the fact that the DAC3 did not cover rulings concerning individuals or domestic arrangements, which might however have an impact on another Member State. It also pointed out the possibility of circumventing the DAC3 reporting obligations by submitting information on ATR/APA only after (and not in advance of) making a transaction, creating a permanent establishment or filing returns. Moreover, the study also mentioned the annual net turnover threshold of EUR 40 million, under which old tax rulings for non-financial or investment corporations do not need to be reported.

In respect of legal obstacles, there were two key issues identified: (1) a public disclosure issue, as there were no public disclosure requirements under DAC3 which would have an impact on the objective of transparency, and (2) a legal interpretation issue, as in the qualitative evidence indicated there could be conflict between how the Directive and the national legislation define the same concepts, for example, an APA for DAC3.

---

46 EC Evaluation (n 28) 123.

47 EC Evaluation (n 28) 126.

48 EPRS Study (n 33).

Regarding practical obstacles linked to DAC3, the problem related to the summary information contained in the Central Directory was confirmed: it was often too brief to be used without requesting additional information from the issuing state. What is more, tax authorities could decide to categorise an ATR or APA as being non-cross-border and hence not upload them to the central directory.[49]

In September 2021 the European Parliament released the Resolution on the implementation of the EU requirements for EOI, which presented similar weaknesses. It also provided a set of recommendations that could increase the effectiveness of DAC3, such as: (1) widening the scope of AEOI to include informal arrangements, but excluding 'advance' rulings (for example, post-transaction agreements or after filing the returns), individuals[50] and rulings which were still valid, but which were issued (amended or renewed) before 2012; (2) a mechanism of specific notification to be sent to the tax administrations where a company benefiting from a tax ruling in the scope of DAC3 had a taxable presence; (3) renegotiating by EU Member States and not agreeing to any future international tax agreements which do not permit the disclosure of APAs; (4) broadening the scope of information exchanged under tax agreements with third countries, such as Andorra, Liechtenstein, Monaco, San Marino and Switzerland; and, (5) developing guidelines on what tax administrations should provide as a summary, which should include all relevant direct and indirect tax implications, such as the effective tax rates.[51]

Last but not least, the Resolution deplored the practice of shadow tax rulings in Luxembourg, exposed by the 2021 'LuxLetters' revelations,[52] which led to

---

49 EPRS Study (n 33) 22, 24 and 120.

50 The extension of the scope of AEOI to cross-border tax rulings concerning wealthy individuals (HNWIs) is foreseen in the DAC8 Proposal, see: European Commission, 'New transparency rules require service providers to report crypto-asset transactions' (date issued 8 December 2022), <https:// taxation -customs .ec .europa .eu/ news/ new -transparency -rules -require -service -providers -report -crypto -asset -transactions-2022-12-08_en> accessed 7 December 2023.

51 European Parliament (n 38) 126–32.

52 In 2015 Luxembourg amended its law and nowadays the issuing of tax rulings in this country is subject to precise procedural regulations. However, the 2021 'LuxLetters' revealed the existence and application of secret tax practices in Luxembourg that breach EU transparency rules. In response, Luxembourg provided assurances that the country is compliant with both EU and international standards in the field of EOI of tax rulings. Luxembourg also declared that the number of such tax rulings decreased significantly (over 90% in the period 2015–2020), see: Patrick Mischo and Franz Kerger, 'After "Lux Leaks": Welcome Changes to Luxembourg's Tax Ruling Practice' (2015) 77 Tax Notes International 1197; Wojciech Morawski, 'Will the European Union Put an End to the "Golden Age" of Tax Ruling?' (2020) 3 Acta Universitatis Carolinae Iuridica 61; Tax Justice Network, 'EU and OECD half-measures fail to

informal arrangements not being reported under DAC3 provisions. Next, it urged the Commission to assess the potential breach of the DAC3 requirements (both by Luxembourg and the other Member States with similar practices) and to launch infringement proceedings in necessary cases.

The Resolution confirmed that certain blind spots of DAC3 may have unintended negative effects, such as tax administrations not exchanging information on tax rulings if these are too favourable; or tax administrations resorting to informal arrangements in order to avoid exchanges. To improve the objectives of the provision, emphasis should be placed on closing existing gaps in implementation and monitoring rather than on creating new rules.

12.4 CONCLUSIONS

Reducing the scope for harmful tax competition and increasing the transparency of national tax systems were the reasons behind implementing the DAC3 measures that extended the AEOI to international tax rulings. The main findings of the chapter show that the analysed provisions were transposed by all Member States and triggered the exchange of a substantial amount of information, which increased over the years. Despite its relatively recent implementation, DAC3 has already started contributing to the capacity of Member States to fight tax evasion and avoidance, thanks to the new EOI instruments it placed at the disposal of Member States. At the same time, this has so far not affected the average behaviour of tax authorities in granting advanced tax rulings and pricing agreements nor the attitude of firms demanding for these rulings. In this light, while no significant challenges emerged that would require a short-term legislative revision, some amendments could be made in order to close the loopholes and increase the effectiveness of the provision.

detect Luxembourg's shadow tax rulings' (date issued: 1 July 2021), <https://taxjustice.net/press/eu-and-oecd-half-measures-fail-to-detect-luxembourgs-shadow-tax-rulings> accessed 7 December 2023; Luxembourg Government, 'LuxLetters. Statement by the Luxembourg Government on press articles published about tax rulings and so-called information letters' (date issued: 4 July 2021), <https://gouvernement.lu/en/dossiers/2021/luxletters.html> accessed 7 December 2023.

13. DAC4 on CbCr: a powerful tool in the hands of tax administration with regard to transfer pricing

Vasiliki Athanasaki

13.1 INTRODUCTION

In recent years, within the frame of the modern, highly digitalised global tax era, tax avoidance and tax evasion phenomena have been rapidly increasing.[1] Aggressive tax planning techniques and harmful tax practices not reflecting economic reality and real economic substance have become increasingly elaborate and, thus, very difficult to identify and properly scrutinise. Nowadays, international commerce is mainly conducted through big multinational groups ('MNE Groups' or 'MNEs'). Consequently, many transfer pricing issues arise from a tax perspective, resulting in many transfer pricing[2] disputes.

Tax authorities need comprehensive and relevant information on MNE Groups regarding their overall structure, transfer-pricing policy and internal intra-group transactions,[3] given that the lack of quality data on corporate taxation is a major limitation to measuring the fiscal and economic effects of tax avoidance, making it difficult for authorities to carry out transfer pricing assessments on transactions between associated companies and even more

---

1 See European Commission, 'Combatting corporate tax avoidance: Commission presents Tax Transparency' (Press Release, 18 March 2015), <https://ec.europa.eu/commission/presscorner/detail/en/MEMO_15_4609> accessed 7 December 2023.

2 See also Vikram Chand, 'Transfer Pricing Aspects of Intra-Group Loans in Light of the Base Erosion and Profit Shifting Action Plan' (2016) 44(12) Intertax 885.

3 See Office of the Commissioner for Revenue, 'Guidelines for the implementation of The EU Council Directive 2016/881/EU of 25 May 2016 amending Directive 2011/16/EU as regards mandatory automatic exchange of information in the field of taxation (DAC4) in Malta and the 2015 Final Report on Action 13 of the OECD/G20 Base Erosion and Profit Shifting Project, version 1.3.' <https://cfr.gov.mt/en/inlandrevenue/itu/Documents/CbCR%20Guidelines_Version%204.pdf> accessed 7 December 2023.

difficult to carry out audits.[4] As transfer pricing is not an exact science,[5] it seems that the intensification of the international, cross-border activity entails a significant reconstruction, recreation and evolution of the whole architecture of the international tax law.

In this respect, it is clear that increased tax transparency and effective administrative cooperation and assistance between states is of vital importance, as these factors are crucial to tax stability, tax certainty and tax justice. In the present chapter, the tax framework concerning the automatic exchange of the CbCr introduced under DAC4 will be thoroughly examined. First, an overview of DAC4's origins will be presented, followed by an analysis of its main provisions, and, lastly, some critical remarks will be given in this respect.

13.2 THE ORIGIN OF THE DAC4: THE OECD PERSPECTIVE

Action 13 of the OECD/G20 BEPS Action Plan on Base Erosion and Profit Shifting ('BEPS Action Plan' or 'BEPS') introduces a minimum standard whereby all large MNE groups with combined revenues of €750 million or more are required to prepare an annual return, the so-called country-by-country report (CbCr),[6] with aggregate data on the global allocation of income, profit, taxes paid and economic activity among the tax jurisdictions in which it operates.[7] This CbCr breaks down the key elements of the MNE group's financial statement by jurisdiction, providing local tax authorities with useful information for transfer pricing and BEPS risk assessment[8] as well as for tax audit and resource allocation purposes. In essence, the preparation of a CbCr constitutes

---

4 OECD, 'Country by country reporting' (Taxation and Customs Union, n.d.), <https:// taxation -customs .ec .europa .eu/ country -country -reporting _en> accessed 7 December 2023.

5 OECD, Transfer Pricing Guidelines for Multinational Enterprises and Tax Administrations 2017 (OECD Publishing 2017) para 4.8.

6 See James M. Stewart, 'CbC reporting and measuring effective tax rates' (2021) 102(9) Tax Notes International 1213.

7 See also Arco C.P. Bobeldijk and Paul Klaassen, 'Country-by-Country Reporting and the Effective Tax Rate: How Effective Is the Effective Tax Rate in Detecting Tax Avoidance in Country-by-Country Reports?' (2019) 47(12) Intertax 1057. According to the authors, a low effective tax rate in combination with a high profit can be an important indicator of possible tax avoidance. The authors conclude that the effective tax rate calculated based on the country-by-country report cannot be accurately used in high level risk analyses.

8 See OECD, *Country-by-Country Reporting Handbook on Effective Tax Risk Assessment* (2017), <https:// www .oecd .org/ tax/ beps/ country -by -country -reporting -handbook-on-effective-tax-risk-assessment.pdf> accessed 7 December 2023.

a tax reporting obligation, with additional reporting obligations being implemented in both the banking and extractive industries sectors.[9]

The CbCr includes information for every tax jurisdiction in which the MNE group operates, on the amount of revenue, the profit before income tax, the income tax paid and accrued, the number of employees, the stated capital, the retained earnings and the tangible assets.[10] The CbCr is a highly useful tool of modern taxation, which analytically depicts the geographical allocation of specific critical elements among various group entities around the world. It provides for a template for multinational enterprises (MNEs), which was officially released with the September 2014 BEPS Report on Action 13 to report annually and for each tax jurisdiction in which they do business the information set out therein.[11]

In response to this requirement, a three-tiered standardised approach to transfer pricing documentation has been developed,[12] which comprises the master file, the local file and the CbCr. The CbCr should be drafted by large multinationals and should include specific elements on an annual basis, as well as an identification of all the group entities per tax jurisdiction along with a description of the exact business activities carried out respectively. Taken together, these three documents require taxpayers to articulate consistent transfer pricing positions and provide tax administrations with useful information to assess transfer pricing risks, make determinations about where audit resources can be most effectively deployed, and, in the event audits are called for, provide information to commence and target audit enquiries.[13]

CbCrs are primarily filed in the jurisdiction of the headquarters of the parent entity and, in the case that said jurisdiction has not implemented CbC reporting, a surrogate parent entity must be determined and must undertake the filing procedure instead. The relevant information is exchanged electronically in the

---

[9] Deloitte, *Country by Country Reporting, the FAQs* (2016), <https:// www2 .deloitte.com/content/dam/Deloitte/global/Documents/Tax/dttl-tax-country-by-country -reporting-faqs.pdf> accessed 7 December 2023.

[10] OECD, 'Country by country reporting' (Taxation and Customs Union, n.d.), <https:// taxation -customs .ec .europa .eu/ country -country -reporting _en> accessed 7 December 2023.

[11] OECD/G20 base Erosion and Profit Shifting Project, *Action 13: Country-by-Country Reporting Implementation Package* (2015), <https:// www .oecd .org/ctp/transfer-pricing/beps-action-13-country-by-country-reporting-implementation -package.pdf> accessed 7 December 2023.

[12] See OECD/G20 Base Erosion and Profit Shifting Project, *Transfer Pricing Documentation and Country-by-Country Reporting, Action 13 – 2015 Final Report* (OECD Publishing 2015) <http://dx.doi.org/10.1787/9789264241480-en> accessed 7 December 2023.

[13] See OECD (n 12).

CbC XML Schema[14] format[15], in order to ensure the uniformity and quality of information exchanged.

13.3 ANALYSIS OF THE PROVISIONS OF DAC4

13.3.1 Introductory Remarks

'DAC4'[16] extended the scope of the DAC when it comes to automatic exchange of information, in order to also include the automatic exchange of tax information included in the CbCrs at EU level, following the BEPS Action 13 report and the minimum standard it introduced.[17] DAC4 should have been adopted and published by Member States by 4 June 2017, and Member States should have begun applying those measures from 5 June 2017 onwards.

---

[14] Extensible Markup Language (XML) is a markup language and file format for storing, transmitting, and reconstructing arbitrary data. It defines a set of rules for encoding documents in a format that is both human-readable and machine-readable. The design goals of XML emphasise simplicity, generality, and usability across the Internet. See <https://en.wikipedia.org/wiki/XML> accessed 7 December 2023.

[15] The OECD has published a new reporting form for CbC reporting, the CbC 2.0 form, effective as from February 2021.

[16] Based on statistics provided by the OECD, more than 100 countries have now introduced CbCR obligations and over 3,000 relationships are in place for the exchange of CbCrs between countries. In July 2021, the OECD published a new set of aggregated and anonymised data from CbCRs, providing information on the global tax and economic activities of around 6,000 multinational enterprise (MNE) groups. See OECD, *Corporate Tax Statistics* (3rd edn, OECD 2021) 42 <https://www.oecd.org/tax/tax-policy/corporate-tax-statistics-third-edition.pdf> accessed 7 December 2023); OECD, New OECD data highlights the importance of the international tax reform discussions – OECD (*Tax Policy Analysis*, 29 July 2021) <https://web-archive.oecd.org/2021-07-29/595143-new-oecd-data-highlights-the-importance-of-the-international-tax-reform-discussions.htm> accessed 7 December 2023; Susanne Verloove, Peter Hoving and Roberto Aviles Gutierrez, 'EU Public Country-by-Country Reporting' (2022) 29(3) Intl. Transfer Pricing Journal 1.

[17] Cécile Remeur, 'Briefing, EU Legislation in Progress: Country-by-Country Reporting for multinational enterprise groups' (European Parliamentary Research Service (EARPS) April 2021), <https://www.europarl.europa.eu/EPRS/EPRS-Briefing-580914-Country-by-country-reporting.pdf> accessed 7 December 2023.

13.3.2 Scope and Conditions of Mandatory Automatic Exchange of CbCrs

Pursuant to the DAC4, a new article, Article 8aa has been inserted in the DAC, as regards the scope[18] and conditions of mandatory automatic exchange of information on the CbCr. Under this article, each Member State shall take the necessary measures to require the Ultimate Parent Entity (UPE) of an MNE Group that is resident for tax purposes in its territory, or any other Reporting Entity, to file a CbCr with respect to its Reporting Fiscal Year within 12 months of the last day of the Reporting Fiscal Year of the MNE Group. The competent authority of a Member State where the CbCr was received shall, by means of automatic exchange and within a specific deadline, communicate the CbCr to any other Member State in which, on the basis of the information in the CbCr, one or more Constituent Entities of the MNE Group of the Reporting Entity are either resident for tax purposes or subject to tax with respect to the business carried out through a permanent establishment.

The aforementioned article stipulates the ambit of the new reporting requirements and sets the timeframe of the fulfilment of the relevant reporting and notification obligations. According to Section I of Annex III of DAC4, the UPE means a Constituent Entity[19] of an MNE Group that meets specific criteria enumerated there. The deadline for the communication of the CbCr is 15 months of the last day of the Fiscal Year of the MNE Group to which the CbCr relates. The reporting entity should proceed to the completion of the CbCr in a reasonable, practical and consistent manner and should ensure that such a report is accurate, complete and filed in a timely manner.

13.3.3 Aim and Mission of Automatic Exchange of the CbCrs

Information communicated between Member States shall be used for the purposes of assessing high-level transfer-pricing risks and other risks related to BEPS, including assessing the risk of non-compliance by members of the MNE Group with applicable transfer pricing rules, and where appropriate for

---

[18] It has been stressed that the automatic sharing of the CbCrs lies 'beneath' the original scope of the OECD template, according to which different CbCrs should be drafted for one MNE-Group. See the Federal Ministry of Finance's concerns about the DAC4 proposal in Marc Alms, Stefano Bognandi, Jens Brodbeck et al., *Transfer pricing & the new world of country-by-country reporting* (Tax and 2017) <https://www.taxand.com/wp-content/uploads/2017/09/tp_the_new_world_of_cbc_reporting.pdf> accessed 7 December 2023.

[19] The term 'Constituent Entity' is defined in Annex III, Section I, number 5, 'Defined Terms'.

economic and statistical analysis.[20] The core mission of the new reporting and notification obligations refers to the need for increased transparency, more effective administrative cooperation and more efficient tax and transfer pricing risk assessment, under conditions compatible with the proper functioning of the internal market. Although it is clarified that transfer pricing adjustments by the tax authorities of the receiving Member State shall not be based on the information exchanged pursuant to Article 8aa, the use of information communicated between Member States as a basis for making further enquiries into the MNE Group's transfer-pricing arrangements or into other tax matters in the course of a tax audit is not prohibited as such. Consequently, appropriate adjustments to the taxable income of a constituent entity may be made in this respect.[21]

The increase of tax transparency could operate as a disincentive for the multinational groups to engage in aggressive tax planning and base eroding tax techniques, and could play a decisive role in effectively tackling tax avoidance and tax evasion,[22] by better ensuring that companies will pay their fair share of tax in the jurisdiction where profits actually arise.[23] Nevertheless, the rights of the taxpayers should be protected accordingly, pursuant to the respective case-law of the ECJ[24] and the ECHR.[25] The increasing amount of tax data

---

20 DAC4 art 16, para 6.

21 ibid.

22 League of Nations, *Technical Experts to the Economic and Financial Committee Double Taxation and Tax Evasion Report and Resolutions submitted by the Technical Experts to the Financial Committee Document F.212* (Geneva, February 1925).

23 See also Paul B.W.L. Lamberts, 'Fair Taxation: Truth is in the Eye of the Beholder' (2017) 45(1) Intertax 49. According to the author, the critical factor is where taxes are actually paid; in other words, the geographical allocation of taxes plays a very important role.

24 See Case C-184/05 *Jiří Sabou v Finančníředitelství pro hlavníměsto Prahu* [2007] ECLI:EU:C:2013:678; Case C-276/12 *Jiří Sabou v Finanční ředitelství pro hlavní město Prahu* [2013] ECLI:EU:C:2013:678; Case C-682/15 *Berlioz Investment Fund SA v Directeur de l'administration des contributions directes* [2017] ECLI:EU:C:2017:373; Joined Cases C-245/19 and C-246/19 *Luxembourg v B* [2020] ECLI:EU:C:2020:795, on an indicative basis. Moreover, as regards exchange of information in the field of VAT, see Case C-419/14 *Web Mind Licenses Kft v Nemzeti Adó- és Vámhivatal Kiemelt Adó- és Vám Főigazgatóság* [2015] ECLI:EU:C:2015:832; Case C-189/18 *Glencore Agriculture Hungary v Nemzeti Adó- és Vámhivatal Fellebbviteli Igazgatósá* [2018] ECLI:EU:C:2019:861 on an indicative basis.

25 See relevant case law of the ECtHR on the exchange of tax information, for example *Othymia Investments BV v The Netherlands* (2015) App. No 75292/10 (EctHR, 9 July 2015; *Brito Ferrinho Bexiga Villa-Nova v Portugal* (2015) App. No 69436/10 (EctHR, 1 December 2015); *MN & Others v San Marino* (2015) App. No 28005/12 (EctHR, 7 July 2015); *GSB v Switzerland* App no 28601/11 (EctHR, 22 December 2016) on an indicative basis.

exchanged between tax administrations will create new tax disputes before both national and European courts.[26]

CbCr information is a powerful tool in the hands of a tax administration authority; it provides a key opportunity for tax authorities to take a global perspective of MNE groups in their jurisdiction, and, as it is of vital importance for tax authorities to use this information actively for high-level risk assessment, has been designed with tax administrations in mind.[27] CbCrs alone do not provide evidence that an MNE group is engaged in BEPS but, read alongside the master file, local file and other information available to tax authorities, and interpreted in light of a tax authority's knowledge and experience of an MNE group's activities and attitude to tax risk, they can reveal important indicators as to where tax risks may exist.[28] For example, they may show whether no real substance exists in a certain jurisdiction and whether excess profits are not aligned with value creation. Each tax authority must determine how to make the best use of CbCrs in conducting tax risk assessments.[29]

The impact of the CbCr on the various organisations it concerns and their strategic choices is remarkable. This is also reflected in their effective tax rate (ETR), although this entails serious challenges, mainly at the level of tax management. It could, thus, be argued that the CbCr is a valuable driver of future business decisions.

13.3.4 Liable Persons

The entity that bears the obligation to submit a CbCr for any period of time (the 'Reporting Entity') is an entity that is a member of an MNE Group which fulfils the following two cumulative conditions: (a) the group includes two or more entities with tax residence in different jurisdictions; and (b) the group had an annual total consolidated income of €750 million or more over the immediately preceding fiscal year, as reflected in the consolidated financial statements of the Group, irrespective of whether the Group has its registered office within the EU or not.[30] Moreover, any Constituent Entity of an MNE Group is required to submit a notification, stating its actual status and the identity and

---

26 Katerina Savvaidou, 'Exchange of information on the field of taxation in the light of fundamental rights' (AD On-line Classroom on EU Tax Law, EJTN March 2021).

27 See OECD (n 10).

28 ibid.

29 ibid.

30 Independent Authority for Public Revenue (IAPR), 'Country-by-Country Reporting' (*Frequently Asked Questions*, 7 July 2022), <https:// www .aade .gr/ sites/ default/ files/ 2022 -07/ CbCR _FAQs _EN _07 _2022 _V1 .pdf> accessed 7 December 2023.

tax residence of the Reporting Entity to the competent tax authority of its state of residence for each fiscal year, no later than the last day of the Reporting Fiscal Year of the MNE Group.[31]

DAC4 entails a certain obligation for Member States to include a secondary mechanism if the ultimate parent does not file the CbCr, whereas the OECD only provides the possibility for such an obligation.[32] Moreover, the treatment of the MNE group is determined pursuant to the applicable accounting consolidation rules. Consequently, in the case that such rules apply to a partnership, then that partnership may be a Constituent Entity of an MNE group and subject to CbC reporting. Besides, in the case of an entity[33] that is owned and/or operated by more than one unrelated MNE Group, the treatment of such an entity for CbC reporting purposes should be determined under the accounting rules applicable to each of the unrelated MNE Groups separately. If the applicable accounting rules require an entity to be consolidated into the consolidated financial statements of an MNE Group, the entity would be considered as a Constituent Entity of that group and, accordingly, the financial data of such an entity should be reported in the CbCr of the MNE Group.[34]

13.3.5 Penalties

The penalties imposed for infringements of the respective framework shall be effective, proportionate and dissuasive. Reference to the principle of proportionality and effectiveness highlights that the penalties provided and imposed should be appropriate, necessary and proportionate *stricto sensu*, i.e., in the

---

31 DAC4 (n 20) Section II of Annex III paras 3 and 4.

32 Alms et al. (n 18).

33 As per other special categories of entities, such as investment funds, no general exemption is provided for, and therefore, the governing principle to determine an MNE Group is to follow the accounting consolidation rules. In case the accounting rules instruct investment entities not to consolidate with investee companies (e.g. because the consolidated accounts for the investment entity should instead report fair value of the investment through profit and loss), then the investee companies should not form part of a Group or MNE Group or be considered as Constituent Entities of an MNE Group. This principle applies even where the investment entity has a controlling interest in the investee company. On the other hand, if the accounting rules require an investment entity to consolidate with a subsidiary, such as where that subsidiary provides services that relate to the investment entity's investment activities, then the subsidiary should be part of a Group and should be considered as a Constituent Entity of the MNE Group (if one exists). See OECD (n 11) para 55 and Office of the Commissioner for Revenue (n 3).

34 Office of the Commissioner for Revenue (n 3).

narrow sense.[35] While the choice of penalties remains within the discretion of the Member States, the penalties provided for should be effective, proportionate and dissuasive. This broad discretion of the Member States highlights and intensifies the tax uncertainty among Member States and could potentially undermine fair tax competition within the internal market, due to the resulting lack of uniformity when it comes to the penalties imposed.[36]

13.3.6 Determination of the CbCr format, necessary content and templates

The automatic exchange of information on the CbCr shall be carried out using the standard form provided in Tables 1, 2 and 3 in Section III of Annex III to DAC4, which provides for CbCr templates, for the sake of consistency and uniformity.[37] In more detail, Table 1 depicts an overview of the allocation of income, taxes and business activities by tax jurisdiction,[38] Table 2 contains

---

35 'The last test of proportionality is the "proportional result" or "proportionality stricto sensu" (*Verhältnismässigkeit im engeren Sinne*)'. See Aharon Barak, *Proportionality Constitutional Rights and their Limitations* (Cambridge University Press 2012) 340–70; Richard H. Fallon, 'Individual Rights and the Powers of Government' (1993) 27(2) Georgia Law Review 343; Aharon Barak, *Purposive Interpretation in Law* (Princeton University Press 2005); and Selene Mize, 'Resolving Cases of Conflicting Rights under the New Zealand Bill of Rights Act' (2006) 22 New Zealand University Law Review 50.

36 For example, in Greece the penalty for late/inaccurate filing of the CbCr is set at EUR 10,000, while the penalty for the non-filing of the CbCr amounts to EUR 20,000. In France, failure to provide the French tax authorities with complete CbCr will result in a penalty of up to EUR 100,000. In Italy, penalties are levied in case of missed or untrue communication (ranging from EUR 10,000 to EUR 50,000). Luxembourg tax authorities may impose a penalty of up to EUR 250,000 in case of no filing, late filing, or incorrect filing of either the CbCr or notification(s). See PwC, 'Worldwide Tax Summaries Online' (*Tax Summaries*, 2023) <https:// taxsummaries .pwc .com/> accessed 7 December 2023. In Germany, for failure to comply with CbCr requirements, penalties up to EUR 10,000 may be imposed. See Deloitte, 'International Tax Germany Highlights 2023' (*Tax guides and highlights*, January 2023) <https://dits.deloitte.com/#TaxGuides> accessed 7 December 2023. Note that the aforementioned penalties are presented on an indicative basis.

37 See also DAC4 (n 20) recital 12. The countries that proceed to the automatic exchange of the CbCrs are the EU tax jurisdictions incorporating DAC4, the signatories of the Multilateral Competent Authority Agreement on the Exchange off CbCrs (CbC MCAA), within the frame of OECD and the United States, pursuant to its legal framework (such as its Double Tax Conventions, its tax information exchange agreements and its Convention on Mutual Administrative Assistance in Tax Matters).

38 Per jurisdiction, the following information needs to be provided: revenues (differentiated by revenues from unrelated parties, related parties and the total revenues), profits before income tax, income tax paid (on a cash basis), income tax accrued for the

a list of all the Constituent Entities of the MNE Group included in each aggregation per tax jurisdiction,[39] and Table 3 provides additional information in brief.

13.3.7 Accounting Treatment and Technical Issues

The treatment of an entity for CbC reporting purposes should be in accordance with accounting treatment.[40]MNE Groups have flexibility in identifying the data sources and reference standards they use, as long as the data is derived from reliable sources, consistent with the use of the same sources from year to year and the same sources are used for all jurisdictions.[41] In this respect, the columns as well as the respective items of the CbCr should be completed accordingly, taking into account the proper accounting treatment. For example, when financial statements are used as the source of the data to complete the CbC template, the item 'revenues' in Table 1 should include all revenue, gains, income or other inflows shown in the financial statement prepared, in accordance with the applicable accounting rules relating to profit and loss, such as the income statement or profit and loss statement.[42] Moreover, the governing principle to determine an MNE Group is to follow the accounting consolidation rules. The respective information included in the CbCrs shall be provided by electronic means using the common communication network 'CCN'.[43]

current year, stated capital, accumulated earnings, the number of employees and tangible profits other than cash and cash equivalents.

[39] As such, per jurisdiction a list of resident constituent entities should be included. For each entity, it should be determined what is its tax Jurisdiction of establishment or incorporation – if that is different from its tax jurisdiction of residence. Per entity, the main business activities should be specified. To that end, Table 2 distinguishes between the following activities: research and development, holding or managing intellectual property, purchasing or procurement, manufacturing or production, sales, marketing or distribution, administrative/management/support services, provision of services to unrelated parties, internal group finance, regulated financial services, insurance, holding shares or other equity instrument, dormant, and other. In case the entity checks the 'other' box, Table 3 should be used to specify the nature of the activity.

[40] Office of the Commissioner for Revenue (n 3).

[41] See Independent Authority for Public Revenue (IAPR) (n 30).

[42] OECD/G20 Base Erosion and Profit Shifting Project, Guidance on the Implementation of Country-by-Country Reporting: BEPS Action 13 (October 2022), <https://web-archive.oecd.org/2022-10-17/407167-guidance-on-the-implementation-of-country-by-country-reporting-beps-action-13.pdf> accessed 7 December 2023.

[43] DAC1 art 21(6).

13.4 A CRITICAL APPROACH TOWARDS DAC4

13.4.1 Coordinated Rules on Tax Transparency

In order to better safeguard the proper functioning of the internal market, it is necessary to ensure that Member States adopt coordinated rules on the transparency obligations of MNE Groups.[44] Tax transparency plays a vital and decisive role in tax compliance and tax effectiveness, being inextricably intertwined with tax morale and tax consciousness. Thus, it should constitute a central part of the design of the most appropriate and efficient tax policy, which represents the tax mix adopted in a certain jurisdiction.

Low levels of transparency in corporate taxation enable harmful tax practices to remain unchallenged. The exploitation of the gaps and mismatches of the various tax systems in the current globalised tax environment results in the artificial shifting of taxable profits to low or even zero tax jurisdictions, where no real economic substance exists and no real economic activity is carried out. Therefore, the increase in tax transparency has been regarded by the European Commission as a top priority at the political agenda, aiming at tackling tax avoidance and tax abuse through the re-establishment of the link between taxation and economic substance. Consequently, greater openness will be achieved into the various tax systems of the EU Member States, which will enable taxpayers to better comply with their tax responsibilities.[45]

Furthermore, the newly-proposed Public CbCR Directive[46] will have a significant impact on both EU-headquartered MNEs and non-EU-headquartered MNEs operating in the EU. Thus, it is considered to constitute a significant step in the tax transparency environment, where by more stakeholders as well as civil society will require increased public tax reporting by businesses.[47]

---

44 DAC4 (n 20) Preamble, para 10.

45 See also the Commission's Tax Transparency Package on automatic exchange of information between Member States on their tax rulings, of March 2015, and the action plan for a fair and efficient corporate tax system in the EU of June 2015.

46 Commission, 'Proposal for a Directive of 12 April 2016 amending Directive 2013/34/EU as regards disclosure of income tax information by certain undertakings and branches' COM (2016) 198 final, according to which MNEs are obliged to publish information on where they make their profits and where they pay their tax in the European Union on a country-by-country basis. See also Directive EU 2021/2101 of 24 November 2021 amending Directive 2013/34/EU [2021] OJ L 429/1 (Public CbCR Directive). As regards disclosure of income tax information by certain undertakings and branches, see Verloove et al. (n 16). In order to avoid creating an administrative burden, the Public CbCR Directive allows MNEs to publish a report based on the reporting instructions of the DAC4 under art 48c(3).

47 See Verloove et al. (n 16).

Using tax data analytics, business leaders will be able to extract new organisational insights and correlations from the respective data reported, which could be leveraged in strategic planning purposes.[48]

13.4.2 The Cost of Compliance for Taxpayers and the Administrative Burden for the Tax Administrations

This newly introduced tax reporting framework with regard to the CbCrs implies high compliance costs and a significant administrative burden. A good deal of resources should be attributed to the proper preparation of the CbCrs as well as their filing, particularly regarding employees which will undertake and handle this work as well as the allocation of working hours, as a CbCr combines information coming from many different departments and tax jurisdictions. Thus, it is not always straightforward to collect such information and report on it properly. On the other hand, a significant administrative burden also arises for the tax administrations, which are the competent authorities to assess all the information included in the CbCrs within the framework of their tax audits, as well as to proceed to the timely exchange of the reports.

The respective tax framework could in general be characterised as rather complicated and technical. Moreover, the respective processes of data collection and aggregation need to be highly standardised and centralised, and entail a lot of practicalities that need to be resolved. In order to minimise costs and administrative burdens for both tax administrations and MNE Groups, it is necessary to provide rules that are in line with international developments and can contribute positively to their implementation.[49]

13.4.3 Automatic Exchange of CbCrs and Tax Uncertainty

Tax certainty is an essential element in the protection of taxpayers' rights,[50] and features such as the stability and simplicity of the tax system are crucial in

---

[48] Deloitte (n 9).

[49] More specifically, the OECD BEPS Action Plan, including the 2015 Final Report on Action 13 and the 2015 OECD package. The work on Action 13 of the BEPS Action Plan resulted in a set of standards for providing information for MNE Groups. See DAC4 Preamble, paras 13, 14 and 17.

[50] Arias Esteban Isaác Gonzalo, Vargas David, and Cremades Ugarte Luis, 'Cooperative Tax Relationship or Compliance: Current situation in the CIAT member countries of Latin America, the Caribbean, Africa and Asia' (2015) International Cooperation & Tax Directorate Working Papers 2 <https://biblioteca.ciat.org/opac/?v=5373> accessed 7 December 2023; CIAT, *Manual on Tax Collection and Recovery* (CIAT, GIZ and IDB 2016); G20 *Communiqué of G20 Finance Ministers and Central Bank Governors* (Baden-Baden, 17–18 March 2017); IMF and OECD, *Tax Certainty:*

order for it to be considered favourable for investments.[51] The data collection process requires all stakeholders to have the same understanding of their contribution as well as the varying notions and parameters governing the requested data. However, interpretations of the definitions for some of the CbC reporting information could cause uncertainty and concerns regarding integrity; these definitions must be clarified upfront in order to achieve interpretational uniformity. It has been observed that where ambiguity exists, most companies opt to rely upon their own existing internal definitions. This practice could potentially further jeopardise tax certainty.[52]

In the case of DAC4, tax uncertainty is caused by various aspects, such as the fact that it is not always crystal-clear which entity is liable to prepare and file the CbCr (i.e., the UPE, the constituent entity or the surrogate parent entity), due to this being a fact-sensitive matter and the relevant legal framework being rather technical, detailed and complicated. However, Section II of Annex III analytically describes the general reporting and notification requirements, and deals with the issue of how the entity that is liable to file the CbCr is determined based on the facts and circumstances of each particular case. Moreover, detailed guidance has been issued from the competent tax authorities, clarifying the respective obligations and, therefore, the respective risk is effectively mitigated to a certain extent.

As regards the calculation of the amounts to be reported, the reporting MNE shall consistently use the same sources of data from year to year in completing the template. In fact, the reporting MNE may choose to use data from its consolidation reporting packages from separate entity statutory financial statements, regulatory financial statements, or internal management accounts. It is not necessary to reconcile the revenue, profit and tax reporting in the template with the Consolidated Financial Statements.[53] However, uncertainty arises from the fact that each MNE is using its own GAAP and accounting principles. More specifically, given the fact that the liable entities have enough flexibility in selecting the source of information as well as the respective reference standards they use, provided that the sources are reliable, it should be carefully

IMF/OECD Report for the G20 Finance Ministers (Washington, DC, IMF and OECD 2013); OECD, *Co-operative Compliance: A Framework from Enhanced Relationship to Co-operative Compliance* (OECD 2008): OECD, *Study into the Role of Tax Intermediaries* (OECD 2008). Also see Part I, Chapter 5 of this book on taxpayer's rights.

[51] Katerina Savvaidou and Vasiliki Athanasaki, 'Contemporary challenges of tax certainty in the ever-evolving tax environment: digital tax, GAARs and tax rulings in the field of fiscal state aid' (2021) 2 Rivista di Diritto Tributario Internazionale: International Tax Law Review 93–115.

[52] Deloitte (n 9).

[53] See DAC4 (n 20) Section III Annex III.

explained in Table 3 (titled 'Additional Information') which accounting principles and sources of data and information have been selected, any respective change compared to the previous year and the exact reason for this, as well as the average exchange rate for the year that is being declared. Moreover, the respective principles should be relied upon on a consistent basis, without deviations from year to year or among the various jurisdictions.

Characteristic examples of items that raise uncertainty when it comes to their estimation are the 'revenues' of Table 1, which should be interpreted using the broadest possible concept of the term,[54] the 'income tax paid', which should also include withholding taxes paid,[55] and the 'income tax accrued', which should include only the amounts for the current tax year, without any Deferred Tax Assets (DTA) or provisions for Uncertain Tax Liabilities (AHY).[56] Further, other terms used should also be defined carefully, such as the term 'stated capital', which should include not only paid-up and called-up share capital but also the premium; the term 'accumulated earnings', which should be interpreted as including retained earnings and other reserves (e.g. tax-exempt reserves); and the term 'tangible assets', which should be interpreted as including real estate investments but not including cash or cash equivalents, intangible assets and financial assets[57] and should be based upon their net book value. Moreover, questions arise concerning the tangible assets of permanent establishments, which should refer to the tax jurisdiction where the permanent establishment is located.

Last but not least, detailed explanations and clarifications should also be provided regarding the entities regarded as 'related parties' for the purpose of completing the column 'revenues' in Table 1, as well as the depiction of 'domestic intragroup transactions' in Table 1, which should be effected on an aggregated basis, per tax jurisdiction, given that the consolidation eliminates intercompany transactions, the reference date for the calculation of the number of employees[58] as well as the determining factors for the 'core business activity' of the group's constituent entities (when it comes to the completion

---

54 OECD/G20 Base Erosion and Profit Shifting Project (n 11).

55 OECD (n 4).

56 ibid.

57 ibid.

58 This figure may be reported either as at the end of the tax year, based on the average level of employment for the year, or on any other basis, as long as it is the same for all jurisdictions and the same rule is used from year to year. According to the BEPS Action 13 Final Report, self-employed persons engaged in the normal operational activities of the Constituent Entity may be referred to as employees. It is up to the Reporting Entity to decide which of the counterparties are involved in the normal operating activities of the business and should therefore be included in the number of employees when completing the CbCr.

of Table 2). In particular, when 'other' activity is selected for one or more entities, the Reporting Entity must specify the nature of that entity's activity in Table 3 of the report. In any case, Table 3 could be used for the purpose of better explaining in detail the criteria used for the completion of the report.

In order to eliminate the resultant tax uncertainty, detailed and consistent guidance, providing all the necessary technical details and including all necessary clarifications, should be issued by the tax administrations. According to the practice followed thus far, the majority of EU jurisdictions have proceeded to the issuance of specific guidelines regarding the process of filing, submitting and exchanging the CbCrs.[59] In this respect, it is highly important for the MNEs to make reconciliations as well as the necessary adjustments, if required, not only with respect to CbCr filing but to the overall business strategy and the respective business model in place. In any case, local specifications released by the competent national tax authorities should be carefully monitored and considered.

13.4.4 Confidentiality and Privacy Issues

Another highly important issue that arises regarding DAC4 is the issue of confidentiality and the subsequent limitation of use, since the liable entities disclose a significant amount of crucial information about their operations and their business activity worldwide through the CbCr. The issue of confidentiality is an inevitable drawback of enhancing tax transparency through public disclosure and automatic exchange of information. This is also recognised by the legislator, who highlights in the preamble of DAC4 that the information exchanged under this directive does not lead to the disclosure of a commercial, industrial or professional secret, a commercial process or information the disclosure of which would be contrary to public policy.

It has been supported in relevant literature that exchanging tax information between countries is nothing new.[60] Moreover, a lot of countries consider that exchanging tax information is justified in order to fight tax evasion and ensure tax compliance. The central question that arises in this regard is whether and to

---

[59] For example, Independent Authority for Public Revenue, *Country-by-Country Reporting* (2022), <https:// www .aade .gr/ sites/ default/ files/ 2022 -07/ CbCR _FAQs _EN_07_2022_V1.pdf> accessed 7 December 2023; Office of the Commissioner for Revenue (n 3).

[60] Ants Soone, 'Exchange of Tax Information and Privacy in Estonia' (2016) 44 Intertax 279.

what extent, automatic exchange of tax information encroaches on the right to privacy,[61] bank secrecy and confidentiality proportionately.[62]

It is true that the CbCr usually contains sensitive information as well as business and industry secrets and, in general very, important confidential economic data with regard to liable MNE groups, which should be respected and properly safeguarded. No such information should be further notified to any third, unauthorised, party. This is the so-called 'appropriate use' of CbCrs, which, according to both DAC4 and the OECD BEPS Action 13 minimum standard, should be used only for high-level transfer pricing risk assessment, the assessment of other BEPS-related risks, and, where appropriate, for economic and statistical analysis.[63]

13.5 Conclusions

The equilibrium between the tax administration and the taxpayers, which had been largely restored by the introduction of a taxpayer rights framework by the OECD,[64] was once again overturned by the economic crisis and the significant international developments in tackling tax evasion, tax avoidance and aggressive tax planning. In this context, new highly elaborated anti-tax abuse provisions were enacted, based on which the powers of the tax administrations were strengthened again to the detriment of the taxpayers' rights.[65]

The current tax landscape is rapidly evolving. Fair taxation, emphasis on the real economic substance and alignment of the tax results with the value creation[66] lie at the core of the latest developments in international and EU tax law.[67]

---

61 See Case C-201/14 *Smaranda Bara and Others v Preşedintele Casei Naţionale de Asigurări de Sănătate, Casa Naţională de Asigurări de Sănătate, Agenţia Naţională de Administrare Fiscală (ANAF)* [2015] ECLI:EU:C:2015:638; Case C-73/16 *Peter Puškár v Finančné riaditeľstvo Slovenskej republiky, Kriminálny úrad finančnej správy* [2016] ECLI:EU:C:2017:725. Also see Part I, Chapter 4 of this book on Privacy.

62 See Soone (n 60) according to whom there are those who believe the automatic exchange to be the end of bank secrecy.

63 OECD, *BEPS Action 13 on Country-by-Country Reporting: Guidance on the appropriate use of information contained in Country-by-Country reports* (2017) accessed 20 April 2023; Office of the Commissioner for Revenue (n 3).

64 See also OECD, Centre for Tax Policy and Administration, *Tax guidance series: General Administrative Principles – GAP001 Principles of Good Tax Administration, Principles of Good Tax Administration – Practice Note (Prepared by the OECD Committee of Fiscal Affairs Forum on Strategic Management*, (OECD 2001).

65 Savvaidou and Athanasaki (n 51).

66 Patricia Hofmann and Nadine Riedel, Debate: Comment on J. Becker & J. Englisch, 'Taxing Where Value Is Created: What's "User Involvement" Got to Do with It?' (2019) 47(2) Intertax 172.

67 Savvaidou and Athanasaki (n 51).

Administrative cooperation[68] concerns the tax and customs administrations of EU Member States cooperating with one another to share and exchange information. Close cooperation is vital to detect and reduce tax fraud.[69]

Taking into account that the fight against tax avoidance and tax evasion necessitates drastic measures, increased transparency is inevitable, in light of the current tax developments at international level. The automatic exchange of CbCrs within the framework of DAC4 as well as their publication – pursuant to the recent public CbCr directive,[70] which highlights a significant progress towards greater visibility of the tax results of the MNEs – facilitate the competent tax authorities' ability to gain access to invaluable sources of information and tax data, in order to be able to better review and assess them within the course of the tax audits they conduct. Both the automatic exchange of the CbCrs and their publication entail a remarkable reverse of the burden of proof, since it is the taxpayers who are required to declare the necessary information, without any former official request. Although compliance implies a significant administrative burden and it could also become cost-bearing, it could potentially lead to greater tax fairness[71] and, therefore, better ensure tax justice, provided that all necessary safeguards are in place.

Tax reporting, apart from being a tool to fight tax avoidance and evasion, is also increasingly used as a tool for driving sustainable development and

---

68 The European Court of Auditors (ECA) published a special report on 26 January 2021. It highlights the insufficient sharing of tax information between Member States for the purpose of ensuring fair and effective taxation. It also states that the information exchanged is of limited quality or is under-used and calls for more support to the Member States. It criticises the Commission for its insufficient focus on the issues of: (i) poor data quality, and (ii) the low impact of sanctions on non-compliance. Additionally, it considers that there is no EU framework for monitoring achievements and that there is a lack of a uniform set of performance indicators throughout the EU to measure how effective tax information is exchanged between Member States. See Miroslava Karaboytcheva, 'Briefing, EU Legislation in Progress: Advances in administrative cooperation in the field of taxation' (European Parliamentary Research Service (EARPS) April 2021) <https://www.europarl.europa.eu/RegData/etudes/BRIE/2021/679099/EPRS_BRI(2021)679099_EN.pdf> accessed 7 December 2023.

69 Savvaidou (n 26).

70 Willemien Netjes and Dominik Freyer, 'Policy Note: Tax Transparency Is Here to Stay: An Analysis of the Public CbCR Directive' (2022) 50(8) Intertax 612, according to whom, publishing such information can lead to greater scrutiny and can potentially harm a company´s reputation, thus causing major reputational risk for the liable entities. Pursuant to the view expressed by the author, this contribution is a formal discourse of how the Public CbCR Directive initiative is a logical consequence of years of corporate tax transparency discussions and how it fits into broader global environmental, social, and governance (ESG) trends.

71 See also Paul B.W.L. Lamberts, 'Fair Taxation: Truth is in the Eye of the Beholder' (2017) 45(1) Intertax 49.

ESG goals and behaviour.[72] The achievement of greater transparency, efficient data mapping and enhanced reporting requirements definitely contribute to the global tax reset, given that they strengthen tax administrations' visibility regarding the MNE's tax positions and general economic and business activity worldwide. Provided that the taxpayers' rights are effectively respected and that the uncertainties ensued are properly clarified and dealt with, the requirements enacted pursuant to DAC4 as well as the proposed next step, the public CbCr directive, constitute a significant step towards the formation of a more transparent and stable global tax environment in the future.

---

72 See Verloove et al. (n 16).

14. The challenges of DAC5: access to anti-money-laundering information by tax authorities – taxation is no crime fighting!

Almut Breuer

14.1 INTRODUCTION

Ever since the conviction of Al Capone in 1931,[1] governments have been aware that fighting organised crime might very well succeed by investigating seemingly minor white-collar crimes, like tax fraud and money laundering. Following this path, after 9/11, more advanced anti-money laundering regulations have been introduced as a major tool in the fight against terrorism.[2] In response to these developments, the EU introduced the so-called Anti-Money Laundering Directive (AMLD), which aims at collecting and exchanging information which is deemed useful in combatting money laundering and terrorism.[3] Then, in 2014, the Investigative Consortium of Journalists published their Lux Leaks investigation, [4] followed, in 2016, by their Panama Papers

[1] See FBI, 'Al Capone' (*Famous Cases and Criminals*, 2023) <https://www.fbi.gov/history/famous-cases/al-capone> accessed 7 December 2023.

[2] See IMF, 'Anti-Money Laundering/Combatting the financing of Terrorism' (*About the IMF*, 2023) <https://www.imf.org/external/np/leg/amlcft/eng/aml1.htm> accessed 7 December 2023.

[3] Directive (EU) 2015/849 of the European Parliament and of the Council of 20 May 2015 on the prevention of the use of the financial system for the purposes of money laundering or terrorist financing, amending Regulation (EU) No 648/2012 of the European Parliament and of the Council, and repealing Directive 2005/60/EC of the European Parliament and of the Council and Commission Directive 2006/70/EC [2015] OJ L 141, 73-117 (AMLD4), as amended by Council Directives (EU) 2018/843 (AMLD5) and (EU) 2019/2177.

[4] See ICIJ, 'Luxembourg Leaks: Global Companies' Secrets Exposed' (Investigations, 2023) <https:// www .icij .org/ investigations/ luxembourg -leaks/ > accessed 7 December 2023.

investigation,[5] laying bare the extensive scope of international tax avoidance and tax evasion by both multinational enterprises and private individuals. These developments made clear that the tax authorities were also in great need of more information on international money streams. By the end of 2016, the Directive on administrative cooperation in the field of taxation (DAC) was amended by DAC5 in order to grant the tax authorities of EU Member States access to information collected under the AMLD. However, when comparing both directives, the different goals become apparent: the AMLD serves the purpose of crime fighting and the DAC serves the purpose of facilitating correct taxation. The legal challenges arising from these differences should not be underestimated.

This chapter provides an overview of the obligations of Member States laid down in DAC5, and analyses its challenges. DAC5 refers to the AMLD through a dynamic reference, meaning that it automatically includes all amendments to the AMLD.[6] Both directives are therefore closely intertwined. The first part of the chapter explains which information must be provided by credit and financial institutions and certain other persons carrying out professional activities under the current AMLD. For DAC5 purposes, the relevant information concerns the so-called 'customer due diligence' information, including information on the beneficial owners of certain entities and legal arrangements. The second part of the chapter contains an analysis of challenges originating from the close interaction between DAC5 and the AMLD. Literature on this topic is unfortunately very scarce, with studies mainly focusing on the interplay between the AMLD and DAC2.[7]

Since – as mentioned above – both directives have different goals – DAC promoting correct taxation and the AMDL targeting crime – it will be examined whether this close interaction causes problems regarding: (i) the effectiveness of DAC5 from a legal perspective, and (ii) the guarantee of fundamental rights of taxpayers. Subsequently, possible ways to meet the identified challenges will be presented, which mainly include providing for clear, aligned definitions and a limitation of the scope of DAC5.

---

5 See ICIJ, 'The Panama Papers: Exposing the Rogue Offshore Finance Industry' (Investigations, 2023) <https://www.icij.org/investigations/panama-papers/> accessed 7 December 2023.

6 DAC5 recital 4.

7 See M. Müller-Dragovits and M. Somare 'Interplay between automatic exchange of information and AML requirements' in Michael Lang and Peter Haunold, *Transparenz – Eine neue Ära im Steuerrecht* (Linde 2016); Irene Schiefer, *Interplay Between Anti-Money Laundering Provisions and Exchange of Information for Tax Transparency Purposes at EU Level,* European Union Law Working Papers No. 56, Stanford-Vienna Transatlantic Technology Law Forum (2022).

14.2 DAC5 EXPLAINED

14.2.1 General

DAC5 has already been around for a little while – it had to be implemented in national law by 1 January 2018 at the latest. The purpose of DAC5 is to regulate access to anti-money laundering information for tax authorities who execute their duties under the scope of DAC. For this purpose, one provision has been added to Article 22 of the DAC (headed 'Specific Obligations'). This article requires EU Member States to, among other things, guarantee the proper functioning of administrative cooperation arrangements, as well as to establish direct cooperation with the tax authorities of the other EU Member States. The provision thus applies to all forms of assistance.[8] DAC5 introduces a new paragraph in Article 22 of the DAC that grants tax authorities access to the mechanisms, procedures, documents and (anti-money laundering) information referred to in certain articles of the AMLD.

DAC5 is of particular importance regarding the information included in DAC2. Under Article 1(2)(b) of DAC2 (Article 8(3a) of the DAC), financial account information is automatically exchanged between EU Member States in accordance with the so-called Common Reporting Standard (CRS).[9] On the basis of the CRS, information on financial account holders is provided to the (Member) State of which the account holder is a resident. If an account holder is a so-called passive non-financial entity (passive NFE),[10] information

---

[8] See also in this regard: Proposal for a Council Directive amending Directive 2011/16/EU as regards access to anti-money laundering information by tax authorities [2011] COM(2016) 452 final, ch 2 Explanatory Memorandum (under 'legal basis').

[9] The CRS is an identification and reporting standard and is part of the global standard for the automatic exchange of financial information developed by the Organization for Economic Co-operation and Development. This Standard consists of a model Competent Authority Agreement (CAA), providing the international legal framework for the automatic exchange of CRS information, the Common Reporting Standard itself, the Commentaries on the CAA and the CRS and a schematic user guide, see: OECD, 'Common Reporting Standard (CRS)' (Automatic Exchange Portal, 2023) <https://www.oecd.org/tax/automatic-exchange/common-reporting-standard/> accessed 7 December 2023; see also Part II, Chapter 11 of this book; see from a US perspective: Joseph Scarfone and Madison Kerr, 'Paved Paradise: Analysis of the Common Reporting Standard to Combat Tax Avoidance' (2018) 4(1) 'Liberated Arts: a journal for undergraduate research', Article 4.

[10] An NFE is an entity that is not a financial institution. A passive NFE is: (i) an NFE that is not an active non-financial entity (active NFE); and (ii) an investment entity that is not a financial institution in a so-called Participating Jurisdiction, being a jurisdiction with which a country will exchange data on the basis of the CRS. Depending on the type of income or activities, an NFE can be passive or active.

about the so-called ultimate beneficial owner(s)[11] of that entity might also be exchanged. For that purpose, the CRS contains an identification and reporting obligation for financial institutions. In order to fulfil this identification obligation, in some cases the information collected through the so-called AML/KYC procedures[12] (hereinafter also: anti-money laundering information) must be consulted. In fact, the identification of the ultimate beneficial owner(s) of a passive NFE is done entirely through anti-money laundering information. In order to increase the effectiveness of monitoring the correct application of the DAC, tax authorities should have access to this anti-money laundering information. DAC5 provides this access.

14.2.2 Link Between DAC5 and DAC2

DAC5 is of particular importance regarding the information included in DAC2.[13] With regard to tackling tax avoidance and evasion, under DAC2, financial account information is automatically exchanged between EU Member States in accordance with the CRS.

CRS information includes, for example, the balance of an account, the value of a capital or annuity insurance policy, and the total gross amount of interest, dividends and other income generated in respect of (assets associated with) a financial account. In addition, it may also include identifying data concerning the account holder and (in certain cases) the ultimate beneficial owner(s) are exchanged, including the name, address, tax country of residence and tax identification number. This is necessary in order to link the relevant financial account to the correct person.

Financial account information and personal data are exchanged about a beneficial owner if the account holder is a passive NFE, and the beneficial owner(s) thereof is/are resident for tax purposes in a country other than the country where the financial institution (where the account is held) is located. Under the CRS, the ultimate beneficial owners are called 'controlling persons' and defined as natural persons who exercise control over an entity.[14] In the case of trusts, this means the settlor(s) of a trust, the trustees, any protector(s), the beneficiary(ies) or category(ies) of beneficiaries and any other natural persons

---

[11] Ultimate beneficial owners (UBOs) are also referred to as beneficial owners in the AMLD.

[12] AML stands for 'anti-money laundering' and KYC stands for 'know your customer'.

[13] DAC2 recitals 1–20.

[14] See DAC1 Annex I, Section VIII, Section D(5) and FATF, International Standards on Combating Money Laundering and the Financing of Terrorism & Proliferation: The FATF Recommendations (Paris, FATF 2012–2023).

who exercise ultimate effective control over the trust. In the case of legal arrangements other than a trust, this means persons in the same or a comparable position. The term 'controlling persons' must be interpreted in a way that is compatible with the recommendations of the Financial Action Task Force (FATF).[15] While the FATF recommendations do not use the term 'controlling persons', they do define the term 'beneficial owner' as being the natural person who ultimately owns or effectively controls an entity or arrangement. The definition is phrased in a very similar, yet not identical way as in Annex I of the DAC1.[16] For the purpose of the exchange of information based on the CRS, the identification rules state how a financial institution must determine in which state the account holders, or in the case of a passive NFE the beneficial owners, are resident or established for tax purposes. A distinction is made here between so-called existing accounts and new accounts, between accounts of natural persons and those of entities and between low value accounts (existing accounts of natural persons of not more than USD 1,000,000) and high value accounts (existing accounts of natural persons of more than USD 1,000,000).[17] In principle, an existing account is understood to mean a financial account that is already held by a financial institution on 31 December 2015 and a new account is a financial account that was opened on or after 1 January 2016. For high-value accounts, for existing entity accounts and for new accounts of natural persons and entities, the determination of the tax residence takes place on the basis of the information already available, which includes the anti-money laundering information.[18]

For example, for new accounts to be opened (by natural persons and by entities), a so-called self-certification must be obtained from the account holder, stating the (fiscal) country of residence or country of residence of the account holder.[19] This self-certification may be kept as part of the account opening documentation that also includes anti-money laundering information obtained as part of the so-called AML/KYC procedures. AML/KYC procedures are the customer due diligence procedures that reporting financial institutions are required to perform in the context of the anti-money laundering or similar requirements and is therefore in line with the anti-money laundering regulations. The concept of anti-money laundering information will be developed further in the next section. The financial institution can compare the tax residence(s) indicated in the self-declaration with that documentation and assess its accuracy and then determine whether the account holder must be reported

---

15 ibid.
16 ibid.
17 See C DAC1 Annex I, Section VIII(C)(14) and (15).
18 See ibid Annex I, Sections III(C)(3), IV(A), V(D), VI(1) and (2).
19 See ibid Annex I, Section IV(D)(5).

to the tax authorities. In fact, identifying the beneficial owner(s) of a passive NFE – both for existing entity accounts and for new entity accounts – can be done entirely through the anti-money laundering information. In order to subsequently determine whether the relevant beneficial owner is a person who must be reported, a financial institution can rely on a self-certification of the account holder or ultimate beneficial owner or, in the case of an existing entity account with a balance of not more than USD 1,000,000, on the anti-money laundering information that is already on file.

To sum up, DAC5 provides the necessary access for tax authorities to anti-money laundering information needed to fulfil exchange of information requirements, which, in this context, specifically means that they are able to check whether the CRS data provided to the financial institutions are correct and complete.

14.2.3 Link Between the AMLD and DAC5

But what exactly is meant by anti-money laundering information? To define this notion, DAC5 establishes a dynamic link with the AMLD in its current version, referring to its Articles 13, 30, 31 and 40.

Articles 13 and 40 of the AMLD concern customer due diligence measures by so-called obliged entities and the retention of supporting documents in this regard. The term 'obliged entities' means, in short, credit institutions (banks), financial institutions (other financial undertakings) and certain natural or legal persons acting in the course of their professional activities. Obliged entities are required to investigate clients and the background and purpose of a proposed business relationship[20] or transaction. With these measures, obliged entities should prevent their services from being misused for money laundering or terrorist financing and should recognise transactions that should be considered unusual in that regard.

The customer due diligence measures as mentioned in Article 13 AMLD include:

1. the identification of the customer and the verification of his identity on the basis of documents, data or information from a reliable and independent source;
2. identifying the beneficial owner and taking reasonable steps to verify that person's identity and, in the case of legal entities, trusts, partnerships, foundations and similar legal arrangements, taking reasonable steps to

[20] A business relationship is a business, professional or commercial relationship related to the professional activities of an obliged entity, and which is believed to last for some time at the time the contact is established.

obtain an understanding of the ownership and control structure of the client;
3. assessing and obtaining information about the purpose and intended nature of the business relationship;
4. ongoing monitoring of the business relationship, including a close review of transactions conducted throughout the relationship, including, if necessary, the origin of funds, and updating of records, data or information, in the possession of the obliged entity.

In short, with a view to preventing, detecting or investigating possible cases of money laundering or terrorist financing, obliged entities are required to provide copies of the documents and information necessary for compliance with customer due diligence requirements and the supporting documents, and to keep records of transactions necessary to identify a transaction for a period of five years from the end of the business relationship with their client or from the date of an incidental transaction.[21]

Based on Article 1 of DAC5 (Article 22(1a) DAC1), tax authorities must be granted access by the obliged entities to the anti-money laundering information they keep in order to be able to check whether the CRS data supplied by the financial institutions is correct and complete.[22] After all, the financial institutions must use the anti-money laundering information to fulfil their identification and reporting obligations under the CRS. Moreover, tax authorities must be granted access to central register(s) that contain information on beneficial owners.

Articles 30 and 31 of the AMLD concern the obligation to keep information on beneficial owners in a central register (this may be a trade register, a company's register, or another public register).[23] To this end, adequate, accurate and up-to-date information about who the ultimate beneficial owners are needs to be collected and maintained, including details of the economic interests held by the ultimate beneficial owners.[24] The general definition of ultimate beneficial owners in Article 3(6) in the AMLD defines a beneficial owner as 'any natural person(s) who ultimately owns or controls the customer and/or the natural person(s) on whose behalf a transaction or activity is being

---

21 See Directive (EU) 2015/849 (n 3) art 40(1).

22 See also DAC5 recitals 4 and 5.

23 Two regimes for the registration of beneficial ownership information apply here: a regime relating to the beneficial ownership of companies and other legal entities incorporated within the territory of an EU Member State (this concerns Article 30 of the AMLD) and a regime with regard to the ultimate beneficial owners of so-called express trusts and of legal constructions comparable to trusts (this concerns Article 31 of the AMLD).

24 For further reference, see the AMLD.

conducted'. Subsequently, three parts are included, in which an elaboration is given of what should be understood as a minimum by an ultimate beneficial owner for corporate entities, trusts and legal entities such as foundations and legal constructions that are comparable to trusts. This is a non-exhaustive list of who qualifies as the ultimate beneficial owner in those cases.

The definition of a beneficial owner in the AMLD is largely similar to the concept of an ultimate beneficial owner in the CRS, as both definitions are closely related to the aforementioned FATF recommendations. However, there are differences which lead to challenges that will be addressed in the following section.

14.3 THE CHALLENGES ARISING FROM THE INTERACTION OF DAC5 AND THE AMLD

14.3.1 The Effectiveness of DAC5 from a Legal Perspective

The effectiveness of DAC5 has, thus far, not been extensively evaluated, as it is still relatively new. However, in a resolution on the implementation of the EU requirements for exchange of tax information,[25] which is based on a report on the effectiveness of the DAC1,[26] the European Parliament (EP) touched upon the topic. The EP appears concerned that the effectiveness of the DAC1 is undermined by the incorrect implementation of both the DAC1 and the AMLD. Particularly with regard to the AMLD, it can be observed that many Member States have not implemented the (amendments to) the directive in time. The European Commission (EC) had to start infringement procedures against no less than 16 Member States.[27] One example would be the Netherlands, where the register for trusts was introduced only as per 1 November 2022, instead of 10 March 2020, as required by the fourth amendment of the AMLD.[28]

---

[25] European Parliament Resolution of 16 September 2021 on the implementation of the EU requirements for exchange of tax information: progress, lessons learnt and obstacles to overcome, Committee on Economic and Monetary Affairs [2021] 2020/2046(INI).

[26] Eckhard Binder (ed), *Implementation of the EU requirements for tax information exchange: European Implementation Assessment* (Study, PE 622.603, EPRS- European Parliamentary Research Service 2021).

[27] European Parliament Resolution of 16 September 2021 (n 25) para 21.

[28] See Besluit van 19 oktober 2022 tot vaststelling van het tijdstip van inwerkingtreding van de Implementatiewet registratie uiteindelijk belanghebbenden van trusts en soortgelijke juridische constructies en het Implementatiebesluit registratie uiteindelijk belanghebbenden van trusts en soortgelijke juridische constructies [2022] Staatsblad 2022, 405.

Furthermore, the resolution stressed:

> the lack of effective enforcement and the remaining weaknesses in the AML framework such as (i) the fact that beneficial ownership is not determined for individual accounts held through active non-financial entities (NFE), (ii) the lack of beneficial ownership information for real estate properties and life insurance contracts, (iii) the lack of inter-connected national registries in particular real estate with beneficial ownership registries, and (iv) the lack of common definitions for beneficial ownership, due diligence and tax crime.[29]

The resolution also indicates that the AML measures have not been effectively applied in many Member States, with only Spain being rated as having a 'substantial' level of effectiveness, and no Member State attaining a 'high' level of effectiveness.[30]

Furthermore, the resolution expresses the view that there should be no threshold for beneficial ownership in terms of effectivity.[31]

When it comes to the interaction between the DAC1 and the AMLD, the resolution notes that:

> the DAC, as it concerns tax matters, is an intergovernmental dimension of European integration; recalls, however, that tax policies are structural for the fulfilment of strategic EU objectives, mainly related to AML, terrorist financing, combating tax fraud and evasion, etc.; deplores the Council's position on consecutive DAC1 revisions, based on the repeated mitigation of Commission proposals and disregard of Parliament's positions; calls on the Council to review its attitude towards the Parliament on tax matters and, specifically, on DAC1 revisions; urges the Council to grant access to relevant information on DAC1 implementation in order to guarantee proper democratic scrutiny by the Parliament; Understands that the DAC1 has a dual effect: detecting fraud through information sharing and deterring it by making fraudsters more likely to be identified while not letting them go unpunished; recognises that it is more difficult to quantify such deterrent effect, but invites the Commission to further consider this aspect of the DAC in its future evaluations.[32]

The abovementioned concerns have also been discussed in literature.[33] In particular, the lack of common definitions has been described as a serious challenge regarding the effectiveness of DAC5. The AMLD intends to combat money laundering and refers to 'any proceeds derived from criminal activity'

---

29 European Parliament Resolution of 16 September 2021 (n 25) para 20.

30 ibid para 22; FATF, *4th Round Ratings* (November 2020).

31 European Parliament Resolution of 16 September 21 (n 25) para 23.

32 European Parliament Resolution of 16 September 21 (n 25) paras 53 and 54.

33 See, inter alia, Andrea Zaccagna, 'Tax Crimes Inclusion in 'Criminal Activity' Definition' in Domenico Siclari (ed), *The New Anti-Money Laundering Law* (Springer International Publishing 2016) 67–76; Schiefer (n 7).

that need to be tracked down. According to AMLD4, 'criminal activity' also includes tax crimes. However, no further definition is provided. Thus, it is for the Member States to decide what a 'tax crime' is. Given this lack of a common definition of tax crime across EU Member States, it is possible that obliged entities may not be required to keep the relevant information if transactions do not fall under the national definition of tax crime where they are subject to the AML provisions. As a consequence, tax authorities will not be able to receive this information for tax purposes.[34]

As regards the identification of real beneficial ownership, a clear definition that encompasses all beneficial owners is lacking.[35] For example, when it comes to corporations, a person holding 25% or less of shares, voting rights or ownership interest is generally not considered a 'beneficial owner' according to the AMLD, unless that person has control via 'other means'.[36] What exactly is meant by 'other means' remains vague and is to be defined by the Member States. As both the definition of beneficial owner in the AMLD and the definition of 'controlling person' as used in the DAC for CRS purposes are rooted in the FATF Recommendations, this vagueness also exists under the DAC. Similar issues arise concerning the determination of the beneficial owner of a trust, where settlors may be regarded as beneficial owners, irrespective of the fact whether they are just 'dummy settlors', i.e., persons who are legally the settlor while the economic settlement has been done by another person who remains hidden.[37]

These inconsistencies certainly have a negative impact on the effectiveness of the interaction between DAC and AML provisions and thus the exchange of information for tax purposes.[38]

14.3.2 Fundamental Rights of Taxpayers

In the recitals of DAC5, the importance of fundamental rights is stressed:

> This Directive respects the fundamental rights and observes the principles recognised by the Charter of Fundamental Rights of the European Union. Where this Directive requires that access to personal data by tax authorities be provided by law, (…) such a law should be clear and precise, and its application should be clear and foreseeable (…).[39]

---

34 See Binder (n 26) 115.

35 See, inter alia: ibid 115–16.; Schiefer (n 7) 68–74.

36 DAC5 art 3(6)(a)(i). The 25%-threshold is also recommended by FATF (n 30) 65.

37 See Binder (n 26) 73.

38 See Schiefer (n 7) 75.

39 DAC5 recital 6.

Specifically with regard to the right to privacy and data protection,[40] as laid down in Article 8 EMRC and Articles 7 and 8 of the Charter, DAC5 faces, however, some challenges.

DAC5 regulates (full) access for the tax authorities to anti-money laundering information for the implementation and enforcement of the legislation for the implementation of the DAC. This anti-money laundering information may also include personal data, which includes any information relating to an identified or identifiable natural person. The customer due diligence measures – to which the tax authorities are given access – include, among other things, the identification of the customer (including natural persons) and the verification of their identity on the basis of documents, data or information from a reliable and independent source, for example, a valid passport or a valid identity card. In addition, ultimate beneficial owners must be identified on the basis of these customer due diligence measures.[41] Furthermore, tax authorities will, upon request, have access to the information about ultimate beneficial owners that is kept or maintained in a central register. This raises the question of to what extent the interference with privacy associated with the processing of personal data is necessary in relation to the purpose it pursues, which is the public interest of combating (cross-border) tax avoidance and evasion, and whether it does not go beyond what is necessary for that purpose. Access to anti-money laundering information is directly related to the obligations of EU Member States to implement the DAC.

In this regard, the recent judgment of the CJEU on public access to beneficial ownership information based on Article 30(5) of the AMLD is of particular importance.[42] In this judgment, the Grand Chamber of the CJEU decided that the public access to beneficial ownership data as required by Article 30(5) AMLD constitutes a serious interference with the fundamental rights of Articles 7 and 8 of the Charter. Consequently, this provision of the AMLD was declared invalid to the extent that public access to the data is granted.[43] The

40 Viktoria Wöhrer, 'Data Protection and Taxpayers' Rights: Challenges Created by Automatic Exchange of Information' (2018) European and International Tax Law and Policy Series 10; Iakovina Kindylidi, *The Data Protection Implications of the EU AML Framework: A Critical Overview & the Case of AI* (Privacy Technologies and Policy: 10th Annual Privacy Forum, APF 2022, Warsaw, 23–24 June 2022, Springer-Verlag 2022) 37–49. Lecture Notes in Computer Science. Springer International Publishing, 2022; see also Part 1, Chapter 4 of this book.

41 See Section 14.2.3 above.

42 Joined Cases C-37/20 and C-601/20 *WM and Sovim SA v Luxembourg Business Registers* [2022] ECLI:EU:C:2022:912.

43 See Katerina Pantazatou, 'A Never-Ending Battle Between Privacy and Transparency: The Case of Registers of Beneficial Ownership Before the CJEU' (2023) 32(3) 'EC Tax Review' 103.

CJEU did not have to decide on the access to the data by competent authorities as provided in DAC5. It did, however, explain in paragraph 84 of the judgment that access to anti-money laundering information by competent authorities and obliged entities is necessary in order to properly combat money laundering and terrorist financing.

The same reasoning should be applicable with regard to DAC5. Full access to the anti-money laundering information is necessary to verify that the CRS data provided by the financial institutions is correct and complete. Only if the tax and customs administration is given full access to the anti-money laundering information can it adequately check whether the CRS data provided is correct and also whether certain data has been wrongly not provided.

The question is how broad the word 'access' in this sentence should be interpreted. It seems logical that the term includes both accessing and using the anti-money laundering information, but to what extent should personal data be collected and processed? Based on the aforementioned judgment of the CJEU, and its willingness to enforce the fundamental rights of the Charter even when it comes to legislative acts of the EU itself, the proportionality test should be taken very seriously in this respect.[44] Therefore, the collection and processing of personal data in the context of DAC5 should only be lawful to the extent necessary for the purpose of implementing and enforcing the DAC and to ensure the functioning of the administrative cooperation it provides.

Processing of the aforementioned personal data may, in principle, only take place within that purpose. This means that personal data that are not relevant may in principle not be processed further than is necessary for the purposes for which they were initially made accessible, thus guaranteeing the minimum data processing. Non-relevant information is then disregarded. If the tax authorities want to use the anti-money laundering information in the context of providing assistance to another EU Member State on request or spontaneously, that would only be lawful if such information is expected to be relevant for the taxation of that other EU Member State.[45] The purpose of that criterion is to provide for the widest possible exchange of information in the tax field, while at the same time clarifying that EU Member States cannot freely conduct so-called fishing expeditions and request information that is likely not relevant for the taxation of the EU Member State concerned.[46] Fishing expeditions refer to situations in which the connection between the requested information and one (or more) specific taxpayer(s) cannot be made sufficiently plausible.

---

[44] Joined Cases C-37/20 and C-601/20 (n 42) paras 65 and 65; Case C-401/19 *Poland v Parliament and Council* EU:C:2022:297, paras 65–67.

[45] This is guaranteed by DAC arts 5a and 9.

[46] See ibid recital 9.

Finally, it should be noted in this regard that Regulation (EU) 2016/679 (General Data Protection Regulation, GDPR)[47] applies to this provision insofar as it results in the processing of personal data. The personal data in question are processed for a specific, legitimate purpose in accordance with the GDPR, given the legal basis in the DAC. In principle, the data are also adequate, relevant and limited to what is necessary for the purpose outlined. The processing is, however, only lawful if any non-relevant personal data in the information to which access has been granted will not be processed further than is necessary (meaning that the initial access was necessary in that specific case, but the subsequent use was not), thus ensuring minimal data processing.[48]

Another relevant fundamental right is the right to client-attorney privilege as laid down in Article 8 of the ECHR and Articles 7 and 47 of the Charter. This is an issue that stems from the AMLD, because attorneys and tax advisors are considered as obliged entities and, therefore, the tax authorities have the right to access their anti-money laundering information. While the AMLD recognises legal privilege, that privilege is limited to 'the strict extent that those persons ascertain the legal position of their client, or perform the task of defending or representing that client in, or concerning, judicial proceedings, including providing advice on instituting or avoiding such proceedings.'[49] Attorneys at law providing tax advice may, therefore, find themselves in a position where they are obliged to collect anti-money laundering information on their clients, and through DAC5, tax authorities are permitted to request that information. Given the fact that the purpose of the AMLD is combating crime, and that the purpose of the DAC1 is promoting correct taxation, one could ask the question of whether it is proportionate that tax authorities have the right under DAC5 to violate legal privilege, at least in cases where the information request is not concerned with (potential) criminal charges.[50] In this respect, a case that the Belgium constitutional court brought before the CJEU may be of interest.[51] The *Orde van Vlaamse Balies and Others* case concerns DAC6, and the fact that it raises the issue of the infringement of legal privilege is

---

[47] Regulation (EU) 2016/679 of the European Parliament and of the Council of 27 April 2016 on the protection of individuals with regard to the processing of personal data and on the free movement of such data, and repealing Directive 95/46/EC(General Data Protection Regulation) [2016] OJ L 119/1.

[48] See ibid art 6.

[49] Directive (EU) 2015/849 (n 3) art 14(4).

[50] Tomáš Sejkora, 'Does the Implementation of DAC 5 Represent a Breach of Attorney Confidentiality?' in Gábor Hulkó and Roman Vybíral (eds), *European Financial Law in Times of Crisis of the European Union* (Ludovika University Press 2019) 525–34.

[51] Case C-694/20 *Orde van Vlaamse Balies and Others v Vlaamse Regering* [2022] ECLI:EU:C:2022:963.

also of relevance here, as the CJEU decided that legal privilege precluded the application of DAC6 to the extent that lawyers and advisers falling under legal privilege have to disclose certain information about their clients.[52]

14.4 HOW TO FACE THE CHALLENGES

The abovementioned challenges have already sent a signal to the European Commission in recent years. The EC has come up with a large package in order to strengthen the uniformity of AML supervision. On 20 July 2021, the EC proposed the so-called Anti-Money Laundering and Countering Financing of Terrorism AML/CFT package, which consists of four legislative proposals:[53]

1. A Regulation establishing an EU AML/CFT Authority in the form of a decentralised EU regulatory agency;
2. A new Regulation on AML/CFT, containing directly applicable AML/CFT rules, including a revised EU list of entities subject to AML/CFT rules (known as Obliged Entities);
3. A Directive on AML/CFT, replacing the existing EU AMLD (and containing provisions not appropriate for a Regulation and requiring national transposition, such as rules concerning national supervisors and Financial Intelligence Units in Member States);
4. A recast of the 2015 Regulation on Transfers of Funds (Regulation 2015/847).

With these measures, the EC aims to put into place a set of uniform rules governing money laundering issues and guide Member States in executing those rules. By largely using the legal form of a regulation, the issues of different or delayed implementation, as has occurred with the (amendments to) the directives in the field, can be avoided.[54]

As DAC5 contains a dynamic reference to the relevant AMLD rules, it would probably not need to be significantly changed in order to properly refer to the new set of rules. However, it might be recommendable to integrate

---

[52] See Part II, Chapter 15 of this book.

[53] See Proposal for a Directive of the European Parliament and of the Council on the mechanisms to be put in place by the Member States for the prevention of the use of the financial system for the purposes of money laundering or terrorist financing and repealing Directive (EU) 2015/849 [2021] COM(2021) 423 final; see also the recent press releases of the European Council dated 13 December 2023 and 18 January 2024 at <www.consilium.europa.eu>, according to which an agreement has been reached between the Council and the European Parliament that includes some amendments to the 2021 proposals.

[54] See also Schiefer (n 7) 83.

the relevant definitions of the new set of rules into the DAC by amending or changing the definitions article. This is specifically true for the notion of 'beneficial ownership'.

Another relevant step that should be taken would be the strengthening of taxpayers' rights. As discussed in this article, the fundamental rights to privacy, data protection and legal privilege could be violated by DAC5. The main issue here is proportionality, given the fact that the primary objective of the DAC1 is not crime fighting. Much could be gained if the access granted to tax authorities under DAC5 were limited to financial institutions and central registers on beneficial ownership, thus excluding other obliged entities. This would also be in line with the CRS obligations under DAC2, which only concerns financial institutions.

14.5 CONCLUSION

DAC5 does not stand on its own, but needs to be read in conjunction with DAC2 and the AMLD. The purpose of DAC5 is to enhance the exchange of information between tax authorities by granting tax authorities access to anti-money laundering information which has been collected by obliged entities, in particular financial institutions, under the AMLD. This information contains, inter alia, client verification and beneficial ownership data as well as data on certain transactions conducted throughout the business relationship, including – if necessary – the origin of funds.

While the effectiveness of DAC5 has not been thoroughly assessed due to its relatively short existence, there has been an assessment of the DAC1 as a whole, with particular attention given to anti-money laundering information. The concerns raised were, essentially, that the directives have not been implemented in a timely manner, that there is a lack of uniform and clear definitions (e.g., when it comes to the notions of 'tax crime' and 'beneficial ownership'), and that the information obtained may not be very accurate. Many of the concerns regarding effectiveness will be addressed by the proposed AML/CFT package of the EC, in which uniformity through regulations is envisaged, leaving behind implementation issues that always exist with directives. Once those clear definitions and rules are in place, it would be recommendable to also include the most important definitions in the DAC1, in order to improve uniformity and accuracy.

As regards fundamental rights, DAC5 potentially violates the right to privacy, data protection and legal privilege. The latter is of special concern, given the fact that legal professionals are in certain cases also obliged entities under the AMLD, and the anti-money laundering information they gather is accessible by tax authorities through DAC5. Given the recent judgments of the CJEU in the *Vlaamse Balies and Others* case, it would be advisable to consider limiting the scope of DAC5 to financial institutions and access to central registers, and to preclude the tax authorities from access to information that stems from legal professionals.

15. DAC6: reportable cross-border arrangements

Marianne Malmgrén

15.1 INTRODUCTION

Directive 2018/822 amending Directive 2011/16/EU as regards mandatory automatic exchange of information in the field of taxation in relation to reportable cross-border arrangements (DAC6) is part of the system of mandatory automatic exchange of information in the field of taxation.[1] Its purpose is to increase transparency and make it less attractive for intermediaries to design, market and implement potentially aggressive tax structures. DAC6 imposes on tax authorities within the European Union (EU) Member States the obligation to collect certain information on reportable cross-border arrangements. The reportable arrangements are mainly reported to the national tax authorities by intermediaries, which are defined as any person that designs, markets, organises, or makes available for implementation or manages the implementation of a reportable cross-border arrangement.[2] The reported information is exchanged between Member States on a quarterly basis. DAC6 sets a minimum standard allowing the Member States a certain flexibility with implementation.[3]

DAC6 is based on the OECD Base Erosion and Profit Shifting (BEPS) project, Action 12, aiming to prevent aggressive tax planning and international tax evasion.[4] It incorporates the model rules set out in the 2018 OECD report 'Model Mandatory Disclosure Rules for CRS Avoidance Arrangements and

---

[1] See Viktoria Wöhrer, *Data protection and taxpayers' rights: Challenges created by automatic exchange of information* (IBFD 2018) 95 in relation to the development of automatic exchange of tax rulings under DAC in general.

[2] DAC6 art 3(21).

[3] Stan Stevens, 'Cutting-Edge Techniques to Collect Information from Taxpayers' in Funda Basaran Yavaslar and Johanna Hey (eds), *Tax Transparency* (IBFD 2020), section 5.4.3 in which the mandatory disclosure rules are reviewed.

[4] OECD/G20 *Base Erosion and Profit Shifting Project, Mandatory Disclosure Rules, Action 12, 2015 Final Report*, (OECD Publishing 2015).

Opaque Offshore Structures'[5] to EU legislation. Thus, DAC6 has an essential connection to the measures implemented to restrain aggressive tax planning.[6]

DAC6 was to be implemented by 31 December 2019 at the latest and applied from 1 July 2020. It has been implemented in the meantime by all Member States in their national legislation. The first exchange of information applied to an extended reporting period between 25 June 2018 and 1 July 2020, and was due by 31 October 2020.[7]

The aim of this chapter is to discuss the legality of DAC6, its hallmarks (i.e., the list of features and elements of the reportable transactions), as well as the main benefit test (MBT), the reporting procedure, and the penalties for neglecting the obligations that it imposes. The chapter will also consider the interaction between DAC6 and taxpayers' fundamental rights. Throughout the chapter, reference will also be made to the implementation of DAC6 in individual Member States.

---

[5] OECD, *Model Mandatory Disclosure Rules for CRS Avoidance Arrangements and Opaque Offshore Structures* (OECD 2018).

[6] DAC6 recital 9, which links the hallmarks in DAC6 Annex IV to aggressive tax planning by stating the Directive endeavours to capture potentially aggressive tax planning arrangements through the compiling of a list of the features and elements of transactions that present a strong indication of tax avoidance or abuse rather than to define the concept of aggressive tax planning. See also Bart Peeters and Lars Vanneste, 'DAC 6: An Additional Common EU Reporting Standard?' (2020) 12(3) World Tax Journal 499, section 2, which refers to the arts 113 and 115 of the Treaty on European Union and the Treaty on the Functioning of the European Union, as the legal ground for DAC6. The authors state accurately e.g., that the concept of aggressive tax planning is not defined in DAC6 even though the Directive several times refers to 'aggressive tax planning', 'aggressive tax arrangements' and 'aggressive tax practices'.

[7] Council Directive (EU) 2020/876 of 24 June 2020 amending Directive 2011/16/EU to address the urgent need to defer certain time limits for the filing and exchange of information in the field of taxation because of the COVID-19 pandemic [2020] OJ L 204/46 granted a suspension to the filing limits due to COVID-19. The optional suspension meant that the Member States were allowed to postpone the first information to be communicated by 30 April 2021. The amendment to the Directive also included a possibility for an additional three-month extension which could have been implemented by the Council depending upon how the pandemic unfolded. However, further suspensions were considered unlikely in the amendment to the Directive.

15.2 BACKGROUND AND MAIN OBJECTIVES OF DAC6

15.2.1 DAC6's Background

The existing national mandatory disclosure rules (MDR), which provide a modular framework for jurisdictions without MDR to design a regime to obtain early information on potentially aggressive and abusive tax planning schemes and their users, were the basis of OECD BEPS Action 12. In the 2015 OECD Report, the existing national MDR in several jurisdictions were reviewed.[8] The OECD recommendation related to MDR was not a BEPS minimum standard (i.e., jurisdictions were free to choose whether to introduce the recommendation or not). One could argue that, since MDR were not a BEPS minimum standard, they were not considered to be central in the OECD BEPS work. However, the EU adapted the recommendation and implemented it through DAC6. One reason for this might have been that rules related to administrative co-operation in tax matters between Member States are relatively easy to implement and, as such, are likely to be approved by all Member States. Administrative and other procedural rules on the EU level have a longer tradition within EU tax directives than directives such as ATAD, which comprise substantive income tax rules. However, there is no reference to this reasoning in DAC6 recitals.

In the 2015 OECD BEPS Action 12 Report, it is stated that the main purpose of MDR is to increase transparency by providing information regarding potentially aggressive and abusive tax planning schemes at the earliest possible stage and to identify the promoters[9] and users of such schemes; to identify schemes, and the users and promoters of the schemes; and to act as a deterrent, i.e., to reduce the promotion and use of avoidance schemes. In that sense, cross-border tax planning aims to benefit from tax arbitrage (i.e., benefit from the differences in national tax legislation) and thus it often erodes the jurisdictional tax base. Shifting of profits to low-tax jurisdictions and base erosion

---

8 OECD (n 5) 23 stating that amongst the OECD and G20 countries, MDR were introduced in the United States, Canada, South Africa, the United Kingdom, Portugal, Ireland, Israel, and Korea at the time of drafting of the 2015 OECD Report. The United States was the first jurisdiction to introduce MDR in 1984. In Annex E of the 2015 OECD Report, a comparison table between the MDR in the United Kingdom, United States, Ireland, Portugal, Canada, and South Africa is presented.

9 In the 2015 OECD Report (n 4), the 'promoters' refer to those who promote a tax shelter or avoidance scheme in the traditional sense, and intermediaries (such as material advisors) who facilitate the implementation of a reportable scheme.

may also distort the internal market and cause unfair competition.[10]. As several jurisdictions have implemented both a number of the results from the BEPS actions and, for EU Member States, the related EU directives, it has become increasingly difficult for enterprises to benefit from tax arbitrage. Thus, there is a preventive or deterrent element in the MDR as well as in DAC6 reporting.

15.2.2 DAC6's Main Objectives

By adopting DAC6, the EU embedded at least the essential content of OECD BEPS Action 12 Report into the EU EOI framework. DAC6 Recital 2 states that Member States find it 'increasingly difficult to protect their national tax bases from erosion as tax-planning structures have evolved to be particularly sophisticated and often take advantage of the increased mobility of both capital and persons within the internal market'. The recital also refers to that tax planning arrangements often take place in cross-border situations.[11] This recognition was also one of the basic ideas behind the OECD BEPS project.

In that sense, the primary objective of DAC6 was to ensure the proper functioning of the internal market.[12] The aim was to increase transparency and enable tax authorities to get access to correct information at an early stage to, e.g., improve their risk assessment. In addition, its purpose was to enable, depending on the applicable national legal framework, either authorities or legislators, when necessary, to close loopholes and prevent a loss of tax revenue in relation to reportable cross-border arrangements.[13]

DAC6 increases transparency by providing the legal framework for the disclosure of certain schemes. Taxpayers need to recognise that schemes they plan or execute may need to be reported to the tax administration and the information will be forwarded to other Member States' tax authorities due to the exchange of information system. This may result in further scrutiny of the taxpayer's schemes, some of which may be non-compliant with the national tax legislation in the jurisdictions involved. Additionally, DAC6 reporting of

---

[10] Peeters and Vanneste (n 6).

[11] Andrea Purpura, 'DAC6: Some (potential) Incompatibility Profiles with Article 6 ATAD' (2023) 51(1) Intertax 62, in relation to the interaction of DAC6 and Council Directive (EU) 2016/1164 of 12 July 2016 laying down rules against tax avoidance practices that directly affect the functioning of the internal market [2016] OJ L 193/1 (ATAD).

[12] DAC6 (n 6) recitals 10 and 19.

[13] See Explanatory Memorandum of Proposal for a Council Directive amending Directive 2011/16/EU as regards mandatory automatic exchange of information in the field of taxation in relation to reportable cross-border arrangements COM (2017) 335 final.

reportable cross-border schemes may result in national legislative changes to prohibit at least some of the reported arrangements.

In the DAC6 recitals it is stated that the reporting of potentially aggressive cross-border tax-planning arrangements can contribute effectively to efforts in creating an environment of fair taxation in the internal market.[14] This relates to the principle of subsidiarity and was used as an argument in recital 19 for the implementation of MDR with a directive. Further, the principle of proportionality relates to the legality of DAC6. However, all in all, the legality of DAC6 has been criticised.[15]

In the DAC6 recitals it is emphasised that the European Commission needs to have access to adequate information to monitor the proper functioning of DAC6. According to Article 27 DAC, the Commission has an obligation to submit a report on the application of the Directive to the European Parliament and Council.[16] It is further stated that in cross-border situations, due to the potential impact on the functioning of the internal market, the need for enacting a common set of rules is justified. This argumentation is, as such, reasonable, as international co-operation on tackling cross-border aggressive tax planning is essential, especially in the field of exchange of information. However, as explained below, the differences in Member States' implementation of DAC6 reduce the benefit to the internal market.

15.3 ARRANGEMENTS TO BE REPORTED

15.3.1 Overview

It is important to note, at the outset, that the reporting obligation exists not only in the case of an implemented cross-border arrangement, but also when cross-border advice is given.[17] In general, the reporting obligation applies when an (i) arrangement is considered to be (ii) cross-border, (iii) required

---

[14] DAC6 (n 6) recital 6.

[15] Werner Haslehner and Katerina Pantazatou, *Assessment of recent anti-tax avoidance and evasion measures (ATAD & DAC6)* (Publication for the Subcommittee on tax matters (FISC), Policy Department for Economic, Scientific and Quality of Life Policies, European Parliament 2022) 33, including reference also to additional bibliographic sources.

[16] Committee on Economic and Monetary Affairs, 'Report on the implementation of the EU requirements for exchange of tax information: progress, lessons learnt and obstacles to overcome' (2021) 2020/2046(INI)), in which the European Parliament expresses its rejection to it not being granted an access to the documents on the implementation of DAC in relation to information provided to it by the European Commission in its DAC-related reports.

[17] Stevens (n 3), section 5.4.3.1.

hallmarks are fulfilled, and (iv) MBT are met when required in connection to the applicable hallmark. Thus, DAC6 has four conditions to be fulfilled before the reporting obligation arises.

As a starting point, it should be observed that several issues related to DAC6 are presently under the scrutiny of the Court of Justice of the European Union (CJEU) in the *Belgian Association of Tax Lawyers* case.[18] In particular, the Court will need to consider the relationship of the scope of taxes covered in the Belgian legislation implementing DAC6 in relation to Article 6(3) TFEU and Articles 20 and 21 of the Charter of Fundamental Rights of the European Union (the Charter).[19] Furthermore, the national court reflected on whether the concepts of 'arrangement' (and therefore the concepts of 'cross-border arrangement', 'marketable arrangement' and 'bespoke arrangement'), 'intermediary', 'participant', 'associated enterprise', 'cross-border', the different 'hallmarks' and the 'MBT' in DAC6 are sufficiently clear and precise. Thirdly, the Court is asked to decide whether the starting point of the 30-day period during which the intermediary or relevant taxpayer must fulfil its reporting obligation in respect of a cross-border arrangement is fixed in a sufficiently clear and precise manner. In both of these items under review the benchmark is that of Article 49(1) of the Charter and Article 7 of the European Convention of Human Rights (ECHR). Finally, issues related to the national implementation of an optional waiver for legal professionals based on legal professional privilege under the national law of that Member State arise as a possible interference with the right to respect for the private life of intermediaries and relevant taxpayers in relation to Article 7 of the Charter and Article 8 of the ECHR.[20] In the case *Orde van Vlaamse Balies*, the CJEU already judged that the application of legal professional privilege by advocates should have as a consequence that the notification requirement under DAC6 is contrary to fundamental rights.[21]

In the *Belgian Association of Tax Lawyers* case that is currently pending, essential issues are thus raised in relation to the legality of DAC6. The first one is the scope of the taxes concerned and the second one the clarity of a number

---

[18] Case C-623/22 *Belgian Association of Tax Lawyers and Others v Premier ministre/ Eerste Minister* (pending). See further Pieter J. Wouters, 'EU Disclosure Regime on Cross-Border Tax Planning Arrangements: Pending Decision Court of Justice of the European Union (ECJ) on Legal Professional Privilege and Constitutionality of the Directive on Administrative Cooperation (DAC6)' (2022) 76(12) Bulletin for International Taxation 589, including a detailed review of the preliminary questions presented to CJEU.

[19] Charter of Fundamental Rights of the European Union (2012) OJ C 326/02.

[20] This point is in general further reviewed below in Section 15.4.1.

[21] Case C-694/20 *Orde van Vlaamse Balies and Others v Vlaamse Regering* [2022] ECLI:EU:C:2022:963.

of provisions related to certain concepts and timelines. The clarity of concepts is an especially important issue as it relates to legal certainty and has a connection with the Constitutions of the individual Member States which usually require enacting the provisions in law with certain accuracy. The questions raised also relate to the principle of good governance and the burden of proof.

15.3.2 Arrangements and Cross-border Arrangements

The term 'arrangement' is not defined in DAC6.[22] It can be argued that to some extent 'an arrangement' is defined through hallmarks in Annex IV.[23] In recital 8 of DAC6 there is a reference to 'a reportable cross-border transaction or a series of such transactions', which could be interpreted as somewhat explaining the meaning of an arrangement by referring to transactions.

DAC6 is restricted to cross-border arrangements. Purely domestic arrangements are out of scope of the directive, even though some EU Member States included domestic arrangements in scope of the domestic implementation of DAC6, like Poland and Portugal.

According to Article 3(18) DAC, the parties of a cross-border arrangement need to be in different jurisdictions, either in more than one Member State or in a Member State and a third country (i.e., a non-EU jurisdiction). An additional condition for the cross-border element is that at least one of the below conditions contained in Article 3(18)(a)–(18)(e) is met:

(a) not all of the participants in the arrangement are resident for tax purposes in the same jurisdiction;
(b) one or more of the participants in the arrangement is simultaneously resident for tax purposes in more than one jurisdiction;
(c) one or more of the participants in the arrangement carries on a business in another jurisdiction through a permanent establishment (PE) situated in that jurisdiction and the arrangement forms part or the whole of the business of that PE;
(d) one or more of the participants in the arrangement carries on an activity in another jurisdiction without being resident for tax purposes or creating a PE situated in that jurisdiction;

---

[22] See Case C-623/22 (n 18) and Wouters (n 18) 332, where it is stated that the absence of the definition of what constitutes an 'arrangement' is intentional.

[23] See also Peeters and Vanneste (n 6), section 3.1.1.1 reviewing as one possibility to define 'arrangement' according to BEPS Action 12 as 'any agreement, scheme, plan or understanding, whether or not legally enforceable'. The authors conclude that 'the scope of an "arrangement" is far from clear'. In addition, they note that Member States are free to determine the term in their domestic legislation.

(e) such arrangement has a possible impact on the automatic exchange of information or the identification of beneficial ownership.

The above points contained in Article 3(18)(a) and (18)(b) are based on reviewing the state of tax residence and not the state of corporate law residence. The reporting obligation can be applied, e.g., when two entities are established according to the corporate law of Member State A and, according to Member State A's national tax legislation, both entities are tax resident in State A due to place of corporate registration. If one of the entities has its place of effective management (PoEM) in Member State B or third country C and is, as a consequence of its PoEM, considered to be tax resident in Member State B or third country C as well (i.e., a dual resident) the cross-border requirement is fulfilled.

15.3.3 Reportable Cross-border Arrangements

'Reportable cross-border arrangement' is defined in Article 3(19) DAC as any cross-border arrangement that fulfils at least one of the hallmarks set out in Annex IV. In addition, for an arrangement to be reportable some of the hallmarks need to fulfil the MBT explained below in Section 15.3.4. Hallmarks (i.e., the list of features and elements related in the Directive to the reportable cross-border transactions) are listed in Annex IV to the directive.

The hallmarks present an indication of a potential risk of tax avoidance. In Annex IV the hallmarks are categorised as follows:[24]

A. Generic hallmarks linked to the MBT;
B. Specific hallmarks linked to the MBT;
C. Specific hallmarks related to cross-border transactions;
D. Specific hallmarks concerning automatic exchange of information and beneficial ownership;
E. Specific hallmarks concerning transfer pricing.

Hallmarks in the categories A, B and in relation to category C (1), under points (b)(i), (c) and (d) are subject to the MBT explained below. They are only reportable if the MBT is also met. Generic hallmarks in category A include the use of a condition of confidentiality in the arrangement, a fee linked to a tax advantage, and standardised documentation and/or structures of the

[24] Peeters and Vanneste (n 6), section 3.1.1.3.2 reviews the hallmarks in more detail. See also Jasper Korving and Joep Verbaarschot 'Mandatory disclosure in the Netherlands – To disclose or not to disclose: That's the question' (2019) 59(10) European Taxation 461, where the implementation of DAC6 in the Netherlands is discussed including a detailed review of e.g., the DAC6 hallmarks in Dutch legislation.

arrangement available for more than one relevant taxpayer without a need for substantially customised implementation. Specific hallmarks in category B include the trade in loss-making companies in order to utilise those losses, conversion of income into capital, gifts or other categories of revenue and circular transactions resulting in round-tripping of funds.

Hallmarks C partly,[25] as well as hallmarks D and E, result in a reporting obligation without having to meet the MBT. Hallmarks in category C include mismatches of a payment meaning, e.g., that a deduction does not result in taxing the corresponding income in another jurisdiction. Some of the hallmarks in category C relate to transactions between associated enterprises. Category D covers, e.g., situations where reporting obligation according to EU legislation is undermined based on agreements with third countries. In category E, hallmarks include, e.g., arrangements involving the use of unilateral safe harbour rules, the transfer of hard-to-value intangibles, and cross-border intragroup transfers of functions, risks or assets resulting in a drop of the expected earnings before interest and taxes (EBIT) of the transferor(s).

In general, the hallmarks can be argued to be ambiguous. In the pending *Belgian Association of Tax Lawyers* case, the principle of legal certainty is discussed in relation to the hallmarks and MBT. In relation to DAC6, the principle of good governance and the burden of proof is also to be reviewed from the perspective of proportionality. The principle of good governance is not served when rules are unclear as in DAC6. Distribution of the burden of proof in DAC6 could be addressed by extending the MBT to all hallmarks.[26] However, this might result in further unclarity of the rules, since the interpretation of the MBT is not clear either.

Ambiguous rules are subject to interpretation, potentially resulting in a situation in which all reportable arrangements are not reported if the party liable for reporting interprets the requirements in such a way that no liability to report arises. Neglecting to report may also result in penalty sanctions. However, the result of this uncertainty in the interpretation of several seminal concepts in DAC6 may also be over-reporting (i.e., reporting arrangements which should not be reported).[27]

---

25 Excluding category C(1) points (b)(i), (c) and (d) of paragraph 1 which, as stated earlier, are subject to MBT explained below.

26 Wouters (n 18) 597.

27 Antti Kurikka, Seurantaraportti rajat ylittävien järjestelyjen raportoinnin kokemuksista (VN/17648/2022-VM-1, Valtiovarainministeriö Finansministeriet 2022) on the reportable cross-border tax arrangements based on a resolution issued by the Finnish parliament when the legislation implementing DAC6 was accepted in the Parliament. The Finnish progress report was conducted by the Finnish Ministry of Finance as an enquiry addressed to five Finnish organisations serving both business

Ambiguous hallmarks can also result in different interpretations in different Member States. In principle, the interpretation of EU law lies with the CJEU. The interpretation by the CJEU should aid in reducing differences in interpretation among the Member States. In the case of DAC6, it fails to provide a homogeneous interpretation, as some Member States have altered the hallmarks.[28] The alteration of hallmarks in a Member State means that the level playing field and harmonisation within EU is not obtained in relation to DAC6. It also increases the administrative burden for the taxpayers since the reporting obligation differs depending on the Member State.

In 2017, the EU Commission services issued a meeting document, 'Examples and origin of the Hallmarks' to the Working Party on Tax Questions (Direct Taxation-DAC).[29] The document provides some detail on how the hallmarks were supposed to be interpreted, at least at the time of drafting and negotiations on DAC6. In addition, tax authorities in several Member States have issued guidelines related to DAC6 including information on how to interpret the hallmarks when identifying the reportable transactions.[30] From a wider perspective, the national guidelines may be of minor importance when trying to find a common interpretation between the Member States since DAC is a minimum standard and there are local differences in the implementation. In DAC6 recital 13 it is stated that OECD work on MDR could be used as a source of illustration and interpretation.[31]

The Economic and Monetary Affairs Subcommittee on tax matters (FISC) has requested an assessment of recent anti-tax avoidance and evasion measures

---

and advisors, and Finnish Tax Administration. In the Finnish progress report, Finnish tax administration stated that reportability of national transaction could be limited to arrangements with certain transactions where intermediaries are involved. On page 23 of the Finnish Progress Report the parties representing intermediaries etc. responsible for reporting state that the responsibilities for reporting are complex resulting in that exhaustive and expensive processes and tools are required to get to know and to fulfil the responsibilities.

[28] Such as Poland.

[29] Commission Services, Examples and origin of the Hallmarks WK 9981/2017 INIT (Brussels, Council of the European Union General Secretariat 2017).

[30] René Offermanns and Rita Botelho Moniz, 'European Union – DAC6 in a Selection of EU Member States: The Practical Application of the MBT and Its Hallmarks' (2021) 61(6) European Taxation 229, for a comparison of the practical application of the hallmarks and the MBT in Belgium, France, Germany, Ireland, Luxembourg, the Netherlands, Portugal and Spain. See also Jasper Korving, 'A Guide to the Netherlands DAC6 Guidelines' (2021) 61(1) European Taxation 12.

[31] See e.g. Dennis Weber and Jorn Steenbergen, 'The (Absence of) Member State Autonomy in the Interpretation of DAC6: A Call for EU Guidance' (2021) 30(5) EC Tax Review 254.

including DAC6.[32] The assessment states that, according to some authors, the very broad hallmarks included in DAC6 may result in the situation that perfectly legitimate transactions are being caught by the reporting obligation.[33] This has led authors to wonder, e.g., whether the measures are meaningful and necessary to ensure the functioning of the internal market.[34]

15.3.4 Main Benefit Test

The MBT related to hallmarks A, B and C (1) points (b) (i), (c) and (d) in Annex IV compares the tax advantage of a transaction to other benefits of a transaction. The test is satisfied if the main benefit or one of the main benefits which, having regard to all relevant facts and circumstances, a person may reasonably expect to derive from an arrangement is the obtaining of a tax advantage.[35] In relation to hallmarks under category C (1) points (b) (i), (c) and (d), the presence of conditions set out in category C in itself cannot be a reason for concluding that an arrangement automatically satisfies the MBT.

The MBT is to be evaluated based on objective criteria, meaning observable facts and circumstances. Even an outsider should be able to see that a person may reasonably expect to derive a tax advantage from the arrangement. The evaluation is based on facts and circumstances known by the intermediary or taxpayer upon the design phase of the arrangement and relies on obtaining the benefit and not in the purpose of the arrangement. However, it can be argued that subjective elements are relevant as well, such as the phrase in Part I of Annex IV: 'what a person may reasonably expect to derive'. In the first instance, the MBT is to be interpreted by the party liable to report the cross-border arrangement, i.e., the intermediary. If the tax administration, in the case of non-reporting, makes it probable that obtaining a tax advantage was one of the main benefits, the intermediary, or the relevant taxpayer can provide evidence to the contrary. As regards the hallmarks and other definitions, there is a lack of a precise definition of MBT.[36]

---

32 Committee on Economic and Monetary Affairs (n 16).

33 See the Finnish Progress Report (n 27) 23 section 5.2 where some of the parties related to the taxpayers and intermediaries state that the reported arrangements are not tax driven.

34 Committee on Economic and Monetary Affairs (n 16) 33.

35 DAC6 (6) Annex IV, part I.

36 Peeters and Vanneste (n 6), section 3.1.1.3.1 stating among others that the definition of the MBT defers from the GAAR provision in ATAD. The authors also refer to DAC6 recital (14) addressing ATAD. Also, the question of the interaction of the MBT with the EU term 'wholly artificial arrangements' raises questions.

The highlights of the test can be illustrated with the below flow chart (Figure 15.1).[37]

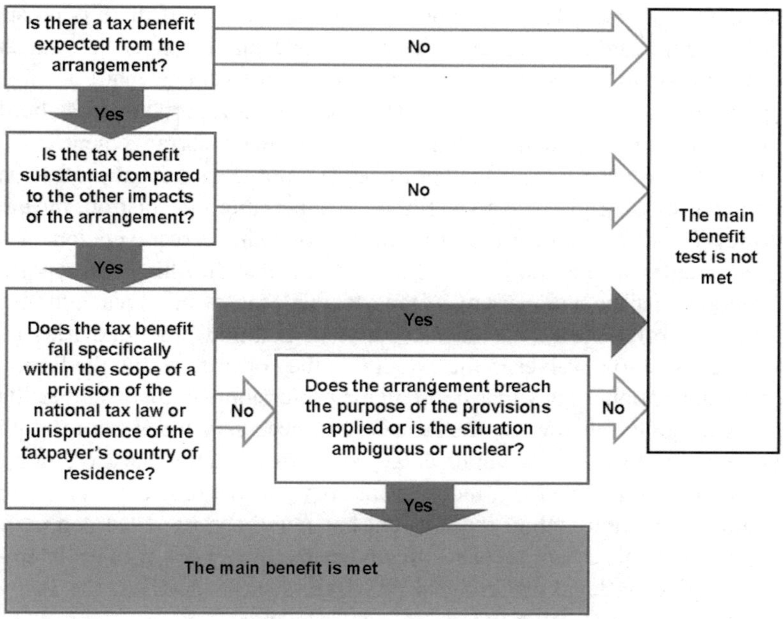

Source: Finnish Tax Administration.

Figure 15.1 Main Benefit Test according to Finland

15.4 PROCEDURAL ASPECTS

15.4.1 Who is Responsible for Reporting?

Article 8ab DAC includes provisions on who has the obligation to report the reportable transactions. The main principle is that the reporting obligation lies with the intermediary. The concept of an 'intermediary' is defined in Article 3(21) as 'any person that designs, markets, organises, or makes available for implementation or manages the implementation of a reportable cross-border

---

37 See Vero Skatt, 'Reportable cross-border arrangements' (Date issued 12/9/2022), <https://www.vero.fi/en/detailed-guidance/guidance/84830/reportable-cross-border-arrangements2/> accessed 8 December 2023, section 3.2 MBT.

arrangement'. In case there is no intermediary, or the intermediary notifies the relevant taxpayer or another intermediary of the application of a waiver under Article 8ab(5), the obligation to file information on a reportable cross-border arrangement lies with the other notified intermediary, or, if there is no such intermediary, with the relevant taxpayer. 'Relevant taxpayer' means any person to whom a reportable cross-border arrangement is made available for implementation, or who is ready to implement a reportable cross-border arrangement or has implemented the first step of such an arrangement.

Based on Article 8ab(5), Member States can opt to give legal professional intermediaries the right to waiver filing the reportable information, meaning that they would not have a reporting obligation. The implementation of the waiver is optional and subject to the condition that fulfilling the reporting obligation under the national law of the Member State would breach the legal professional privilege of the intermediary. In addition, intermediaries may only be entitled to a waiver to the extent that they operate within the limits of the relevant national laws that define their professions. If the Member State chooses to apply the waiver, it shall take the necessary measures to require intermediaries to notify, without delay, any other intermediary or, in case there is no such intermediary, the relevant taxpayer that they have a reporting obligation. This notification requirement has now been regarded contrary to fundamental rights where it relates to advocates. In respect of other intermediaries relying on legal professional privilege, such as notaries, the *Belgian Association of Tax Lawyers* judgment is still pending.

The Belgian notification requirement was contested before the CJEU in the *Orde van Vlaamse Balies* case. The Belgian Order of Attorneys had requested whether it was in line with client-attorney privilege that a legal professional informs another intermediary about their reporting obligation and whether according to the national legislation the name of the legal professional who has the right to waiver from filing may be included in the report filed by the intermediary. After all, in the report the name of the legal professional was required to be disclosed. The CJEU stipulated, with reference to Article 7 of the Charter, that DAC6 is unlawful to the extent that it requires a lawyer acting as an intermediary to notify other intermediaries that are not their client of the fact that they are exempt from reporting, and the reporting requirement shifts to another intermediary, in view of the right to respect for communications between a lawyer and their client. In the abovementioned *Belgian Association of Tax Lawyers* case, the CJEU has been asked whether the same goes for other legal professions – besides lawyers – that may rely on legal professional privilege.

The ruling in *Orde van Vlaamse Balies* has had a major impact on the waiver clauses already implemented in the legislation of several Member States, with the result that such clauses cannot be applied.[38] Even though EU legislation has primacy over conflicting national law, it is to be hoped that national legislations are amended accordingly.[39] The waiver for legal professionals based on Member States professional privilege under the national law has been implemented in Austria, Belgium,[40] Bulgaria, Croatia, Cyprus, Denmark, Estonia, Finland, France,[41] Germany, Greece, Hungary, Ireland, Italy, Latvia, Lithuania, Luxembourg, Malta, the Netherlands, Poland, Portugal, Romania, Slovak Republic, Slovenia, Spain, and Sweden. The Czech Republic does not apply the waiver for legal professionals to marketable arrangements.[42]

15.4.2 Timing of the Reporting

Intermediaries shall file the information on reportable cross-border arrangements that are within their knowledge, possession, or control with the competent authorities within 30 days, beginning:[43]

1. on the day after the reportable cross-border arrangement is made available for implementation; or

---

[38] Reparation of DAC6 following the *Orde van Vlaamse Balies* judgment has been adopted via DAC8.

[39] See the Spanish Supreme Court order ATS 2181/2023, 27 February 2023, following Case C-694/20 (n 21) adopting as a precautionary measure a suspension of DAC6's Article 8ab(5) transposed in Spanish national rules as Article 45.4.b of the General Regulation on the Application of Taxes (RGAT). According to the order, legal professionals do not need to inform other intermediaries that they are exempt from reporting of a cross-border arrangement due to their right to waiver and are thus allowed not to follow the RGAT provision.

[40] See Case C-694/20 (n 21) and pending Case C-623/22 (n 18) related to among other the legal professionals' waiver as implemented in the Belgian legislation. The case is examined above in Section 15.3.1.

[41] See Case C-398/21 *KT, NS v FTI Touristik GmbH* [2021] ECLI:EU:C:2023:10, where the French Supreme Administrative Court requested a preliminary ruling from CJEU related to Article 8ab(5) and its relation to the right a fair hearing guaranteed by Article 47 of the Charter of Fundamental Rights of the European Union and Article 6 of the European Convention for the Protection of Human Rights, and the right to private life guaranteed by Article 7 of the Charter of Fundamental Rights of the European Union and Article 8 of the European Convention for the Protection of Human Rights. In the meantime, the case has been removed from the CJEU registry.

[42] IBFD, Tax research database, DAC6 - DAC7 Implementation Status according to which UK, which is no longer an EU Member State, has also implemented the waiver for legal professionals.

[43] See Case C-623/22 (n 18) in which the starting point of the reporting obligation is also under review of the CJEU. See also Wouters (n 18) pointing out that it can be unclear which the starting point of the reporting timeline is e.g., when a reportable arrangement includes series of arrangements.

2. on the day after the reportable cross-border arrangement is ready for implementation; or
3. when the first step in the implementation of the reportable cross-border arrangement has been made, whichever occurs first.[44]

Intermediaries referred to in the second paragraph of Article 3(21) DAC shall also be required to file information within 30 days beginning on the day after they provided, directly or by means of other persons, aid, assistance, or advice.[45]

In the case of marketable arrangements, a periodic report is to be made by the intermediary every three months providing an update which contains new reportable information as referred to in points (a), (d), (g) and (h) of paragraph 14 that has become available since the last report was filed.[46]

If the reporting obligation is on the relevant taxpayer, they shall file the information within 30 days, beginning on the day after the reportable cross-border arrangement is made available for implementation to that relevant taxpayer, or is ready for implementation by the relevant taxpayer, or when the first step in its implementation has been made in relation to the relevant taxpayer, whichever occurs first.[47]

The automatic exchange of information shall take place on each quarter within one month of the end of the quarter in which the information is filed.[48]

15.4.3 Where to Report

Where the intermediary has an obligation to file information on the reportable cross-border arrangement with the competent authorities of more than one Member State, the information shall be filed only with the competent authorities of the Member State that features first in the list below:[49]

1. the Member State where the intermediary is resident for tax purposes;
2. the Member State where the intermediary has a PE through which the services with respect to the arrangement are provided;
3. the Member State which the intermediary is incorporated in or governed by the laws of;
4. the Member State where the intermediary is registered with a professional association related to legal, taxation or consultancy services.

---

44 DAC6 art 8ab(1).
45 DAC6 art 8ab(1).
46 DAC6 art 8ab(2).
47 DAC6 art 8ab(10).
48 DAC6, art 8ab(18).
49 DAC6, art 8ab(3).

When there are multiple reporting obligations, the intermediary shall be exempt from filing the information if it has proof, in accordance with national law, that the information has been filed in another Member State.[50] Each Member State shall take the necessary measures to require that, where there is more than one intermediary, the obligation to file information on the reportable cross-border arrangement lies with all intermediaries involved in the same reportable cross-border arrangement.[51]

Similar provisions as those explained above in relation to intermediaries are included in Article 8ab(7) DAC in relation to the relevant taxpayers.

15.4.4 Content of the Report

The information to be communicated by the competent authority of a Member State shall contain the following:[52]

1. the identification of intermediaries and relevant taxpayers, including their name, date and place of birth (in the case of an individual), residence for tax purposes, TIN and, where appropriate, the persons that are associated enterprises to the relevant taxpayer;
2. details of the hallmarks set out in Annex IV that make the cross-border arrangement reportable;
3. a summary of the content of the reportable cross-border arrangement, including a reference to the name by which it is commonly known, if any, and a description in abstract terms of the relevant business activities or arrangements, without leading to the disclosure of a commercial, industrial or professional secret or of a commercial process, or of information the disclosure of which would be contrary to public policy;
4. the date on which the first step in implementing the reportable cross-border arrangement has been made or will be made;
5. details of the national provisions that form the basis of the reportable cross-border arrangement;
6. the value of the reportable cross-border arrangement;
7. the identification of the Member State of the relevant taxpayer(s) and any other Member States which are likely to be concerned by the reportable cross-border arrangement;
8. the identification of any other person in a Member State likely to be affected by the reportable cross-border arrangement, indicating to which Member State such person is linked.

---

50 DAC6, Art 8ab(4).
51 DAC6, Art 8ab(9).
52 DAC6, Art 8ab(14).

15.4.5 Penalties

Article 25a DAC includes clauses related to penalties applicable to infringements of national provisions related to reportable cross-border arrangements. According to the provision, the penalties in national legislation shall be effective, proportionate and dissuasive, which leaves the level of the penalties to the discretion of the Member States.

Since there is no precise amount for penalties, the amounts included in national legislations differ quite extensively.[53] The range of penalties varies between €3,000 and €4,700,000. From this perspective, it would be preferable that there be some guidance on the EU level about the range of the penalties. In case of high penalties, for example, it can be argued that they are disproportionate when reviewed under EU legislation.[54]

15.5 DIFFERENCES IN NATIONAL IMPLEMENTATION

The national implementation of DAC varies from Member State to Member State.[55] Some of the differences in national implementation are discussed below.

In DAC, most indirect taxes are excluded from the scope of reporting.[56] Poland and Portugal, however, have even expanded the scope of DAC6 by covering in their legislation a wider range of taxes, including VAT. They have also opted to include domestic transactions among the reportable arrangements. Poland has in addition increased the number of hallmarks.[57] Some of the alterations made by Portugal and Poland may be such that they conflict with, e.g., the principle of proportionality, especially if applied to cross-border situations, and the Charter.[58]

---

53 Andrea Ballancin and Francesco Cannas, 'The "DAC6" and Its Compatibility with Some of the Founding Principles of the European Legal System(s)' (2020) 29(3) EC Tax Review 117 conclude that there is no legal basis for a common penalty system in EU hard law and suggest relying on soft law.

54 Haslehner and Pantazatou (n 15) 33. See also IBFD, Tax research database, Tax Dossier, DAC6 - DAC7 Implementation Status which includes among others details of the amounts of penalties per Member State.

55 Kristin Resenig, 'The current state of DAC-6 implementation in the European Union' (2020) 60(12) European taxation 527, and Offermanns and Botelho Moniz (n 30).

56 DAC art 2(2).

57 Haslehner and Pantazatou (n 15) 35.

58 In the pending Case C-623/22 (n 18) described above in Section 15.3.1 issues related to the scope of taxes etc. are under scrutiny.

In Finland, the Government Proposal for implementing of DAC6 also considered whether similar rules should be implemented in purely domestic arrangements.[59] It was concluded that purely domestic arrangements should not be covered in the implementation, among others since the content (i.e., the hallmarks) of the domestic arrangements would most likely need to be different from cross-border arrangements.[60] It was concluded that the reportability of domestic arrangements should be reviewed separately later.[61] Also Germany and Sweden contemplated to include domestic arrangements to reportable arrangements in their legislative process but they both abandoned the plan to expand the scope as well.[62]

15.6 THE FUNDAMENTAL RIGHTS OF TAXPAYERS

In the OECD BEPS Action 12 discussions, issues relating to taxpayer's fundamental rights were considered. Fundamental rights relate to, e.g., legal certainty and legitimate expectations, the right to legal advice and legal representation, as well as the right against self-incrimination; and the right to privacy and data protection.[63] Similar issues have arisen in relation to DAC6. Below, self-incrimination will be discussed. Above also client-attorney privilege has been briefly discussed.[64]

In Annex B to the 2015 OECD Report on BEPS Action 12, the compatibility of self-incrimination and MDR was examined. The conclusion was that MDR should not give rise to concerns with respect to self-incrimination. It was argued that the concerns would not be greater than those which would arise under the exercise of other information collection powers, such as an investigation or audit into a tax return. Reference was also made to the fact that the

---

59 DAC6 (n 6) recital 10 states the following 'A Member State could take further national reporting measures of a similar nature, but any information collected in addition to what is reportable in accordance with this Directive should not be communicated automatically to the competent authorities of the other Member States. That information could be exchanged on request or spontaneously according to applicable rules.'

60 *Finnish Government Proposal HE 69/2019*, Section 4.1, <https://www.eduskunta.fi/FI/vaski/HallituksenEsitys/Sivut/HE_69+2019.aspx> accessed 8 December 2023.

61 Kurikka (n 27) 6 and 7 where Finnish tax administration stated that reportability of national transactions could be limited to arrangements with certain transactions where intermediaries are involved.

62 Haslehner and Pantazatou (n 15) 35.

63 Nevia Čičin-Šain, 'New Mandatory Disclosure Rules for Tax Intermediaries and Taxpayers in the European Union – Another "Bite" into the Rights of the Taxpayer?' (2019) 11(1) World Tax Journal 77, where these issues are comprehensively and profoundly reviewed. Also see Part I, Chapters 4, 5 and 6 of this book.

64 See Section 15.4.1.

types of transactions targeted for disclosure under MDR will not generally be the types of transactions that will give rise to criminal liabilities.[65]

An assessment made at the request of the Economic and Monetary Affairs Subcommittee on tax matters (FISC) refers to the fundamental rights of privacy (Article 7 Charter),[66] the protection of personal data (Article 8 Charter), together with the right against self-incrimination (Articles 47 and 48 Charter) in relation to DAC6. It is stated in this assessment that it is doubtful whether a violation of one of the previously mentioned rights would withstand the proportionality test in Article 52 (1) of the Charter, for reasons of protection against potential tax avoidance.[67]

Self-incrimination may also be an issue under the constitutions of Member States – for example, according to the Finnish Government Proposal implementing DAC6, with respect to the provisions in Constitution, protecting the right to fair trial and good administration include protection against self-incrimination. The Finnish Constitutional Law Committee, however, concluded that the proposal was in line with the Constitution regarding the provisions on disclosure and notification obligations and penalty fees.[68]

15.7 CONCLUSIONS

The aim of DAC (i.e., increased transparency and prevention of aggressive tax planning) is reasonable and justified. Whether the aim has been reached can be measured with many different criteria, such as the amount of reported

---

[65] See Čičin-Šain (n 63) 77, who states that 'when the obligation to report is passed on to the taxpayer himself, there is a valid concern that its application could violate the taxpayer's right not to self-incriminate (nemo tenetur), which is a very important principle of criminal law. The same concerns apply for the situation in which a tax intermediary can potentially face a charge for being an accomplice to a tax crime.' The conclusion is partly based on that an arrangement reported may qualify as a tax fraud. Ballancin and Cannas (n 53), where the authors arrive at pretty much the same conclusion as in the OECD Report 2015 described in the text with reference to case law of e.g., European Court of Human Rights.

[66] See also Case C-694/20 (n 21) para 46 stating that 'Even if the notification obligation established by Article 8ab(5) of DAC6 (n 6) is indeed capable of contributing to the combating of aggressive tax planning and the prevention of the risk of tax avoidance and evasion, it must be held that that obligation cannot, however, be regarded as being strictly necessary in order to attain those objectives and, in particular, to ensure that the information concerning the reportable cross-border arrangements is filed with the competent authorities.'

[67] Haslehner and Pantazatou (n 15) 33.

[68] PeVL 13/2019 vp. <https://www.eduskunta.fi/FI/vaski/Lausunto/Sivut/PeVL_13+2019.aspx> accessed 8 December 2023.

transactions per country and proposed changes to the national legislation to fight potentially aggressive tax planning.

The preventive impact is more difficult to measure, as it is not possible to obtain information about arrangements which have not been 'marketed' by intermediaries or implemented by taxpayers. However, the 2015 OECD Report on BEPS Action 12 argues that even though the extent of deterrent effect is difficult to measure, such an effect exists. There is also evidence that several BEPS actions have changed the tax planning climate especially on a macro level.[69] DAC6 is likely to have increased the caution of taxpayers and, thus, fulfils the aim of deterrence.

Making an impact assessment of DAC6 at EU level is important. Some work related to an EU assessment has already been done.[70] The EU report discloses important points related to the functionality or non-functionality of DAC. Some national reports have also been published, such as the one in Finland.[71] In addition, the CJEU has reviewed or is reviewing some specific questions related mainly to the legality of the DAC6 provisions.

DAC6 puts in the spotlight the taxpayer's fundamental rights and the importance of considering the compatibility of legislative proposals in general with these rights. The fundamental problems with DAC6 are its ambiguity or the lack of definitions. This may to a certain extent stem from the minimum standard nature of DAC. It can be questioned whether, from the perspective of clarity and harmonisation within the EU, it would be better to have one set of rules for all Member States without the option for national deviations which are enabled through the minimum standard approach. The unclear provisions have resulted in preliminary ruling requests to the CJEU in which the compatibility of DAC6 provisions is under review from the point of view of taxpayers' fundamental rights. These issues also relate to legal certainty and the principle of good governance. A major issue has been the removal of professional privilege of lawyers and other legal professionals and the related obligation to notify other intermediaries on the exemption to report. Furthermore, DAC6 has raised national constitutional questions which have initiated preliminary ruling requests before CJEU in those Member States which have constitutional courts. In others, the issues have been discussed in the process of DAC6 implementation but may later emerge also in courts depending on the applicable national legal framework.

---

[69] Renata Legenzova, Kristina Levisauskaite and Edidijus Kundelis, 'Estimating an impact of base erosion and profit shifting (BEPS) countermeasures – a case of business group' (2017) 8(4) Oeconomia Copernicana 621.

[70] Haslehner and Pantazatou (n 15).

[71] Kurikka (n 27).

The constitutional requirements related to how tax legislation is enforced may differ between jurisdictions. For example, in Finland, as a civil law country, the rule of law entails that possible loopholes in taxation, in most cases, needs to be tackled by legislative changes and cannot be removed by administrative decisions issued by the tax administration. This also has an impact on how swiftly potential tax avoidance schemes can be tackled and on how effectively early information reported under DAC6 can be used to amend legislation. One possibility in relation to legislative changes might be to have an EU-wide approach to limit the recognised new aggressive tax planning transactions, as the focus is on cross-border arrangements. However, to do this, one should recognise the tax structures which include one or more common features. Having the common features as a frame of reference, the issues could be tackled within a common EU-wide approach instead of by individual Member State measures. One problem with an EU-wide hard law approach is that it is time consuming to adopt and implement.

Additional issues stem from the differences in the national implementation of DAC6 which are at least partly related to the minimum standard approach of DAC. An advantage of the minimum standard approach is that the Member States can consider the differences in national legislation which impact the implementation. This is essential as income taxation is under the jurisdiction on individual Member States. Further harmonisation of direct taxation on the EU level is likely to be difficult, as often the central aim of tax legislation is fiscal i.e., to bring in revenue to cover public expenditure. The harmonisation of public expenditure is also limited e.g., in relation to the public health and other social welfare services. At the same time, one should not forget the major disadvantages of reduced harmonisation and increased uncertainty of interpretation.

Finally, one of the downsides of DAC6 is the increased administrative burden for the taxpayers. Additional expenses also emerge for tax administrations and governments as a result of setting up the reporting system, reviewing the reports, and from the legislative changes needed to implement national legislation to prohibit aggressive tax arrangements.[72] At the same time, DAC6 may decrease the need for tax audits and assist data analysis to detect tax avoidance and identify groups of taxpayers to be audited, as pointed out in the 2015 OECD Report. Thus, DAC6 may result in better targeting when choosing taxpayers for tax audit.

[72] Kurikka (n 27) 23 where the parties representing those responsible for reporting state exhaustive and expensive processes and tools are required to get to know and to fulfil the responsibilities.

16. DAC7 rules for platforms: a proportionality and legal certainty assessment

Juan Manuel Vázquez[1]

16.1 INTRODUCTION

The present chapter assesses DAC7's rules for online platforms in light of the EU general principles of legal certainty and proportionality. The chapter is structured as follows. Section 16.2 provides a brief description of DAC7's main provisions with a particular focus on those related to digital platforms. Section 16.3 goes on to identify some definitions that are unclear under DAC7 and assesses whether the uncertainties created by these could amount to a violation of the EU principle of legal certainty. Section 16.4 then shifts the analysis to the issue of proportionality: first, it briefly describes this general principle of EU law and then it explains how it has been assessed in different contexts by the Court of Justice of the EU (CJEU). On this basis, the section offers a particular assessment of DAC7's proportionality, differentiating between its substantive, procedural and penalty-related rules and drawing insights from existing CJEU case law regarding similar reporting obligations introduced by Member States at the domestic level. The proportionality

[1] This work has been developed within the framework of the Amsterdam Centre for Tax Law (ACTL) research project 'Designing the tax system for a cashless, platform-based and technology-driven society' (CPT project). The CPT project is financed with university funding and funds provided by external stakeholders (i.e., businesses and governments) interested in supporting academic research to design fair, efficient and fraud-proof tax systems. Stakeholders participating and financing this project include the private commercial organisations Ernst & Young (EY), Gatti Pavesi Bianchi Ludovici, Loyens & Loeff, Microsoft, Netflix and NEXI Group; Other organisations financing this initiative are the Dutch Association of Tax Advisers (NOB) and the Dutch Branch of the International Fiscal Association (IFA). Part of the CPT project is also financed by the Netherlands legal research agenda 2019–2025 on Digital Legal Studies. For more information about the CPT project and its partners, please visit its website <https://actl.uva.nl/cpt-project/cpt-project.html> accessed 8 December 2023.

analysis referred to above includes an assessment of whether DAC7, when considered jointly with other similar (and partially overlapping) reporting obligations applicable to platform operators (e.g., VAT reporting for Electronic Interfaces and PSPs, domestic reporting regimes, etc.), could in fact amount to a violation of the proportionality principle. Finally, in Section 16.5, a short conclusion on the topic is offered.

16.2 DAC7 IN A NUTSHELL

After being amended several times in recent years, on 22 March 2021 the Council of the EU introduced a new amendment to the DAC by means of the adoption of Council Directive 2021/514/EU (DAC7).[2] The most prominent element of this sixth amendment to the DAC is the expansion of the existing EU administrative cooperation framework to improve tax transparency and enforcement within the sharing and gig economy.

The main objective of DAC7's reporting rules for platforms is to exploit the opportunities created by digital platforms' involvement in the sharing and gig economy for the sake of improving tax transparency and enforcement within that specific sector.[3] In particular, DAC7 aims to address the tax revenue losses[4] caused by the fact that: (1) some taxpayers using digital platforms did not report (or misreport) the income they earn via such interfaces;[5] and, (2) existing tax reporting frameworks were unsuitable to detect these

---

[2] Inspired by the work of the OECD, on 7 February 2020, the EU Commission published an Inception Impact Assessment (Roadmap) to strengthen the EU exchange of information framework at the EU level. This initiative was part of a package for fair and simple taxation supporting the recovery of the EU. Later on, a public consultation took place from 10 February–6 April 2020. Based on the input from stakeholders, on 15 July 2020, the Commission tabled the DAC7's legislative proposal (COM(2020) 314 final) together with its supporting documents. Following the special EU legislative procedure for direct tax initiatives (Article 115 TFEU), the Council unanimously approved DAC7 on 22 March 2021.

[3] Digital platforms provide governments with a gateway to detect underlying economic transactions that were previously carried out in the informal cash economy.

[4] Within the EU, the tax gap in all sectors of the digital platform economy has been estimated to reach EUR 2.7 – 7.1 billion in 2018. Commission Staff Working Document – Impact Assessment: Tax Fraud and Evasion – Better Cooperation between National Tax Authorities on Exchanging Information,' Accompanying the DAC7 Proposal [2020] SWD(2020) 131 final 11.

[5] The lack of transparency and enforcement in the sharing economy provided platform sellers with an advantage compared to sellers who are not active on platforms and pay their fair share of taxes. Thus, DAC7 also aims to ensure a level playing field for competition within the EU. Moreover, DAC7 aims to have a deterrent effect and foster voluntary compliance by platform sellers.

tax evasion and/or avoidance cases (especially when platform sellers used foreign platforms).[6] In addition, DAC7 aims to introduce a single set of rules at the EU level to curb the proliferation of unilateral reporting requirements that were already spreading in several Member States and creating significant administrative and compliance burdens for platform operators.

In addition to the rules for platforms, DAC7 also introduces several specific amendments to the DAC in order to address some general inefficiencies of the existing framework in terms of cooperation and data exploitation. The following sub-sections provide a brief overview of all these amendments.

16.2.1 Rules for Digital Platforms

In a nutshell, DAC7 rules for platforms introduce: (1) a standardised reporting requirement for platform operators; together with (2) an extended automatic exchange of information (AEoI) mechanisms for tax authorities. The former requirement is introduced in Annex V of DAC7 (i.e, Due Diligence Procedures, Reporting Requirements and other Rules for Platform Operators), which includes inter alia 'definitions' laying down the subjective, objective and territorial scope of the rules for platforms (Section I).[7] Inspired by the OECD's '*Model Rules for Reporting by Platform Operators with respect to Sellers in the Sharing and Gig Economy*'[8] (MRs), DAC7 requires both EU and non-EU platform operators[9] to collect, verify (due dili-

---

[6] It is important to clarify that the challenges and risks identified above arise when platform sellers are deemed to be self-employed entrepreneurs and not employees of the platform.

[7] Annex V has four sections which include (a) 'definitions' laying down the subjective, objective and territorial scope of the legislative initiative (Section I); (b) the due diligence procedures that platforms shall apply for the purpose of identifying reportable sellers (Section II); and (c) the reporting requirements that platforms must comply with (Section III). In addition, the Annex to this directive provides specific rules for effective implementation (Section IV).

[8] After the publication of several studies focused on the tax enforcement challenges raised by the sharing and gig economy (which were, first, mainly focused on VAT/GST and later on direct taxation), on 3 July 2020 the OECD published a 'Code of Conduct: Co-operation between tax administrations and sharing and gig economy platforms' together with the final version of the OECD MRs, which were complemented by an 'International Exchange Framework and Optional Module for Sale of Goods' published on 22 June 2021 and a XML Schema and User Guide for Tax Administrations published on 29 March 2022.

[9] Non-EU digital platform operators fall in scope of DAC7 only where either: (1) there is an EU-based seller, and/or (2) the activities involve the rental of immovable property located in the EU. In such a case non-EU digital platform operators need to register in an EU MS of choice. In order to avoid double and foreign reporting, DAC7

gence),[10] monitor, store and report to EU tax authorities specific information items regarding certain sellers[11] carrying out any of four specific activities via platforms (i.e., rental of immovable property in the EU; provision of personal services; rental of any mode of transport or the sale of tangible goods). DAC7 covers both cross-border and pure domestic transactions and all B2B, B2C, C2B and C2C transactions.

The data items to be reported under DAC7 include personal information relevant to the correct identification of the seller (e.g., name, registered office, TIN, VAT number, date of birth, business registration number, each MS of residence of the seller) and financial information relevant to the determination of the profits realised by the reportable seller through the platform (e.g., the amount of the consideration paid to the seller and the number of activities for which it was paid, the account number where the consideration is credited, the addresses of the property being rented out and the number of days).

The information must be reported by the platform operator to the competent EU tax authority by 31 January of the year following the calendar year in which the seller is identified as a reportable seller. The rules also require platform operators to inform the relevant sellers about the information reported to the tax authorities. To ensure compliance, DAC7 foresees the application of penalties to both platform operators and sellers who do not comply with their relevant obligations.[12] Once platform operators have

---

contains a coordination or 'switch off' mechanism' for non-EU platform operators that already fulfil reporting obligations in their own country of residence, and as long as these obligations are equivalent to the DAC7 requirements and the information is exchanged with EU Member States.

[10] Regarding the timing to comply with the due diligence obligations (collection and verification of sellers' information) DAC7 states that RPOs have to collect and verify the required information on the Reportable Sellers by 31 December of each year.

[11] Sellers either having a primary address, a tax identification number (TIN), or a PE in an EU Member State (for entities), are all considered EU residents and therefore subject to tax information reporting. Sellers, whether EU resident or not, who rent out immovable property located in an EU Member State must also be reported under DAC7. In turn, DAC7 provides an exclusion for certain type of sellers (e.g., governmental and stock listed entities, large-hotels and small sellers).

[12] Despite the choice of penalties remains within the discretion of the Member States, DAC7 states that penalties shall be effective, proportionate and dissuasive. DAC further provides that where a Seller does not provide the information required after two reminders following the initial request by the platform operator, but not prior to the expiration of 60 days, the latter shall: (1) close the sellers' account and prevent him/her from re-registering on the Platform; or (2) withhold the payment of the Consideration to the Seller as long as he/her does not provide the information requested. In the case of the reporting platforms, and referring particularly to non-EU platforms, DAC7 sanc-

reported the required information to the relevant tax authorities, the rules mandate the latter to automatically exchange it with the jurisdiction that would be entitled (under substantive tax rules) to tax the seller's income (i.e., jurisdiction of residence of the Seller or/and jurisdiction of location of the immovable property). The information reported under DAC7 will be exchanged via the existing EU's common communication network (CCN). DAC7 regulates this AEoI mechanism in the new Article 8ac added to this Directive. Regarding its implementation, DAC7 had to be transposed into MS national legislation by 31 December 2022. The reporting rules for platforms apply as of 1 January 2023.

16.2.2 Other Amendments to Improve Administrative Cooperation

In addition to the rules on digital platforms, DAC7 (which is mainly a direct taxation tool) extends the AEoI to the field of Value Added Taxes (VAT)[13] and other indirect taxes, and introduces several specific amendments to the DAC in order to address some general inefficiencies of this framework in terms of cooperation and data exploitation. These changes include, inter alia, the following:

1. New definition of 'foreseeable relevance' (Article 5a): DAC7 introduces a new definition of 'foreseeable relevance' which states that the requested information is foreseeably relevant where at the time the request is made the requesting authority considers that, in accordance with its national law, there is a reasonable possibility that the requested information will be relevant to the tax affairs of one or several taxpayers, whether identified by name or otherwise, and be justified for the purposes of the investigation. DAC7 also provides time limits in which the requested authority has to respond to the request and clarifies that the standard of foreseeable relevance does not apply to requests for additional information following an exchange of information of an advance cross-border ruling or an advance pricing arrangement.
2. Group Requests (Article 5a): In addition, DAC7 introduces the ability to ask for information on a group of taxpayers who cannot be identified individually by name or otherwise but merely described on the basis

tions include, inter alia, the revocation of the registration and the prevention of the platform from being able to operate within the Union as a last resort.

[13] In the preamble, the Directive states that VAT is significant for the functioning of the internal market and, therefore, an amendment is made to Article 16 of the DAC so that the information exchanged under DAC7 may also be used for the assessment, administration and enforcement of VAT in the MS.

of a common set of characteristics. DAC7 indicates the minimum information that the requesting competent authority shall provide to the requested authority when asking for information in cases involving a group of taxpayers. This includes a detailed description of the group and how the requested information would be helpful for the requesting Member State.

3. Royalties (Article 8): DAC7 adds to the list of information that EU Member States will automatically exchange information about royalty payments. The term 'royalties' follows the definition provided in the EU Interest and Royalty Directive.
4. Cross-border rulings and advance pricing arrangements (Article 8a paragraph 5a): DAC7 also amends the DAC so that the mandatory AEoI takes place without delay after the advance cross-border rulings or advance pricing arrangements have been issued, amended or renewed and, at the latest, three months following the end of half of the calendar year during which these were issued, amended or renewed.
5. Presence of foreign officials and simultaneous controls (Articles 11 and Article 12, paragraph 3): Moreover, DAC7 strengthens the rules regarding the presence of officials of one Member State in the territory of another Member State and the carrying out of simultaneous controls by two or more Member States in order to ensure the effective application of those provisions.
6. Joint audits (Article 12a): DAC7 also amends the legal framework of joint audits to strengthen the current provisions regarding administrative enquiry conducted by two or more tax authorities.

Despite their being important developments, due to space constraints, the present chapter does not discuss the various amendments to the DAC briefly described in the previous sub-section. Therefore, from this point onwards, the focus of the discussion is solely placed on DAC7 rules for platforms and, more specifically, on their alignment with the principle of legal certainty and proportionality. For a more granular analysis of DAC7 rules for platforms and their operational and fundamental implications, please see a previous contribution of the author on this topic.[14]

---

[14] Juan Manuel Vázquez and Nevia Čičin-Šain, 'Tax Reporting Obligations Imposed on Platforms in Relation to Sellers in the Sharing and Gig Economy: Operational and Fundamental Implications of DAC7 and the OECD Model Rules' in Dennis Weber (ed), *The Implications of Online Platforms and Technology on Taxation* (GREIT Series, IBFD 2023).

16.3 A LEGAL CERTAINTY ASSESSMENT OF DAC7

Evidently, there are manifest and unquestionable public interests behind the adoption of DAC7's rules for digital platforms. However, even when, prima facie, these rules appear to be necessary and justified, it is important to analyse whether the specific provisions they introduce entail a violation of general principles of EU law. One such principle is the principle of legal certainty, which could potentially be affected by the fact that some of DAC7's definitions (which are key in determining its scope) are not clear enough and lead to uncertainty when attempting to apply them to particular cases.

16.3.1 Some General Considerations about Legal Certainty

The principle of legal certainty is a fundamental principle of EU law and serves to ensure that legal rules are clear and precise and also that the legal situations and relationships governed by Community law are foreseeable.[15] Accordingly, this principle safeguards the ability of interested parties to ascertain what their legal rights and obligations are at a given moment, which, in turn, ensures that they can be certain as to the legal and economic consequences of their actions.[16] The CJEU has considered that 'the principle of legal certainty is a fundamental principle of Community law (...) which requires in particular that rules imposing charges on a taxpayer be clear and precise so that he may be able to ascertain unequivocally what his rights and obligations are and take steps accordingly.'[17] Furthermore, the CJEU has recognised the principle of legal certainty as a corollary of the rule of law recognised in Article 2 of the TEU.[18]

The principle of legal certainty has been the subject of discussion in a number of (tax) cases concerning both EU and Member States' actions.[19]

---

[15] Case C-63/93 *Fintan Duff, Liam Finlay, Thomas Julian, James Lyons, Catherine Moloney, Michael McCarthy, Patrick McCarthy, James O'Regan, Patrick O'Donovan v Minister for Agriculture and Food and Attorney General* [1995] ECLI:EU:C:1995:170 Opinion of Advocate General Cosmas, para 20.

[16] ibid paras 23–25.

[17] Case C-143/93 *Gebroeders van Es Douane Agenten BV v Inspecteur der Invoerrechten en Accijnzen* [1994] ECLI:EU:C:1994:283 Opinion of Advocate General Elmer. In the *van Es* judgment (a customs case), a Regulation could not be applied to certain tax assessments because the Commission had not adjusted this Regulation and, as a result, a taxpayer was unable to precisely determine his legal position.

[18] Case C-157/21 *Poland vs European Parliament and Council of the European Union* [2022] ECLI:EU:C:2022:98, paras 319-321.

[19] Case C-788/19 *European Commission v Kingdom of Spain* [2022] ECLI:EU:C:2022:55; Case C-504/19 *Banco dePortugal and others v VR* [2022]

Although usually applied autonomously, it is important to mention that, in some cases, the principle of legal certainty has also been assessed as part of the proportionality test applied by the CJEU. As identified by Hilling, since the *SIAT* case[20] (which was the first case in the area of direct taxation in which legal certainty was assessed by the CJEU as part of the proportionality test), the former principle has occasionally been used by the CJEU to supplement the latter.[21]

Under settled CJEU case law, the principle of legal certainty is infringed whenever a rule leads to uncertainty because it is not clear ('not clearly');[22] or is unclear by the absence of a statutory definition, or because of the absence of instructions,[23] or it leads to 'a degree of confusion'. In addition, legislation has usually been found to be contrary to the principle of legal certainty by the CJEU whenever: (1) the representatives of the Member State (or the EU) expressly admitted during the procedure before the CJEU that the rule in question was not clear, precise and predictable; and, (2) the case involved another contravention of EU law and the contravention with the legal principle of legal certainty was an extra argument.[24]

It is important to mention that the principle of legal certainty has a strong connection with the principle of legality. Indeed, in the recently decided *Fiat*

ECLI:EU:C:2021:335, point 51; Case C-178/05 *Commission of the European Communities v Hellenic Republic* [2007] ECLI:EU:C:2007:317; Case C-318/10 *Société d'investissement pour l'agriculture tropicale SA (SIAT) v État belge* [2012] ECLI:EU:C:2012:415; C-282/12 *Itelcar – Automóveis de Aluguer Lda v Fazenda Pública* [2013] ECLI:EU:C:2013:629; Case C-17/03 *Vereniging voor Energie, Milieu en Water and Others v Directeur van de Dienst uitvoering en toezicht energie* [2005] ECLI:EU:C:2005:362, para 80 and Joined Cases C-72/10 and C-77/10 *Criminal proceedings against Marcello Costa and Ugo Cifone* [2012] ECLI:EU:C:2012:80. Dennis Weber, 'The Reasonableness Test of the Principal Purpose Test Rule in OECD BEPS Action 6 (Tax Treaty Abuse) versus the EU Principle of Legal Certainty and the EU Abuse of Law Case Law' (2017) 10 Erasmus Law Review <http://www.elevenjournals.com/doi/10.5553/ELR.000081> accessed 8 December 2023.

20 Case C-318/10 (n 18).

21 Although apparently disconnected from the core of the proportionality test, Hilling notes that legal certainty has been included as part of the proportionality test. Pursuant to this author, the most convincing explanation for this is that the CJEU follows a trend named 'the proceduralisation of proportionality' that has become apparent in other areas of EU law in recent years. The existence of such a trend indicates that the proportionality test is sometimes supplemented with demands about, for example, legal certainty and transparency. Maria Hilling, 'Justifications and Proportionality: An Analysis of the ECJ's Assessment of National Rules for the Prevention of Tax Avoidance' (2013) 41 Intertax 294, 304.

22 Case C-178/05 (n 18).

23 Case C-318/10 (n 18).

24 Weber (n 18).

Chrysler case, the CJEU reiterated the importance of the latter principle by stating that 'the principle of legality of taxation, which forms part of the legal order of the European Union as a general principle of law, requiring that any obligation to pay a tax and all the essential elements defining the substantive features thereof must be provided for by law, the taxable person having to be in a position to foresee and calculate the amount of tax due and determine the point at which it becomes payable'.[25] Although the CJEU judgment refers to substantive taxation, the considerations made above are equally applicable in relation to tax reporting obligations imposed on third parties.

The CJEU has further clarified the scope of the principle of legality and the need for legal certainty in the recently decided case on Luxembourg's Beneficial Owner (BO) Registers. In this case, the CJEU stated that

> any limitation on the exercise of fundamental rights must be provided for by law, this implies that the act which permits the interference with those rights must itself define the scope of the limitation on the exercise of the right concerned, bearing in mind, on the one hand, that that requirement does not preclude the limitation in question from being formulated in terms which are sufficiently open to be able to adapt to different scenarios and keep pace with changing circumstances and, on the other hand, that the Court may, where appropriate, specify, by means of interpretation, the actual scope of the limitation in the light of the very wording of the EU legislation in question as well as its general scheme and the objectives it pursues, as interpreted in view of the fundamental rights guaranteed by the Charter.[26]

In the context of the DAC, Belgium's Constitutional Court has also recently relied on the principle of legal certainty (and legality) to invalidate the Belgian legislation implementing DAC6.[27] The legal certainty issues identified in relation to DAC6 (which have also been flagged in relation to the recently proposed Unshell Directive) are – perhaps at a minor level – transferable to the DAC7 context. Unlike DAC6, DAC7 does include definitions which evidently contribute to achieving increased legal certainty and facilitate a more homogenous implementation across Member States.[28] However, since certain key definitions laying down DAC7's subjective and objective

---

[25] Joined Cases C-885/19 P and C-898/19 P *Fiat Chrysler Finance Europe v Commission* [2022] ECLI:EU:C:2022:859, para 97.

[26] Joined Cases C-37/20 and C-601/20 *WM and Sovim SA v Luxembourg Business Registers* [2022] ECLI:EU:C:2022:912, para 47.

[27] Belgian Constitutional Court, judgment concerning the implementation of DAC6 into Belgian legislation (Judgment n° 103/2022 of 15 September 2022, Nos 7407, 7409, 7410 and 7412).

[28] Werner Haslehner and Katerina Pantazatou, *Assessment of Recent Anti-Tax Avoidance and Evasion Measures (ATAD & DAC6)* (Publication for the Subcommittee

scope suffer from a lack of clarity and precision – which makes it difficult to determine whether a certain businesses/activity are covered by the rules – the question may be raised as to whether DAC7 could also amount to a violation of the legal certainty principle.

16.3.2 Are DAC7's Definitions Unclear Enough to Violate the Principle of Legal Certainty?

The unclear definitions included in DAC7 mainly[29] refer to those of the terms 'Platform',[30] 'Relevant Activity',[31] 'Personal Service',[32]

---

on tax matters (FISC), Policy Department for Economic, Scientific and Quality of Life Policies, European Parliament 2022).

[29] In addition to the definitions mentioned above, other specific concepts of DAC7 (e.g., 'Qualified Non-Union Jurisdiction' and 'Qualified Non-Union Platform Operator') which are relevant for applying its switch off or relief mechanism for reporting by non-EU RPOs also create unclarities and complexities.

[30] In relation to the term 'Platform', uncertainty arise in relation to, inter alia: (1) the scope of this definition in cases when the Platform Operator (herein after referred to as 'PO') allow Sellers to be connected to other users for the purpose of carrying out a Relevant Activity in an 'indirect' way; and (2) the wording used by the Directive for listing the carveouts from the definition of platform (alternative vs. cumulative criteria).

[31] Regarding the term 'Relevant Activity', confusions arise in relation to the wording used in such definition. Although activities 'carried out by a seller acting as an employee of the Platform Operator or a related entity of the Platform Operator' are not regarded as a Relevant Activity under DAC7, it is not clear if all activities of a related entity or, rather, if merely activities of sellers who are employees of the related entities are excluded. This lack of clarity on DAC7's scope creates uncertainties in relation to, for example, cases involving: (1) entities within a group facilitating the sale of goods or services held by a different entity in the group to third parties; (2) intra-group procurement platform where third-party service providers register in a website operated by one entity of a group to provide services or sell goods to other entities within the same group; (3) entities making sales under franchise agreements, etc.

[32] Concerning the definition of 'Personal Service', DAC7 is not entirely clear on whether such concept (which mainly refers to services involving time- or task-based work performed by one or more individuals, independently or on behalf of an entity, at 'the request of a user') refers both to: (1) standardised type of services that users request but cannot influence (e.g., a theatrical, musical or stand-up presentation made by a seller who uses a platform to commercialise the tickets and reach more audience); and (2) customised type of services requested by users and in relation to which they do have an influence (e.g., hiring a tutor via a platform to learn to play to play the guitar). In addition, the application of DAC7's Personal Service definition does not provide criteria for classifying activities (e.g., services or other type of activity). Thus, the application of this definition becomes challenging when considering certain specific activities involving, for example, multipurpose vouchers or gift cards, website/mobile applications, renewable energy certificates, insurance services, pre-recorded or pre-produced content (e.g., songs, videos, books, website templates, off-the-shelf software, etc.), etc.

'Excluded Sellers',[33] and 'Consideration'.[34] Because of their relevance in determining the application of the rules, the unclarities related to the aforementioned definitions are critical when applying DAC7 to particular cases.

Even when DAC7 provides a long list of definitions (which, in comparison to DAC6, can contribute to a more homogenous implementation of the Directive across the EU), the lack of clarity and precision of them still creates great uncertainties. Evidently, there are cases in which the uncertainties in relation to DAC7 arise in very rare and niche cases (e.g., unclarities of the definition of Excluded Sellers in relation to partially quoted entities or unclarities in relation to businesses that fall under two or three carve outs of the Platform definition). In the author's opinion, those cases are minor unclarities that arise from the practical application of the rules and would not amount to a violation of the legal certainty principle. In any case, it would be the role of the courts, where appropriate, to specify, by means of interpretation, the actual scope of these provisions in the light of the very wording of DAC7 as well as its general scheme and the objectives it pursues.

However, the author considers that the conclusion expressed above does not necessarily apply to more serious uncertainties that were identified in relation to the terms 'Platform', 'Relevant Activity' and 'Personal Service'. In these cases, the uncertainties are much more serious because they not only refer to key general definitions laying down DAC7's subjective and

---

The Directive is also silent in relation to transactions involving both Personal Services and components that are not subject to reporting under the Rules (e.g., non-personal services, crowdfunding, lease of movable property, sale of intangible assets, etc.).

33 In the case of 'Excluded Sellers' what creates difficulties is the reference to stock listed entities and the lack of clarity on whether partially quoted companies (e.g., an entity having 50% of the shares quoted whereby the remaining 50% of the shares are (indirectly) held by a private individual) are within the reach of this carve-out.

34 Regarding the definition of 'Consideration' and, more specifically, its reference to an 'amount of which is known or reasonably knowable' it is not certain how this should be understood when, for example, a price is negotiated online, but the final sale of goods is made offline and, therefore, discounts may be applied or tips may be given. This could happen in marketplaces such as Marktplaats.nl, Willhaben.at and similar. The questions in these cases are how much certainty should a Reporting PO (RPO) have on the amount of the consideration that is being paid? And if discounts, tips, etc. are unknown to the RPO, the amount of the consideration would still be deemed as 'know or reasonably know' by it? The definition of the term 'Consideration' is important for determining DAC7's applications since, if as a consequence of its business model or the type of consideration, a PO does not have, or cannot reasonably have, knowledge of the consideration paid or credited to a seller in connection with the relevant activity, the consideration element is not met. In the absence of knowledge of whether a transaction has taken place or in the absence of a consideration, there is also no relevant activity, which means that in that case there is also no 'platform' as referred to in DAC7 and, therefore, no reporting obligation.

objective scope, but mainly because they impact a much broader range of cases and situations and could potentially lead to the imposition of penalties. Thus, the author believes that DAC7's imprecisions in relation to the terms 'Platform', 'Relevant Activity' and 'Personal Service' could indeed amount to a violation of the EU legal certainty principle.

It must be acknowledged that a certain degree of uncertainty is inherent to every language and to every legal provision and that the principle of legality (and legal certainty) does not preclude legislation from being 'formulated in terms which are sufficiently open to be able to adapt to different scenarios'.[35] However, in the author's view, the uncertainty created by DAC7's definitions mentioned above, is serious enough and goes beyond mere language unclarities or openly drafted provisions. Even when, based on the CJEU case law, it is difficult to envision a court striking down DAC7 on the bases of legal certainty, such outcome should not be completely discarded, especially if the case also involves another contravention of EU law and the Member State (or the EU) expressly admits this unclarities before the CJEU.

In any case, because of the relevance of the provision involved, it is reasonable to expect that (as experience has already demonstrated) Member States will try to overcome the unclarities of DAC7 definitions by issuing their own guidance/rules. This could lead to the Directive having a different scope depending on the Member States involved which would further exacerbate the uncertainty in its application.

16.4 A PROPORTIONALITY ASSESSMENT OF DAC7

16.4.1 The Proportionality Principle under EU law: A Balancing Act

Together with supremacy, direct effect, and state liability, proportionality is one of the core general principles of EU law.[36] Originating from the jurisprudence of the Prussian Supreme Administrative Court, proportionality initially appeared within the European Community's (now Union) legal order as a general principle of law[37] and was subsequently codified in the EC

---

[35] Joined Cases C-37/20 and C-601/20 (n 25) para 47.

[36] Wolf Sauter, 'Proportionality in EU Law: A Balancing Act?' (2013) *TILEC Discussion Paper* 2013-003, 442.

[37] The principle of proportionality first appeared in the CJEU's case law in 1955 in the *Fédéchar* case (Case 8/55 *Fédération Charbonnière Belgique v High Authority* [1956] ECLI:EU:C:1956:7, para 299). At this early stage it was predominantly applied within the sphere of inter-institutional dealings, especially the Community law making process: Adam Zalasiński, 'The Principle of Proportionality and (European) Tax Law'

Treaty as amended by the Maastricht Treaty. Article 5(3) EC Treaty (now Article 5(4) TEU)[38] supplemented the principle of subsidiarity in delimiting law-making powers of the Community and of Member States in the field of non-restricted competences.[39]

The proportionality principle mainly serves as a framework to determine whether and/or to what extent rights can be limited by governmental intervention (such as legislation) that is motivated by public interests.[40] In other words, it serves as a judicial test for determining the limits on the exercise of public authorities' competences and prerogatives that interfere with private individuals' rights and liberties. The principle requires that the actions of public authorities should be proportionate to their aims and the least intrusive for private individuals and entities.[41]

The principle of proportionality contains three sub-principles: the principles of appropriateness, necessity, and proportionality in a narrow sense.[42] Under the most general statement of the test in EU law (in which a thumb is firmly placed on the scale in favour of EU discretion, in particular where the relevant powers have been centralised):[43]

1. an appropriate (or suitable) measure;
2. in pursuit of a legitimate objective;
3. which does not exceed the limits of what is necessary ('necessity') or, in other words, it constitutes the 'less restrictive measure' ('LRM');
4. not manifestly disproportionate in terms of a costs versus benefits balance (proportionality '*stricto sensu*' test).

Although always requiring a 'balancing act', the proportionality analysis is not uniform and depends significantly on the specific context of the case involved.

Considering the general observations about the proportionality principle made in Part I, Chapter 3 of this book, the next sub-sections make an assess-

---

in Cécile Brokelind, *Principles of Law: Function, Status and Impact in EU Tax Law* (IBFD 2014) 1.

[38] This article now provides that, '[u]nder the principle of proportionality, the content and form of Union action shall not exceed what is necessary to achieve the objectives of the Treaties […]'.

[39] Zalasiński (n 36) 1–2.

[40] Sauter (n 35) 440.

[41] Zalasiński (n 36) 1.

[42] See e.g. Robert Alexy, 'On the Structure of Legal Principles' (2000) 13(3) Ratio Juris 294; Joaquin R.-Toubes Muniz, 'Legal Principles and Legal Theory' (2002) 10(3) Ratio Juris 267.

[43] Sauter (n 35) 448.

ment of DAC7's proportionality under the criteria commonly used by the CJEU to review EU secondary law measures (i.e., the 'manifestly disproportionate test' (MDT)).

16.4.2 The Public and Private Interests Affected by DAC7

Applying the proportionality test requires weighing the interests of two different sectors (i.e., the interest of the private sector (in tax cases represented by a taxpayer) on the one hand, and the public sector (in tax cases represented by a tax authority) on the other). Therefore, the first step in applying this test is to previously identify such opposing interests.[44]

The public interests behind DAC7's adoption are manifest and do not need an extensive elaboration. These are: (1) fighting tax avoidance and evasion by platform sellers to help secure national and EU revenues and make EU tax systems fairer; (2) ensuring a proper functioning of the internal market by establishing fair competition and a level playing field for all businesses active in the EU; and (3) simplifying tax compliance for digital Platform Operator (PO) across the EU and different taxes.[45] As already widely recognised, tax avoidance and evasion affect all EU citizens and businesses. It leads to fewer resources to fund social services of public utility, such as education, healthcare, pensions and infrastructure. It also affects compliant taxpayers 'who do the right thing' and pay their fair share of taxes.[46]

On the other hand, the private interests impacted by DAC7's rules are principally POs' and sellers' fundamental rights and freedoms, such as their right to conduct a business, their property rights, their right to privacy and data protection, the EU freedom to provide services, etc. As suggested by EU law specialists such as De Búrca and Jans, identifying such private interest and the intensity of their restriction is of great significance as the manner in which the CJEU will apply the proportionality principle is set by the nature of the interest harmed and the level to which that interest to be protected is actually affected. In this sense, 'the seriousness of the restriction will affect the intensity of the test'.[47]

---

44 Adam Zalasiński, 'Proportionality of Anti-Avoidance and Anti-Abuse Measures in the ECJ's Direct Tax Case Law' (2007) 35 Intertax 310, 312.

45 EU Commission (n 3) 19.

46 ibid 12.

47 Gráinne de Búrca, 'The Principle of Proportionality and its Application in EC Law' (1993) 13(1) Yearbook of European Law 105, 126; Jan H. Jans, 'Proportionality Revisited' (2000) 27(3) Legal Issues of Economic Integration 239, 246 and 253.

Thus, since the impact of DAC7 on the aforementioned rights and freedom may not be of great enough significance to amount to an interference to their enjoyment, a more detailed analysis of this impact is provided in Section 16.4.4.1. of this chapter.

16.4.3 DAC7's suitability and necessity

Having provided an overview of both elements of the proportionality test and the public/private interest at play when dealing with DAC7, this 4-step test will now be applied to the latter. As explained above, the first two steps of this assessment are to determine whether DAC7 is indeed an 'appropriate (or suitable) measure in pursuit of a legitimate objective'.

Based on the three public interest objectives protected by DAC7 which were identified in the previous sub-section, it seems manifestly clear that this EU Directive can be deemed as a measure adopted in pursuit of a legitimate objective. However, even when public actions of this kind have a legitimate objective, the end does not necessarily justify the means. Thus, it is also important to determine, whether the DAC7 is an appropriate (or suitable) measure. The 'suitability requirement' is concerned with the relationship between the objectives pursued and the means employed to achieve it.

Considering the base-line scenario before DAC7's adoption, its general and specific objectives (see Section 16.2), as well as the chosen policy option (i.e., legislative intervention), the author considers that DAC7 is a 'partially' appropriate (or suitable) measure. This is because, on the one hand, DAC7 uses appropriate means (i.e., a standardised EU reporting requirement plus AEoI) to achieve the objectives pursued. DAC7 is evidently a suitable measure to deter tax avoidance/evasion or encourage tax compliance by platform sellers, facilitate the detection of these fraudulent cases by tax authorities, align reporting requirements among MS, reduce the compliance costs for PO, etc.

However, on the other hand, DAC7 has only gone halfway to achieving some of its core objectives, such as: (1) curbing the proliferation of unilateral reporting requirements among Member States and (2) 'simplifying compliance' for PO by ensuring that they only need to comply with one set of reporting obligations across different taxations fields within the EU.[48]

Concerning the first objective, it should be noted that DAC7 does not include a provision dealing with existing reporting regimes in Member States and their potential withdrawal. Thus, after DAC7's adoption, and even when

---

[48] EU Commission (n 3) 20.

Member States may align their relevant legislation to the directive, it could still be the case that they either conserve or introduce specific regimes of tax information reporting by platforms for particular industries and/or purposes. A good practice in this regard is the one followed by the Italian transposing legislation, which introduces a coordination rule aimed at avoiding overlap between the reporting obligations under DAC7 and those established by the national legislation on short-term rentals.[49]

In relation to the second objective, and as explained above, DAC7 has failed to streamline reporting obligations 'across different taxations fields' within the EU and, on the contrary, it has created a new reporting regime which has its own complexities and continues to apply – with some level of overlapping – alongside other frameworks (i.e., VAT reporting and domestic reporting regimes).

The latter shortfall of DAC7 also becomes relevant for assessing the 'necessity' component of the proportionality test (i.e., if there is a choice between measures that are all suitable, preference must be given to the least onerous one). The CJEU has applied the LRM element of the proportionality test in recently decided cases regarding Luxembourg's public BO Registers and Belgium's DAC6's notification obligation.[50] However, in general, the use of the LRM as part of the proportionality test is rarely applied (at least explicitly) to EU actions. In any case, it is worth mentioning that when comparing the adopted DAC7 to a hypothetical version of such directive which would have actually streamlined tax reporting 'across different taxations fields' (i.e., the 'Improved DAC7'), preference should have been given to the latter version which is clearly the least onerous one.

For the reasons given above, the author believes that, despite being, in general, a suitable measure, DAC7 should not have stopped halfway and, instead, should have gone 'all the way' by introducing a single and streamlined EU reporting obligation for platforms across different taxation fields (i.e., income tax, VAT, tourist taxes, etc.). Such a regime would be suitable enough to achieve the objectives sought by this initiative, which includes keeping the legislative and administrative burden to a necessary minimum

---

[49] See Article 16 of the Italian draft Law Decree (Schema di decreto legislativo di attuazione della direttiva (ue) 2021/514 del consiglio del 22 marzo 2021, recante modifica della direttiva 2011/16/ue relativa alla cooperazione amministrativa nel settore fiscale) and page 22 of its accompanying explanatory memorandum (Relazione Illustrativa).

[50] Joined Cases C-37/20 and C-601/20 (n 25) paras 66–68, 47; Case C-694/20 *Orde van Vlaamse Balies and Others* [2022] ECLI:EU:C:2022:963, paras 41–42.

and avoiding hampering businesses in the European market with too much red tape.[51]

16.4.4 The Proportionality Stricto Sensu Assessment

Considering that, in general, DAC7 can be deemed as a suitable measure adopted in pursuit of a legitimate objective, and since the LRM test is rarely applied to EU level actions, the next step of the proportionality assessment is to apply the 'proportionality's *stricto sensu* test'. When a measure is both suitable and necessary, it can still be quashed if the harm caused to the party concerned is disproportionately higher than the advantage gained in the public interest. As described by Freyer, in the majority of cases, the CJEU simply omits the *stricto sensu* component.[52] Moreover, in most cases involving EU actions, the CJEU substitutes the full version of the proportionality test with a completely different standard (i.e., the 'manifest inappropriateness' standard).[53]

Thus, the issue to be addressed herein is whether, under the 'proportionality's *stricto sensu* test', DAC7 is 'manifestly disproportionate' or not in terms of a costs-versus-benefits balance. This implies assessing whether DAC7 rules amount to a (disproportionate) interference of PO's rights and EU freedoms. For this purpose, it is thus necessary to analyse in more depth the extent to which the substantive, procedural and sanctions-related rules of DAC7 may interfere with the private interests of PO.

To determine the level of intensity of such interference in a rational and objective way, the author relies on the values assigned under the mathemat-

---

[51] Manuel Vázquez and Čičin-Šain (n 13).

[52] Pursuant to such authors, the reasons for the reluctance of the CJEU to apply the *stricto sensu* analysis are twofold. First, in the context of the acts of EU institutions, Article 5(4) TEU simply states that these measures must not go beyond what is necessary to achieve a Treaty objective without referring to the *stricto sensu* analysis. Second, the proportionality analysis in internal market case law involves balancing the objective of establishing an internal market, on the one hand, with other Treaty objectives represented by justifications, on the other. The notion of 'harm caused', which the *stricto sensu* analysis refers to, does not fit well with EU law, as there is no real harm or disadvantage involved. Instead, the CJEU searches for a balance between two theoretically equal Treaty objectives and, therefore, conducting the *stricto sensu* analysis may not be simple. Dominik Freyer, 'The Proportionality Principle under EU Tax Law: General and Practical Problems Caused by Its Extensive Application – Part 1' (2017) 9 European Taxation 385.

[53] See Joined Cases C-154/04 and C-155/04 *The Queen, on the application of Alliance for Natural Health v Secretary of State for Health* [2005] ECLI:EU:C:2005:449, para 52.

ical notation built up by scholars like Robert Alexy and others[54] for forming the proportionality 'balancing test'.[55] These values range from 'light' to 'intermediate' and 'serious' interferences.

16.4.4.1 Areas of potential interference of DAC7 with taxpayers' fundamental rights and EU freedoms[56]

16.4.4.1.1 Fundamental rights

Imposing additional reporting and record keeping obligations on POs may potentially infringe some of their fundamental rights, as codified in the Charter of Fundamental Rights of the European Union (hereinafter referred to as the 'Charter'). The rights that first spring to mind are, inter alia, those of an 'economic nature', namely the freedom to conduct a business (Article 16 of the Charter) or the right to property (Article 17 of the Charter).[57] In addition, the reporting of platform sellers' information can also impact their individual rights and freedoms with regard to the processing of personal data under Articles 7 and 8 of the Charter and the General Data Protection Regulation ('GDPR'). These issues are briefly addressed in the forthcoming sub-sections.

16.4.4.1.1.1 Freedom to conduct a business

The jurisprudence of the CJEU has clarified that the freedom to conduct a business, enshrined now in Article 16 of the Charter, is composed of several

---

[54] Robert Alexy, *A Theory of Constitutional Rights* (Oxford University Press 2002) 231; Ahron Barak, *Proportionality: Constitutional Rights and their Limitations* (Cambridge University Press 2012); David M Beatty, *The Ultimate Rule of Law* (Oxford University Press 2004); Alec Stone Sweet and Jud Matthews, 'Proportionality Balancing and Global Constitutionalism' (2008) 47 Columbia Journal of Transnational Law 68, 73.

[55] This is based on the notion that the test consists of three rules: first, the value of the interference of the individual interest; second, the value of satisfying the public interest; and, third, whether the importance of satisfying the public interest can justify the detriment to the individual's right. The values assigned range from light to intermediate and serious, and by ranking them in this manner, balancing decisions can be made more rational. This is considered a 'weighted' test.

[56] The analysis in this section is largely based on the analysis made by Vazquez and Čičin-Šain on the fundamental aspects of DAC7. Manuel Vázquez and Čičin-Šain (n 13).

[57] Article 15 (freedom to engage in work) could also hypothetically be invoked. However, since DAC7 reporting obligations affect companies and the content of the freedom to engage in work can (to a certain extent) be encompassed by the broad concept of 'business' contained in the freedom to conduct a business, Article 15 of the ECFR is not addressed here.

elements.[58] The CJEU has determined that it encompasses the freedom to exercise an economic or commercial activity, and the freedom of contract and free competition.[59] In addition, freedom of contract includes, in particular, the freedom to choose with whom to do business,[60] as well as the freedom to determine the price of a service.[61] The term 'conducting a business' has been interpreted as involving all the stages of a cycle of a business – from its setting up to its operation and finally liquidation.[62] Moreover, nothing in the wording of Article 16 of the Charter prevents either individuals and companies from relying on this particular fundamental right. It should also be clarified that, unlike the EU fundamental freedoms (which protect against discrimination of cross-border activities compared to comparable domestic situations), the freedom to conduct a business is not restricted to cross-border scenarios only.[63]

In the literature, freedom to conduct a business is often argued to be a weak right, in the sense that great discretion is left to the public authorities creating the potential restrictions to this right. This means that the freedom can only be violated when a certain measure fully prevents one from carrying on a business activity as such. As long as the affected person could conduct a business, even the most severe limitation to the way in which it is performed would not cause the freedom's requirements to be at stake.[64]

In other words, the freedom to provide business is not absolute and is recognised to the extent that a business is conducted in accordance with Union law and national laws and practices. Hence, the freedom is subject to legitimate limitations imposed on entrepreneurs in the EU to guarantee the fulfilment of EU and domestic policy objectives and the social function of

---

[58] The CJEU invoked the freedom to pursue trade or professional activities long before the Charter came into existence, as early as the mid-1970s, on the basis of rights stemming from the common constitutional traditions as well as the EU common market freedoms Case 44/79 *Liselotte Hauer v Land Rheinland-Pfalz* [1979] ECLI:EU:C:1979:290, paras 31–33.

[59] Case C-283/11 *Sky Österreich GmbH v Österreichischer Rundfunk* [2013] ECLI:EU:C:2013:28, para 42.

[60] Joined Cases C-90/90 and C-91/90 *Jean Neu and others v Secrétaire d'Etat à l'Agriculture et à la Viticulture* [1991] ECLI:EU:C:1991:303, para 13.

[61] Case C-278/94 *Commission of the European Communities v Kingdom of Belgium* [1996] ECLI:EU:C:1996:321, para 51.

[62] European Union Agency for Fundamental Rights, *Freedom to Conduct a Business: Exploring the Dimensions of a Fundamental Right* (Luxembourg, Publications Office of the European Union 2015).

[63] ibid 21.

[64] Svitlana Buriak and Dennis Weber, 'Investment Obligations and Levies on VOD Media Service Providers and Cultural Policies of Member States' (2023) 15 World Tax Journal 255, 263.

law.[65] For this reason, the doctrine found the freedom to conduct a business to be rather weak and incapable of being invoked meaningfully for the purpose of setting aside any national or EU provisions.[66]

In this legal context, the author considers that, despite its flaws and shortcomings, the administrative burden created by the reporting and due diligence obligations under DAC7 do not seem to severely infringe the freedom to conduct a business to the extent that POs cannot continue carrying on their business. Therefore, from a legal perspective, there may be few grounds to challenge DAC7's substantive provisions as a restriction to the freedom to conduct a business (this is because it would also be unlikely that the CJEU would consider an eventual infringing measure as a 'manifest error').[67] When assessed under Alexy's mathematical notation, this DAC7's interference with the PO's freedom to conduct a business can be labelled as 'light'.

However, the author highlights that the aforementioned conclusion may not apply when considering DAC7's sanctions-related rules. In this case, the author envisions two potential circumstances. The first could be that Member States adopt sanctions that in practice are not proportionate and, when applied to a SME operating a start-up platform, would prevent this SME from

---

[65] See, to that effect, judgment in Case C-544/10 *Deutsches Weintor eG v Land Rheinland-Pfalz* [2012] ECLI:EU:C:2012:526, para 54; Case C-157/14 *Société Neptune Distribution v Ministre de l'Économie et des Finances* [2015] ECLI:EU:C:2015:823, para 56.

[66] In any case, it is interesting to mention that even in the absence of an infringement to the freedom to conduct a business at the 'restriction' stage of the Court assessment, the CJEU has anyway applied the proportionality test to assess whether the measure was the least restrictive possible to achieve the goal of the provision (*Sky Österreich* (Case C-283/11 (n 58))). An interesting part of the decision is that a Directive itself was challenged and not an implementing provision of a Member State. The court applied the proportionality principle as 'the least restrictive measure' test while usually the Court assesses EU measures under the manifestly inappropriate test (which is much higher). In this regard, Buriak and Weber noted that 'the application of the proportionality test, even when no infringement of the core essence of the freedom to conduct business is found, appears to be an important characteristic of the case law on Article 16 of the Charter. The 'restriction' stage of an assessment whether a measure is in breach of freedom to conduct a business sets a very high standard – a person has to be fully precluded from carrying an activity as such, which can be justified only in extreme circumstances (e.g., when such an activity is hazardous to the public order or other essential public interests). Mostly, restrictions to freedom to conduct a business are not absolute; hence, the proportionality stage would not have any relevance had it be pre-conditioned to the 'restriction' stage of the Court's assessment'. Buriak and Weber (n 63) 264.

[67] The legality of a measure adopted in that sphere can be affected only if the measure is *manifestly inappropriate* having regard to the objective which the competent institution is seeking to pursue, Case C-343/09 *Afton Chemical Limited v Secretary of State for Transport* [2010] ECLI:EU:C:2010:419, para 46.

continuing to carry on its business. The second envisioned case relates to DAC7's express authorisation for Member States to prevent non-compliant Reporting POs (RPOs) from 'being able to operate within the Union as a last resort' and to 'clos[e] the Sellers' account, preventing his/her re-registration or withholding the payment of the consideration'. Evidently, the application of this sanction would prevent POs from continuing to carry on their business and, thus, it would affect their freedom to conduct a business. Although such relation will usually be justified; it cannot be ruled out that this maximum penalty may end up being misapplied (e.g., as a consequence of a minor fault or without a due process). In both cases envisaged above, the author considers that DAC7's rules would amount to a serious infringement of PO's freedom to conduct a business and other fundamental rights.

16.4.4.1.1.2 Property rights

The other fundamental right that could potentially be infringed by the reporting obligations imposed by DAC7's rules is the right to property, which is enshrined in Article 17 of the Charter. It should be noted that, in CJEU case law, this fundamental right (laying down the principle of free use of resources by entrepreneurs in the EU) is usually invoked in conjunction with the freedom to conduct a business, which is analysed above.[68]

This right was already protected by the CJEU in the 70-ties in the landmark decision *Nold*,[69] based on the common constitutional traditions of the Member States, as well various international treaties, including, in particular, the Convention for the Protection of Human Rights and Fundamental Freedoms of 4 November 1950 (hereinafter referred to as the 'Convention') and the Protocol to that Convention of 20 March 1952.

Mandatory reporting rules could not only interfere with POs' right to the peaceful enjoyment of its possessions in view of the forced allocation of human, technical and financial resources necessary to operationalise the said rules, but could also be viewed as interfering with the peaceful possession of the data itself. Indeed, it is increasingly being debated whether data itself can be treated as property, as evidenced by a recent IFA Report.[70]

Generally speaking, raw data is protected by data protection regulations, but not by copyright or intellectual property rights, as it is equated to

---

[68] Case C-134/15 *Lidl GmbH & Co. KG v Freistaat Sachsen* [2016] ECLI:EU:C:2016:498, para 21.

[69] Case 4-73 *J Nold, Kohlen- und Baustoffgroßhandlung v Commission of the European Communities* [1974] ECLI:EU:C:1974:5.

[70] Gary D. Sprague, *Big data and tax - domestic and international taxation of data drive business* (Vol 106 B, IFA Cahiers de Droit Fiscal International, Kluwer Law International 2022).

information and lacks an original creation component. The data collected under DAC7's rules can be considered to be a 'structured database', as POs collect and verify data (e.g., cross-match the data with their own records or a Government Verification Service), monitor changes, and transmit a specific data set on their seller or on the rented immovable property to the tax administration.

EU law provides protection of structured databases under Directive 96/9/EC on Legal Protection of Databases.[71] For databases representing an original intellectual creation, it provides protection through copyright, which guarantees the creators' exclusive right to reproduce, adapt, and distribute the database or any variation of it. The *structure* of the database is protected, rather than its content.

Evidently, the structured databases created by POs are not protected by the aforementioned copyright law as they lack the 'creative component'. Nevertheless, the same Directive also offers a certain protection to 'non-original' structured databases. This *sui gėneris* protection of the structure of the 'non-original' database can prevent the extraction and/or reuse of the whole or a substantial part of the database's content. To obtain this *sui generis* protection, the makers or right holders of the database must be EU nationals or residents of the EU. The beneficiaries need to prove that they have made a substantial investment (financial, material and/or human) in either the obtaining, verification or presentation of the database content.[72]

The IFA Congress Report 2022 reveals that, on a national level, some jurisdictions are considering the creation of *sui generis* ownership rights in data, in some cases making distinctions between various types of data, including raw data, personal data, machine data, etc.[73] In addition, AG Bobek recently stressed in the opinion rendered in the *SS SIA* case[74] (which is addressed in more detail in the following sub-section) that 'in increasingly data-driven modern economies, it is only a matter of time before data is recognised as a type of possession, or even property, the same way a number of other immaterial assets of economic value have become, including various types of intellectual property.'[75]

---

[71] See Directive 96/9/EC of the European Parliament and of the Council of 11 March 1996 on the Legal Protection of Databases [1996] OJ L 77/20.

[72] In view of the value of data as well as the extensive due diligence checks, this conditions in case of DAC7 would be most probably fulfilled.

[73] Sprague (n 69) 18.

[74] Case C-175/20 *SIA 'SS' v Valstsieņēmumudienests* [2021] ECLI:EU:C:2021:690 Opinion of AG Bobek, para 95.

[75] In this context, the AG reminds that the European Court of Human Rights has already opened the stance to the inclusion of various types of 'possessions' within the

In view of the value of the data to be reported under DAC7, as well as the extensive due diligence checks that must be conducted as part of this framework, the aforementioned conditions for benefiting from the protection of the structure of the 'non-original' database have a high likelihood of being fulfilled. Therefore, data collected by POs under DAC7 should not automatically be excluded from the potential qualification as 'possessions' under Article 17 of the Charter, defining the right of property.

However, it is important to consider that pursuant to both Article 1(2) of Protocol No. 1 of the Convention, as well as Article 17(1) of the Charter, the right to property may be limited in cases of public interest. The Convention in this aspect even explicitly mentions taxes, stating that the 'right to peaceful enjoyment of possessions may not in any way impair the right of a State to enforce such laws as it deems necessary to control the use of property in accordance with the general interest or to secure the payment of taxes or other contributions or penalties'.[76]

This exception for 'public interest' purposes can serve as a shield protecting the tax authorities from potential judicial intervention when enforcing reporting obligations such as those imposed by DAC7. Furthermore, in the rare cases where the ECtHR has found a breach of the right to property in the context of taxes, this breach was largely caused by administrative procedural mishaps involving, for example, the refusal of the right to deduct input VAT. Because of this exception and the limited cases referred to above, it is highly questionable whether a taxpayer's claim that DAC7 infringes the 'right to peaceful enjoyment of possessions' would succeed in court.

Nevertheless, since the obligations imposed by DAC7 can have an effect on both the entry into the EU market of certain businesses and their operation, as well as hindering the right to property, these rights may eventually be called upon to challenge substantive provisions of the Directive. When assessed under Alexy's mathematical notation, DAC7's interference with the PO's property rights on non-original structured databases can be labelled as light.

16.4.4.1.1.3 Privacy and data protection rights

Reporting obligations such as those introduced by DAC7 can also have an impact on the protection of platform users' rights and freedoms with regard

scope of Article 1 of the First Additional Protocol citing the judgment of the ECtHR of 11 January 2007, *Anheuser-Busch Inc v Portugal* App no 73049/01 (ECtHR, 11 January 2007), paras 63-65, relating to trademarks or appellation of origins.

[76] See e.g. *Bulves AD v Bulgaria* App no 3991/03 (ECtHR, 22 January 2009).

to the processing of personal data under Articles 7 and 8 of the Charter, the GDPR[77] and other regulations in this field.[78]

In line with the opinion issued by the European Data Protection Supervisor ('EDPS')[79] in relation to the DAC7 legislative proposal, the author considers that – in general – this Directive does not flagrantly violate platform users' data rights.

First, DAC7 appears to respect the principle of data minimisation,[80] as the set of data elements to be transmitted to tax administrations captures only the minimum data necessary to detect non-compliant underreporting or non-reporting, in line with the with the GDPR obligations. It should be noted that a provision of the draft version of DAC7 proposal was indeed amended during the adoption process in order to make it compliant with the data minimisation principle and limit the information reported by RPOs to that of a financial nature.[81] Nevertheless, it cannot be denied that certain data elements that remained within DAC7's scope (e.g., date of birth of the seller

---

[77] Regulation (EU) 2016/679 of the European Parliament and of the Council of 27 April 2016 on the protection of natural persons with regard to the processing of personal data and on the free movement of such data, and repealing Directive 95/46/EC (GDPR) [2016] OJ L 119/1.

[78] Regulation (EU) No 2018/1725 of the European Parliament and of the Council of 23 October 2018 on the protection of individuals with regard to the processing of personal data by the Community institutions and bodies and on the free movement of such data and repealing Regulation (EC) No 45/2001 and Decision No 1247/2002/EC [2018] OJ L 295/39, in particular art 42(1).

[79] European Data Protection Supervisor (EDPS), *Opinion 6/2020 on a Proposal for an Amendment of Council Directive 2011/16/EU Relating to Administrative Cooperation in the Field of Taxation* (DAC7) (EDPS 2020) 2.

[80] GDPR (n 76) art 5(1)(c) and Regulation (EU) 2018/1725 (n 77) art 4(1)(c), which provide that personal data must be 'adequate, relevant and limited to what is necessary in relation to the purposes for which they are processed'.

[81] Section III.B.2.(c) of Annex V of the Proposal indicated that each RPO shall report with respect to each Reportable Seller that carried out Relevant Activity, other than immovable property rental, the following information: 'where different from the name of the Reportable Seller, the name of the holder of the financial account to which the Consideration is paid or credited, to the extent available to the Reporting Platform Operator, as well as *any other identifying information available to the Reporting Platform Operator with respect to that account holder*'. The EDPS recommended amending this provision to better define the 'identifying information' to be reported and limiting the information required to that of financial nature. In addition, it recommended the Commission to: (1) ensure compliance of the secure central interface with the provisions on security of processing under Regulation (EU) 2018/1725, in particular following the EDPS 'Guidelines on the protection of personal data in IT governance and management of EU institutions'; (2) with regard to the secure central interface, to reconsider the reference to the role of the Commission as 'processor'. European Data Protection Supervisor (n 78) 7–8.

or fees charged by the PO) are questionable as they do not appear necessary for the purposes of detecting non-compliant underreporting. In this sense, and considering the principle of minimalisation of data, the interference of DAC7 with data protection rights can be labelled as intermediate.

Second, it is welcomed that DAC7 has expressly provided for data protection safeguards within the DAC.[82] Furthermore, in order to prevent data breaches[83] and limit potential damage, DAC7 also includes rules with a specific procedure to be followed by Member States and the Commission in the event of a data breach in a Member State, as well as in cases where the breach occurs in the CCN. Such procedures include measures such as requesting the suspension of the exchange of information with the Member State where the data breach occurred, or suspending access to the CCN for one or more Member States until the data breach is remedied.

Third, DAC7 also appears to be in line with the principle of storage limitation established in Article 5(1)(e) of the GDPR,[84] as it expressly specifies a minimum and a maximum retention period for the records of the steps undertaken and the information relied upon for the reporting requirements.

Fourth, it is worth mentioning that in the recently decided *SS SIA* case, the CJEU delivered its judgment on the application and compatibility of the GDPR with a request for information issued by the Latvian tax authorities to an internet advertising platform (SS SIA) in relation to information held by the latter in relation to its clients.[85] In its decision, the CJEU concluded that the GDPR does not preclude the tax authority of a Member State from requiring an internet advertising platform to supply information on taxable persons who have placed advertisements in one of the sections of its internet portal,

---

[82] In particular, Article 1(18) of DAC7 amending Article 25 of the DAC establishes an obligation for MSs to ensure that its competent authority or each RPO, as the case may be, complies with the right of information by informing 'each individual concerned that information relating to this individual will be collected and transferred in accordance with the Directive', and providing 'to each individual all information that he/she is entitled to from the data controller in sufficient time for the individual to exercise his data protection rights and, in any case, before the information is reported'.

[83] Pursuant to DAC7, 'data breach' means a breach of security leading to destruction, loss, alteration or any incident of inappropriate or unauthorised access, disclosure or use of information, including but not limited to personal data transmitted, stored or otherwise processed, as the result of deliberate unlawful acts, negligence or accidents. A data breach may concern the confidentiality, availability and integrity of data; Council Directive (EU) 2021/514 of 22 March 2021 amending Directive 2011/16/EU on administrative cooperation in the field of taxation (DAC7) [2021] OJ L 104/1.

[84] Pursuant to this principle, personal data shall be kept in a form which permits identification of data subjects for no longer than is necessary for the purposes for which the personal data are processed.

[85] Case C-175/20 (n 73).

provided that: (1) the information in question is necessary for the specific purposes for which it is collected; and (2) the period during which such data is collected does not exceed what is strictly necessary to achieve the public interest objective behind such collection.[86] Although the *SS SIA* case refers to a national reporting obligation arising from a specific request by a Member State's tax authority (and not to an EU level regime which imposes generalised reporting obligations), the elements addressed therein become unquestionably relevant for this chapter as they could be also applied in conducting a DAC7-GDPR analysis.

In principle, DAC7 provides for a clear and precise legal basis. It precisely determines the circumstances and conditions under which the scope of the obligations and data rights provided for in Article 5 GDPR may be restricted.[87] Thus, even when DAC7 evidently restricts data rights, this restriction can be labelled as light and, as explained below, would ultimately be both justified and well balanced with the public interest involved (i.e., preventing tax fraud).

Finally, it is worth mentioning that there are also other practical elements of DAC7 that have raised GDPR concerns among POs during the implementation process (e.g., collection of information on certain sellers without a legal basis to do so).[88] Further GDPR concerns have been raised in relation to exchanges of information with countries outside the EU, which do not have solid data protection frameworks. In these cases, an adequate level of protection should be required as part of the 'equivalency test' and as

---

[86] Loyens & Loeff, 'EU Tax Alert 193 - SS SIA - Case C-175/20' (*News*, 20 March 2022), <https://www.loyensloeff.com/insights/news--events/news/eu-tax-alert-193/> accessed 8 December 2023.

[87] See Part I, Chapter 4 of this book for a broader insight.

[88] As explained above, among DAC7's 'Excluded Sellers' there are those for which 'the PO facilitated less than 30 Relevant Activities by means of the sale of Goods and for which the total amount of Consideration paid or credited did not exceed EUR 2 000 during the Reporting Period'. Evidently, in order to determine the existence of such an Excluded Seller, platforms have no other choice but to identify and monitor these sellers before they effectively exceed the relevant reportable sales thresholds. This leads to platforms having to collect, process and record personal data on sellers at a moment in which there is no legal obligation to do so (which is a requirement under the GDPR to be allowed to process personal data). For this reason, platforms have argued that collecting, processing and recording personal data in those circumstances (i.e. without a legal basis and with no legal obligation) would conflict with GDPR. Dutch Ministry of Finance, 'Decision Memorandum Implementation Act DAC7- Memorandum in Response to the Report' (23 June 2022) <https://open.overheid.nl/repository/ronl-db2d69e1d4508b724357241a62d6fc332214c4fd/1/pdf/implementatiewet-dac7-nota-naar-aanleiding-van-het-verslag.pdf> accessed 8 December 2023.

a condition for data transfers to third countries.[89] As a consequence of this issue, Member States are currently examining whether an adaptation can or should be made in national legislation to meet this GDPR requirement. When assessed under Alexy's mathematical notation, these specific interferences under DAC7 with the Sellers' data rights can be labelled as intermediate.

16.4.4.1.2 EU fundamental freedoms

In addition to impacting taxpayers' fundamental rights, DAC7 could also lead to restrictions of PO's fundamental freedoms. In order to assess this Directive's interference with fundamental freedoms, it is necessary to analyse how the CJEU has weighed the public and private interests at play when assessing national reporting obligations similar to those included in DAC7. In this latter situation, the proportionality test appears in a very specific context, namely in the application of the CJEU's rule of reason in the interpretation of the fundamental freedoms.[90]

Like any other taxpayer, POs may seek protection under the fundamental freedoms of the TFEU, as well as under secondary EU law such as the E-Commerce Directive[91] and the Services Directive.[92] Generally speaking, under said sources, service providers are not to be subject to market access or other requirements, such as authorisation schemes and licensing requirements, unless they are non-discriminatory, necessary to attain a clearly identified public interest objective[93] and proportionate to achieving this interest (i.e., imposing no more requirements than strictly needed).[94] In the recent cases *Airbnb Ireland UC v Région de Bruxelles-Capitale*[95] and *Airbnb*

[89] The CJEU confirmed this in its *Schrems* judgments. However, the extent to which this assessment also applies to the area of taxation remains to be seen. See most recently Case C-311/18 *Data Protection Commissioner v Facebook Ireland Limited and Maximillian Schrems* [2020] ECLI:EU:C:2020:559. Juliane Kokott, Pasquale Pistone and Robin Miller, 'Public International Law and Tax Law: Taxpayers' Rights' (2021) 52 Georgetown Journal of International Law 381, 419.

[90] Zalasiński (n 43) 312.

[91] Directive 2000/31/EC of the European Parliament and of the Council of 8 June 2000 on certain legal aspects of information society services, in particular electronic commerce, in the Internal Market [2000] OJ L 178/1.

[92] Directive 2006/123/EC of the European Parliament and of the Council of 12 December 2006 on services in the internal market (Services Directive) [2006] OJ L 376/36.

[93] For a list of overriding reasons relating to the public interest under the Services Directive see ibid art 4(8).

[94] See ibid recital 39 and art 4(6) on the concept of 'authorisation'.

[95] Case C-674/20 *Airbnb Ireland UC v Région de Bruxelles-Capitale* [2022] ECLI:EU:C:2022:303.

Ireland and Airbnb Payments UK vs Agenzia delle Entrate,[96] the CJEU addressed this precise matter.

When considering the aforementioned Airbnb case law in the context of DAC7, the issue of whether the CJEU's line of argumentation can be translated to a potential claim of incompatibility of such a Directive with the fundamental freedoms is questionable. As stated above, the CJEU previously ruled that a measure is not capable of hindering the fundamental freedom to provide services as laid down in Article 56 TFEU if it has a universal application to all traders on the territory, it does not regulate market access, and its restrictive effects on the freedom to provide services are too uncertain and indirect. First, it is evident that, contrary to the Belgian and Italian national reporting rules, DAC7 will clearly not apply to all intermediaries operating on the national territory in the same way, but will rather target only digital intermediaries. Therefore, it is immediately possible to legitimately claim that DAC7 creates a discrimination between digital intermediaries and traditional intermediaries. Second, what is less obvious but is worth exploring is whether the conclusion reached in the Airbnb cases in which the CJEU qualified the national reporting rules as *not being conditions* for the provision of intermediation services, but 'merely' information collection obligation *after* the service has been provided, would be transposable to DAC7. Admittedly, DAC7 rules would prima facie also 'merely' oblige the service provider to retain the particular items of information for the purposes of the accurate levying of the tax relating to the individual sellers. However, one should keep in mind that the quantity and quality of information required under the DAC7 warrants setting up sophisticated systems, oftentimes leading to outsourcing due to the inability to comply with the obligations in-house. Moreover, the information items to be collected, validated, stored and reported by DAC7 are not necessarily 'already stored by intermediaries', as the CJEU held in these cases. In this sense, DAC7 goes far beyond a mere 'data transfer' and, in many cases, will require POs to collect further information items that they would not collect in the normal course of their business.

For the reasons explained above, the author questions whether it may be premature to conclude that the CJEU's conclusion in the Airbnb cases (according to which the reporting rules are not part of the conditions in which intermediaries have to provide their services) is equally applicable to DAC7. This would be particularly true for SME platforms for which such legislative requirements may indeed create conditions under which they would have to

[96] Case C-83/21 *Airbnb Ireland and Airbnb Payments UK* [2022] ECLI:EU:C:2022:1018.

provide their services and which could end up preventing such SME platforms from entering the market.

When assessed under Alexy's mathematical notation, and depending on the circumstances of the case, this interference by DAC7 with the PO's freedom to provide services can be labelled as intermediate. In any case, and as further elaborated below, the author considers that the CJEU would probably try to defend DAC7, likely by finding that the Directive does not 'manifestly' contravene the freedom to provide services under Article 56 TFEU in the first place. This would be similar to the conclusions in the Airbnb cases, as DAC7 is also a measure that affects in the same way the provision of services between Member States and the provision of services within one Member State. Therefore, the CJEU would most likely end the analysis here.

16.4.4.2 Level of satisfaction of the public interests

Having identified and labelled DAC7's levels of interference with taxpayers' fundamental rights and freedoms, it is now time to look at the other side of the 'scale' or 'balance' and assign values to the different public interests at play, based on their levels of satisfaction. Here again the mathematical notion proposed by Alexy indicates that the level of satisfaction assigned to each public interest can be low, intermediate or high.

The first public interest behind DAC7 is tackling tax avoidance/evasion within the sharing and gig economy. Although, at this stage, it is not possible to assess the level of satisfaction of this interest (in other words, to what extent a measure like DAC7 is indeed effective for tackling these harmful practices), it is reasonable to expect that the Directive will be reasonably effective and have a deterrent effect that will lead to greater tax compliance by platform sellers. For that reason, the author considers that the satisfaction of this interest can be labelled as high. Nevertheless, this conclusion may change if a future assessment of DAC7 would show some level of ineffectiveness (as occurred in relation to DAC 1–5),[97] in which case the level of satisfaction of this interest could drop to intermediate.

The second public interest behind DAC7's rules is ensuring a fair competition and a level playing field among taxpayers. It is true that, by extending an existent transparency framework to a new sector, the Directive creates a more level playing field among taxpayers operating in different industries. By applying DAC7 to all EU and non-EU platforms and covering both cross-border and non-cross-border activities, the Directive also seems to prevent unfair competition. In this sense, the author considers that the level

---

[97] European Court of Auditors, Special Report No 03/2021: Exchanging tax information in the EU: solid foundation, cracks in the implementation (Vol 03, 2021).

to which DAC7 satisfies the 'fair competition' interest is high. However, when considering that the Directive applies only to certain activities and equally to large and small platforms (there is no carve-out for small platforms), certain questions arise. First, one could argue that, if leaving out other 'relevant activities' does not provide taxpayers doing or facilitating activities with a competitive advantage in relation to those doing or facilitating activities covered by DAC7. Second, the lack of a carve-out for small platforms could severely increase the barrier to entry for new operators into the digital platform business (start-up digital platforms rarely consider in their business models that they will also have to be a seconded tax authority).[98] This could create a competitive advantage for large platforms that have the necessary structure and enough resources to comply with several reporting frameworks. In relation to these latter aspects, the author considers that the level to which DAC7 satisfies the 'fair competition' interest drops to intermediate.

Third, another public interest sought by DAC7 is to simplify tax compliance for platform business operators. Referring to the considerations made in Section 16.4.3. above, the author deems that the level to which DAC7 satisfies the 'simplification' interest is intermediate.

16.4.4.3 The balancing act

Having identified and labelled DAC7's levels of interferences with taxpayers' fundamental rights and freedoms on the one hand, and its levels of satisfaction of the public interests in play on the other, it is now time to complete the proportionality 'balancing test'. This means determining whether the identified detriment to the private interests can be justified and are proportional to the level of satisfaction of the public interests in play.

For such purpose, it is worth remembering that EU courts apply a more lenient approach towards EU secondary law than towards national law, when assessing its compatibility with primary EU law. The CJEU almost never strikes down provisions of secondary EU law unless there are 'manifest errors'.[99] This is because, first of all, the CJEU's understanding is that 'when the EU legislature adopts a tax measure, it is called upon to make political,

---

[98] Lachlan Wolfers and Philippe Stephanny, 'The Future of Indirect Taxation in a Digital World Proposition 6: Digital Platforms – KPMG Global' (*KPMG*, 14 November 2022) <https://home.kpmg/xx/en/home/insights/2022/09/proposition-6-digital-platforms.html> accessed 8 December 2023.

[99] The legality of a measure adopted in that sphere can be affected only if the measure is *manifestly inappropriate* having regard to the objective which the competent institution is seeking to pursue, Case C-343/09 (n 66) para 46.

economic and social choices, and to rank divergent interests or to undertake complex assessments. Consequently, it should, in that context, be accorded a broad discretion, so that judicial review of compliance with the conditions set out in the previous paragraph of this judgment must be limited to review as to manifest error'.[100]

In applying the proportionality test to EU level measures, the CJEU follows the same logic and, as explained above, it usually applies a higher benchmark, namely the 'manifestly disproportionate standard'.[101] Because the manifestly disproportionate test sets the bar so high, this, in practice, means that only a marginal review of the EU's actions is made, which generally promotes integration. Indeed, there are few instances of an EU measure being declared manifestly disproportionate (e.g., the *ABNA* case[102] and the recently decided cases on public BO registers[103] and on DAC6's requirement for notifying other intermediaries in the case of legal professional privilege).[104]

That being said, it should be considered whether DAC7 could be one of these instances. For such purposes, the provisions of the Directive are separately assessed based on whether they involve substantive, procedural or penalty-related aspects.

16.4.4.3.1 Substantive aspects

The discussion about the proportionality of DAC7's substantive provisions (i.e., the obligations imposed on POs to collect, review, store, and report to the tax authorities certain information) involves considering the related burdens (costs) that these administrative obligations create on POs. The issue of costs, touched upon briefly in the previous sections, not only concerns the issue of market access, but also the expenses a platform will incur during the operation of the intermediation services on an ongoing basis.

The way in which the CJEU assessed the proportionality of the costs arising from the reporting obligations referred to in the previously commented cases raises several comments. On the one hand, the CJEU, in the author's opinion, erroneously dismisses the issue by stating that tax obliga-

---

[100] Case C-390/15 *RPO* [2017] ECLI:EU:C:2017:174.

[101] Case C-491/01 *The Queen v Secretary of State for Health ex parte British American Tobacco (Investments) Ltd and Imperial Tobacco Ltd* [2002] ECLI:EU:C:2002:741, para 123 and the references cited therein.

[102] Joined Cases C-453/03, C-11/04, C-12/04 and C-194/04 *ABNA Ltd et al v Secretary of State for Health et al* [2005] ECLI:EU:C:2005:74, paras 80–84; Sauter (n 35) 450.

[103] Joined Cases C-37/20 and C-601/20 (n 25) para 47.

[104] Case C-694/20 (n 49).

tions create additional cost.[105] It is true that 'your own tax obligations (have a) cost', however, in this case, it is not the tax of the PO that is being determined.[106] To the contrary, POs are merely unpaid assistants of tax administrations that somehow outsource the task of determining the tax of the platform sellers. In any case, the author considers that the CJEU opens the door to the proportionality analysis of this and similar reporting obligations, with respect of the information readily available to the platform operator, as opposed to information that is not. In the *Airbnb* cases, the CJEU concluded that the information demanded by the Belgian legislation is easily accessible to (and already stored by) the platform in question. However, whether the same holds true for the information under DAC7 (e.g., VAT number, date of birth of the individual seller, the number of days each property listing was rented, the type of each property listing or its respective land registration number) is questionable. In addition, smaller platforms, or those already in business for a longer period of time, may not dispose of all the information needed under DAC7 and will have problems and additional costs in order to get this information.

In view of all these reasons, the CJEU would most likely defend DAC7's substantive provisions (due diligence and reporting obligations) in the face of claims of disproportionality, supporting its argument that even though this reporting requirement may create additional costs (in particular in connection with the search for and storage of the data concerned), the way in which digital businesses collect data permits them to obtain, review, and report the information at a limited cost. Whether this approach would be true in all cases remains open.

The judicial forecast offered in the previous sub-section is somewhat confirmed by the application of Alexy's mathematical notion for assessing proportionality to DAC7. This is because the values assigned to DAC7's interferences to taxpayers' rights and freedoms are largely light, whereas the values assigned to the levels of satisfaction of the public interest at play are largely high or intermediate.

---

[105] Case C-674/20 (n 94) para 45: 'Next, it should be noted that, by their very nature, tax obligations entail additional burdens for service providers'.

[106] A similar argument was indeed used by Airbnb in the Italian case (Case C-83/21 (n 95) Opinion of Advocate General Spuznar, see recital 55) but in relation to the obligation to withhold taxes. To such claim, the AG responded 'that argument is not unfounded, at least as far as the obligation to withhold tax is concerned'. However, as explained above, the AG then considered that the obstacle generated by the withholding obligation is fully justified by the need for effective collection of taxes and the prevention of tax evasion and that it is not disproportionate.

16.4.4.3.2 Procedural aspects

The conclusion arrived at above is not necessarily applicable to DAC7 rules regulating procedural aspects. In this field, the existence of procedural guarantees of individual rights can play a role in the proportionality assessment of a court with regard to EU acts. In fact, this area represents one of the two exceptions to the predominance of the 'manifestly disproportionate test', as the CJEU has generally been more open to strike down EU measures as 'disproportionate' because there was no procedural safeguard enabling the individuals affected to bring their case before the competent authorities.

In relation to procedural rights, the essence of such rights also plays an important role in how the CJEU applies the proportionality test. This is because when, for example, the essence of individual rights (e.g., the right to be heard)[107] is at issue, the CJEU is stricter than when primarily economic entities were concerned[108] (although essentially similar property rights and rights to appeal against administrative discretion are usually involved).[109] The existence of procedural guarantees can therefore be significant in the context of a manifestly disproportionate test (even if proportionality itself may not be well-suited to establishing procedural rights).[110]

Based on the above, it should be considered that DAC7 does not include specific and detailed provisions on procedural aspects. This is because it is a competence of EU Member States to establish their own national procedural rules to govern the exercise of EU law. The only procedural rules included in DAC7 are those related to instances where a Seller does not provide the information required (i.e., after two reminders following the initial request by the RPO, but not prior to the expiration of 60 days, the RPO shall close the account of the Seller and prevent the Seller from re-registering on the Platform or withhold the payment of the Consideration to the Seller as long as the Seller does not provide the information requested). Although not expressly provided as such, from the wording of this provision it can be inferred that the aforementioned procedure (i.e., 'request' plus the 'two reminders' after a two-month period) entails a procedural safeguard that

---

[107] Joined Cases C-402/05 P and C-415/05 P *Yassin Abdullah Kadi and Al Barakaat International Foundation v Council and Commission* [2008] ECLI:EU:C:2008:461, para 369 ff; Case T-85/09 *Yassin Abdullah Kadi v Commission* [2010] ECLI:EU:T:2010:418, para 194.

[108] Joined Cases C-154/04 and C-155/04 (n 52).

[109] Sauter (n 35) 452.

[110] Sacha Prechal, 'Free Movement and Procedural Requirements: Proportionality Reconsidered' (2008) 35 Legal Issues of European Integration 201, who advocates the general principles of effective judicial administration and sound administration as a more appropriate foundation for procedural rights than proportionality. ibid 451.

would enable individuals (Sellers) affected to put their case to the competent authorities and exercise their right to be heard. If that would not be the case, then the author believes that an unjustified and therefore disproportionate restriction of the Sellers' (individual) fundamental rights could evidently arise. It should be noted that, in relation to the enforcement of DAC7 rules on foreign POs and the application of the last resort sanction included for such purposes (not being able to operate within the EU), DAC7's rules do not include any provision related to the PO's procedural rights.

16.4.4.3.3 Aspects related to penalties

Similarly to procedural rights, the conclusion arrived in relation to DAC7's substantive provisions are not necessarily applicable to its penalty-related rules. Although DAC7's penalties fall within the powers of the Member States, such systems should not have the effect of jeopardising taxpayers' fundamental rights, freedoms and general principles of EU law.[111]

Pursuant to settled CJEU case law, the imposition of penalties, including criminal penalties, may be considered to be necessary in order to ensure compliance with national rules, subject, however, to the condition that the nature and amount of the penalty imposed is, in each individual case, proportionate to the gravity of the infringement that it is designed to penalise.[112]

Thus, proportionality has regularly been used by applicants claiming that a penalty or other financial burden is excessive. Indeed, this area represents the second exception to the predominance of the 'manifestly disproportionate test', as these penalty-related cases will commonly involve the annulment of either a single administrative act or of a particular article of a regulation without calling into question the more general legislative schema. As with procedural rules, the considerations that operate to limit the proportionality review of discretionary policy choices are largely absent here (with some minor exceptions).[113]

---

[111] Case C-482/18 *Google Ireland Limited v Nemzeti Adó- és Vámhivatal Kiemelt Adó- és Vámigazgatósága* [2020] ECLI:EU:C:2020:141, para 47 and the case-law cited; see also Case C-431/21 *X GmbH & Co. KG v Finanzamt Bremen* [2022] ECLI:EU:C:2022:792.

[112] Case C-431/21 (n 110).

[113] Craig notes that while the general approach is that set out above, there are cases concerned with penalties, where the CJEU has applied the manifestly disproportionate test derived from Fedesa. This approach seems to be adopted when the penalty is an integral substantive part of a discretionary policy, which is itself subject to the Fedesa test: Paul Craig, 'Proportionality I: EU' in Paul Craig (ed), *EU Administrative Law* (Oxford University Press 2012).

With this in mind, it is necessary to assess whether the penalties imposed under DAC7 are too drastic or disproportionate. The appropriateness and necessity of a penalty can best be determined in light of the legislative objectives pertaining to the particular area. In the case of DAC7, the objectives to be considered are inter alia the detection and countering of cross-border tax evasion/avoidance as well as the enhancement of voluntary compliance by means of causing a deterrent effect. Since non-compliance with DAC7's core obligation (i.e., RPOs' non-compliance with their registration, reporting and re-registration obligations and Sellers' not providing the information requested) implies a serious offense, the author deems that the 'last resource sanctions' included in DAC7[114] are commensurate and appropriate.

However, since the choice of DAC7's penalties remains within the discretion of Member States (even if the minimum penalties proposed under DAC8 are adopted),[115] the proportionality assessment of this Directive also needs to consider whether the national legislation implementing DAC7 provides for penalties that are commensurate with the seriousness of the offenses (especially when these are minor, or refer, for example, to delays or the reporting of an incorrect data point). Due to DAC7 being in the process of transposition and because of the limited scope of this contribution, such particular analysis of Member States' penalties under their domestic DAC7 legislation is not provided herein.

In any case, it is worth considering that, while countries like Ireland impose fines on POs of €19,045 for failure to comply with the reporting liability,[116] other countries, such as the Netherlands, set a maximum penalty of € 900,000 (this applies for wilful or grossly culpable breach of the reporting obligation and not merely for not reporting on time, in a complete or correct way). This gap between the level of penalties among the Member States may also motivate companies to adapt their planning and choose the friendliest Member State in which to concentrate its reporting.

---

[114] In the case of RPOs: (1) the revocation of the registration and (2) the prevention of the RPO from being able to operate within the Union as a last resort. In the case of Sellers: (1) close the sellers' account and prevent him/her from re-registering on the Platform; or (2) withhold the payment of the Consideration to the Seller as long as he/her does not provide the information requested.

[115] See Part II, Chapter 17 of this book on DAC8.

[116] Under Irish Finance Bill 2021, Section 898O shall apply to: (1) a failure by a RPO to make a return required, and(2) the making of an incorrect or incomplete return. Such section states that a person shall be liable to a penalty of €19,045 and, if the failure continues that person shall be liable to a further penalty of € 2,535 for each day on which the failure continues.

A particular element of DAC7 that could lead to a disproportionate application of its penalties and a serious violation of taxpayers' rights is the situation in which two jurisdictions impose their sanctions on the same PO for insufficient or non-compliance with the administrative obligations included in those rules. The Directive is silent on the application of penalties in these cases.

Finally, it is important to mention that the problem addressed above would not be completely solved by the introduction of minimum levels of financial penalties with respect to serious non-compliance with the DACs (including DAC7), as suggested by the DAC8 proposal published on 8 December 2022. This is because the minimum penalty amounts would not prevent Member States from applying more stringent (and potentially disproportionate) sanctions for serious infringements to DAC7, as the imposition of penalties for non-compliance will remain under the sovereign control of the individual EU MS.[117]

16.4.5 Other Reporting Obligations Imposed on Platforms: When Considered Together with DAC7, are they Proportional?

Within the EU context, proportionality not only has the role of a benchmark to assess possible infringements of fundamental rights or freedoms, but – as explained in Section 16.4.1. above – it can also be viewed as a standalone general principle of EU law.

In the previous sub-section, it has already been stated that, when applying the proportionality test to individual EU actions (e.g. DAC7) or national measures that impose reporting obligations on POs, it is unlikely – although not impossible – that the CJEU would conclude that each of these frameworks entails an unjustified and (manifestly) disproportionate measure. Similar conclusions can apply when assessing, individually, other reporting obligations that may apply to PO together with DAC7.

As widely acknowledged, in the post-BEPS era, there has been a proliferation of new tax transparency frameworks both in the field of direct and indirect taxation. These frameworks include not only the OECD's Common Reporting Standard (CRS) implemented in the EU under DAC2,[118] but also:

---

[117] European Commission 'Taxation: New transparency rules require service providers to report crypto-asset transactions' (Press Corner, 8 December 2022) <https://ec.europa.eu/commission/presscorner/detail/en/ip_22_7513> accessed 8 December 2023.

[118] Council Directive 2014/107/EU of 9 December 2014 amending Directive 2011/16/EU as regards mandatory automatic exchange of information in the field of taxation [2014] OJ L 359/1.

(1) VAT reporting obligations imposed on Payment Service Providers (PSPs) under the PSP Directive (which amended the VAT Directive);[119] and the (2) VAT record-keeping obligations imposed on electronic interfaces under Article 242a of the VAT Directive.[120] In addition, at the level of Member States' national tax regimes, there are also reporting regimes applicable to digital platforms that may apply alongside the EU rules mentioned above. Outside the field of taxation, there are also other frameworks such as the recently adopted EU Digital Service Act (DSA)[121] and general Anti Money Laundering/Know your Customer (AML/KYC) regulations,[122] which apply to platforms and provide for their own reporting obligations.

All of the aforementioned packages and measures interact with each other and have created a quite complex and fragmented regulatory environment for platform businesses operating in the EU. Due to several commonalities between these packages/measures and the fact that they all impact platform businesses, the question of whether they create overlapping and inefficient reporting obligations is raised. In addition to this question, it is particularly interesting whether it is possible to make a proportionality assessment of the cumulative effect of several due diligence and reporting obligations imposed on POs under all these frameworks. The author believes that, even when this

---

[119] New article 243a–243d were introduced into the VAT Directive by Council Directive (EU) 2020/284 of 18 February 2020 amending Council Directive 2006/112/EC as regards introducing certain requirements for payment service providers [2020] OJ L 62/7; and, Council Regulation (EU) 2020/283 of 18 February 2020 amending Regulation (EU) No 904/2010 as regards measures to strengthen administrative cooperation in order to combat VAT fraud [2020] OJ L 62/1.

[120] Although DAC7 emerged and is designed as a 'direct tax' transparency tool, it must be underlined that this Directive explicitly amended Article 16(1) of the current DAC and specified that information communicated between MSs may also be used for the assessment, administration and enforcement of VAT and other indirect taxes (see recital 30 and partially recital 8 of DAC7).

[121] Under the adopted DSA, Strict requirements for online platforms that allow consumers to conduct distance contracts with traders, to ensure that traders can only offer goods and services via their platforms after strict Know Your Customer procedures. Platforms must keep information about the traders to help track down sellers of illegal goods or services. Moreover, such legal framework also includes its own transparency reporting obligation applicable to PO.

[122] In this respect Beretta, points out that an important flaw common to the OECD and EU initiatives relates to the lack of coordination with other instruments for collection and exchange of information already available to tax administrations (e.g., information exchanged with tax authorities by means of electronic invoicing or due to AML/KYC reporting). Duplicative reporting should be avoided. Giorgio Beretta, 'The New Rules for Reporting by Sharing and Gig Economy Platforms Under the OECD and EU Initiatives' (2021) 30 EC Tax Review 31, 38.

assessment would rarely be made by a court,[123] the outcome of the proportionality test in such a case could be quite different.

This approach of considering the several due diligence and reporting obligations imposed by the aforementioned frameworks 'collectively' rather than 'individually' could be built upon: (1) A theory supported by some scholars[124] and applied by Advocate General Saugmandsgaard Øe, in line with German case law,[125] which adopts a holistic approach to the protection of fundamental rights by considering that a measure might be deemed as necessary and proportionate if assessed independently, but could become excessive if taken together with others intrusive measures; and on (2) an analogous application of the CJEU 'taken together' approach that was introduced in *Marks & Spencer*,[126] and is used by the CJEU for assessing the justifications of measures that were found to restrict a right or a freedom. In this sense, one could argue that if the CJEU has accepted this 'taken together' approach for justifying a restriction, the same approach should also be accepted for determining whether the light and/or intermediate restrictions created by several legal frameworks 'taken together' amount to a (manifestly) disproportionate measure.

Evidently, an important part of this assessment requires comparing the multiple legal frameworks at play in order to identify their differences, similarities/areas of overlapping, and inefficiencies. In any case, it cannot be

---

[123] This would require that a taxpayer who is impacted by some of these frameworks presents the case to a Court and demonstrate that existence of overlapping reporting requirements leads to a disproportionate compliance burden.

[124] Lauren E. Elrick, 'The Ecosystem Concept: A Holistic Approach to Privacy Protection' (2021) 35 International Review of Law, Computers & Technology 24; Fanny Coudert, 'The Europol Regulation and Purpose Limitation: From the 'Silo-Based Approach' to … What Exactly'?' (2017) 3 European Data Protection Law Review 313, 317.

[125] See Franziska Boehm and Mark Cole, *Data Retention after the judgement of the CJEU* (Study funded by the Greens/EFA Group in the European Parliament, 30 June 2014) 96; and Joined Cases C-203/15 and C-698/15 *Tele2 Sverige AB v Post- och telestyrelsen and Secretary of State for the Home Department v Tom Watson and Others* [2016] ECLI:EU:C:2016:572, Opinion of Advocate General Saugmandsgaard Øe.

[126] This case involved the issue of whether the refusal of United Kingdom's tax authorities (HMRC) to extend the benefits of the group relief cross-border constituted, according to the CJEU, a restriction of the freedom of establishment. Three justifications were presented by the UK: a balanced allocation of taxing rights, the need to prevent tax avoidance and the risk that losses will be considered twice. The ECJ noted that these 'taken together' were capable of justifying the restriction. Case C-446/03, *Marks & Spencer plc v David Halsey (Her Majesty's Inspector of Taxes)* [2005] ECLI:EU:C:2005:763, para 51.

denied that, taken together, all the aforementioned multiple and fragmented reporting obligations across Member States hinders the automation of data processing by POs. Evidently, this has a substantial impact on compliance costs borne by digital platforms operating with very large databases of users and transactions.[127]

Based on the above, the author concludes that – depending on the circumstances of the case and the ability of a taxpayer to demonstrate this – when 'taken together', the multiple due diligence and reporting obligations applicable to POs in the EU could be deemed as 'manifestly disproportionate' by an EU Court. Even if these proportionality considerations do not find reception at the level of the CJEU (mainly because the CJEU usually does not strike down merely inefficient legislation), the author strongly believes that they should at least be addressed at a policy level by the EU legislator. This is because, as demonstrated above, there is significant room for improving these various reporting obligations by streamlining them into a single reporting system for POs for all direct and indirect tax (and why not for AML) purposes.[128]

16.5 CONCLUSION

As has arisen from the considerations made throughout this chapter, the protection of the collective interest to counter tax evasion and avoidance via the collaboration of intermediaries has generally been accepted and can be deemed as a justification for reporting and due diligence obligations imposed on private platforms under DAC7. However, this Directive still raises fundamental questions, such as: (1) whether the lack of clarity and precision of certain definitions could amount to a violation of the principle of legal certainty; and (2) whether its substantive, procedural and penalty-related rules (whether or not in combination with those arising from analogous frameworks applicable to platforms) could amount to a violation of the general principle of proportionality.

When analysing whether the specific provisions introduced by DAC7 may entail a violation of the principle of legal certainty, the author concludes that, even though DAC7 provides a long list of definitions, the lack of clarity

---

[127] European Commission. Directorate General for Taxation and Customs Union. and others, *VAT in the Digital Age: Final Report. Volume 2, The VAT Treatment of the Platform Economy* (Publications Office 2022).

[128] It should be noted that, in AML regulation, the general focus is on due diligence obligations rather than on reporting obligations (except for the cases in which an obligations is placed on business to report unusual transactions).

and precision of some of these indeed creates great uncertainties. In some cases, the identified uncertainties are minor and arise in very rare and niche cases. Thus, in those cases the author understands that the lack of clarity would not amount to a violation of the legal certainty principle. However, in other cases, more serious uncertainties were identified. These relate to the terms 'Platform', 'Relevant Activity' and 'Personal Service', which are key general definitions laying down DAC7's subjective and objective scope. Since these latter uncertainties are central to the Directive's application and impact a much broader range of cases and situations, the author believes that this unclarity could indeed amount to a violation of the EU legal certainty principle.

Concerning the proportionality question, after analysing the issue from the perspective of both CJEU case law and the theoretical framework proposed by Alexy, the author concludes that: (1) when applying the proportionality test to DAC7 or national measures that impose reporting obligations on POs, it is unlikely – although not impossible – that the CJEU would conclude that, considered individually, these frameworks entail an unjustified and (manifestly) disproportionate measure; (2) the aforementioned conclusion does not apply equally to DAC7's rules referred to procedural rights and penalties, where proportionality issues are likely to arise and be assessed by EU courts with a more favourable standard, which could lead to the annulment of either a single administrative act or a particular provision, while preserving DAC7's general legislative schema; and (3) depending on the circumstances of the case and the ability of a taxpayer to demonstrate this, when 'taken together', the cumulative effect of several due diligence and reporting obligations applicable to POs in the EU could be deemed 'manifestly disproportionate' by an EU Court. Even if these proportionality considerations do not find reception at the level of the CJEU (mainly because the CJEU usually does not strike down merely inefficient legislation), the author strongly believes that they should at least be addressed at a policy level by the EU legislator.

Finally, the author highlights that the aforementioned conclusions are not affected by the fact that, during 2022, the EU has witnessed some winds of change in relation to both: (1) the CJEU's openness to strike down EU measures because of their being deemed as 'disproportionate' (see cases on public BO registers in Luxemburg[129] and on DAC6's requirement for notifying other intermediary in case of professional privilege);[130] and (2) other stakeholders' reluctance to support legislative proposals that are not

[129] Joined Cases C-37/20 and C-601/20 (n 25) para 47.

[130] Case C-694/20 (n 49).

efficient and are found to 'go beyond what is necessary' (e.g. the proposal for an Unshell Directive).[131]

[131] Proposal for a Council Directive laying down rules to prevent the misuse of shell entities for tax purposes and amending Directive 2011/16/EU [2021] COM(2021) 565 final.

17. DAC8: track and exchange of information on crypto-assets as a new tool to achieve tax compliance

Anne Van de Vijver, Luisa Scarcella[1] and Alessia Tomo

17.1 INTRODUCTION

Crypto-asset and e-money markets are growing rapidly in an increasingly digitised world. Initially driven by the perception that the traditional financial system was closed and the objective of making means of payment more accessible, virtual currencies were subsequently used as speculative investments and sometimes, because of their (pseudo-)anonymity, for criminal or illegal activities. Today, these assets are gradually becoming mainstream and their growth is increasing exponentially, even though their value continues to fluctuate widely.[2] Prior to the COVID-19 pandemic, Bitcoin's market capitalisation was about $130.6 billion, a drop from its previous high of about $320.6 billion in December 2017. During the pandemic, Bitcoin's market capitalisation rose again, followed by a significant decline. In August 2022, Bitcoin's market capitalisation was approximately $404.8 billion.[3]

Crypto-assets can be defined as digital representations of value or rights, which may be transferred and stored electronically, using distributed ledger technology – a type of technology that supports the distributed recording of encrypted data[4] – such as blockchain.[5] Specific characteristics of the

[1] This contribution is in my personal capacity and does not reflect the views of ICC.

[2] OECD, *Crypto-Asset Reporting Framework and Amendments to the Common Reporting Standard* (OECD 2022) 9.

[3] US Department of the Treasury, *Crypto-assets: Implications for Consumers, Investors, and Businesses* (US Department of the Treasury September 2022) 13–14.

[4] ibid art 3(1)(1).

[5] Proposal for a Regulation of the European Parliament and of the Council on Markets in Crypto-assets, and amending Directive (EU) 2019/1937 [2019] COM/2020/593 final (MICA) art 3(1)(2).

crypto-asset and e-money markets are virtual nature, decentralisation, anonymity or pseudonymity.

Crypto-assets are virtual in nature as they intrinsically rely on distributed ledger technology (DLT) and cryptography.[6] The World Bank Group defines DLT as 'a novel and fast-evolving approach to recording and sharing data across multiple data stores (ledgers), which each have the exact same data records and are collectively maintained and controlled by a distributed network of computer servers, which are called nodes'.[7] Blockchain is a specific kind of DLT[8] that underpins many different applications, including many virtual currencies, such as Bitcoin.

DLT allows for transactions and data to be recorded and shared in a synchronised and decentralised manner across network participants, without the need to rely on traditional financial intermediaries or central administrators.[9] These characteristics are linked with the undisclosed identity (anonymity) of the cryptocurrency users, as they use a digital identity that can in principle not be linked to their real-world identity (pseudonymity).

These characterising features of crypto-assets result in a lack of information at the level of the national tax administrations regarding the use of crypto-assets, which entails a significant risk of revenue loss. Some countries have embarked on developing guidelines for the treatment of crypto-assets. However, most countries lack comprehensive guidance or a framework for the treatment of these assets for tax purposes, and, if guidance exists, it is usually insufficient, only addressing certain fragments of the relevant areas.[10]

This chapter will, first, discuss crypto-assets and the stakeholders involved, after which, the main tax compliance challenges will be identified. Lastly, the rules proposed by the OECD and the EU to increase transparency and compliance will be examined, with the aim of underlining future legal challenges related to DAC8.

---

[6] OECD, *Taxing Virtual Currencies: An Overview of Tax Treatments and Emerging Tax Policy Issues* (OECD 2020) 7, 10.

[7] World Bank Group, 'Distributed Ledger Technology (DLT) and blockchain' (2019) *FinTech Note* No. 1.

[8] For a definition of blockchain, see Robby Houben and Alexander Snyers, *Cryptocurrencies and blockchain Legal context and implications for financial crime, money laundering and tax evasion* (Study Requested by the TAX3 committee Policy Department for Economic, Scientific and Quality of Life Policies, European Parliament 2018).

[9] OECD (n 1) 9; Tina Ehrke-Rabel and Lily Zechner, 'VAT Treatment of Cryptocurrency Intermediation Services' (2020) 48 Intertax 498–514.

[10] OECD (n 5) 8, 16.

17.2 MAPPING THE CRYPTO-WORLD

17.2.1 A Crypto-asset Taxonomy

During the last decade, there has been seemingly exponential growth in the number of online coins and tokens, with just a handful of crypto-assets in 2013, to more than 2,800 by the end of 2019, to nearly 10,400 as of early 2022.[11] The classification and the tax compliance relating to crypto-assets is complicated due to the potential use of assets for investments and/or payments. In addition, the constant and rapid development of crypto-assets and their use makes it challenging to determine definitions. Different types of crypto-assets have developed at different rates,[12] but, in general, a distinction can be made between three sub-categories of crypto-assets, payment tokens, utility tokens and security tokens.[13]

Payment tokens operate as a unit of account and means of payment. These 'virtual currencies' or 'E-money tokens' aim to stabilise their value by referencing only one fiat currency. Such crypto-assets are electronic surrogates for coins and banknotes and are used for making payments. Well-known examples are Bitcoin and Ethereum. The term 'virtual currency' also includes payment tokens that are backed with real assets (e.g., securities or fiat currencies), which aim to be more stable and are therefore called 'stablecoins'.

Utility tokens intend to provide digital access to a good or service, available on DLT, and are only accepted by the issuer of that token. Such 'utility tokens' have non-financial purposes related to the operation of a digital platform and digital services. An example is Storj, a token that provides access to a peer-to-peer network cloud storage service.[14]

Security tokens represent a tradeable financial instrument (equity, debt or hybrid) that has been issued to raise capital (or a derivative thereof) and are held for investment purposes or traded by investors.[15] Examples include Spice, tZero and BCAP.[16]

---

11 US Department of the Treasury (n 2) 13 and 14.

12 ibid.

13 MICA (n 4), Explanatory Memorandum; OECD (n 1) 9.

14 OECD, Taxing Virtual Currencies (n 5).

15 Joachim Englisch, 'Editorial: VAT Goes Virtual: Security Tokens' (2022) 31 EC-Tax Review 232.

16 OECD (n 5).

These categories exist on an overlapping spectrum (hybridity) and there are also several types of crypto-assets that can be classified under multiple categories.[17]

17.2.2 Stakeholders Involved in the Crypto-world

17.2.2.1 Miners and forgers

Miners and forgers are involved in the creation of crypto-assets. Miners are responsible for validating transactions and rely on a proof of work (PoW) validation mechanism. This process consists of a kind of race, with the main goal of solving complex equations under a protocol, ensuring that transactions are properly verified. For their work, they receive a reward consisting of the transaction fee relating to the transaction itself and they are entitled to create a certain quantity of new Bitcoins that are attributed to them.[18] Proof of work is used with the Bitcoin blockchain, and currently most DLTs.[19]

Forgers operate on a system that relies on a proof-of-stake (PoS) protocol. A proof of stake system assigns shares of validation rights to users according to the stake they have in the blockchain. Stakes can be measured differently (number of tokens owned, holding period, amount of assets locked in the blockchain as collateral). Forgers or stakers must have a minimum stake in the blockchain to be able to participate in the verification process: they 'stake' their own tokens to have the right to verify a transaction and are credited a transaction fee or new tokens. Therefore, no mathematical equations are required to verify a transaction. This makes the verification process considerably more energy efficient than a proof of work mechanism. Proof of stake is, for instance, used with the Peercoin blockchain.[20]

17.2.2.2 Cryptocurrency users

Cryptocurrency users obtain their assets in several ways: from mining, from cryptocurrency exchange, directly from cryptocurrency users on trading platforms, from the selling of goods or services on trading platforms, via gift or donation or via hard fork of coin's blockchain.[21] In principle, they remain anonymous because they use a digital identity that cannot be linked to their real identity. However, providers of online wallets or exchange platforms

---

[17] Cambridge Centre for Alternative Finance, *Global Cryptoasset Regulatory Landscape Study* (2019).

[18] Allison Christians, 'Tax Cryptographia: Exploring the Fiscal Design of Cryptocurrencies' (2019) 64 McGill Law Journal 683.

[19] OECD (n 5).

[20] ibid.

[21] ibid.

usually require the real identity of the cryptocurrency investor to enter into transactions.[22] Users obtain crypto-assets for two main reasons: (1) to buy virtual or real goods or services; or (2) to hold for investment purposes.[23]

17.2.2.3 Service providers

Crypto-asset service providers are persons whose business is the provision of crypto-asset services to third parties on a professional basis.[24] In consideration for their services, they receive a commission.[25] Crypto-asset services may be divided into two categories.

A first category of such services consists of the following: ensuring the operation of a trading platform for crypto-assets; exchanging crypto-assets against fiat currencies that are legal tender or other crypto-assets by dealing on own account; and the service, on behalf of third parties, of ensuring the custody and administration of crypto-assets or ensuring the control of means to access such crypto-assets. For example, the most prominent cryptocurrency exchange platforms are Binance, Bitfinex, HitBTC, Kraken and Coinbase GDA.[26] Wallet providers offer digital 'wallets', which individuals can use to store their crypto-assets via authorisation through public and private keys. These services may either be provided in online (i.e., 'hot') wallets, or via service providers offering products that allow individuals to store their crypto-assets offline on downloaded (i.e., 'cold') wallets.[27]

A second category of such services is the placing of crypto-assets, the reception or transmission of orders for crypto-assets, the execution of orders for crypto-assets on behalf of third parties, and the provision of advice on crypto-assets.[28]

17.3 TAX CHALLENGES RELATED TO CRYPTO-ASSETS

Several tax challenges arise as a result of the increasing use of crypto-assets. The first challenge is the identification of the taxable event, which is then followed by the need to determine the applicable provision. However, the characterising features of crypto-assets, such as decentralisation, anonymity

---

22 Houben and Snyers (n 7).

23 Marwan Ahmed, 'Cryptocurrency Tax Compliance in the European Union: Reality or Mirage' (2021) 61 European Taxation 491.

24 MICA (n 4) art 3(1)(8).

25 Houben and Snyers (n 7).

26 Ahmed (n 22).

27 OECD (n 1).

28 MICA (n 4) Explanatory Memorandum.

or pseudonymity, as well as their virtual nature, can compromise the correct application of such provisions. Non-habitual users may be unaware of the applicable rules, especially in a cross-border situation. Similarly, tax administrations may not be able to enforce the applicable rules.

In the following subsections, these main challenges will be analysed in order to offer an overview of the key problems that led policymakers to look for new solutions in the area of exchange of information to be applied in relation to crypto-assets.

17.3.1 Identifying the Taxable Event

As indicated by the OECD in 2020, it is critical that policymakers provide comprehensive guidance aimed at addressing the major taxable events and income forms associated with virtual currencies.[29] The taxable events in the area of crypto-assets can thus be divided into three main stages in alignment with the lifecycle of digital tokens: creation, acquisition and disposal.

Crypto-assets are usually created through mining or forging, depending on whether the underlying blockchain relies on a PoW or proof of stake PoS validation system. Depending on this, different stakeholders will be involved, and the types of activities and resources used will differ. Miners (PoW) will generally invest in equipment such as 'mining rigs' and will incur high energy expenses in order to participate in the validation process and obtain the resultant crypto-assets. In this case, the validation process consists of a form of 'race', with the main goal of solving complex equations under a PoW protocol ensuring that transactions are properly verified. Conversely, 'forgers' operate on a system that relies on a PoS protocol. Under this protocol, they will risk the forfeiture of the tokens which they stake. Based on these different protocols, 'miners' or 'forgers' will have different roles in keeping the system running smoothly. They will also be compensated with crypto-assets for their efforts in doing so. Consequently, the payment for their efforts, whether in the form of validation or participation with 'stakes', will constitute a taxable event.

The type of activity required for the creation of crypto-assets can be interpreted in different ways. In the case of PoW, such as the one of cryptocurrencies like bitcoin, scholars have considered it as a gambling activity. Similarly, courts have also begun to qualify it as such. This is, for instance, the case in Austria, where the Federal Finance Court in the area of VAT defined cryptocurrency mining as a 'gambling activity'.[30] However, the qualification

---

[29] OECD (n 5); Ahmed (n 22).

[30] Bundesfinanzgericht [BFG] [*Mag Stefan Raab and Leopold Pichlbauer v Austrian Tax Office*] 20 August 2021 RV/5100226/2021.

of cryptocurrency mining is debated by scholars and commentators alike.[31] Indeed, the subsequent tax treatment will depend on the qualification adopted in a certain jurisdiction and by its tax and legal framework.

An example of differing qualifications relating to the creation of crypto-assets for income tax purposes may be found in Singapore, where the tax authority, in its e-Tax Guide, has distinguished mining activities as recreational or hobby mining on the one hand, and mining activities where there is a habitual and systematic effort to make a profit on the other hand.[32] If there is no habitual effort to make a profit, individuals will be considered to be engaging in 'hobby mining' by default and will not be taxed.

Crypto-assets may be acquired in different ways. Based on the experience of the past several years, there are mainly three ways to do so. The most straightforward way is acquisition through purchase via fiat currencies or other crypto-assets, but also through 'airdrops' or remuneration of labour. Through airdrops, typically, small amounts of these new digital tokens are sent to the digital wallets of active members of the blockchain community for free or in return of a small service, which can be in the form of retweeting or sharing posts regarding the project associated to the new digital tokens on other social media. The fact that this type of transaction may require a service in return can lead to a taxable event and questions relating to the type of income and the applicable tax treatment.

In relation to the work activity, most of the countries have considered that payment in the form of crypto-assets would still fall under the labour income definition adopted according to their legal system.[33]

The third life phase of a crypto-asset is the disposal or transfer. The transfer generally takes place where a token is exchanged and sold for goods and services, other digital tokens, or fiat currencies. Users might want to buy and sell cryptocurrencies to make profits out of the constant volatility of the market. In these cases, taxable events may arise, and tax provisions on capital gains may thus be applicable. The taxability of any gains deriving from the disposal of crypto-assets will depend on both how the disposal is carried out and the

---

31 Among scholars, a debate on the nature of mining has started already in 2017. Natalie Enzinger, 'Mining von Kryptowährunge' (2017) 23/24 Steuer- und Wirtschaftskartei 1013; Matthew Petutschnig, 'Sind Bitcoins ertragsteuerpflichtig?' (2014) 14 Österreichische Steuerzeitung 357; Tina Ehrke-Rabel, Iris Eisenberger, Elisabeth Hödl and Lily Zechner, 'Bitcoin-Miner als Prosumer: Eine Frage staatlicher Regulierung?' (2017) 3 Austrian Law Journal 188.

32 Inland Revenue Authority of Singapore (IRAS), *IRAS e-Tax Guide: Income Tax Treatment of Digital Tokens* (IRAS 2020).

33 To mention some examples, this is the case for Estonia, Germany, Italy, United Kingdom and United States.

underlying intention, from which it will be derived whether the taxpayer can be considered a 'trader' or not. There are a set of indicia in tax rules, the use of which indicia would depend on the country, which are used to assess whether a taxpayer shall be considered a trader. Similarly, capital gains provisions may differ in their design among countries – some jurisdictions have general clauses, while others rely on a specific and limited list. In any case, if a taxpayer is considered to be a 'trader', and all other requirements provided by the capital gain provisions applicable are fulfilled, then gains from the buying and selling of cryptocurrency will be taxable trade income. Capital gains provisions can also contain requirements based on an amount, or on a holding period requirement under which those assets should have been held before being transferred.

Finally, additional activities relating to the disposal phase of crypto-assets where taxable events can arise are so-called crypto-lending[34] and through gifts and inheritance, depending on the rules applicable in the single jurisdictions.

17.3.2 Identifying the Applicable Tax Provisions

Based on the taxable event arising from the activities involving the use of crypto-assets, it is then of fundamental importance to identify the applicable tax provision. The identification of the relevant provision will indeed depend on the tax rules in place in the relevant jurisdiction, but will also need to take into account Treaty rules in the case of a cross-border situation. The wide variety of methods by which digital tokens may be commercially used makes it untenable to assume that the classification of an asset as a digital token will, in itself, indicate anything about how it might be taxed. Conversely, having a clear understanding of the crypto ecosystem's key activities and stakeholders is essential in order to identify where possible tax events can arise. The characteristic features of crypto assets, such as decentralisation, anonymity or pseudonymity, and their virtual nature, increase difficulties in understanding the tax treatment of the possible income arising from activities involving them. Nonetheless, despite these difficulties, it is vital to understand whether the application of more traditional tax principles and provisions is being disrupted by this technology or whether, conversely, there is still room for the application of these principles and rules.

Applicable rules will also depend on the ways in which the stakeholders carry out their activities. For instance, miners and forgers can operate alone or organised in mining or staking pools. Some jurisdictions have already begun

---

[34] Crypto-lending can be defined as the process of depositing cryptocurrency that is lent to borrowers in return for regular interest payments.

to question themselves on the applicable rules based on how stakeholders organise themselves. This is the case in Germany, where the guidelines of the Ministry of Finance specifically highlight how the applicability of the general principle for a so-called '*Mitunternehmerschaft*' will differ based on the underlying agreement of the pool:[35] if operators merely provide computational powers in return for compensation, this relationship will be considered as a provision of services.

Aside from this example, more generally, the approaches adopted in single countries have diverged, taking into account the complexities in qualifying crypto-assets and the pre-existing provisions in their legal system. Generally, extensive interpretation of existing provisions has been applied in courts, such as the CJEU in the leading *Hedqvist* ruling for bitcoin,[36] but also in guidelines produced by ministries of finances and tax authorities,[37] as well as in answers to ruling requests presented by taxpayers and released by tax authorities as a result of general interest.[38]

17.3.3 Tax Compliance

The distinguishing features of crypto-assets as listed above (such as their decentralisation, anonymity or pseudonymity, and virtual nature) not only make it more difficult to identify the applicable rules, but also aggravate tax compliance by users and the correct application of rules by tax administrations.

On the one hand, when it comes to the difficulties faced by users, who might be unsure of the correct rule to apply, it is important to increase certainty on the applicability of the relevant tax provisions. This will require increased guidance from policymakers and tax authorities, which many countries have already begun to put in place. On the other hand, some taxpayers could take advantage of the uncertainty surrounding the applicability of existing rules to a certain taxable event. Especially given their digital nature, anonymity and global dimension, it could be difficult for tax authorities to gain insight into a certain tax situation, as well as to keep track of the different transac-

---

[35] BMF, *Einzelfragen zur ertragsteuerrechtlichen Behandlung von virtuellen Währungen und von sonstigen Token* (2022).

[36] Case C-264/14 *Skatteverket v David Hedqvist* [2015] ECLI:EU:C:2015:718; Tina Ehrke-Rabel and Lily Zechner, 'VAT Treatment of Cryptocurrency Intermediation Services' (2020) 48 Intertax 498.

[37] BMF, *Einzelfragen zur ertragsteuerrechtlichen Behandlung von virtuellen Währungen und von sonstigen Token* (2022); IFRS, *Holdings of cryptocurrencies* (2019); IRAS (n 31).

[38] See e.g. in Italy, Agenzia delle Entrate, Risoluzione n. 72 /E, 2.9.2016; Agenzia delle Entrate, Risposta n. 437/2022; Agenzia delle Entrate, Risposta n. 397/2022.

tions related to it, and whether taxable events have arisen in their respective jurisdictions.

Consequently, there are import tax compliance issues that cannot be addressed in unilaterally. As has been the case with anti-money laundering legislation, the need to effectively address the issues arising from the increasing use of crypto-assets requires a multilateral solution. Existing standards and international rules concerning administrative cooperation among tax authorities have gained renewed relevance. Nevertheless, adjustments still need to be made in order to facilitate international tax cooperation. Indeed, the current framework is not able to tackle these issues and needs to be updated.

17.4 NEWLY ADOPTED AND MOST RECENT PROPOSALS TO IMPROVE TAX COMPLIANCE

The challenges described in the previous section have led policymakers at both the OECD and EU level to investigate to what extent current frameworks can be modified and updated, and whether a completely new set of rules should be adopted. Concrete steps were taken in 2021, when the European Commission published a public consultation to collect more information on the proposal for a new update to DAC, which could include rules targeted at challenges related to crypto-assets. Following this public consultation, in Spring 2022 the OECD published a public consultation on a crypto-asset reporting framework, also known under the acronym CARF. In October 2022, the OECD released the final CARF rules.

Then, largely following CARF's scheme, the EU Commission adopted the new DAC8 proposal in December 2022, in order to include crypto-assets in the EU's automatic exchange of information mechanism.

17.4.1 OECD Crypto-assets Reporting Framework

The Common Reporting Standard (CRS) was adopted by the OECD in 2014, with the aim of promoting tax transparency with respect to financial accounts held abroad. However, due to the continual evolution of financial markets, the standard needed to be revised in order to take into account new investment and payment practices, which include the rise in the use and circulation of crypto-assets. The CARF was a response to the request by the G20 for the OECD to develop a framework for the automatic exchange of information on crypto-assets between countries. It was approved by the OECD Committee on Fiscal Affairs in August 2022,[39] along with a set of amendments to the CRS. Its main goal is to provide a set of new rules governing the reporting of tax information on transactions that involve crypto-assets in a standardised manner so that they can be automatically exchanged with the jurisdictions of residence of taxpayers on an annual basis. The CARF consists of rules and commentary that can be transposed into domestic law to collect information from Reporting Crypto-Asset Service Providers with a relevant nexus to the jurisdiction implementing the CARF. In addition to the rules and commentary, the OECD is also working on an implementation package to ensure the consistent domestic and international application of the CARF. The CARF has a very linear structure and includes rules and commentary grouped under four building blocks: the scope of crypto-assets, entities and individuals which are subject to data collection and reporting requirements, transactions that will fall under the reporting requirement and the information that will need to be reported, and due diligence procedures.

Considering the scope of crypto-assets under the CARF, the proposed definition focuses on the use of cryptographically secured distributed ledger technology, as this is a distinguishing factor underpinning the creation, holding and transferability of crypto-assets. Endeavouring to build a future-proof standard, the definition also refers to 'similar technology' in order to include new technological developments that will emerge in the future and that might raise similar tax risks. According to the OECD, this definition should be able to identify all those assets that can be held and transferred in a decentralised manner, without the intervention of traditional financial intermediaries. While this definition seems comprehensive for the crypto-environment, there are still three categories that are not included under the definition, and which, according to the OECD, would pose limited tax compliance risks. The first category relates to those crypto-assets that the Reporting Crypto-Asset Service Provider have adequately determined cannot be used for payment or investment purposes. This exclusion takes inspiration from the scope of the virtual asset definition of the Financial Action Task Force (FATF) and seeks to exclude crypto-assets that do not have the capacity of being used for payment or investment purposes.[40] The second category are Central Bank Digital Currencies, representing a claim in fiat currency on an issuing Central Bank or monetary authority, which function similarly to money held in a traditional bank account. The third category covers Specified Electronic Money Products that represent a single fiat currency and are redeemable at any time in the same

---

[39] OECD, *Crypto-Asset Reporting Framework and Amendments to the Common Reporting Standard* (OECD 2022).

[40] ibid 11.

fiat currency at par value as a regulatory matter. The reason for these last two exclusions from the CARF is justified by the fact that they will be included within the scope of the CRS' new changes.

The alignment with the FATF Recommendations definition is indeed to be welcomed, as it is aimed to facilitate compliance with due diligence requirements, which operators will also need to fulfil under existing AML/KYC obligations.[41] The alignment with FATF rules can also be found in relation to the definition of intermediaries and other service providers that will fall under the CARF rules. The reason for focusing on these intermediaries and service providers is based on the fact that, by facilitating transactions, they are expected to have the best and most comprehensive access to the value of the relevant crypto-assets and the exchange transactions. The definition includes intermediaries and other service providers that facilitate exchanges between relevant crypto-assets, as well as between crypto-assets and fiat currencies. Thus, those entities or individuals that provide business services effectuating exchange transactions in relevant crypto-assets, for or on behalf of customers, will fall under the scope of CARF. The definition appears to be quite comprehensive, as it includes not only exchanges but also other intermediaries as well as other service providers, such as brokers, dealers and operators of crypto-asset ATMs. However, despite the CARF building upon the latest changes adopted in the FATF commentary regarding decentralised exchanges, questions may still arise in relation to these issues.

In order to determine whether there is a reporting nexus, the following elements will need to be considered. More specifically, the nexus will be present if operators are both tax resident in, both incorporated in, or both organised under the laws of a jurisdiction adopting the rules, and have legal personality or are subject to tax reporting requirements in, managed from, having a regular place of business in, or effectuating Relevant Transactions through a branch based in, a jurisdiction adopting the rules.

In order to avoid duplicative reporting when a provider has a nexus with more than one jurisdiction, the CARF has also created a hierarchy of nexus rules and a rule to be applied where an operator has a nexus in two jurisdictions based on the same type of nexus.

In terms of reporting requirements, the CARF identifies three relevant types of transactions: (1) exchanges between relevant crypto-assets and fiat currencies, (2) exchanges between one or more forms of relevant crypto-assets, and (3) transfers (including reportable retail payment transactions) of relevant crypto-assets. Transactions will be reported on an aggregate basis according to the type of relevant crypto-asset, differentiating between outward and inward

---

41 ibid.

transactions. Crypto-asset service providers responsible for reporting will also need to categorise transfers by transfer type, if they have access to such knowledge. In terms of value determination in crypto-asset-to-fiat currency transactions, the fiat amount paid or received is reported as the acquisition amount or gross proceeds. Moreover, for crypto-asset-to-crypto-asset transactions, it is proposed that the value of the crypto-asset (at acquisition) and the gross proceeds (upon disposal) must (also) be reported in fiat currency.

Taxpayers' holdings and transfers of relevant crypto-assets outside the scope of reporting crypto-asset service providers subject to reporting are also relevant to tax authorities. Thus, the CARF requires reporting of the number of units and the total value of transfers of relevant crypto-assets effectuated by a reporting crypto-asset service provider, on behalf of a crypto-asset user, to wallets not associated with a virtual asset service provider or a financial institution. Moreover, the CARF also applies to certain instances where a reporting crypto-asset service provider processes payments on behalf of a merchant accepting Relevant Crypto-Assets in payment for goods or services, focusing on high-value transactions (i.e., Reportable Retail Payment Transactions). In such instances, the reporting crypto-asset service provider is required to treat the customer of the merchant as a crypto-asset user (provided the reporting crypto-asset service provider is required to verify the identity of the customer on the basis of domestic anti-money laundering rules and by virtue of effectuating the reportable retail payment transaction), and report with respect to the value of the transaction on that basis. According to the OECD, this information could be useful to provide tax administrations with information on cases where Relevant Crypto-Assets are used to purchase goods or services, therewith realising a capital gain on the disposal of such Relevant Crypto-Assets.

Finally, in terms of due diligence procedure, the CARF contains rules that need to be followed by reporting crypto-asset service providers in the identification of their crypto-asset users, the determining of the relevant tax jurisdictions for reporting purposes, and the collection of relevant information needed to comply with the reporting requirements under the CARF. The goal is to allow reporting crypto-asset service providers to efficiently and reliably determine the identity and tax residence of their individual and entity crypto-asset users, as well as of the individuals controlling certain entity crypto-asset users.

17.4.2 EU DAC8

The aim of DAC1 was to contribute to efficient tax controls aided by the exchange of information between Member States. Since its adoption, Directive 2011/16/EU has been amended six times, the purpose of this always being to strengthen the entire system of administrative cooperation.[42] The adoption of a new, seventh, amendment, known as DAC8, is currently pending.[43] Several institutional initiatives, such as the '2020 Action Plan for Fair and Simple Taxation Supporting the Recovery Strategy' adopted by the EU Commission,[44] and the 'Exchanging tax information in the EU: solid foundation, cracks in the implementation in 2021' adopted by the European Court of Auditors,[45] underlined the risk that crypto-assets and e-money undermine the progress made on tax transparency and pose substantial risks for tax evasion.[46] As this new technology is used to create, hold and transfer financial assets without traditional financial intermediaries, this could lead to the erosion of the integrity of DAC2, which provides exchanges of financial account information. Indeed, DAC2 was adopted and implemented when it was impossible to predict the rise of the crypto-market, and the crypto-market was not covered under earlier DAC provisions.[47]

Hence, on 8 December 2022, the EU Commission adopted its new proposal for a directive that aims to enable tax administrations to obtain necessary information, to further improve cooperation across administrations, and to keep compliance costs to a minimum through a common EU reporting standard, including the exchange of information related to gains and profits made from crypto transactions by European users for direct tax purposes. To this end, DAC8, largely following the CARF's provisions and definitions of the Regulation of the European Parliament and of the Council on Markets in Crypto-assets (MiCa),[48] sets out rules for reporting on crypto-asset service providers. In more detail, reporting crypto-asset service providers must report

---

42 Andrea Ballancin and Francesco Cannas, 'The "DAC 6" and Its Compatibility with Some of the Founding Principles of the European Legal System(s)' (2020) 29 EC-Tax Review 117; Nevia Cicin-Šain and Joachim Englisch, 'DAC 7: An Entire New Framework for Joint Audits in the EU: How Do the Taxpayers Fare?' (2022) 50 Intertax 7.

43 Proposal for a Council Directive amending Directive 2011/16/EU on administrative cooperation in the field of taxation [2011] COM(2022) 707 final.

44 Communication from the Commission to the European Parliament and the Council. An Action Plan for fair and Simple Taxation Supporting the Recovery Strategy [2020] COM(2020) 312 final.

45 Special report 3/2021 'Exchanging tax information in the EU: solid foundation, cracks in the implementation' [2021] OJ C 31/05.

46 ibid.

47 EPRS-European Parliamentary Research Service, *Tax transparency rules for crypto-asset transactions (DAC8)* (Briefing, European Parliament 2023).

48 Regulation (EU) 2023/1114 of the European Parliament and of the Council of 31 May 2023 on markets in crypto-assets, and amending Regulations (EU) No 1093/2010 and (EU) No 1095/2010 and Directives 2013/36/EU and (EU) 2019/1937 [2023] OJ L 150/40.

information on crypto-asset users (who use the service provider to trade and exchange crypto-assets) to the relevant competent authority. The aim is to enable the communication of the reported information by the authority of the Member State that received the data from the reporting crypto-asset service provider, to the competent authority of the Member State where the reportable crypto-asset user resides.

As in the case of the CARF, the proposed rules may be grouped under four blocks: the scope of crypto-assets; the intermediaries subject to the reporting requirements; what and whose transactions are reportable; and due diligence procedures.

The definition of crypto-assets in the scope of DAC8 is largely based on the MiCa definition. Therefore, the Commission also proposes an abstract and sufficiently open definition, in order to cover all relevant assets and to be future-proof.[49] Nevertheless, it is argued in the literature that the Commission opted for a narrower definition of 'reportable crypto-asset,' than that of 'crypto-asset'.[50]

DAC8 explicitly identifies two types of intermediaries which, irrespective of their size or location, are obliged to report to the local tax authorities (RCASPs, 'reportable crypto-asset service providers'): the 'crypto-asset providers' and the 'crypto-asset operators'. In line with the definition provided by MiCA, DAC8 defines 'crypto-asset providers' as any legal person whose professional activity consists of providing one or more crypto-asset services to third parties. However, contrary to MiCA, the proposal also includes 'crypto-asset operators', such as providers of crypto-asset services other than a crypto-asset service provider.[51] Again, the proposed definition seems to be relatively open to being future-proof.

The proposal identifies two types of transactions, namely exchange transactions and transfers of reportable crypto-assets, and specifies that both domestic

---

[49] European Commission and DG Taxation and Customs Union, Platform for tax good governance (European Commission, 2021).

[50] Dennis Post and Claudio Cipollini, 'The DAC8 Proposal and the Future of Crypto-Asset Reporting: Some Preliminary Thoughts' (*Kluwer International Tax Blog*, January, 2023) <https://kluwertaxblog.com/2023/01/09/the-dac8-proposal-and-the-future-of-crypto-asset-reporting-some-preliminary-thoughts/> accessed 9 December 2023.

[51] However, the Commission specified that 'DAC8 has a different purpose from that of MiCA. DAC8 covers both crypto-asset service providers regulated under MiCA and those that are not. Without regulating entities as such, DAC8 provides rules for the reporting of information of crypto-asset service providers and crypto-asset operators': <https://ec.europa.eu/commission/presscorner/detail/en/qanda_22_7517> accessed 9 December 2023.

and cross-border transactions are in its scope and are aggregated based on the type of reportable crypto-assets.

To identify whose transactions are reportable, i.e., who the 'reportable users' are, the proposal requires information on individuals or entities resident in EU Member States. Therefore, intermediaries are liable to report transactions by clients residing in the EU. Indeed, due to the inherent mobility of crypto-asset intermediaries extra attention is paid to the level playing field, also concerning third countries.[52] It is worth noting that, as with platforms under DAC7, these RCASPs (Reporting Crypto-Asset Service Providers) are obliged to report if they have reportable users within the EU, regardless of their residence, even if they are located in a non-EU Member State. As the proposal explains, the aim of this is to 'avoid that service providers engage in forum made shopping'.

In terms of its due diligence procedure, the proposal identifies practices that reporting crypto-asset service providers shall comply with to identify reportable users. Their identification will occur through self-certification, enabling the reporting crypto-asset service provider to determine information on crypto-asset users.

Unlike the CARF, DAC8 requires providers to act when a crypto-asset user fails to provide the requested data after two reminders, although not before a 60-day deadline. This provision seems to prove providers' 'strong' involvement as third parties. In other words, the reporting crypto-asset service providers are to prevent the crypto-asset user from performing exchange transactions. Therefore, DAC8 appears to be in line with the 'trend' of a constant and increasing involvement of private parties in collecting data to be transferred to tax administrations, already visible in DAC6 and DAC7. Once again, arguably, providers are required to verify the truthfulness of the received information.

As for the legislative process, the proposed DAC8 is subject to a special legislative procedure and requires the unanimous support of the Council. During the meeting of the Economic and Financial Affairs Council on 16 May 2023, the Council agreed on its position (general approach) on the amendments made during negotiations to DAC8. Therefore, the consultation of the Parliament is currently pending. The proposal has been assigned to the Economic and Monetary Affairs (ECON) Committee and its vote is supposed to take place by the end of June 2023.

As suggested by the Commission and supported by the Council, the reporting arrangements would begin from January 2026.

---

[52] European Commission and DG Taxation and Customs Union (n 48).

17.4.2.1 DAC8 and legal challenges

The interest objectives pursued with the adoption of DAC8 are undoubtedly legitimate. Nevertheless, it appears necessary to consider the new legal challenges related to protecting taxpayers' fundamental rights and providers' activities. As for the former, the possible vulnus to taxpayers' data protection is clear. The proposal underlines explicitly that, among other things:

> The Directive includes specific provisions and safeguards on data protection. The proposed amendments will continue to follow and respect these safeguards. The relevant IT and procedural measures ensure that personal data are protected in line with the GDPR. The exchange of data will pass through a secured electronic system that encrypts and decrypts the data and, in every tax administration, only authorised national officials should have access to this information (…).

Nevertheless, it remains to be seen whether the increasing amount of data that will be collected (from third parties), stored, and exchanged, will be compatible with the GDPR – especially considering the data minimisation principle[53] – and, consequently, with the proportionality principle. It might also be helpful to take into account some hints from the European Court of Auditors,[54] which underlined the lack of exchange of information in the field of crypto-assets, but at the same time highlighted that 'information is generally under-used'. This observation appears crucial in reflecting on whether the collection and exchange of more and more data can be considered proportionate.

As for the providers' activities, the proposal extends the number of private third parties involved in the taxation process. This could lead to some issues, such as the 'unfair' lack of compensation for this additional compliance burden, and the lack of information for the taxpayers. Moreover, high-risk taxpayers might opt for a different provider not yet included in the proposal scope. Indeed, as argued, the definition of 'reportable crypto-asset' adopted by the Commission is narrower than that of 'crypto-asset'.[55] This might lead to the users opting for crypto-assets not covered by the directive.

17.5 CONCLUDING REMARKS

The EU Commission estimated that implementing DAC8 could raise additional tax revenue of between €1 billion and €2.4 billion per year. As argued in this chapter, several institutional papers have recently pointed out the necessity

---

53 Article 5(1) GDPR sets out the principles that must be applied when processing personal data, such as lawfulness, fairness and transparency; purpose limitation; storage limitation; data minimisation; accuracy; integrity and confidentiality.

54 Special report 3/2021 (n 44).

55 Post and Cipollini (n 49).

of an EU intervention in this field, as the value deriving from crypto-assets is largely untaxed. However, the adoption of DAC8 poses various issues.

On the one hand, in terms of its scope, the classification of crypto-assets is complicated for several reasons, such as the potential use of assets for investments and payments, the rapid development and evolution of crypto-assets, and the inherent mobility of crypto-asset intermediaries. On the other hand, as pointed out in the previous section, the adoption of DAC8 is likely to entail several legal challenges. Regarding these challenges, it seems appropriate to recall some considerations raised by the Advocate General of the Court of Justice of the EU in the case SS Sia.[56] There seems to be a steeply increasing involvement of third parties under DAC6, DAC7 and DAC8, contributing to the increasing, and potentially disproportionate, collection and processing of more and more data. The main issue is whether this remains in line with the principles of Article 5 of the GDPR. Another concern is the increasing compliance burden for intermediaries. As the Advocate General noted, the involvement of private third parties has cost implications and requires organisational effort. Therefore, although the proposal specifies that it is possible to 'claim that the proposed initiative represents a proportionate answer to identified loopholes in the Directive and also aims to tackle the problem of tax evasion', the doubts related to ascertaining whether 'a sledgehammer was [or will be] used to crack a nut'[57] remain.

---

[56] Case C-175/20 *SIA 'SS' v Valsts ieņēmumu dienests* [2022] ECLI:EU:C:2021:690, Opinion of Advocate General Bobek.

[57] Walter Jellinek, *Gesetz, Gesetzesanwendung und Zweckmässigkeitserwägung* (Mohr 1913).

Conclusions: *exchange of information in the EU – taxpayers' rights, transparency and effectiveness*

Marina Serrat Romaní, Jasper Korving and Mariolina Eliantonio

The overarching objective of this book has been to provide a comprehensive analysis of the exchange of information (EOI) procedures for tax purposes within the European Union from both a theoretical and a practical perspective, taking into account both the general administrative law and tax law angles on the matter. These concluding reflections aim to highlight the main overarching themes which emerge from the chapters, by focusing on the key aspects that contributed to shaping the current state of the EU EOI system, including its transparency, the digitalisation process, the influence on taxpayers' rights, the possible gaps in judicial protection and the effectiveness of the current legal framework.

THE INFLUENCE OF THE OECD ON THE EU EXCHANGE OF INFORMATION

A first theme which emerges from various chapters is the multi-level nature of the EOI mechanism. Access to information is crucial to correctly assess and collect taxes, making EOI a vital mechanism in cross-border situations, as international law prohibits unilateral legal actions of any kind in foreign jurisdictions. As Wenz, Koegl and Zotkaj explain, the necessity to agree on common standards and approaches to tackle tax fraud, tax evasion and tax avoidance became especially apparent after 2008's economic recession that was accompanied by the discovery of 'aggressive' tax planning strategies by multi-national enterprises (MNEs) as well as tax evasion cases, many of them related to uncooperative jurisdictions with solid tax and banking secrecy regulations. This situation has led the EU to create a list of non-cooperative jurisdictions that heavily relies on OECD data and criteria.

The influence that the OECD has played on the EU legal system is undeniable. The main inspiration can be found in the EOI provisions contained in the OECD Model Tax Convention (MTC) and OECD soft law. The EU has adapted and, in most cases, expanded the limits of these standards and methods to exchange information for tax purposes. The growing interest from the EU institutions and its Member States in exchanging information as a critical tool to enhance the effectiveness of international cooperation and as a mechanism to combat fraudulent and borderline tax practices has created a symbiotic relationship with the OECD. The EU and its Member States' market power, as Geringer points out, have tried (and most likely will continue trying), somehow, to nurture and influence the OECD to expand the advancement of such mechanisms as well, with the aim of levelling the legal playing field internationally and influencing the alignment between both tax policies. This alignment, in some ways, still represents unfinished business, as with the lists of non-cooperative jurisdictions (NCJs). As Báez Moreno and Wenz explain, although the EU List of NCJs is still a non-binding instrument, it is a helpful tool to show coherent criteria for Member States to respect, since national lists still contain asymmetric criteria when carrying out the listing process. As Wenz, Koegl and Zotkaj point out, achieving a level playing field regarding EOI and transparency criteria to identify NCJs and enhance mutual assistance should be regarded as necessary, not only within the EU, but also for non-EU jurisdictions, to achieve a coherent international policy to tackle the above-mentioned malpractices.

TRANSPARENCY, 'FORESEEABLE RELEVANCE' AND THE QUEST FOR PROPORTIONALITY

A second issue which several chapters touch upon is that of the 'correct' amount of transparency which EOI procedures ought to ensure. The need to increase the amount of information considered relevant for tax purposes is the ultimate reason behind the reforms of tax transparency standards; however, this process has created an ongoing debate about the limits of such tax transparency. When talking about transparency in the legal field, the concept evokes 'quality' and trustworthiness. Transparency laws are fundamental to guarantee public accountability of institutional activities, as they are intended to guarantee citizens a more visible form of law-making. Nonetheless, within the field of taxation, transparency is commonly understood in a double sense. On the one hand, transparency is seen as the requirement of clarity to improve quality and bring about simplification of taxation rules. It is, thus, a requirement for governmental bodies. On the other hand, transparency also refers to an obligation for taxpayers to provide tax administrations with all kinds of information necessary to make taxpayers and third parties comply with their duty to contribute or to facilitate access to relevant data that may be useful for tax authorities to carry out tax collection or tax procedures, even though this obligation is limited by the boundaries set by primary EU law and fundamental rights, such as the right to privacy. It is this last approach to tax transparency which belongs within the framework of administrative cooperation and international mutual assistance that has been in the spotlight of the international tax framework.

As EOI foresees an increasing use of the EU's Common Communication Network and the individual Member States continue working on national Information and Communications Technology (ICT) systems, transparency is also of increasing relevance in that sense. Specifically focusing on the transparency debate in connection with technological developments, the chapter by Serrat Romaní explains how ICT has not only shaped the way economic and social relations work, but at the same time how it has considerably simplified and accelerated the process of data collection and analysis. For this reason, technology has been a critical element in enforcing the new tax transparency standards. Such standards were initially designed to give effect to transparency in relation to the exchange of information upon request, as originally provided for in Article 26 of the OECD MTC. As this provision has been amended over time to increase the amount of exchangeable information, and AEOI mechanisms have gained increased relevance, an important question still remains regarding what information is relevant for tax purposes. In that sense, a recurring theme that several chapters have directly or indirectly referred to is the role played by 'foreseeable relevance' as well as the limits for the exchange of information for tax purposes. The ultimate objective of the notion of foreseeable relevance is to try to find a balance between the interest of the Member States in enforcing the duty of the taxpayers to provide information or to contribute, and taxpayers' rights.

DAC1 sought to align the EU legislation regarding administrative cooperation with the international framework led by the OECD and to improve its minimum standards, including the foreseeable relevance of the requested information as the main term of reference. As Pantazatou and Bianco explain, the EOIR in DAC1 has, however, a broader scope regarding the information to be exchanged compared to EOI under the OECD MTC. The latter seems to be more restrictive not only in relation to the amount of information to be exchanged, but also regarding who can access that information, as an express consent from the state of origin of such information is required. The latter does not appear to be a criterion under DAC1.

For a long time, no official definition of 'foreseeable relevance' was included in DAC, but this situation changed following the adoption of DAC7, which includes a definition of that concept, as further discussed in the chapter by Vázquez. However, before a definition was finally included in the DAC itself, the CJEU has played a crucial role in shaping the notion of 'foreseeable relevance'. In particular, as highlighted in the chapters by Moreno González,

Antoniou, and Dorigo and Cinotti, the *Berlioz*, *Grand Duchy of Luxembourg v B and FC* and *Grand Duchy of Luxembourg v L* cases helped shape the boundaries of the concept of 'foreseeable relevance' by setting certain objective criteria. The identity of the taxpayer or any person holding relevant information for the investigation, the motivation and requirements behind the investigation and the necessity for particular information are the key elements for tax authorities when evaluating a request to exchange certain information. Eventually, an official definition – aligned with the CJEU's case law and the Commentaries on Article 26, paragraph 1 of the 2012 OECD MTC – was included in DAC7. Although this codification has brought more certainty for taxpayers, Moreno González argues that this is a missed opportunity to establish an official homogenous statement of reasons granting minimum standards to argue that there are sufficient grounds and relevance for requesting the information in question. Having such a guide would have struck a more proportional balance between the taxpayers' rights and the concept of foreseeable relevance.

EXCHANGE OF INFORMATION AND PROCEDURAL RIGHTS

Article 26 OECD MTC and its commentaries does not contain specific provisions concerning the protection of taxpayers' rights in EOI procedures, and leaves the level of protection at the discretion of each sovereign state. This practice is also present in other international tax treaties, such as the Tax Information Exchange Agreements (TIEAs) or the Convention on Mutual Administrative Assistance in Tax Matters. The TIEAs do, however, contain a *numerus clausus* list of procedural rights that need to be recognised by the signatory states. However, as pointed out by Dorigo and Cinotti, such a list is recognised only as long as these procedural rights do not impede or delay the exchange of information processes. In general, the chapters in this volume reveal that international instruments do not offer adequate and balanced protection of procedural rights during information exchanges.

In a manner similar to the way of proceeding at the international treaties level, the DAC proclaims in its preamble its respect for the fundamental rights and principles of the Charter. However, the Directive directs taxpayers towards the domestic legislation of Member States. This creates protection at different levels across the EU, since some Member States grant extensive procedural rights, while others grant only a minimum level of protection. This legal context has inevitably created conflicts over which the CJEU and the ECtHR have had to adjudicate. Before the CJEU, conflicts have mostly revolved around Article 47 of the Charter and the extension of the right to a fair trial and the right of defence among taxpayers and third parties involved in EOI procedures. Cases such as *Sabou* have set an important precedent, where the

CJEU ruled that it is in line with EU law to restrict access to justice for claims brought against the exchange of information itself. *Berlioz* and *Grand Duchy of Luxembourg v B and FC* confirmed this position. In these rulings, the CJEU went even further, adding that taxpayers cannot challenge the orders addressed to third parties to collect information within the framework of their investigation. A similar approach is also observed in the ECtHR case law. The ECtHR has always been very cautious in extensively granting taxpayers procedural rights, even though the most recent case law shows some openings towards the recognition of more procedural rights to taxpayers. Finally, it should be noted that, despite the update of Article 25 DAC, together with the adoption of the General Data Protection Regulation (GDPR), having arguably improved the overall legal protection of taxpayers, the chapters by Moreno González, Serrat Romaní, Dorigo and Cinotti, Antoniou and Vázquez still conclude that the current framework does not really achieve a suitable balance between the standards of transparency and exchange of information and taxpayers' protection. Therefore, they urge further steps be taken in the harmonisation of rights connected to EOI procedures.

THE RELATIONSHIP TO SUBSTANTIVE RIGHTS

EU instruments ultimately grant taxpayers an essential layer of common protection not only for procedural but also for substantive rights. Nonetheless, the fact that the judicial protection system still largely depends on each individual Member State's legal system creates a fragmented protection throughout the EU. This issue has been noted from both tax law and general administrative law perspectives. Indeed, as the chapter by Dubos, Eliantonio and Ivanchykava explains, EOI procedures, seen as composite procedures and as generating transnational administrative acts, challenge the current mechanisms of judicial protection, based on the principle of territoriality and separation of jurisdictions. As such, they, generate gaps in judicial protection.

Furthermore, the fragmentation of judicial protection proves ineffective when it comes to striking a balance between effectiveness of cooperation and taxpayers' protection, also because, as discussed in the chapter by Antoniou, several taxpayers' rights linked to ensuring the right to judicial protection are not fully guaranteed by EU law or ECHR law. What is more, there is an inconsistency between the CJEU and the ECtHR, which further undermines the position of taxpayers and the availability of judicial protection.

Access to justice in the context of EOI becomes all the more crucial in the current context of digitalisation and datafication, which brings new risks, linked especially to automatic EOI, such as the transfer of large amounts of data, the exchange of unnecessary data or the lack of a guarantee of total data security. The only remedy currently available, *ex post* appeal, requires complementary – *ex ante* – methods to ensure the respect for fundamental rights. In that sense, as concluded by Moreno Gonzáles and Debelva, the update of DAC7 recognising the right of the data subject to be informed *ex ante* about the processing and transmission of personal data, together with the adoption of the GDPR, can be considered an improvement of the overall legal protection of taxpayers. Yet, Debelva also observes that the GDPR still provides many – possibly unnecessary – restrictions on taxpayers' rights. Therefore, as proposed by Serrat Romaní, it is not unreasonable to consider a relaxation of the limits of the rights of access, rectification, cancellation or opposition of personal data as a complementary *ex ante* protection instrument, especially in relation to automatic EOI procedures.

COMPLIANCE AND EFFECTIVENESS OF THE DAC AND ITS AMENDMENTS

A final aspect which several authors touch upon is the effectiveness of the information exchange measures. Undoubtedly, the DAC is a necessary instrument that aims to prevent cross-border tax fraud, evasion and avoidance, thus incentivising tax compliance. Particularly, as explained in the chapter by Pantazatou and Bianco, DAC1 and DAC2 laid the foundations for these objectives and, due to their development, they have become one of the most relevant tools to pursue such aims. These objectives are commendable, yet the effectiveness of DAC1 and its amendments is still up for debate. Even though the EOI system foreseen in DAC1 is solid in its implementation and results, DAC2 appears not to be as effective, since its success depends to some extent on the decisional capacity of financial institutions. This can be problematic, especially in respect of foreign-held bank accounts, casting some doubts on the measure's overall effectiveness, as Boei and Douma conclude.

In the case of DAC3, as Brodzka indicates, reports show that DAC3 information in the EU Central Directory was mostly completed but little used by the Member States, and, apparently, the reporting obligation has influenced neither the behaviour of tax authorities in granting advanced tax rulings and pricing agreements nor the attitude of companies demanding these rulings.

DAC4 intends to facilitate access to valuable sources of information about MNEs. However, as Athanasaki explains, the high compliance costs and significant administrative burdens due to the amount of information that needs to be provided prove to be an obstacle to the measure's effectiveness. At the same time, there are no up-to-date results concerning how DAC4 has impacted the behaviour of MNEs, hence any conclusion on its effectiveness remains somewhat speculative.

DAC5 can be considered an additional control tool to the targeted information on DAC2. It has not caused difficulties in its implementation and has not added extra compliance burdens, even though a lack of uniform and clear definitions and regulatory coordination between the Anti-Money Laundering Directive and DAC have been identified in the chapter by Breuer. The author also concludes that these mismatches may also indirectly affect the effectiveness of the measure. An overall positive assessment emerges also regarding DAC7's obligation for digital platforms, discussed in Vásquez' chapter. He foresees DAC7 becoming a complementary instrument to effectively contrast the income declared by digitally present businesses. When it comes to the awaited DAC8 on crypto-assets and its effectiveness, Van de Vijver, Scarcella and Tomo's chapter remains open: it is too early to draw any conclusions.

The most significant issues regarding effectiveness are foreseen for DAC6. Both Vásquez and Malmgrén lament, in particular, its lack of clarity regarding the interpretation of its core terms and mismatches in definitions, as well as high compliance costs, all inevitably leading towards legal uncertainty for taxpayers. The vagueness of the definitions, concepts and hallmarks, besides the fear of penalties, varying in maximum amounts across the Member States, become a dangerous cocktail that might lead to the overreporting of unnecessary information. This can, in turn, bring about dangers concerning the right to privacy and the overall effectiveness of the measure, as the amount of information might become unmanageable for tax authorities. Indeed, Van de Vijver, Scarcella and Tomo remark that the newest amendments of the DAC, (i.e., DAC6, DAC7 and DAC8) are greatly increasing the involvement of third parties contributing to the ever greater, and potentially disproportionate, collection and processing of more and more data. This involvement of third parties not only raises doubts about its intersection with the GDPR principles, but it also creates concerns about the amount of effort, costs and compliance burden, especially for intermediaries. Most likely, as Debelva points out, in the near future, such involvement of intermediaries will make the privilege against self-incrimination (or *nemo tenetur*) in the context of EOI procedures all the more relevant.

SOME FINAL WORDS

Overall, the chapters collected in this volume agree on the fact that exchanges of information within the DAC framework seem to have had a preventive effect on malpractices and increased tax compliance levels. However, many authors are also concerned about the management of massive amounts of data that tax administrations need to handle and the time they need to be fully prepared for this task. If the information exchanged cannot be adequately processed due to the amount of data and ICT not being fully able to handle that, the question can be raised as to what the purpose of DAC actually is. On this basis, our conclusion is, therefore, that the DAC can be an effective preventive measure, yet due to the complexity of information management, the unclear interpretation of core concepts used therein, and the struggles national tax administrations experience to use and act upon the information received, the DAC cannot yet display all its effectiveness in detecting malpractices.

Index